Seizing Power

Seizing Power

The Strategic Logic of Military Coups

NAUNIHAL SINGH

Johns Hopkins University Press

Baltimore

To my parents

Johns Hopkins University Press
2715 North Charles Street
Baltimore, Maryland 21218-4363

ISBN 13: 978-1-4214-1336-5
ISBN 10: 1-4214-1336-1

Library of Congress Control Number: 2013949132

A catalog record for this book is available from the British Library.

Special discounts are available for bulk purchases of this book. For more information, please contact Special Sales at 410-516-6936 or specialsales @press.jhu.edu.

Johns Hopkins University Press uses environmentally friendly book materials, including recycled text paper that is composed of at least 30 percent post-consumer waste, whenever possible.

Contents

Figures and Tables

Acknowledgments

Thanks are due first to my advisors, the intellectual godfathers of this book, Robert Bates, Jorge Dominguez, Bear Braumoeller, and Samuel Huntington. To this number should be added a fifth, Adam Brandenburger, who served as the unofficial advisor for the game theoretic parts of the argument.

This book would not have been written without the generosity of the retired officers and enlisted men of the Ghanaian armed forces, who taught me almost everything I know about coups. Each footnote should be read as extending fulsome and effusive thanks to the individual cited. In addition, particular thanks should be extended to Eboe Hutchful, K. F. Gyimah-Boadi, General Edwin Sam, Kwesi Pratt, and Kweku Baaku, without whom the oral history I collected would not have been possible.

Funds for the field research in this book came from a Social Science Research Council International Predissertation Fellowship (1999–2000) and an Institute for the Study of World Politics Doctoral Dissertation Fellowship. Additional support was received for dissertation writing from the John M. Olin Institute and for postgraduate writing from the Kellogg Institute for International Studies at the University of Notre Dame.

Thanks also to the many students who worked with me to collect data on every single coup attempt around the world between 1945 and 2005. This part of the project took four years and required the considerable efforts of Colleen Mallahan, John Busch, Andy Bramsen, Katherine Moran, Shannon Coyne, Daniel Sportiello, Katherine Cessar, Krystin Krause, David Partida, Joe Brutto, Christina O'Donnell, Amber Herkey, and Jenna Farmer. That research was generously supported by the Kellogg Institute.

Along the way, I have benefited from the intellectual and personal support of a large number of friends and colleagues. Although they are too numerous to name individually, I want them to know that I am very grateful for all their help.

This book has reached completion largely due to the work of two editors. Suzanne Flinchbaugh at Johns Hopkins University Press believed in this project and championed it through the editorial process, and Jeanne Barker-Nunn helped me cut the fat in the manuscript and find my voice.

And last, thanks beyond all measure to my long-suffering parents, who did so much to support me, even at one point hand-counting all the words in the manuscript. There is no way to thank or appreciate them enough.

Seizing Power

Chapter 1

Introduction

In 1991, in a last-ditch effort to save the Soviet Union from dissolution, a coalition of the top military and civilian leaders in the country tried to seize power from Premier Mikhail Gorbachev. The conspirators included every major official in the state apparatus except the premier himself, including the defense minister, interior minister, KGB chief, the prime minister, the secretary of the central committee, and the chief of the president's staff (Odom 1998, 310). Despite the overwhelming force the coup makers had at their disposal—including troops from the regular armed forces, the interior ministry, and the KGB—the coup attempt failed. The party, army, and intelligence services that had so ably defended the Soviets against the Nazi invasion were dismantled, and the USSR was no more.[1]

Almost ten years earlier, on New Year's Eve 1981, a young retired flight lieutenant named Jerry Rawlings led a very different military coup, in Ghana. In this attempt, Rawlings and just a handful of men managed to take control of a military of 9,000 and a country of 11,000,000. Unlike the Soviet conspirators, who commanded virtually the entire security apparatus and represented the entire state, Rawlings attacked with only ten men carrying small arms and broader alliances with mainly disgruntled enlisted men and student radicals. He staged his attack against a fairly elected (albeit highly unpopular) democratic regime at a time when Ghanaians were fed up with military intervention. His radio appeals for soldiers and civilians to join his "holy war" and "revolution" were met largely with indifference within the military and, for the first time in Ghana, even produced opposition from civilians, who had greeted prior successful coups with public jubilation. Yet, despite all these seeming obstacles, Rawlings prevailed.

Why did the 1991 USSR coup attempt fail and the 1981 Ghana coup attempt succeed? Despite an extensive scholarly literature on civil-military relations in general and coups in particular, the question of the determinants of coup outcomes has been almost entirely ignored. To address this gap, this book offers the first

---

[1] Making this outcome even more puzzling, there is no evidence of either widespread defection to Yeltsin or significant disobedience within the armed forces to the commands issued by the junta (Brusstar & Jones 1995, 52-53).

sustained theoretical and empirical treatment of why some coup attempts fail while others succeed. Based on almost 300 hours of interviews with coup participants and an original dataset of all coup attempts around the world between 1950 and 2000, this analysis develops and tests a novel theory of coup dynamics and outcomes.

The Importance of Understanding Coups

There are several reasons for scholars to care about coups, the most significant one being that some coup attempts have been pivotal moments in world history. At stake in the 1991 Soviet coup attempt, for example, was nothing less than the survival of the Soviet Union, a superpower that covered more territory than any other country in the world and which had a nuclear arsenal twice as large as its nearest competitor. Because this coup failed, the USSR was dismembered and the communist party dismantled, conclusively ending the Cold War. Similarly, the success of Portugal's 1974 Carnation Revolution led to the democratization of Portugal, the independence of the large Lusophone colonies, and the Third Wave of democratization around the world (Huntington 1991). And if the July 1944 coup attempt against Hitler had succeeded, the war in Europe might have ended very differently, with consequences for both civilians along the Eastern Front and those being slaughtered in the concentration camps. In these and other cases, the trajectory of world politics was determined by the outcome of a single coup attempt.

Even when a coup attempt does not cast a large shadow internationally, it can have a substantial impact on the lives of those who live within the affected country's borders. Some of the most cruel and venal dictators in the world have taken power via a coup, such as Indonesia's President Suharto, who killed between a half-million and a million Indonesians in the first year of his rule (Valentino 2004, 71) and is estimated to have embezzled between 15 and 35 billion dollars during his time in office (Transparency International 2004, 13). Saddam Hussein and Idi Amin were able to retain power (and murder vast numbers of their citizens) because the coup attempts that brought them to power succeeded and numerous subsequent coup attempts against them failed.

Although not every coup attempt is of critical importance domestically or internationally, the cumulative impact of coup attempts on the politics of the latter half of the twentieth century has been undeniable, with a majority of countries in the world experiencing at least one coup attempt during that period.[2] On a regional basis, 80% of countries in sub-Saharan Africa, 76% of countries in North Africa and the Middle East, 67% of countries in Latin America, and 50% of countries in Asia had at least one coup attempt during this period. Between 1950 and 2000, 471 coup

---

[2]To be precise, 55% of countries with populations more than 100,000 had at least one coup attempt between 1950 and 2000.

attempts occurred in independent countries with populations over 100,000, 238 of which succeeded and 233 of which failed. During this period, there was an average (both mean and median) of 9 coup attempts each year, ranging from a low of 3 attempts in 1998 to a high of 19 attempts in 1975. And while the frequency of coup attempts has decreased, between 1950 and 2012 there was not a single year without a coup attempt somewhere in the world. It puts these numbers in perspective to note that, between 1950 and 2000, non-Western countries had at least 30% more coup attempts than democratic elections for the executive.[3]

As their frequency and ubiquity suggest, coup attempts are the basic mechanism for most of the regime change and irregular leadership removal in the world. Indeed, coups are responsible for roughly 75% of democratic failures, making them the single largest danger to democracy (Goemans & Marinov 2008).[4] Nor are military coups restricted to democracies: since 1946, all monarchies that have ended have been ousted by their own armed forces (Geddes 2009), and coups are also the most common form of irregular leadership change in dictatorships. In fact, during the period addressed in this study, two-thirds of dictators were removed by coups. Despite the popular image of dictators being brought down by mass demonstrations, this is the exception rather than the rule: coups were more than six times more likely to end a dictatorship than was a popular uprising (Svolik 2008).

Successful military coups are also the primary source of regime change in general. When any regime subtype fails—whether a parliamentary democracy, presidential democracy, mixed democracy, or civilian dictatorship—it is most likely to be succeeded by a military regime (Cheibub 2007, 145). Because all military regimes are the result of successful coups but not all successful coups lead to military regimes (and some failed coups also lead to regime changes), the high rate of transition to military regimes clearly demonstrates the impact of coups. Military governments themselves are not spared the destabilizing effects of coups. To the contrary, it is well established that both military rulers and military regimes have a shorter tenure than other kinds of authoritarian regimes, lasting around four years, while other types of dictatorships stay in power at least twice as long (Brownlee 2007, Gandhi 2008, Geddes 2003, Geddes 2009, Svolik 2008). In fact, each successful coup increases the odds of a further coup, suggesting that each military government carries within it the seeds of its own removal (Londregan & Poole 1990).

---

[3]The estimate of the relative number of coups and democratic elections was calculated using data from the Quality of Governance Dataset. Excluding Western Europe, US, Canada, Australia, and New Zealand, the remainder of the world had an estimated 354 democratic elections for executive and 459 coup attempts. The number of executive elections was calculated by looking at democratic elections in presidential democracies, legislative elections in parliamentary elections, and both legislative and presidential elections in mixed systems. Because I erred on the side of treating all elections in mixed systems as executive elections, the estimate of executive elections is probably an overcount, so the number of coup attempts probably exceeds the number of elections by more than 30%.

[4]In addition, all countries which have suffered more than one democratic breakdown did so at the hands of the military (Cheibub 2007, 149).

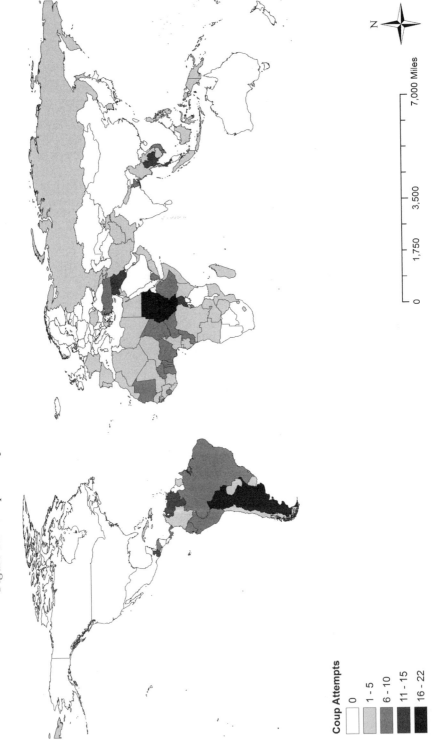

Figure 1.1: Coup attempts around the world between 1950 and 2000

Coup Attempts

- 0
- 1 - 5
- 6 - 10
- 11 - 15
- 16 - 22

0   1,750   3,500   7,000 Miles

Understanding Coup Outcomes and Dynamics

The results of my research reveal a central point that may seem self-evident but which has been largely overlooked by most previous research: the central dynamics of a coup attempt are those that occur within the armed forces. Empirically speaking, coups fail only when they are defeated by another armed actor, who is almost always another faction within the armed forces.[5] Civilian actors have little impact on what happens between the start and end of a coup attempt; when they are able to shape events, it is only to the extent that they can influence intra-military behavior. In practice, civilians alone have no ability to defeat a coup, no matter how many demonstrate and protest. Military units are both able and willing to disperse even extremely large groups of civilians, as the Chinese Army demonstrated in Tiananmen Square.

It is easy to lose sight of the intra-military component of a coup attempt, because scholars and journalists alike commonly describe coup attempts as being committed by "the military," as if armed forces function as a unitary actor. As this book makes clear, however, every military coup attempt is primarily a struggle for power within the armed forces that, if successful, grants the victor control over the state. A coup organized by sergeants, for example, is not a coup by "the armed forces" but a coup by the lowest tier of the armed forces, whose success would threaten everybody above them in the military hierarchy, as well as remove the sitting government from power. The same argument applies at each level of the military hierarchy, as a successful coup attempt would necessarily place the challenger in a position of power over his peers and subordinates. There is an internecine power struggle involved even when officers at the apex of the command structure mount a coup attempt, as such attempts can be rejected by subordinate officers and end in failure. No coup attempt is guaranteed to succeed, no matter what the circumstances; and therefore, any group of challengers must proceed first by establishing control over the rest of the armed forces.

For these reasons, I argue that the key to understanding coup outcomes is understanding coup dynamics. Whether a coup succeeds or fails rests almost entirely upon what happens within the military once the coup attempt begins. Because usually challengers constitute only a small group within the military, so as to avoid detection, the reaction of the rest of the military to the coup attempt is critical to its eventual fate.

The argument presented in this book grows out of field research into the internal workings of coup attempts. This research was conducted in the African country of Ghana, a country with six successful coup attempts and four failed ones. There, through a combination of luck, perseverance, and most of all the generosity of many people, I was able to interview a wide range of participants from both sides in these coup attempts. I was particularly interested in the behavior of key unit

---

[5]Coup attempts are also foiled by the intervention of an external army, but this is infrequent. The main exceptions are the result of French forces stationed on the territory of a former colony and which intervene to protect an allied government from overthrow.

commanders stationed near the capital, since their decisions would have had an important impact on the trajectory and outcome of the coup attempt. The main insight of this book occurred when I asked these members of the military how they had reacted to the news that a coup attempt had begun.

The officers' description of their behavior was surprising to me, and it presented a very different depiction of a coup attempt than is generally found in either scholarly or journalistic accounts. As might be expected, the officers began by discussing the performance of the government, the motives of the coup makers, and the legitimacy of the coup attempt, given the political circumstances at the time—the usual factors invoked by most political scientists who have examined the phenomenon of coups. Surprisingly, however, they then went on to explain that none of these factors had played a role in their choice of which side to back at the start of the attempt. In fact, they believed that it would have been selfish to let their personal political beliefs guide their response. As officers, their first responsibility was to their men, and they felt it was wrong to use their troops, possibly endangering their lives, to support the side they preferred if it was likely to lose. Perhaps equally unexpected from military men, they were emphatic about avoiding what they described as "unnecessary violence." Although they were willing to fight to the last man to defend the country against an *external* invasion, they did not want to engage in fratricidal bloodshed that might damage the military and the country and perhaps spiral into civil war. As a result, they explained, they had cast their support to the side they believed everyone else would back as well, the side that would win rather than the one they might have wanted to win. And until they knew which side that was—the government or the challengers—they had chosen to sit on the fence, gathering information and trying not to make the situation worse.

The strategic dynamic described by these officers is what game theorists call a "coordination game." In a coordination game, each individual has an incentive to do what others are doing, and therefore each individual's choices are based on his or her beliefs about the likely actions of others. The outcome of the game is determined when these beliefs converge among the actors. If you change the players' expectations, you change their behavior as well.

In a coordination game, expectations are powerful because they can become self-fulfilling. Consider the case of a bank run, another situation modeled by a coordination game. In a situation where the bank lacks an external guarantor, depositors leave their money in the bank (and earn interest on it) when they think others will also do so, and they will join in a bank run if they think others are withdrawing their money. When people believe a bank will fail, they will pull their money out, and the bank will fail. What is more, when they believe that other depositors believe the bank will fail, they will withdraw their deposits, leading these expectations about the behavior of other depositors to become true, whether they were accurate originally or not. In other words, no matter what the level of deposits in the bank, it is the depositors' beliefs and meta-beliefs about the bank's possible failure that determine the eventual outcome.

The coordination game model captures the key dynamics of a wide range of collective action situations, whether social, economic, or political. Fads and fashions are obvious examples of coordination games, but so are a wide range of social norms and institutions that have endured for a long time. Rousseau famously described the emergence of society from the state of nature as a coordination game (individuals can choose to hunt hares alone or stags together), and revolutions can be understood in much the same way. In each of these cases, the stability of the system is based on expectations, and change is the result of altered beliefs.

A key way to create or change expectations is via communication. For communication to shape expectations, however, the information conveyed not only has to become known to all parties, but also has to be known to be known by all parties, known to be known to be known by all parties, and so on. That is, it has to create not just knowledge but meta-knowledge (and meta-meta-knowledge, etc.), or what game theorists call "common knowledge." To understand why, consider what is called the "coordinated attack problem," in which two generals are trying to schedule an attack on an enemy encampment from different locations. If they attack together, they can vanquish their foe, but if either attacks alone, they both will lose. The problem they face is that communication between the two is unreliable. It's not enough for the first general to tell the second to attack at dawn, because he doesn't know if the second general will actually receive his message. Even if the message is transmitted, however, the second will not attack without knowing that the first one knows he has successfully received the message. But, even if the second sends an acknowledgment of its receipt, that isn't enough either, because the first has to know that the second knows that the first knows, and so on. In short, coordination requires common knowledge.[6]

Because the generation of common knowledge can lead to collective action, having control over the means of creating such knowledge is very important for those who hold power or those who hope to pry it from them (Chwe 2001, 10). Overthrowing a dictatorship is a coordination game, one in which political actors want to join the protests if others are participating and want to stay at home if others stay at home. For this reason, dictatorships prize outward shows of conformity, especially on ritualized public occasions, because such displays strengthen the expectations that keep the system working. Conversely, they heavily regulate public gatherings and mass media because these can be used to create expectations that could undermine the regime. A single radio broadcast is likely to be far more damaging than a banned cassette tape smuggled hand to hand; one public speech to a group is more of a danger than private conversations with an equivalent number of individuals.

When applied to coups, this understanding of the dynamics of coordination games provides insights into how to make or foil a coup attempt. For challengers, the key is to use common knowledge to shape expectations in a way favorable to

---

[6]Scholars of the epistemology of game theory argue that an infinite tower of meta-knowledge is required, with each level of meta-knowledge equally important (Aumann 1976). In practice, however, humans appear to assume that everybody is boundedly rational and instead use a heuristic which says anything more than three levels deep is plenty (Nagel 1995).

the coup's success. They want to convince military actors that the success of the coup has the support of almost everybody in the institution and thus is essentially a fait accompli. In addition, they want to make it clear that any possible resistance is minor, doomed to fail, and irresponsible, since it would risk an escalating spiral of violence if it persisted. I call this process "making a fact," and I argue that when it is successfully done, members of the armed forces will support, either actively or tacitly, the attempted overthrow of the government.

Making a fact is commonly done by seizing the main radio or other broadcast facility and making a broadcast to the other players. Conversely, to foil the coup attempt, an incumbent government needs to do the opposite: either hold on to broadcasting facilities in the first place or displace the challengers from them and then make a government broadcast to create expectations of the continued survival of the government and the failure of the challengers. Indeed, the officers interviewed were emphatic that controlling the radio station is almost always necessary for coup success and that without it the coup will usually be doomed to failure. Significantly, the purpose of broadcasts is to enable the challengers to seize power (or the government to retain it) and not to convince members of the military to join (or oppose) the coup nor to convince the general public of the coup's legitimacy (or lack thereof). For that reason, what matters is not that the broadcasts reach the public at large but instead that the information in the broadcast is "public" within the military, that is, that the content of the broadcast become common knowledge for members of the armed forces.

Another strategy for accomplishing the same objective is to make a fact at a meeting of the key members of the military. This meeting might be as small as a gathering of just the key commanders in and around the capital or as large as a meeting of all the commanders of fighting units around the country. Anything said by the coup makers in such a meeting acts like a public broadcast to this specific audience, thereby creating common knowledge and shaping expectations. The added benefit of this approach is that not only the broadcast but also the responses of those present are made public to all actors present, making a meeting with commanders even more potent than a radio broadcast at shaping expectations. If the meeting is carefully managed, the challengers not only can assert that there is widespread support for the coup but can seemingly demonstrate it by asking for anyone with objections to speak up. Because no one in the meeting is likely to risk openly challenging the coup makers, the apparent assent of the group to the coup becomes common knowledge among all those present. Having made their consent public among their peers, officers are unlikely to reverse themselves and oppose the coup after leaving the gathering. What's more, the coup's success is ensured even if everybody present is secretly opposed to it, since what matters here are their expectations, not their personal beliefs. After the meeting, there is little loyalists can do to counter the coup, since the expectations formed make it difficult for any participant to oppose the challengers afterwards. Although meetings are a better tool for creating expectations than radio or television broadcasts, they are used less often. Only senior officers have the ability to convene such meetings, and only under the right conditions, which makes them difficult to organize without raising the suspicions of the incumbent.

While the main factors shaping expectations are broadcasts that create common knowledge during a coup attempt (either via the mass news media or a meeting), events that happen beforehand can shape the initial expectations of actors, and thus provide either an advantage or a handicap for the coup makers. Chief among these is the outcome of past coup attempts in the country. Because history is common knowledge, it shapes expectations about behavior during a coup attempt, especially when those precedents are recent, similar, or both (Chwe 2001, 7). This is not to say that the past is doomed to repeat itself over and over again; few countries with more than one coup attempt have experienced only successes or failures. Although what happens over the course of a coup attempt is more important than what comes before it, I argue that challengers will find it easier to make a fact after a recent successful coup attempt than after a recent failure. Similarly, earlier broadcasts can also shape expectations at the start of a coup attempt. When a sitting government uses the broadcast media to warn about the looming danger of a coup, for instance, the seriousness with which it appears to take the opposition can backfire, strengthening the challengers' hand.

As we shall see throughout these chapters, the dynamic of coordination shapes not only initial expectations but also behavior throughout the entire coup attempt, and in a variety of ways. For example, while challengers use force in many coup attempts, it is fruitful only when it results (directly or indirectly) in the creation of expectations favorable to their success. Force is typically used to take control of the radio station or to capture prominent symbolic targets in the capital so as to lend credence to the claims made in the broadcast. This use of force, however, is very different from that which would occur during wartime. Since coordination is driven by a fear of fratricide, both sides take pains to limit violence during skirmishes, even if they incur a tactical cost in the process. Such restraint is evident even at the end of a coup attempt. Even when actors believe they will be executed for their deeds, they almost always surrender or flee rather than make a last stand and try to destroy the opposition. These claims fly in the face of common depictions of coup attempts as intense battles, but I provide evidence over the rest of the book to substantiate them.

All coup makers face essentially the same challenges, but the resources available to them for coup making differ depending on their position within the military. As the following chapters will show, these differences in the organizational position of the challengers within the armed forces hierarchy and the resources flowing from them translate into correspondingly varied tactics, dynamics, and likelihood of success. What is most important to the eventual success or failure of a given coup attempt is not the difference in hard military power among the parties but the resources available for setting and coordinating expectations and making facts.

Challengers from the top (usually generals) are the best placed to successfully mount a coup, because their organizational position gives them greater "soft power," which best allows them to manipulate the expectations of other military actors in a favorable way. As will be discussed in greater detail in chapter 4, the objective of these generals is to ensure that the mid-level officers who actually command fighting units believe that the success of the coup is inevitable, thus guaranteeing their support and making self-fulfilling beliefs around their victory. Such actors have a range of tactics available to them, including the highly effective option of making a coup in a meeting. Coups from the top are generally over quickly, with relatively little chaos and bloodshed.

Coups from the middle are those mounted by majors, lieutenant colonels, and colonels, the officers in charge of the actual fighting units in the military and thus those with the greatest amount of firepower at their disposal. As we will see in chapter 5, challengers from the middle seize symbolic targets in highly symbolic locations and make broadcasts proclaiming broad support for the coup and warning defenders that their loss is an inevitability. These coup makers endeavor to shape the beliefs of both uncommitted officers and the regime's defenders, to convince them that the rest of the military supports or will soon support the coup. This is a more indirect way to manipulate beliefs and depends on the ability to seize and retain control over the targets that serve to demonstrate their credibility. As a result, coups from the middle succeed less often than coups from the top.

Lastly, coups from the bottom, those mounted by enlisted men, non-commissioned officers, and junior officers up to the rank of captain, are essentially mutinies. As discussed in chapter 6, these are the coup attempts least likely to succeed, because the coup makers have neither soft nor hard power and so must unravel the entire structure of the military, knowing they will certainly be opposed by those of higher ranks, whatever their political beliefs, because a mutiny poses an automatic threat to their position. For this reason, coups from the bottom begin with the least initial credibility, and they involve the most violence, threat, and confusion before they can possibly succeed.

Other Theoretical Explanations

As discussed in more detail in the next chapter, previous scholarship on civil-military relations has offered (if sometimes only implicitly) two other approaches to understanding the outcomes and dynamics of coup attempts.[7] One of these approaches emphasizes the tactical aspects of coup making, comparing coups to battles. If this theory is correct, coups succeed when the challengers are able to establish military dominance over loyalists, and therefore coups are usually won by the stronger side. The other perspective on coups emphasizes the legitimacy and popularity of the incumbent, comparing coups to elections. If this approach is correct, a coup succeeds when the challenger attracts more support than the incumbent. After being fleshed out more fully in the next chapter, all three of these

---

[7]Mainly, I draw upon the scholarship on when successful coups occur, work that largely ignores the occurrence of failed coups but some of which can be repurposed to apply to the questions in this book.

approaches will be evaluated using original data, both quantitative and qualitative, in chapters 3 through 7.

Background of Cases

Ghana was originally chosen as a site for this research because it had a high number of coup attempts that were almost evenly split between successes and failures, which is similar to the distribution of coup outcomes worldwide. It also had a variety of potentially relevant background conditions, with, for example, coup attempts against multi-party democracies, one-party states, and military governments. As my research continued, I learned that Ghana also had additional attributes that made it favorable as a case, since it included multiple coup attempts from the top, middle, and bottom of the military hierarchy. In addition, Ghana's coup attempts were recent enough to make conducting oral history feasible, yet far enough in the past that participants were willing to speak freely about events once I had obtained their trust.

Ghana has always attracted considerable scholarly interest because of its historical role as the first independent country in sub-Saharan Africa. Independence from Britain in 1957 was marked with a six-day official celebration with a large number of international dignitaries in attendance, a rarity for Africa in that era. As journalist Martin Meredith said, "No other African state was launched with so much promise for the future. Ghana embarked on independence as one of the richest tropical countries in the world, with an efficient civil service, an impartial judiciary and a prosperous middle class. Its parliament was well established, with able politicians in both government and opposition" (Meredith 2005, 27).

Ghana's first prime minister was Kwame Nkrumah, leader of Ghana's independence movement. At a time when there were only 8,000 black high school graduates in all of sub-Saharan Africa, Nkrumah had two master's degrees from the University of Pennsylvania. He also had already served as prime minister for six years as part of an unusual experiment in self-rule whereby the British government allowed a democratically elected legislature and a period of tutelary democracy, so Ghana was better prepared for independence than most former colonies.

Nkrumah was ambitious, a devoted pan-Africanist who saw himself not just as the leader of Ghana but also as the future president of a United States of Africa. Despite his ties to the West, he was a socialist who set about using the country's wealth to transform and bring the benefits of modernity to the nation. Reaching out to the Eastern Bloc, he attempted to industrialize the country and to diversify the economy from its dependence on cocoa exports. He built schools, clinics, roads, and a new port. He also made sure the country acquired the trappings of modernity, such as a national airline (at a time when there were few if any black pilots flying in the world), a major hydroelectric dam, and a military (with navy and air force) large enough to allow Ghana to participate on the world stage.

But Ghana's early promise soon turned to disappointment. By 1964, it had become a one-party dictatorship, in which Nkrumah was declared president for life and opposition members were imprisoned without trial. The government's development schemes bore little to no economic fruit: the new industries failed, agricultural policy was a disaster, government-owned corporations were inefficient at best, corruption among senior government officials was rife, and when the world price of cocoa slumped, the country became increasingly indebted. Nkrumah moved closer to the Soviet bloc, causing even greater alarm in the West.

There was also increasing tension between Nkrumah and the armed forces, who objected to his direct interference in what they saw as military affairs, his efforts to politicize the military, and the creation of a separate praetorian guard. After years of tension and several aborted plots, in 1966 members of the police and military launched a coup from the middle and overthrew Nkrumah while he was out of the country, en route to an attempt to negotiate peace in the Vietnam War.

For the next fifteen years, as seen in table 1.1, Ghana lurched between civilian and military rule. Three of the civilian governments and three of the military governments were terminated by a successful coup. All of these governments had to deal with the same challenges as had Nkrumah. The split between Nkrumahist socialists and center-right politicians with ties to business and traditional authorities continued to structure civilian politics and even had an impact on military rule. Every head of state since Nkrumah has had to grapple with the challenges posed by an economy overly reliant on a few export commodities whose prices fluctuate wildly. Tensions between ethnic groups have also played an important rule in the country's politics, although the competition between Ashanti and Ewe ethnic groups that has colored so much of that history did not emerge as a significant cleavage until the early 1970s. As elsewhere, urban-rural divisions and intergenerational divisions have also affected Ghana's regular politics.

Of Ghana's ten coup attempts between 1966 and 1983, this book covers the seven from 1967 to 1981. I skip the first attempt because it has already been fairly well documented and omit the last two because they add little original to our theoretical understanding.

Table 1.1: Coup attempts in Ghana, independence to present

Date	Regime	Coup level	Outcome
February 1966	1-Party dictatorship	Middle	Success
April 1967	Military government	Middle	Failure
January 1972	Elected democracy	Middle	Success
October 1975	Military government	Top	Success
July 1978	Military government	Top	Success
May 1979	Military government	Bottom	Failure
June 1979	Military government	Bottom	Success
December 1981	Elected democracy	Bottom	Success
November 1982	1-Party dictatorship	Bottom	Failure
June 1983	1-Party dictatorship	Bottom	Failure

Given the paucity of secondary literature concerning the details of these coup attempts, most of my information comes from the almost 275 hours of interviews I conducted over thirteen months in the country. I obtained multiple perspectives on each coup attempt by speaking to participants and observers on all sides. This included not just those who were trying to overthrow the government and those who were trying to defend it, but also those who were initially passive and through either their action or continued inaction contributed to the outcome. By combining these various accounts for each coup attempt, I was able to build composite histories for each attempted coup, providing both an actor's perspective and a bird's-eye view of the event.

In addition to these Ghanaian cases, the book also presents an extended case study from the Soviet Union, selected both because it was very different from the Ghanaian cases and because, as a coup from the top that failed, it constituted a least-likely case for my theory.[8]

Overview of Chapters

Chapter 2 develops the theoretical basis for this book more fully, discussing in more detail the three explanations for coup dynamics and outcomes, namely that coup attempts are similar to battles, elections, or coordination games. For each, I describe the antecedent literature and central hypotheses each offers about coup dynamics and outcomes. As part of developing the argument that coups are coordination games, I argue that coup makers from the top, middle, and bottom of the military hierarchy possess very different resources with which to make a coup and that these differences lead to three distinct patterns of coup dynamics with different likelihoods of success. This forms the organizing principle for the case studies presented in chapters 4 through 7.

In the third chapter, I use original data on all coup attempts between 1950 and 2000 to examine under what conditions coups are attempted and when these attempts succeed rather than fail. The results show that coups are attempted more often in countries that are poorer, neither democratic nor autocratic, and that have a history of previous coup attempts. Attempts are also more likely in years with elections. Coup outcomes, on the other hand, are predicted only by the rank of the challenger and the history of past failed coups. That is, coup outcomes are solely predicted by the variables associated with coordination. No other factors are statistically significant, whether economic, political, social, or regional. That the predictive factors for attempts and outcomes are disjointed justifies studying the two questions separately and argues that outcomes are not a reflection of the same underlying instability that causes attempts.

---

[8]Information from other cases is presented at various points in the book as well, but few coup attempts are documented in enough depth in the secondary literature to provide material for a chapter-length case study, and field research on this topic is not just difficult but illegal in many countries around the world.

Chapter 4 discusses coups from the top, those by generals. Roughly half of all coup attempts in the world come from the top of the hierarchy. The soft power possessed by senior officers gives them the most leverage to manipulate expectations, and these coup attempts succeed around two-thirds of the time. They do not always succeed, because, although generals are at the apex of the command structure, they must rely on mid-level commanders in charge of fighting units to carry out their orders, and the commanders' obedience is not unconditional during a coup attempt. Even officers at the top have to make a fact. The chapter examines the cases of two coups from the top in Ghana, in 1975 and 1978, which illuminate both the advantages possessed by senior officers and the limitations associated with their position.

Chapter 5 addresses the roughly one-third of all coup attempts worldwide that come from the middle of the military hierarchy, those mounted by majors, lieutenant colonels, and colonels, the officers in charge of the actual fighting units in the military. Coups from the middle unfold with seizures of symbolic targets in highly visible locations and radio broadcasts proclaiming broad support for the coup and warning defenders that their loss is inevitable. Even though these military actors are those with the greatest amount of firepower at their disposal, these attempts succeed only around half of the time because hard power is less suited to manipulating expectations than is soft power. The chapter examines two Ghanaian cases with differing outcomes. The first, in 1967, came very close to succeeding but failed because of a sudden shift in expectations, while the second, in 1972, succeeded easily, bandwagoning so fast that even partisans of the incumbent were ready to support the challengers against rumored resistance.

Chapter 6 examines mutinies, that is, coups from the bottom of the armed forces hierarchy, organized by enlisted men or very junior officers. Of the one in seven coup attempts from the bottom, only about a third succeed, because the challengers have neither soft nor hard power with which to make a fact. The chapter examines three consecutive coup attempts in Ghana (May 1979, June 1979, and December 1981) with almost the same strategies and actors but varying sets of expectations and therefore different outcomes.

Chapter 7 is concerned with the failed Soviet coup of 1991. This was chosen as an out-of-sample case study because it was as different as possible from the Ghanaian cases, was a difficult case for the theory to explain (a coup from the top that failed), and was unusually well documented in the secondary literature. A close reading of the events demonstrates that the conventional explanation for the failure of this coup is flawed and that a critical part of the outcome was the propaganda campaign waged by Russian President Yeltsin's associates to shape expectations within the military.

The concluding chapter summarizes the findings and reviews their implications for broader scholarship in political science. It also reviews more recent coup attempts and draws lessons for the future of attempts in the face of the changing informational landscape that includes deeper penetration by foreign media, the rise of cell phones, and the Internet.

Chapter 2

Theory

Although there is little scholarship on the topic of this book, two arguments are present, implicitly and explicitly, in writing on civil-military relations that can explain the dynamics and outcomes of coup attempts. The first of these explanations claims that coup attempts are like battles, miniature invasions of the country by its own armed forces whose outcomes are determined by tactical dominance. This perspective posits that challengers win when they are stronger than the incumbent and therefore able to establish control over key military targets and suppress opposition. The second argument envisions coup attempts as referendums on the continued rule of the incumbent, a metaphorical plebiscite or vote of no confidence taken within the military. In this view, challengers win when the government is unpopular within the military, either because the incumbent has alienated the citizenry at large or because its policies have antagonized members of the armed forces in particular.

Based on extensive fieldwork and insights drawn from game theoretic literature, this book proposes a third theory, one that understands coup attempts as coordination games within the military. This theory holds that during such an attempt, each military actor wants to be on the same side as everybody else, both because a split within the military could lead to a civil war and because the penalties associated with backing the losing side are severe. In this explanation, challengers win by "making a fact," manipulating the beliefs of other military actors to make the victory of the coup attempt seem inevitable and resistance futile, thus creating self-fulfilling expectations around the coup's success. Doing this requires the ability to make a broadcast to the military, usually on national television or radio. Challengers are also more likely to be successful when they are from higher ranks within the military and when the history of recent attempts creates a favorable precedent.

Coups as Battles

The first of these theories about coup attempts emphasizes their tactical dimension, describing them as brief intense battles fought by armed factions for control of the country.[1] In essence, this perspective views a coup as essentially a civil war or an invasion in which the challenger comes from within the national armed forces. According to this argument, coups are successful when one side establishes clear military dominance over the other, a task that is made easier by having more men with more powerful weapons.[2] Proponents of this position agree with Napoleon's dictum that "God is on the side of the big battalions" (Biddle 2004, 14). As a result, if coup attempts are like battles, then first and foremost, one would expect the coup would be won by the stronger side.

Furthermore, the entire conduct of the coup should look like a short skirmish between two forces at war, one made even more intense by the fact that there is no point in holding any forces back (Luttwak 1979, 147). According to Luttwak, for instance, "The active phase of a coup is like a military operation—only more so" (146). Ghana's General Ocran concurred, saying that "the success or failure of... coups has been dependent on certain factors, amongst which are: secrecy, surprise, simple but sound planning... [and] ruthless offensive action" (Ocran 1977, 74). According to this scenario, successful challengers will exploit the element of surprise, such as by attacking late at night or during a national holiday (Ferguson 1987, 108), giving them a window of opportunity in which to ruthlessly neutralize any loyalist forces that might oppose the coup attempt (Luttwak 1979, 58). An effective challenge along these lines would leave loyalists confused as long as possible as to who is attacking and from what quarter (147).[3]

---

[1] Although there is very little work directly on questions of coup dynamics and outcomes, the argument that coups are like battles is present, explicitly or implicitly, in a variety of scholarly and journalistic writing about coups. The scholar most closely associated with this kind of explanation, and one of the few to write about coup dynamics, is Edward Luttwak. However, since Luttwak mixes claims associated with both battles and elections approaches in his book *Coup d'Etat: A Practical Handbook* (1979), what I have presented here cannot properly be considered Luttwak's analysis. Instead, I have distilled claims from diverse authors, including some who emulate Luttwak, into three brittle hypotheses designed to fairly represent an ideal version of the argument that coup attempts are primarily governed by tactical factors.

[2] Military strategists have enumerated a variety of factors that win battles. Which of these is most important remains debated. However, there is broad agreement that numerical and material superiority plays an important role, even amongst scholars who are critical of preponderance arguments (Biddle 2004, chap. 2). Other factors that are relevant in the context of international war—such as technology, knowledge of terrain, human capital, regime type and culture—matter little during a coup attempt, since they do not vary much within any given military. In addition, many of the caveats to the impact of preponderance have to do with the complexities involved in an extended campaign, most of which would be irrelevant in a short battle with a fairly small amount of territory at stake. For these reasons, my analysis posits that coup attempts should generally be won by the side in control of a preponderance of force.

[3] Some scholars also place a good deal of importance on the role of chance in determining coup outcomes; one even argues that "success in a coup d'etat seems to go to the side which simply made the fewest blunders" (Farcau 1994, 145). For example, Von Stauffenberg's 1944 coup attempt in Nazi Germany ("Operation Valkyrie") is said to have failed because the suitcase bomb that was to kill Adolf Hitler was moved slightly, thus sparing his life. However, such "for want of a nail the kingdom was lost" type explanations likely overstate the importance of minor tactical errors. Such mistakes are not uncommon during either coup attempts or wars, but actors are usually able to recover from them and still attain their objective. For example, the 1953 overthrow of Iran's Prime Minister Mossadegh was so rife with mishaps that it is offered as a lesson in how not to

If coup attempts are best understood as battles, then the goal of the challenger is to establish clear military dominance. It therefore follows that the primary targets during a coup attempt should have tactical importance. Luttwak suggests that coup attempts should target the command centers of the state, such as the headquarters of the armed forces, the central police station, and the presidential palace (Luttwak 1979, 157). Of lesser priority in this account are communications facilities, which should be sabotaged to keep defenders confused, and the least important targets are government buildings and political leaders (Farcau 1994, 96). The only political figure worth targeting during the coup attempt itself, according to this view, is the head of state, since he serves as commander of the armed forces and therefore may play a role in coordinating counter-coup activities.

In this scenario, the national broadcasting facilities have little tactical value during a coup attempt, although they are useful for establishing authority over civilians after the coup is over (Luttwak 1979, 118). Popular opposition is also not of concern, since "coups d'etat down the years have shown how loath people are to confront tanks and armed men with their bare hands" (Ferguson 1987, 61).

Because of the high stakes involved in a coup attempt, "conspirators must be willing to risk high violence levels to achieve their objectives, and government forces willingly use whatever force is seen as necessary to suppress the coup and then punish the perpetrators for their deeds, thus sending a powerful signal to future coup planners" (Kebschull 1994, 576). Another major prediction consistent with this perspective is therefore that the winning side must be willing to crush any resistance ruthlessly. This is not to say that military actors are bloodthirsty or willing to spill blood gratuitously. Challengers may, for example, offer loyalists a chance to surrender rather than engage them in a loud battle that may cost the coup makers the advantage of surprise (Luttwak 1979, 162). The argument here is simply that when penalties for being on the losing side include exile, prison, or execution, military actors have strong incentives to use violent force when it provides tactical benefit.

Coups as Elections

The second theoretical explanation for the success or failure of coup attempts views coups not as battles but as elections, seeing each coup attempt as essentially a plebiscite within the military. As in elections, the incumbents will survive the challenge if they have more support than the challengers and will fail if they do not. This is a preference-based explanation: what matters most to the success or failure of a military coup is how the members of the armed forces feel about the two sides (and the coup attempt itself), rather than the stealth and speed with which the coup attempt is launched and executed. According to this view, a highly popular

stage a coup, yet the attempt succeeded anyway (Hebditch & Connor 2008, 57-67). If such errors matter, they are likely to matter most when the two sides are evenly matched in strength, and less likely to matter the more one side has a preponderance of strength over the other.

government should be able to survive a perfectly executed assault, but an unpopular administration will crumble even if its adversaries are hapless and inept. While scholars holding this view grant that the tactical effectiveness of the coup attempt may matter in the unlikely circumstance that the challengers and defenders are perfectly matched, they see it as largely endogenous to support for the coup. This theory provides a unified approach to both coup attempts and outcomes: coup plots, failed coups, and successful coups are reflections of different levels of discontent with the government in power.[4]

There are two major variants of this approach, both of which are primarily designed to explain the occurrence of successful coups but which have clear implications for understanding both coup dynamics and coup outcomes. The first is a supply-side version, commonly called a "push" explanation, which argues that military intervention is driven by military politics. The second is a demand-side or "pull" explanation, which claims that the armed forces intervene in response to broader public discontent. As we shall see, despite these differences, both supply- and demand-side explanations of coup outcomes argue that coups reflect changes in military attitudes toward the government, differing only on whether discontent within the armed forces reflects organizational issues or broader political trends.

Supply-side explanations argue that militaries intervene in politics to protect their own institutional, class, or ethnic interests from interference by civil authorities. Their analytical focus is therefore on the characteristics of the military that set it at odds with the political leadership. According to Eric Nordlinger, "the great majority of coups are partly, primarily, or entirely motivated by the defense or enactment of the military's corporate interests" (Nordlinger 1977, 78). The military is unique among all branches of the state in having a strong corporate identity that separates it from the civilian world (Finer 1962, Huntington 1957, Nordlinger 1977).[5] As a result, the armed forces sometimes react violently to what they see as violations of their rights by civilians. Military intervention has been justified by a wide range of issues: interference with the military's ability to recruit, socialize, promote, and discipline their members according to internal criteria; cuts in military budgets; and the creation of praetorian guards. Grievances can be as petty as a lack of symbolic respect or as central as threats to abolish the armed forces (Finer 1962, chaps. 4-5). According to Horowitz, "the military [behaves] essentially as a trade union looking out for its own interests. When these are affected—and only then—the officers move to protect their budgets, their autonomy, their promotions, salaries, pensions, and perquisites" (Horowitz 1980, 5-6).

---

[4]In fact, early quantitative analysts of military coups thought it was so obvious that plots, failed coups, and successful coups were simply instances of the same thing that they combined them into a simple weighted additive index (Jackman 1978; Johnson, Slater & McGowan 1984).

[5]The armed forces recruits young men and subjects them to intense socialization designed to produce high levels of solidarity and esprit de corps. It also exercises an extreme level of control over all aspects of soldiers' lives, including matters commonly thought of as private. The military defines much more of its members lives than any other organization except monastic orders.

Factors relating to the recruitment and socialization of military members may also lead to coups (and coup attempts) by creating a gap between military and government preferences regarding key policies. For example, Latin American military coups have often been explained in terms of class conflict between a middle-class military and socialist politicians (Nun 1986). In this view, the military intervenes against oligarchies to open the door for the middle class and intervenes against populist leaders to keep the working class out (Huntington 1968, 222). In Africa, military coups are commonly attributed to ethnic differences between members of the military (who often come from marginal groups) and the political elite; in Europe, they are frequently seen as the result of an ideological cleavage between military and civilian elites.[6]

Demand-side explanations, on the other hand, posit that "the most important causes of military intervention in politics are not military but political and reflect not the social and organizational characteristics of the military establishment but the *political and institutional structure of society*" (Huntington 1968, 194). This theoretical perspective thus emphasizes the degree to which the military is swayed by larger social forces. Macro-level economic, social, and political factors make some countries more coup-prone than others. Poorer, heterogeneous countries with illegitimate governments are most likely to experience military intervention. These factors also function as the proximate cause of coups. Governments are considered more vulnerable during periods of economic or political crisis. Because demand-side explanations make little reference to the armed forces or the act of military overthrow itself, they have a high degree of overlap with explanations for regime change, and also more broadly with theories of civil wars and revolutions (Hegre & Sambanis 2006, Zimmermann 1983). Such explanations are currently the dominant approach to understanding military coups.[7]

For advocates of demand-side explanations, socio-political factors are both necessary and sufficient for military intervention. Such factors are a necessary precondition for a coup, according to Linz (1978, 17), because "it seems unlikely that military leaders would turn their arms against the government unless they felt that a significant segment of the society shared their lack of belief." They are sufficient because once a substantial vacuum of authority develops (what Huntington calls a

---

[6]Huntington (1957) suggests two strategies for reducing supply-side coup attempts. The first, subjective control, reduces civil-military tensions by giving the military the same set of preferences as the rulers. Traditionally, this was done by recruiting the military from the same class, ethnic group, and even family as the political elite (Quinlivan 1999). The second strategy, objective control, relies on a highly professionalized military which gives subservience to civil authority in return for the ability to govern itself in areas of its corporate expertise.

[7]Although there has been a decades-long debate between the advocates of supply- and demand-side explanations for military intervention, it is possible to integrate both approaches. Finer argues that supply-side factors provide the motive for military intervention, while demand-side factors provide the opportunity for it, thus constraining the form that military intervention can take in that society. Failed coup attempts are evidence that military actors were motivated to launch a coup attempt in a situation which was not ripe. Finer argues that the German Kapp Putsch is an example in which "the army, acting alone and in defiance of civilian opinion, was isolated and then defeated by civilian resistances" (Finer 1962, 98).

"praetorian society"), the military is naturally compelled to act, no matter what its characteristics (Finer 1962, Fitch 1977, Huntington 1968, Nordlinger 1977). In this view, the military is no longer an actor with independent preferences but a black box through which social discontent is transmitted.

If either form of this elections approach is correct, then its central proposition is that the outcome of a coup attempt should be determined by whether members of the military prefer the challenger to the incumbent.[8] Since both theories predict military behavior, they can only work through military preferences, regardless of the source of those preferences.

The elections explanation also assumes a mechanism linking individual preferences to outcomes. In an election, it is not enough simply to want the incumbent to win; you have to go and vote in order to make that happen. Similarly, during a successful coup attempt, individuals' actions must reflect their preferences over outcomes. Strongly pro-government officers should act to defend the government, strongly anti-government officers should act in support of the coup attempt, and officers who are indifferent or conflicted should act neutrally. This leads the elections theory to a second proposition, that the behavior of actors will correspond to their preferences.

While the elections theory is less focused on tactics and targets than the battles theory, it does place considerable importance on the ability of coup leaders to communicate and persuade other actors. In this scenario, public broadcasts can be used to sway the military by appealing directly to its members or indirectly by reaching out to the populace as a whole to exert popular pressure on the military to respond.[9] Because the purpose of such broadcasts is to increase the amount of active support for one side and to decrease the same for the other side, coup broadcasts can be viewed as functioning rather like campaign advertisements, informing actors of the benefits of the challengers and the shortcomings of the opposition. Thus, a third assumption that follows from this theoretical perspective is that broadcasts will be used to make appeals for support.

The need to convince members of the military to support or oppose the coup gives civilians a bigger potential role in the election story than the battle story. If supply-side forces are more important, the civilians that matter will be those who have moral authority over members of the military. If demand-side forces are critical,

---

[8]There is some disagreement among scholars concerning how much support is necessary to meet the threshold for victory. Nordlinger (1977, 101) argues that a side wins when it has a majority of support amongst the officer corps, or at least when pro-coup forces combined with neutral officers are a majority. Needler's discussion of the critical role played by a moderate "swing man" evokes images of the median voter and suggests that the support of the majority of the officer corps is required (Needler 1966). Fitch (1986, 159) sets the threshold higher still, arguing that coups succeed when there is a "consensus of opinion among the middle and upper ranks." In this book, I assume that the side with the plurality of support should prevail. The relevant franchise for each election is not, however, restricted to the officer corps; instead, it is defined contextually for each coup attempt.

[9]Even if the dominant side is confident it has sufficient support to prevail without the need for additional last minute appeals, in this scenario it should still seize radio and or television networks in order to deny their use to the other side.

then leaders with the ability to mobilize people to turn out in the streets, in either support of or opposition to the coup attempt, have an important role to play. In the latter case, the number of secondary targets increases dramatically. According to Ferguson, "potentially every cabinet minister, under-secretary and junior minister must be either suborned or neutralized... [and] potentially or actually hostile trades union leaders must be neutralized"(1987, 49-50).

When scholars of civil-military relations have discussed the failure of the 1961 coup attempt against French president Charles de Gaulle, to give an example, they use what is essentially an elections story. In this case, the challengers were militarily stronger than the loyalists, but they lacked popular support and were defeated by the combination of a mass civilian uprising and a pro-government revolt by conscripted soldiers. The conspiracy was organized by four retired Algerian generals in opposition to de Gaulle's decision to withdraw from Algeria, which was widely unpopular among the officer corps, who felt it was a betrayal of both the military and the nation. As a result, the challengers had the support of the most powerful units in the French armed forces. De Gaulle, however, refused either to abandon the planned independence of Algeria or to step down, arguing that the decision to grant independence had been approved by the French populace in a referendum just three months earlier. He then made a direct televised appeal to French citizens, saying, "I forbid all soldiers to obey the rebels ... I shall maintain this legitimate power whatever happens, up to the term of my mandate or until such time as I cease to have necessary means to do so or cease to be alive ... in the name of France I command that all means—I repeat *all means*—be used to bar the way to those men ... *Francaises! Francais! Aidez-Moi!*" (Finer 1962, 97). This was followed by an appeal by Prime Minister Debre, who issued more specific instructions to the populace and started to organize a Gaullist militia. The unions and most of the political parties rallied against the coup, and all of this activity swayed military conscripts, who were not particularly predisposed to support the continuation of the war in the first place and who heard de Gaulle's appeals on their transistor radios (Ferguson 1987, 87).

The generals in Algeria became isolated, as an increasing number of other commanders declared their opposition to the coup. They lacked transport to the metropole by either air or sea and faced the prospect of mass civilian opposition should they arrive in France. Although they still controlled more powerful military units than their adversaries, they had no support from either elite or mass civilian organizations and were a minority within the armed forces. The coup attempt collapsed, and the key conspirators were captured.

Coups as Coordination Games

Contrary to the above accounts, my own research reveals that military actors do not feel free to act directly upon their conscience or political beliefs during a coup attempt, and therefore coup attempts look little like elections. Instead, those military actors are concerned, first and foremost, with what other actors are likely to do and the consequences of their joint actions for themselves, the military, and the country. If an officer feels the government is deeply illegitimate, his desire to strike a blow against injustice is usually outweighed by the costs associated with backing a losing challenge. Even if he is willing to take the chance and support a side that might lose, he will be constrained by the fear that a coup attempt might degenerate into a fratricidal conflict, thus damaging the military and possibly dragging the country into a civil war. This fear of civil war means that coup attempts also look very little like battles, because an unrestrained battle is precisely what both sides are trying to avoid. As a result, the most important consideration in an actor's decision calculus is to support the side he believes everybody else will support, and military strength flows accordingly to that side.

The insight that actors coordinate during a coup attempt has important consequences for the conditions under which we would expect an attempt to succeed. If the strategic logic of a coup attempt is one of coordination, then we would expect a coup to be won by the side that is best at manipulating information and expectations, which is not necessarily the side with the most brute force or popularity. To succeed, the challengers must convince the rest of the military that their victory is a fait accompli, so that each actor believes that the others are likely to support the coup. When this manipulation is done properly, these expectations become self-fulfilling, with actors joining the coup because they believe that others will, thus making these expectations a reality. I call this process of shaping information and expectations so as to herd key actors into consensus around one outcome "making a fact."

Although I arrived at this understanding of coup dynamics primarily based on conversations with coup participants, there is within scholarly literature some support for the argument that coups are best understood as coordination games. Although there is little written on this topic, a few authors have nonetheless recognized that militaries coordinate prior to or during a coup (Geddes 1999, Geddes 2003, Geddes 2009, Lichbach 1998, Nordlinger 1977, Stepan 1974). Of these, my theory owes the greatest debt to Geddes, who states that "most officers... join coups that appear to be succeeding and oppose those that look likely to fail... there is no point in supporting an ideal that is doomed to failure when the cost of failure may be execution for treason, so calculations about the likely outcome of a coup attempt, which depends on what other officers decide to do, always influence decisions" (Geddes 2009, 6). In her work, Geddes treats coordination before and during coups as a general phenomenon, rather than an unusual occurrence, modeling this coordination formally as a coordination game and exploring a number of its implications (Geddes 1999, Geddes 2003, Geddes 2009). Continuing down this general path, this book more extensively develops the theoretical implications of coordination for coup making, based on insights from the field, and then tests the theory with original qualitative and quantitative data.

Why Coordinate?

This description of military behavior during coups is at odds with conventional depictions of military men as unswerving in their commitment, willing to die (or kill) for what they think is right. It is important to observe, therefore, that coordination is not an act of simple cowardice but instead is rooted in both rational concerns and military norms.

The main reason for restraint and coordination during a coup attempt is to avoid escalation into fratricidal conflict. The possibility that a coup attempt may end in a civil war is very real, and that this happens rarely is precisely because of strenuous efforts to avoid it by both sides during a coup attempt. For most members of the military, the benefits associated with having their preferred side win are small compared to the costs involved in a civil war, no matter who prevails in the end.

This rational calculation is reinforced by organizational norms that place great value on order within the armed forces. From the first days of military training, both soldiers and officers are taught that strength comes from coherent coordinated action and that undisciplined behavior during conflict is dangerous. As a result, the instinct to coordinate and avoid chaos is firmly rooted in strong habitual behavior.[10] In addition, norms governing behavior during a coup attempt differ from those to be applied a foreign invasion, when the national armed forces would be willing to fight to the last man (Farcau 1994, 49). During a coup attempt, this would entail killing one's fellow officers, men with whom one may have trained and who may even live in the same military complex. Even when opponents are strangers or feel enmity toward each other, they are still constrained by a common concern for the corporate welfare of the military institution (Geddes 1999, 54).

These pressures, both rational and normative, serve to constrain behavior during a coup attempt, despite the high stakes involved. The leaders of both sides take the possibility of a civil war seriously and are constrained by the desire to avoid it, in part because any such conflict would make their own families direct targets of violence. However, even if they are willing to accept this chance and start a fratricidal conflict in the hope of seizing power, they are constrained by other military actors. Forces that were initially uncommitted, for whom avoiding a civil war is

---

[10]The impulse to bandwagon during a coup attempt also has powerful psychological roots. Pressures to conform have a powerful effect on the actions of individuals, their decision making processes, and even their perceptions of the world. The literature on social influence has documented that the persuasiveness of a message is related to the number of others who are believed to agree with it; messages supported by a near consensus are given more weight, while minority arguments are handicapped (Crano & Prislin 2006). In the 1950s, Solomon Asch demonstrated that experimental subjects would give an obviously wrong answer to a simple factual question (which of three lines was the longest) rather than openly disagree with others in the same group. Later experiments demonstrated that pressures to conform could also operate on a subtler and deeper level, shaping respondents' perceptions at a level previously believed to be physiological (Levine, Resnick & Higgins 1993, 598). From this perspective then, it is unsurprising that actors during a coup attempt—individuals drawn from an organization that prizes conformity, lacking information about what is going on, making decisions under great stress—would want to support the same side that they believe others will support as well.

paramount, may well reject the side that appears to behave rashly, thereby causing that side to lose. In addition, faction leaders cannot fight a war alone; they need the cooperation of their subordinates, men for whom the benefits of victory are lower than they are for the leader but who would still stand to suffer greatly if there were a civil war, one that would endanger the lives of their friends and families. As a result, they may refuse an order to massacre their peers or, worse yet, may defect or even turn against their commanders. The fact that the stakes are high for leaders does not, therefore, automatically mean that factions are willing to behave recklessly during a coup attempt.

The Foundations of Power

This interpretation of military coups as coordination games is consistent with a broader body of literature that uses coordination games to model the dynamics and outcomes of regime changes in political science (DeNardo 1985, Granovetter 1978, Kuran 1997, Kuran 1989), economics (Calvo 1988, Chamley 1999, Cole & Kehoe 2000, Cooper & John 1988, Diamond & Dybvig 1983, Guimaraes & Morris 2007, Katz & Shapiro 1986, Morris & Shin 1998, Morris & Shin 2004, Obstfeld 1996), and sociology (Mackie 1996). Coordination games capture the fact that incumbent regimes depend critically on the compliance (active or passive) of their members. The regime cannot stand if enough members turn against it, but it only makes sense for members to oppose the regime if they believe that enough others will also do so and the challenge will thus succeed. Furthermore, if the tide turns against the regime, then even those members who support it will abandon it. Since the fate of a regime depends on the actions of its members and these in turn depend on their beliefs about each other, information and expectations are more important in determining the outcome of challenges to a regime than either preferences or any measure of fundamentals.

We are most familiar with this dynamic in an economic context, where it is used to explain bank runs and currency crises (Diamond & Dybvig 1983). Money is a store of value; the solvency of any economic regime rests, at bottom, on the confidence of its members rather than on any reserves held in a central bank vault. This confidence is in turn a consequence of the expectations of its members about each others' behavior, not of their opinions about the legitimacy of the system. In the absence of an outside guarantor, the stability of a financial system rests upon self-fulfilling beliefs.

Although political regimes appear to be grounded quite strongly in material reality, such as the number of guns and bullets that a dictator has in his armory, coup attempts expose the foundation of expectations that supports this facade of strength. What matters is less the quantity of arms than the expectations of the people who wield them. "Hard" power relies on "softer" expectations in order to function. No dictator can remain in office if he is abandoned by the men with guns who support him, and those men will stay only if they believe that enough others will support the government for it to survive. The ability of the ruler to wield force

Figure 2.1: Choosing sides during a coup attempt

Pro-Gov't

		Rebel	Defend
	Rebel	9,1	-5,-5
Anti-Gov't			
	Defend	-9,-9	1,9

is contingent upon the existence of the supporting expectations, and this gives coup makers a point of leverage with which to take over the state.

Game Theoretic Models of Coordination

The strategic behavior of military actors during a coup attempt is captured by the kind of coordination game that game theorists have named a battle of the sexes game, one that describes coordination by actors with different preferred outcomes. In the game described below, the military is divided into two factions that have to decide how to respond to a coup attempt. One faction supports the government, the other is opposed to it. Each faction has two possible strategies: to join the coup (rebel) or to oppose it (defend). The numbers used here are chosen arbitrarily for the sake of illustration; what matters here are not the payoffs per se but their relative ordering.

The anti-government faction's favored outcome is one in which the entire military joins in the coup attempt, because then the coup will succeed, which will yield them a payoff of 9. In their second-best outcome, both factions defend the government, which means that the coup makers will surrender and the coup will fail, yielding the anti-government faction a payoff of 1. The worst outcomes are the ones in which the two factions disagree and the military slides into civil war, with the eventual victor being unclear. These outcomes yield negative payoffs for both players. For ease of exposition, the pro-government faction has symmetrical payoffs, preferring that both sides unite to support the government, their second-best outcome being that both sides support the coup, and their worst outcome that the two disagree and the country slides into civil war.

This very simple game captures the most salient features of the more complicated real life experience of a coup. Officers are driven to coordinate even though they have clear preferences over outcomes because of the costs of a non-coordinated outcome. Furthermore, because this is a simultaneous game, it means that each player has to make his choice about which side to support without knowledge of what the others will do, even though their payoffs are determined only jointly. As such, each has to choose his strategy based on his beliefs and on meta-beliefs about the likely behavior of the other actors. The result is a game that has a fundamental indeterminacy. The structure of the situation produces two equilibria in pure strategies, one in which both sides support the government and another in which both sides support the coup, but the structure does not dictate the outcome.

In developing the theoretical argument for this book, I draw upon three bodies of literature within game theory to generate claims about how we would expect to see coordination shape the dynamics and outcomes of military coups. I largely focus on insights drawn from the analysis of the basic battle of the sexes game. As Schelling demonstrated, there is considerable power in even so simple a model because of the parsimonious way in which it encapsulates the key strategic interaction between players. This approach emphasizes the importance of information and expectations, not structural factors, in determining the outcome of the game (Calvo 1988, Cole & Kehoe 2000, Cooper & John 1988, Diamond & Dybvig 1983, Obstfeld 1996). In most of the rest of this chapter I follow Schelling's discussion of strategic moves, applying arguments about the strategic moves that can be used to solve coordination games to provide insight into the actual strategies used by participants in military coups (Schelling 1960, chap. 5).[11]

As is true with many formal models, describing military coups as a battle of the sexes game simplifies many aspects of the real world for the sake of parsimony. This basic game shows only two actors choosing between two strategies at a single point in time, when in fact coup attempts are clearly more complex. In addition, the core game does not formally model information, beliefs, or the entire structure of meta-beliefs necessary for coordination. Unfortunately, there is no extant class of models that includes the key dimensions one would like to see in the formalization of a coup. Lacking such, the analysis in this book works primarily with the simplest possible model and attempts to discuss factors external to it without explicit formalization.

To make sure that arguments drawn from the analysis of simple coordination games are consistent with findings drawn from more sophisticated models of coordination, I also draw upon a subset of findings from the literature on global games, a class of formal models used by economists to model situations such as currency attacks, debt crises, and bank runs. Most global game models are multi-player coordination games in which individuals have to independently choose whether to support an attack on the status quo which will be overturned if the actors opposing it exceed a certain threshold. Global games are useful because they formally model the interactions of a large number of actors and explicitly model the role of infor-

---

[11] As a point of clarification, this theory is not based on the literature on informational cascades. Although both coordination games and information cascades are used to explain regime change and posit that actors bandwagon toward a common outcome, the mechanisms involved are very different. In a coordination game, actors are all trying to be on the same side, but without knowing what others are doing. In an information cascade model, actors do not care about being on the same side, but since they can observe the actions of others, they allow their own choices of which side to back to be informed by the decisions of others. Because of the differences in mechanisms, the dynamics are very different between these two models. For example, actors in information cascades require no public information but are highly sensitive to the sequence in which they receive private information (Bikhchandani, Hirshleifer & Welch 1998).

mation and expectations in determining outcomes. In particular, I draw upon the work of Angeletos, Hellwig, and Pavan (Angeletos, Hellwig & Pavan 2006; Angeletos, Hellwig & Pavan 2007; Angeletos & Pavan 2007) and Edmond (2007, 2008), scholars who extend the classical global game model in ways that make it more relevant for understanding coup attempts. That they find evidence for similar dynamics of coordination while working from different premises lends additional plausibility to the hypotheses in this book.[12]

Lastly, because I am interested in the behavior of real people and not idealized rational actors, I also draw upon results from experimental game theory. This body of research examines how people behave when confronted with the strategic dynamics contained in game theoretic models, paying close attention to the fact that humans are not as rational as the models assume, nor do most people solve complicated mathematical equations before choosing how to act. Although the subjects in such experiments have usually been American undergraduates operating in laboratory settings, that their behavior is generally consistent with the theory provides additional reason to believe that insights drawn from game theory can appropriately be applied to understanding behavior during coup attempts.

Manipulating Expectations during Coup Attempts

This section builds upon the basic intuition that coups are like coordination games to explain the strategic gambits used by participants in coups to manipulate information and expectations in pursuit of victory. Understanding these gambits produces specific hypotheses about the necessity of controlling the means of generating common knowledge, the content of broadcasts made during a coup attempt, the significance of symbolic targets, and the importance of keeping military casualties as low as possible.

---

[12]This book does not, however, draw upon the major body of recent work on global games, because such models contain assumptions, both substantive and formal, that are inconsistent with observed behavior (Carlsson & VanDamme 1993, Goldstein & Pauzner 2005, Morris & Shin 1998). For example, most of these models critically assume that the strength of the incumbent regime is exogenously determined, which is most definitely not the case in military coups. In addition, coordination during a global game involves universal yet private knowledge about the strength of the incumbent. However, precisely because incumbent strength is not fixed, actors in coups do not know how strong the incumbent is, nor do they have good meta-beliefs concerning what others believe the strength of the incumbent to be. As a result of this and other differences between the model and the basic situation confronted by actors during a coup, behavior during a coup attempt does not look like that described by global games. The final problem is that the purpose of the major stream of global games is to find a set of circumstances under which coordination games collapse to a single equilibrium dictated by the extrinsic strength of the regime. Much of the popularity of these models stems from the fact that they take a complicated situation and produce a single answer. While the discovery of such conditions is intellectually interesting, it is not very useful when such conditions do not apply to the condition at hand, and changing minor assumptions or increasing complexity causes multiple equilibria to reappear (Angeletos, Hellwig & Pavan 2006; Angeletos, Hellwig & Pavan 2007). Since such models cannot handle behavior like public broadcasts that contain falsehoods, they are not useful for discussing coup attempts.

Controlling Public Information

If coups are best understood as coordination games, then it follows that the winning side has some way to create expectations favorable to its success and therefore must have some way to generate common knowledge. One canonical method for producing common knowledge is via a mass media broadcast (Chwe 2001). A broadcast is not only heard by everyone, but everybody knows that everybody else has heard it, and everybody knows that everybody knows that everybody has heard it, ad infinitum. The content of a broadcast becomes what I call public information, claims and statements that are common knowledge for members of the target audience.[13]

The importance of public broadcasts is well understood by political leaders around the world, particularly those in young countries where governments are still establishing their authority. In much of the world (both developing and developed), citizens start their day with the morning broadcast of the government news. In poor countries, people with radios turn them up loud enough for their neighbors to hear as well. This shared ritual binds the members of an imagined community into a polity and establishes the authority of the state for all citizens (Anderson 1983).

A coup attempt enacts this ritual in reverse by using public information to create a set of beliefs about the inevitable victory of the challenger and the demise of the incumbent. The key audience for broadcasts during a coup attempt, however, is other military actors, not the citizenry. What matters is that the broadcast become public or common knowledge within the military, not that it be heard by the public. Later broadcasts, made after the coup attempt is over, are intended for the masses.

Because the intended audience of the broadcast is small, usually key unit commanders in the military, some coup attempts also use a face-to-face meeting to create information that is public within this group. Face-to-face meetings, often with everybody sitting in a circle, are the way humans have traditionally coordinated and created common knowledge (Chwe 2001). Although more logistically difficult, meetings are superior to mass media broadcasts for "making facts." In a meeting, not only does the initial claim ("the government is no longer in charge") become common knowledge, but so do the reactions of everybody else present. Since what occurs during these meetings is usually carefully stage-managed, precluding free discussion, the person in charge of the meeting can manipulate the proceedings to create the appearance of unanimous support for the coup. The appearance of unanimous support for the coup instantly becomes common knowledge within the group, making each person present believe that all others are in support, and therefore making it extremely unlikely that any of them will defect afterwards.[14]

---

[13]My use of the word *information* here is colloquial, rather than technical. In game theory, *information* has a precise meaning, referring to accurate, factual knowledge only. I am using the word in a more colloquial fashion, to refer to the broad class of claims and statements that one hears, without presumption to whether they are true or false.

[14]Meetings like this are less common than broadcasts during coup attempts for a number of reasons. They are more logistically difficult to arrange, and the challengers will only organize one when they are convinced that they can manipulate events during the meeting to their satisfaction.

The objective of challengers is not just to make a single broadcast but to monopolize public information for the duration of the coup attempt. This is most easily done in a meeting where the coup makers will be in control of what happens for the time it takes to make a fact. It is also straightforward in countries where there is a media monopoly (even if there are multiple channels), since the coup makers need to control only a single broadcasting facility to ensure their control over the airwaves. If, on the other hand, coup makers are striking in a country where there are multiple broadcasting entities in the capital, they will usually seize the most popular one and either shut the others down or, if they have the requisite manpower, force the others to carry the same recorded message. However, if they are unable to monopolize public information during the course of a coup attempt, the incumbent will be able to create contrary expectations. If there are dueling broadcasts, many military units are likely to sit on the fence, waiting for further developments before choosing which side to support.[15]

A good example of the power of the radio station to make a fact is the 1969 Libyan coup, in which a twenty-seven-year-old Captain Gaddafi and a small number of other low-ranking officers "with only a few revolvers and a mere forty-eight rounds of ammunition" took over the radio station and one other target and managed to bloodlessly overthrow King Idriss (Reed & Stillman 2009, 149).[16]

Using Broadcasts to Make a Fact

While simply making a broadcast shapes expectations, the content of the broadcast also helps (or hinders) the success of the coup attempt.[17] For a successful coup, the

---

In addition, because meetings are so dangerous, incumbents will take great pains to prevent them from occurring if those in power are concerned about the possibility of challenge.

[15] Public information is also critical to equilibrium selection in global games, especially in situations with high levels of strategic complementarity like coup attempts (Angeletos & Pavan 2007, Edmond 2008). Since global games are designed in such a way that actors can coordinate based largely on private information (although this requires that beliefs about the strength of the regime be common knowledge), the fact that public information plays an important role in equilibrium selection even in these models shows how important control of public information is.

[16] There is little information on what actually happened during the coup attempt. One of the few other descriptions makes the plot seem more elaborate, with a greater number of officers attacking a few other targets, but whichever account is correct it is clear that the attackers were tactically fairly weak and could have been stopped had those within the military not bandwagoned in their favor (Simons 1996, 160). The best explanation for the success of this coup lies in the fact that most members of the military had expected a coup attempt by more powerful members of the military at that time, and since the broadcast did not identify who the coup makers were, claiming only that the army had acted to overthrow the government, the expectation was created that the coup's success was a fait accompli.

[17] In theory, it might be enough to whisper "coup" into the microphone at the main broadcasting center for the government to collapse. If there were no other factors that created expectations, a broadcast by the challenger would automatically encourage coordination simply by virtue of providing an arbitrary focal point. An equilibrium formed around the realization of a wholly random variable, one without any intrinsic relevance to the game being played, is known as a sunspot equilibrium (Cass & Shell 1983). In an experiment involving a simulated currency market, which has similar dynamics to a coup, Duffy and Fisher (2005) demonstrate how easily such

content of the broadcast should convey a credible but exaggerated sense of the strength of the challengers relative to the loyalists.[18] The challengers will try to make a fact by claiming that their victory is a fait accompli, that they have broad support within the armed forces, and that any resistance to the coup is on its last legs. This is the part of the broadcast that matters, not the boilerplate justifications offered for the coup, claims that vary remarkably little from one attempt to the next (Kirk-Greene 1981).[19] The same logic works in reverse for loyalist actors trying to defeat a coup.

Whichever side has control over the tools for creating common knowledge will issue a broadcast in the service of making a fact. For example, if the broadcast is made by the challengers, they will claim that their victory is inevitable and that resistance is both futile and dangerous. To do this, they will almost always overstate their strength and tactical position, but in a way that is plausible. This claim will be effective even if the recipients of the message recognize it as an exaggeration, because their primary concern is with coordination, and even a bluff may nudge coordination in one direction or the other.

Note that this is very different behavior from what one would expect if coups were like battles or elections. If coups were like battles, the content of the broadcast would be irrelevant; if they were like elections, an effective broadcast would tell supporters that victory is at hand but that the participation of each and every supporter is necessary to achieve it. In an election, a broadcast that exaggerates strength can backfire, causing supporters to think their involvement is unnecessary. During an interview with an officer who had foiled two coup attempts, I asked him why he didn't make the kinds of broadcasts that were consistent with an election model. He looked horrified by the idea, warning me that doing so would doom any challenger foolish enough to try it.[20]

An example of the importance of the content of a broadcast comes from Admiral Gruber's failed coup attempt against President Perez of Venezuela in November 1992. According to both battle and election theories, this coup attempt should have succeeded. The challengers had a good deal of military strength at their disposal,

---

equilibria can be generated. The experimenters simply flipped a coin and, depending on how the coin landed, broadcast just the word 'high' or 'low' to the players. Players then converged around the corresponding value of the simulated currency, even though they knew that the broadcast was entirely arbitrary and the outcome of the game would affect their monetary payoff. This worked because the broadcast was the only bit of common knowledge possessed by the players, so each assumed that the others would home in on the arbitrary signal.

[18]Although exaggerating strength, the broadcast should not go too far. A bluff works only if it is credible and if the receiver cannot tell how extensive the bluff is even if they determine that the statement is not entirely accurate. A lieutenant cannot claim to have gained control over the key units around the capital, but a colonel or a general might. An admiral cannot claim to have the support of the air force if the two services are known to be antagonistic and there is not a single plane in the sky to back up his claim.

[19]Over the course of my interviews, I did not encounter a single individual who said they changed sides (or even changed their opinion of the desirability of a coup attempt) based on the moral arguments offered. This is why the most elaborate justifications are offered in a separate broadcast announcing the junta, once the challengers have prevailed.

[20]Interview with Major Courage Quashigah. July 26th, 2000. Accra, Ghana.

and an internal survey revealed that the members of the military were deeply dissatisfied. The coup makers failed to effectively make a fact, however, because a logistical mix-up caused a garbled tape to be broadcast on television. Watchers would have been able to tell only that a coup attempt was in progress but not who was involved nor how strong the challengers were. The only information that could be gleaned was that the coup attempt was undertaken by allies of Colonel Hugo Chavez, who was imprisoned awaiting trial for his coup attempt in February of that year. Since Chavez, while popular, had failed in the February attempt, the challengers did not convey that they were strong and their victory was inevitable. Later that morning, President Perez appeared on television to assure the populace that everything was fine, and a few hours later Admiral Gruber surrendered (Gott 2005, chap. 11).

There are two reasons why exaggerated claims of strength are effective even if everybody recognizes that those making the broadcast have an incentive to stretch the truth. The first comes from sophisticated game theoretic models of coordination; it points out that propaganda can be effective at creating coordination as long as the recipients of the broadcast are unsure how much exaggeration there is and are unsure how much others are going to discount the information. As long as actors are concerned that others may be more swayed by the message than they are, they will disregard that the broadcast is not literally true, in order to end up on the same side as other actors.[21] The second reason is that even if it were theoretically possible for a rational actor to filter out the exaggerations in the broadcast, experiments demonstrate that followers' beliefs are strongly influenced by messages even if those messages would not appear to be credible to a Bayesian rational recipient. The reason is that "followers appear not fully to account for leaders' strategic incentives to misrepresent the state of the world in forming their posterior beliefs." (Dickson forthcoming) These experiments also showed that more credible messages had a greater impact on coordination, although the impact of credibility was still modest (Dickson forthcoming). If undergraduates sitting comfortably in a laboratory setting deviate from Bayesian rational behavior, it is reasonable to expect that military officers thinking on their feet in stressful situations will do so as well, making exaggeration even more effective in the real world than in a formal model.[22]

---

[21] This result is demonstrated formally by Edmond (2008). The literature on global games almost uniformly assumes that all signals sent during the game are true, albeit with some noise, and even the distribution of noise is common knowledge. Edmond is the only scholar to tackle the question of what happens to coordination when the game contains credible but false statements.

[22] As an aside, although we should expect the broadcast to exaggerate, this does not necessarily mean that the party making the broadcast is engaging in an intentional bluff. Instead, they may well believe the accuracy of most of their claims, in much the same way that coaches, inspirational business leaders, and revolutionaries believe their overly optimistic utterances. There is little room for self-doubt in the middle of attacking a government; high morale and esprit de corps are essential here. If the person making the broadcast sounded insincere, he would not be persuasive, so in this case self-deception may be advantageous (Johnson 2004, 7). If the person making the broadcast appears to believe what he is saying, this may increase the credibility of the broadcast and therefore its impact.

Figure 2.2: Risk dominance

Player B

		Defend	Rebel
	Defend	2,2	-9,0
Player A			
	Rebel	0,-9	1,1

Shaping Expectations by Capturing Symbolic Targets

Challengers can reinforce the message of their broadcast by capturing prominent symbolic targets, such as the parliament building. These locations are valuable because they are in prominent sites and represent state power, and so their seizure becomes common knowledge if enough actors observe it and believe that others have observed it and so on. Capturing symbolic sites allows the challengers to signal their strength in a public and costly fashion, thus shaping expectations about which side would win if there were a failure to coordinate, which in turn influences the decision of which outcome to coordinate around.

In game theory, an outcome that is chosen because it is safer in the event of a failure to coordinate is called the risk-dominant outcome. Figure 2.2 models a situation in which both undecided actors prefer the government over the challenger; if they both back the government the payoff to each is 2, and if they both back the coup, the payoff to each is 1. (The numbers chosen here are purely arbitrary, chosen for illustration only, although their cardinal values are relevant to this example.) In this example, the fact that both players agree that the government is preferable does not mean that they will both defend the government, contrary to what would happen if coups were like elections. The reason is that neither can assume the actions of the other, and therefore they have to take into account the costs associated with a non-coordinated outcome as well. Each of them knows that if he defends the government while the other backs the rebels, then the military will split, there will be damage to the state, the rebels will probably win and punish anybody who opposed them, and the player will receive a payoff of -9. Meanwhile, if an actor backs the rebels without support from anybody else, he will receive a payoff of 0, indicating that he would have preferred either outcome that did not involve fighting, but he is still better off for having backed the stronger side. As a result, it makes little sense for either actor to support the government unless they are 83% certain that the other will as well. This makes backing the challenger the safer strategy, even though both would prefer to defend the government.[23]

---

[23]The same basic story holds even if the penalties for backing the losing side are not symmetrical. If only player B is afraid of being on the wrong side of the coup, player A will assume that player

When similar games (ones where both sides agree on their preferred outcomes) are played in the laboratory, the effect of risk dominance is also quite pronounced, emerging as often as 98% of the time in some scenarios (Cooper 1999, 3).[24] This finding suggests that this behavior is generic to the way humans coordinate and may be even more pronounced in real life.

The examples above concern situations where players unanimously support one side, but risk dominance exerts an even more powerful influence on equilibrium selection when actors disagree on the ideal outcome, as is true for coups, and the degree of risk dominance predicts the frequency with which the risk-dominant equilibrium is chosen (Cabrales, Garca-Fontes & Motta 2000). More generally, risk dominance predicts equilibrium selection quite well in environments where there is a higher degree of uncertainty about what the other player might do (Cabrales, Nagel & Armenter 2007; Carlsson & VanDamme 1993). Scholars of evolutionary game theory have also found that in environments with continual small stochastic shocks, risk-dominant equilibria emerge as the long-term equilibrium of the population (Kandori, Mailath & Rob 1993). More broadly, risk-dominant equilibria are selected in environments with incomplete information or stochastic noise because they are robust to a wide range of conditions (Peski 2010).[25]

This strategy is a more indirect way to shape expectations than making a broadcast, and therefore is not as effective. It can still play an important supplementary role, however, especially when the challenger has problems of credibility that are common knowledge or when multiple broadcasts are made by the different sides, confusing matters. Risk dominance also illustrates how tactical power can be translated into expectations and why even unanimous preferences of military actors do not automatically determine outcomes.

Lowering Casualties

Although the seizure of symbolic targets may involve force, as may other aspects of the coup attempt, I argue that actors make a deliberate effort to limit the risk of casualties during a coup attempt and that it is enough of a priority that they

---

B will back the challenger, player B will assume that player A assumes that player B will back the challenger, etc. In the end, both players will be likely to coordinate around the safer outcome, even if only one of them is afraid.

[24]Exactly how often the risk-dominant equilibrium prevails over the Pareto-dominant equilibrium in laboratory assurance games is a matter of scholarly debate and is conditional on a number of factors (Devetag & Ortmann 2007). What is relevant for our purpose is that even when there is a payoff-dominant strategy, the risk-dominant outcome is common (Cooper, DeJong, Forsythe & Ross 1990; Cooper, DeJong, Forsythe & Ross 1992, Straub 1995), and players respond more to changes in the level of risk dominance than to the level of payoff dominance (Schmidt, Shupp, Walker & Ostrom 2003). This demonstrates that expectations about what happens off the equilibrium path play an important role in equilibrium selection, even in assurance games.

[25]The importance of risk dominance as a solution criterion for games with multiple equilibria extends beyond situations characterized by friction, however. Scholars using "perfect foresight dynamics" to investigate equilibria chosen by large populations of forward-looking and rational individuals find that generalized versions of risk dominance serve as powerful and stable attractors in situations with very little friction (Kojima 2006, 256).

are willing to accept a tactical cost for doing so. As a result, aggregate military casualties are far lower during a coup attempt than they would be if a similar conflict had occurred as part of either an international invasion or a civil war.[26]

While there is too little reliable data on casualties to establish this claim statistically, incidents like the overthrow of Chile's President Allende in 1973, which resulted in roughly eighty military deaths on both sides, appear to be the exception and not the rule.[27] More common are scenarios like the failed coup attempt against Venezuela's President Chavez in 2002, which led to the deaths of twenty-six civilians but no military deaths.

In part, this restraint is related to the same desire to avoid a bloody fratricidal struggle that motivates coordination during a coup attempt. To unleash unrestrained violence on your adversary is to invite the same in return and to increase the chance of a slide into civil war. In addition, although this may appear counter-intuitive, factions also avoid the indiscriminate use of force during a coup attempt for fear that it will signal weakness. Strong actors should have no need to slaughter their opponents, and therefore an actor who uses a good deal of bloodshed is presumed to be weak. Since coups are about shaping expectations, tactical gains associated with the willingness to use violence are offset by this perception of weakness, which drives uncommitted actors to the other side.

Thus, even at the end of a coup attempt, despite the very real possibility of capital punishment for challengers who fail, challengers will chose to surrender (or flee) rather than fight to the last man. For example, at the end of the failed 1991 Soviet coup attempt, Interior Minister Boris Pugo killed himself and his wife rather than face trial, but he did not use the troops under his command to mount a bloody last-ditch stand. Loyalists behave the same way.

History

Another important factor influencing the expectations of actors during a coup attempt is the outcome of recent coup attempts in the same country. In coordination games, the impact of past coordination affects current behavior because precedent generates common knowledge and therefore shapes expectations (Chwe 2001, 7). For example, in dynamic multiplayer models of coordination, those that allow actors to pause and choose their actions at different points in time, "outcomes ... depend critically on available information and the history of past play" (Angeletos, Hellwig & Pavan 2007, 713). The influence of history is visible not just in mathematical models of coordination but in experiments as well, where the history of past play has been shown to influence current behavior and to provide a basis for coordina-

---

[26]Note that this logic does not extend to civilians, since they are unarmed and therefore their deaths do not increase the risk of conflict escalation within the military.

[27]Even here, one could argue that there was some restraint, given the stakes, since the number who died during the coup attempt was a small fraction of the much larger number who were killed during military rule (Scheina 2003, 326).

tion, even if players only observed previous rounds and did not play those rounds themselves (Schmidt, Shupp, Walker & Ostrom 2003).

The impact of history was mentioned by many interview respondents as an influence on their initial expectations about the likely behavior and beliefs (and meta-beliefs) of other actors. When a coup attempt starts, actors may not know much about what is happening, not even the identity of the challenger, but they know the outcome of past attempts and that this history is common knowledge. They have reason to expect that other military actors will use this history to guide their initial reactions to the coup attempt, especially if the prior attempts were recent and so shaped the personal experience of the officers and men in charge.

As the coup attempt unfolds and new information comes in, actors revise their prior beliefs about the likelihood of the coup's success. History, however, establishes a handicap for challengers. If past attempts failed, it is harder to convince others that your victory is a fait accompli, and therefore challengers have to do more in the present to make a fact. All other things being equal, the history of past coup attempts in a country can determine the difference between the success and failure of a coup attempt by either encouraging or hindering coordination around the challengers.

This argument is distinct from the claim that there is a "coup trap" where one successful coup in a country makes others more likely by breaking the institutional taboo concerning coup making. If coups are coordination games, then not only can a successful coup open the door to other successes but a failed coup can close it again by making future attempts less likely to succeed.[28]

Rank

The final determinant of coup dynamics and outcomes is organizational: the rank level that the challengers occupy within the armed forces. As an empirical matter, coup makers from the top, middle, and bottom of the military hierarchy possess very different resources with which to make a fact, leading to three distinct trajectories with different likelihoods of success.[29] If coups are like coordination games, then

---

[28]There are two other salient points of difference. The first is that the coup trap argument explains both attempts and outcomes, whereas this theory restricts itself to the latter question. Second, while the presence of a coup trap would suggest that the first attempt is less likely to succeed than later attempts (because the normative barrier is not yet breached), the data argue the opposite, namely that the first attempt is more likely to succeed. This points to the importance of looking at failed attempts as well as successes, and it argues that the mechanism involved is informational not normative.

[29]The division of the military into three strata is based on conversations with interview respondents; it is their language and not mine. While arbitrary, it reflects a fundamental functional division of the armed forces. Coups from the middle involve military units with an almost organic unity: they are large enough that they are self-sufficient and can move on their own, but still small enough that the officers and men know each other, train together, and live together. The exact line that separates the middle from the top on one side and the bottom on the other can be debated; an argument can be made that the middle should be more inclusive or that junior officers or junior generals should have their own category. However, to increase the number of categories would cost more in clarity and parsimony than it would gain in precision.

the probability of success should vary directly with the level of the coup attempt, with coups from the top the most likely to succeed and coups from the bottom the least likely. Furthermore, the organizational position of the coup makers should influence the entire character of the coup attempt in distinctive ways.

There are strong structural pressures that make most coup attempts homogenous by stratum. Rank defines all aspects of life within the military, encouraging horizontal ties while discouraging vertical ones through prohibitions against fraternization. Conspiracies develop among men of similar rank because it is easiest to meet with peers and because trust is highest among peers.[30] In addition, conspirators are usually of the same level within the military because officers of very different ranks have a difficult time working together. Such tensions contributed to the failure of the 1981 coup attempt in Spain in which three different conspiracies, one at the middle and two at the top, merged. During one of the critical moments in the coup attempt, however, Colonel Antonio Tejero Molina, who was holding the Spanish parliament hostage, refused to follow the orders of more senior co-conspirator General Alfonso Armada, thus "completely deflating" the chance that the coup would succeed (Aguero 1995, 166).[31]

The way in which rank shapes all phases of the coup attempt is described in greater detail in chapters 4, 5, and 6. What follows here is a survey of major parts of that argument.

Coups from the Top

These coup attempts are the most likely to succeed, because the organizational resources granted to generals enable them to best manipulate the beliefs and expectations of other military actors.

While generals do not command the unconditional obedience of their subordinates during a coup attempt, their position within the institution grants them a good deal of soft power that they can use to make a fact in ways unavailable to challengers from the middle or bottom.[32] For example, they can lay the groundwork for their coup attempt by meeting individually with the major commanders around the capital to tell each one that an internal report has revealed that many

---

[30] At times, this may lead to conspiracies which straddle the barrier between strata, particularly between officers right at the border between the middle and the top of the military. In practice, these conspiracies tend to involve a senior officer who is limited in his ability to use organizational power to make a fact and so collaborates with other officers with command authority to mount what is essentially a coup from the middle. An example of a coup of this sort is the Greek coup of April 1967, in which a brigadier and several colonels jointly moved troops to take control of Athens. The resulting junta was called "the regime of the colonels."

[31] The unwillingness of Colonel Tejero to accept General Armada's orders also underscores the limitations of senior officers during a coup: their hierarchical authority is not sufficient even to guarantee the obedience of more-junior officers who share the same goal.

[32] This soft power is largely the result of the position held by generals within the military and is amplified by the fact that most officers that are promoted to this level have very good people skills. However, it is unrelated to any connections that such generals may or may not have to civilian elites.

other commanders would join a coup attempt, thus making each one more likely to support a coup.

When mounting a coup, generals have a fairly easy time accessing public information, especially if there are mechanisms for making official armed forces broadcasts, such as an internal radio station. They can also take control of public information by holding a meeting of mid-level unit commanders, which is more effective than a radio broadcast at making a fact. When successful, coups from the top are both quicker and less bloody than coups fomented by challengers from lower levels of the military.

Coups from the Middle

These are coup attempts staged by officers in control of fighting units such as battalions, regiments, and brigades. Such officers, usually majors, lieutenant colonels, and colonels, use the hard power at their disposal to try to shape the beliefs and expectations of the other military actors.

Coups from the middle are usually staged in the dead of night, with an attack on the broadcast facilities and key symbolic locations in the capital. As in other types of coups, the challengers will use public information to try to convince the rest of the military that their victory is a fait accompli and that resistance is futile. If they succeed, then other military actors will bandwagon in support and the belief will become self-fulfilling.

Coups from the middle are less likely to succeed than coups from the top because the process of taking over is more indirect. It depends on the ability of coup makers to seize and retain control over targets that serve to demonstrate their credibility, and there are many things that can go wrong in such a process. While strong efforts will be made to keep casualties down, this process also involves more force and therefore increases the possibility of casualties.

Coups from the Bottom

These coup attempts are the least likely to succeed since the conspirators have neither the soft power of generals nor the hard power of colonels and they face challenges that conspirators of higher ranks do not.

The script followed during a coup from the bottom, which is a mutiny with intent to overthrow the government, is closer to that of a coup from the middle than one from the top: mutineers have no bureaucratic prerogatives that can be used to make a fact, but they do have a small amount of force which they can use to seize broadcasting facilities. Even so, the amount of force they have at the start is meager because of the restrictions imposed by their rank. They cannot order armories opened and weapons and ammunition officially disbursed; they must seize them. The same goes for transportation, artillery, and armored vehicles. This makes mutinies particularly easy to stop in their earliest phases.

Even once they seize the broadcasting facilities, mutineers have a harder time manipulating expectations to make a fact. Lacking the tactical strength of coup makers from the middle, they can use risk dominance as a strategy to shape expectations only if the mutiny spreads widely or appears to have done so. Since the mutineers are individually weak and acting without the benefit of institutional coordination, their power is in numbers. However, the need for relatively widespread participation can discourage even sympathetic soldiers from joining, since each will require a fairly high degree of assurance that all the others will join, too. Mutinies tend to be bloodier and more chaotic than the other kinds of coups.

Role of Civilians

Significant civilian actors, either at the elite or mass level, play at best a secondary role in this account of coup dynamics and outcomes. It is true that civilians are often actively involved in military coups, either as founding members of conspiracies or as key members of the post-coup government. However, they are able to support or oppose a coup attempt only when they can shape the expectations of military actors about each other and do so during the brief window of time before the challenge is settled. Moral suasion alone does not create such influence.

The data suggest three circumstances in which civilian actors can influence the trajectory and outcome of coup attempts. The first is when an elite actor, often the head of state, uses the media to make a fact. For example, in 1981, King Juan Carlos played a pivotal role in blocking a coup attempt by making a television broadcast, wearing a military uniform, and stating that he was opposed to the coup and relating the orders he had given to quell the uprising. His broadcast was effective in part because the coup makers had implied that the coup would have the support of the king, and therefore of loyalist officers. Before Juan Carlos's broadcast, most of the military sat on the fence, and the government was having a hard time cracking down on the rebellion (Aguero 1995, 164). After the broadcast, most officers backed the government, and even a key supporter of the coup attempt switched sides (165). The coup makers were then forced to surrender. Most elite civilians, however, are unable to act in such a way.

Second, mass civilian mobilization can be useful in blocking a coup attempt if the civilians' actions are conjoined with widespread expectations that the military will split if they are called upon to attack civilians. This is what happened in the USSR in 1991: the erstwhile junta wrongly believed that the military had already begun to defect to the opposition and would refuse if ordered to fire upon civilian protesters. In this case, however, the effectiveness of public protests relied on an extensive media misinformation campaign by opposition members that created the expectations necessary for the protests to have an impact.

Most of the time, civilian mobilization is not a factor during a coup attempt. It is difficult for civilians to mobilize in a short period of time unless they have organizational structures already in place, such as unions or student organizations, and when they do mobilize against a coup attempt, experience has shown that people power alone is unable to stop a resolute military adversary. Large numbers of civilian protesters can be routed if the military remains unified, and the presence of massive protests does not necessarily lead to a split in the armed forces. For example, authoritarian governments have been easily able to clear very large numbers of protesters. China was able to move over a million protesters from the streets of Beijing in 1989, and to do so with casualties of between a few hundred and a few thousand civilians (BBC News 2009*b*, Kristof 1989). In Iran in 2009, groups of opposition protesters swelled above 100,000 at times, yet the government was able to dispel them without even using the regular military, just the Basij paramilitary (BBC News 2009*a*). These lessons apply just as well during coup attempts, especially since challengers are willing to spill civilian blood even while trying to limit military deaths. For example, in Argentina in June 1955, coup makers bombed and strafed pro-Peronist civilians assembled in the Plaza de Mayo, killing 200 and wounding more (Potash 1980, 188). While this is an extreme example, it shows that even militaries in democratic states are willing to pull the trigger on civilians.[33]

Crowds are effective in one other scenario, when the coup is part of a larger civilian uprising or revolution and a military faction openly backs the protesters against the government. The regime's difficulty in handling protesters is already public, and this causes at least the perception of a division within the armed forces. It is this perception that allows pro-coup forces to generate the belief that many within the military are unwilling to fire upon the protesters and raises the specter of a civil war, as happened recently in Libya. Examples of coups that are part of broader civilian uprisings include the overthrows of President Mahuad in Ecuador 2000, President Ceausescu in Romania 1989, the Shah of Iran 1979, and President Marcos in the Philippines 1986. Although the details of what happened in Tunisia and Egypt in 2011 are not yet clear, it appears that something similar also happened in the successful Arab Spring uprisings. In cases such as this, however, it seems likely that civilians can play a role in helping a coup succeed but not in blocking one.

Conclusion

The three models of coup attempts presented in this chapter offer very different visions of the dynamics of coup attempts and the factors that determine their outcome.

If coups are battles, the goal is to attain tactical dominance, and this is attained by being initially stronger, executing the attack with speed and stealth, and dealing ruthlessly with adversaries. In contrast, if coups are coordination games, challengers prevail not by hiding their presence but by announcing it loudly on the media, advertising and exaggerating their strength. Instead of creating tactical dominance, challengers should aim to take control of symbolic targets but to do so with as little bloodshed as possible. Military strength is useful in this process, but mainly as a tool to capture and retain control over broadcasting facilities and symbolic

---

[33]Why do challengers hesitate to kill military adversaries when they are willing to shoot civilians? The answer is that civilians cannot escalate the conflict into a civil war while members of the military can and will shoot back.

targets. If coups are like coordination games, then strength is neither necessary nor sufficient for victory, and the perception of strength is far more important than actual levels of guns, bullets, and men at the start of the coup attempt. A strong challenger may find his subordinates turning against him if expectations for his coup are unfavorable, and a weak one may find himself unopposed if expectations are favorable. Strength is endogenous to expectations rather than the other way around.

If coups are like elections, on the other hand, then the goal is to win over the hearts and minds of military actors, whether by directly appealing to their institutional, class, or ethnic interests or by making the case that the government lacks legitimacy and the military must step in to fill the vacuum of authority. The less popular the government and the fewer objections members of the military have to coup making, the more likely it is that coups will be attempted and, in fact, succeed. If coups are like coordination games, however, then popularity is neither necessary nor sufficient for victory, because "voting" during a coup attempt is both public and costly. Military actors would rather violate their political convictions than support the losing side or risk dragging the country into civil war. In fact, game theory shows that even when there is unanimity among players, there is no guarantee that they will all support the side they all think is better, especially when the costs for getting it wrong are quite high.[34] The expectation that one side has support is self-fulfilling and therefore matters much more than the preferences of actors. If actors believe everybody is supporting the other side, a side that starts with few supporters will attract supporters or its opponents will refuse to challenge it, while a side that starts with many sympathizers may find its support slipping away. For this reason, successful coups use the media to create the appearance of widespread support rather than to actually court it. In fact, trying to win over supporters during a coup attempt by telling them that their support is necessary for the success of the coup can make the attempt look weak and lead to its collapse.

The next chapter presents the findings of a series of quantitative tests of these models, and the succeeding four chapters examine them qualitatively based on case studies from Ghana and the Soviet Union. As we shall see, the cumulative weight of evidence strongly supports the argument that coups can best be understood as coordination games rather than as battles or elections.

---

[34]The impact of very strong and public preferences on expectations may be part of the reason why there are no coup attempts in wealthy, well-functioning, democratic states like Canada. Still, the impact of opinion, where there is one, has to work through information (it has to be common knowledge) and expectations.

Chapter 3

Counting Coups

This chapter statistically evaluates the three posited theories of coup outcomes using data from an original dataset covering all identifiable coup attempts and their outcomes across the world between 1950 and 2000, the most extensive data collected on coups to date.[1]

The chapter first examines what these data reveal about when coups are attempted. This was done to test the claim of the coups-as-elections theory that coup attempts and successful coups have the same underlying determinants. To do so, it is necessary first to establish the conditions under which coups are attempted so as to test this theory in the context of coup outcomes. This analysis finds robust support for claims that coup attempts are more common in countries that are poor, with governments that are neither highly democratic nor highly dictatorial, and which have experienced recent successful coups.

The second part of the chapter deals directly with the main question of the book, namely which coup attempts will fail and which will succeed. As we shall see, the results of this analysis are quite striking, providing support only for the theory that coups are best understood as coordination games. The analysis also reveals that there is no overlap between factors that predict coup attempts and those that ensure that an attempt will be successful, justifying the treatment of the two questions separately.

Lastly, the chapter examines whether any of the theoretically relevant variables might explain the military level from which the coup attempt originates and thus have an indirect effect on the probability of coup success. Here, the data indicate that the major explanatory factors used by the two other theories to explain coup outcomes are poor at predicting the level of a coup attempt, and therefore coup level is an important explanatory factor in its own right.

Although this analysis is limited by the availability of appropriate proxies for each theory, the chapter will demonstrate that, taken as a whole, the evidence is considerably more consistent with the theory that coups are coordination games than

---

[1]This is the only dataset collected that includes data on the level of the military from which the coup makers came. The data series actually covers the range 1945 to 2005, but independent variable coverage was sparse on either end.

with either of the competing theories. While some factors drawn from the traditional literature on military coups are correlated with the initiation of a coup attempt, none of these variables is useful for predicting the outcome of coup attempts.

Understanding Coup Attempts

Although scholars have long studied successful coups, less attention has been paid to the occurrence of coup attempts more broadly. The interest in successful coups is understandable, given that they have had the most obvious effect on the history and politics of the countries in which they took place. Yet, the apparent lack of interest in all coup attempts is also due to the paucity of reliable data on failed coups, which this chapter hopes to help correct. In this first section, I examine the determinants of coup attempts in order to establish what factors should be included in an elections explanation of coup outcomes in the next section of the chapter. Consequently, this section is empirically driven rather than theoretically driven, agnostically testing all possible explanations for coup attempts. I do not attempt to advance a theory of the motives of coup makers, in large part because a variety of motives exist across coups, within groups of conspirators, and even within the minds of particular individuals. Instead, this section focuses on determining the conditions associated with an increased likelihood of coup attempts.

Theories of Coup Attempts

The existing literature on the causes of successful coups has produced a very wide range of hypotheses that can be applied to the study of coup attempts.[2] In this section, I focus on the subset of claims that can be tested using cross-national proxies, and I generate a list of twenty-one hypotheses concerning the potential economic, political, social, strategic, and military correlates of military coup attempts.

Economic Hypotheses

The first set of these hypotheses concerns the impact of economic factors on the likelihood of a coup attempt in a given country.

There is broad agreement within the literature that successful coups are more frequent in poorer countries. Londregan and Poole go so far as to state that "economic backwardness is close to being a necessary condition for coups" (Londregan & Poole 1990). Since the scholarship posits a variety of mechanisms that link a lack

---

[2]Belkin and Schofer (2003, 601-604) provide a thorough list of hypotheses, encompassing many of the most important explanations given for coups in the literature on civil-military relations. Although it was written decades earlier, Zimmerman (1983) also provides a chapter-long literature review that enumerates almost all of the same arguments, showing how little the literature has changed in the intervening period.

of economic development to successful coups, this analysis assumes that all of these mechanisms should link poverty to coup attempts as well.[3]

Economic hypothesis 1: Coup attempts are more likely in poorer countries.

Various explanations have been provided for the observed connection between low levels of economic development and successful coups. Luttwak (1979, 33-38) argues that poor countries are more likely to experience coups because they have not undergone the social changes associated with modernization. Coups are possible, according to this explanation, only when the bulk of government employees and citizenry are willing to accept a ruler who has come to power via illegal means. This, in turn, is most likely when political power is closely held by a small, educated elite and the masses are largely rural, illiterate, and politically disengaged.

To test this argument, I proxy modernization by the extent of urbanization, as modernization theory regards urbanization as the key social change that precipitates the others and because urbanization has more extensive coverage in the data than other measures of modernization, such as literacy or industrialization.[4]

Economic hypothesis 2: Coup attempts are more likely in more rural countries.

Another explanation for why poorer countries are more coup-prone comes from dependency theory. O'Kane argues that poor countries have more coups because they are export-dependent and therefore more vulnerable to trade shocks. The resulting economic instability "render[s] even the most responsible governments open to accusations of incompetence and corruption, so inviting coups d'etat" (O'Kane 1993, 251). O'Kane's conclusions are supported by more recent work that finds that trade openness is negatively correlated with levels of democracy (Li & Reuveny 2003).[5]

Economic hypothesis 3: Coup attempts are more likely in countries with high trade openness.

In addition to poverty, most scholars assume that poor economic performance increases the risk of a successful coup. Even more than low income, economic decline should be expected to undermine both the popularity of the incumbent and the legitimacy of the regime. Negative growth should also decrease a government's ability to distribute patronage and therefore cause the alienation of key government allies (Kimenyi & Mbaku 1993). Alesina, Ozler, Roubini & Swagel (1996, 203), Collier (2009, 148), and Galetovic & Sanhueza (2000) all find that growth is negatively

---

[3]Surprisingly, Belkin and Schofer (2003, 605) omit wealth from their analysis, arguing that wealth can both increase and decrease the risk of coup attempts, without ever testing this claim. Svolik (2010) is one of the few scholars who tests the impact of GDP per capita, but he does not find it significant.

[4]Not all scholars agree that the risk of coups rises linearly with the extent of modernization. Huntington (1968) argued that both traditional and modern societies are stable and that praetorianism is most likely in modernizing countries where social modernization has outstripped political modernization.

[5]Goemans disagrees, finding that trade openness is negatively correlated with the risk that the leader will lose power through irregular means, most of which is via coup (Goemans 2008, 782).

correlated with the probability of a successful coup. This same logic should apply to coup attempts as well.[6]

Economic hypothesis 4: Coup attempts are more likely in countries with low or negative growth.

The nature of a country's economy may also be linked to the risk of coup attempts. The resource rents associated with large natural resources and the accompanying possibilities for self-enrichment make the presidency a very tempting target. Democratic Sao Tome, for instance, experienced a coup in 2003, soon after oil was discovered, before even a drop had been pumped or sold (Collier 2009, 145). In countries that are already exploiting their natural resources, other sectors of the economy often decline and are crowded out, making control of the government, and therefore control of resource rents, even more important. The literature on the "resource curse" argues that states with large resource endowments have substantially worse governance, which may also increase the likelihood of a coup attempt (Collier & Hoeffler 1998, Karl 1997).[7]

Economic hypothesis 5: Coup attempts are more likely in countries with high levels of natural resources.

Regime Hypotheses

A second set of arguments proposed by earlier scholars concerns the type and subtype of political regime.

Regimes confer legitimacy, to varying degrees, on governments. If popular support for a government is an important element in determining the vulnerability of a government to being overthrown, the probability of a coup attempt should vary systematically with the characteristics of the regime. Regimes also determine the rules for regular leadership replacement. If coup attempts respond to popular demand for leadership change, then regimes can reduce the probability of an attempt by providing institutionalized mechanisms of leadership change.

If the first two claims are true, ceteris paribus, there should be fewer coup attempts in democracies because democratic institutions provide a certain amount of legitimacy, both domestically and internationally, and provide institutionalized means for regular leadership change (Clark 2007, Galetovic & Sanhueza 2000, Goemans 2008, Lehoucq & Lin 2009).[8]

---

[6]Svolik (2010) finds no relationship between growth and the probability of a coup.

[7]Dunning (2008, 141) finds that higher levels of oil production per capita are associated with a greater risk of coup attempts, although he also finds that the impact of natural resources on coup attempts is conditional on the extent of economic inequality. Unfortunately, the limited coverage of the capital share variable that measures inequality means that I am unable to test this second claim. Note that other scholars who have disputed the existence of a resource curse (Wick & Bulte 2009) argue that the existence of a resource curse is conditional upon other factors, such as the ownership structure of the extractive industries (Luong & Weinthal 2006), or provide non-governance-related explanations for its existence (Ross 1999).

[8]Not all scholars find that the presence of democracy lessens the probability of a coup attempt (Moreno, Lewis-Beck & Amoureux 2004, Thyne 2009).

Regime hypothesis 1: Coup attempts are more likely in non-democracies than democracies.

The relationship between democracy and the risk of a coup attempt may not be linear, however. Even if consolidated democracies possess immunity to coup attempts, this does not mean that semi-democratic governments are protected as well. Some scholars argue that the relationship between democracy and political instability is parabolic, with partially democratic states (anocracies) at greater risk than either highly democratic or undemocratic states.

There are several reasons why dictatorships may be less likely to experience coup attempts than anocracies. Highly undemocratic countries may rely on their own effective forms of legitimation that protect them from coup attempts if they are absolutist monarchies or repressive revolutionary states, or they may simply be able to repress threats more effectively than anocracies. Although not even the most powerful leaders can protect themselves from their own coercive apparatus, a highly repressive state can hinder the ability of the conspirators to plot without detection and can credibly promise harsh punishment to erstwhile coup makers (and perhaps their families as well) should they fail. Anocracies, therefore, may have the weaknesses of both democracies and strongly authoritarian governments, without the strengths of either (Fearon & Laitin 2003, Huntington 1968).

Regime hypothesis 2: Coup attempts are more likely in anocracies than either highly democratic countries or highly undemocratic ones.

If the legitimacy of a regime provides protection against coup attempts, then the probability of a coup attempt should vary not just according to regime but also according to regime subtype. For example, military regimes face the problem that they came to power via a coup themselves, so in legitimating their own ascension, they also lend legitimacy to future challengers (Belkin & Schofer 2003, Londregan & Poole 1990). In addition, since military regimes rarely create parties or allow legislative institutions to function, they lack the legitimating abilities of other sorts of civilian dictatorships (Gandhi 2008, Geddes 2003, Geddes 2009, Magaloni 2008, Magaloni & Kricheli 2010). This is consistent with what we know about the fragility of military regimes and the relative robustness of civilian one-party regimes and implies that military governments are the most vulnerable to coup attempts.

Regime hypothesis 3: Coup attempts are more likely under military governments and less likely under civilian dictatorships and civilian democracies.

Similarly, the nature of democratic institutions may also affect the chance of a coup attempt, with some types of democracies being more prone to coup attempts than others. Juan Linz (1990), supported by Stepan and Skatch (1993) and with some caveats by Mainwaring & Shugart (1997), argues that presidential systems are more coup-prone than parliamentary ones.[9] Although this claim is based on multiple arguments, key among them is that presidents, unlike prime ministers, serve fixed terms in office. A vote of no confidence can be called at any time in a parliamentary democracy, but it is much harder to remove a highly unpopular president. As a result, presidential systems are less dynamically responsive to the will of the people, creating a greater chance of irregular methods of leadership change.

Regime hypothesis 4: Coup attempts are more likely under presidential systems than parliamentary ones.

Linz's argument has additional implications: if coups are more likely when there is strong popular demand for the removal of a leader, coups should be the least likely in years when a presidential election is scheduled. The existence of an opportunity to remove the leader via regular means should serve to reduce the pressure to remove him via irregular methods.[10]

Regime hypothesis 5: Coup attempts are less likely in years when there is a scheduled presidential election.

Social Hypotheses

A third set of hypotheses concerns the relationship between social divisions and political instability, with ethnically divided polities assumed to be at higher risk for coup attempts than ethnically homogenous ones. Multiple nations sit uneasily in the breast of a single state, generating social conflict that finds political expression and thus makes ethnic military coup attempts more likely.

Once civilian politics becomes an expression of ethnic interests, scholars such as Horowitz argue, it will be hard for the military to remain above the fray or act as an agent of national unity. Although intervention can be avoided when political elites and the military are drawn from the same ethnic group, this is unlikely because of the way in which colonial powers created the precursors of national militaries as armies of occupation. Soldiers were recruited from "martial races" from the hinterlands, while post-independence political elites are likely to come from either populous or educated ethnic groups that the colonial powers would have considered politically unreliable (Horowitz 1980, chap. 11). As a result, politically dominant ethnic groups rarely dominate militaries in post-colonial states, and the government and armed forces soon find themselves at odds.

In countries that are ethnically polarized, civilian politicians of various stripes will try to ally with or neutralize an ethnically polarized military. Opposition politicians will lobby members of the military from their own ethnic group to strike, while incumbent politicians will try to change the composition of the officer corps to in-

---

[9]Goemans also argues that leaders of presidential systems are more likely to exit irregularly than leaders of parliamentary systems, but it is unclear if this difference is statistically significant from his analysis (Goemans 2008).

[10]Scholars who believe that the military acts on behalf of an elite against the majority would expect the opposite result (Acemoglu & Robinson 2006, Fossum 1967).

clude more members of their own ethnic group by directly intervening in recruitment and promotion, actions that are likely to be seen as threatening by existing officers. In addition to ethnic tensions between the government and the military, there may also be ethnic divisions within the military, with the officer corps being drawn from different ethnic groups than the soldiers and sometimes divisions between senior and junior officers as well. According to Horowitz, "ethnically skewed composition and the close connections between civilian and military affairs lay the foundation for ethnically motivated military intervention" (1980, 471).

Within the literature on successful coups, two arguments have been advanced about the impact of ethnicity. The first is that "the greater the number and cultural diversity of the groups, the greater the elite instability" (Jenkins & Kposowa 1992, 274). This means that the probability of a coup attempt is linear in the extent of ethnic heterogeneity and that countries with the highest level of cultural pluralism are the most likely to experience intervention.

Social hypothesis 1: Coup attempts are more likely in more ethnically heterogeneous societies.

The second argument is that it is more politically destabilizing to have a few medium-sized ethnic groups rather than many small ones. With many small groups, no single group is easily able to dominate the others without alliances, and the pattern of these alliances may be fluid and may even activate cross-cutting cleavages. On the other hand, with a small number of larger ethnic groups, a pattern of ethnic dominance may develop in which a hegemonic group may dominate the others. In this case, the impact of ethnic diversity on military intervention is parabolic, with coup attempts more likely for middle levels of ethnic heterogeneity and less likely in cases of either high heterogeneity or homogeneity.

Social hypothesis 2: Coup attempts are more likely when there is a small number of large ethnic groups.

Strategic Hypotheses

The fourth set of hypotheses concerns the international strategic context in which the coup attempt takes place.

During the Cold War, the superpowers engaged in various proxy conflicts as they jockeyed for geostrategic advantage. CIA involvement is well documented in the 1953 overthrow of the Mosaddeq government in Iran (Risen 2000) and the 1973 overthrow of the Allende government in Chile (Central Intelligence Agency 2000). In addition to the United States, the Soviet Union, Britain, and France are all suspected of involvement in multiple coup attempts. Even when superpowers were not intimately involved in organizing and executing a coup attempt, the struggle between the two sides and the ideological tenor of the period meant that militaries and many elites saw communism as a clear and imminent threat that could justify military intervention, whether to oppose particular policies, to prevent leftists from taking power after winning an election, or even just to replace a government that they felt was doing too little to make the country safe.

Strategic hypothesis 1: Coup attempts were more likely during the Cold War.

In addition to overthrowing rulers they viewed as a threat, the United States and the Soviet Union made extensive efforts to keep key allies in power. The closer the relationship between the patron and client, the more extensive the efforts to protect the client government. Superpowers used a variety of means to assist client states. Beyond official military and developmental aid, they trained members of client militaries and gave them intelligence support in detecting and dealing with threats. Thus, officers were given both incentives to stay loyal and reasons to fear the consequences of being disloyal. If outside support is effective, then we would expect countries closely allied with superpowers to be less prone to coup attempts than those lacking a powerful patron on either side. This claim that super powers worked to protect their allies is not in contradiction with the claim that coup attempts were more likely during the Cold War. It might be that coup attempts were broadly more likely then but that governments with strong external patrons were less likely to experience attempts at military intervention.

Strategic hypothesis 2: Coup attempts are less likely in countries closely aligned with a superpower.

On occasion, external patrons have explicitly guaranteed the survival of allied governments and used their own troops to make good on this promise. France in particular maintained close ties with its former colonies, intervening in Africa nineteen times between 1962 and 1995 to either protect its citizens or keep a friendly government in power. At decolonization, France signed explicit treaties of assistance with most of the countries in its sphere of influence, although some of these treaties were secret and remain secret to this day. It also maintained defense bases in these countries and kept rapid reaction troops ready to intervene as part of its defense structure (Hansen 2008). Where they were not able to deter or prevent a coup attempt, they could often credibly threaten to overthrow any rebel force or coup makers who sought to come to power without France's permission.

Strategic hypothesis 3: Coup attempts are less likely in former French colonies.

The strategic environment is also shaped by the presence of threats to the state, both internal and external. Desch (1999) argues that external threat produces a military that is unified, externally oriented, and receptive to civil control. Internal threat, on the other hand, produces a military that is unified but internally oriented and at odds with civil authorities. When applied to the question of coup attempts, this theory should lead us to expect more coup attempts during periods of domestic conflict and fewer attempts during periods of international conflict.[11]

---

[11]Desch's argument about the effects of international conflict is also supported by Goemans (2008) and Belkin & Schofer (2004), although they posit different mechanisms.

Strategic hypothesis 4: Coup attempts are less likely during conditions of international conflict.

Strategic hypothesis 5: Coup attempts are more likely during conditions of domestic conflict.

Military Hypotheses

The final group of hypotheses concerns the impact of military characteristics on the likelihood of a coup attempt.

The first two arguments link what is known as the centrality of the military, measured by the relative share of national resources (labor and money) it consumes, to its propensity to intervene.[12] Janowitz (1964) argues that militaries that constitute a larger part of society are more likely to intervene in politics.[13] If he is correct, this produces the following two hypotheses concerning the likelihood of a coup attempt:

Military hypothesis 1: Coup attempts are more likely in countries where the armed forces comprise a large portion of the population.

Military hypothesis 2: Coup attempts are more likely in countries that spend a large percentage of their GDP on the military.

Another argument in the literature states that a military's experience with intervention in the past will shape its propensity to intervene in the future (Londregan & Poole 1990). Among scholars there is "near universal consensus that past coups ... are a cause of future [successful] coups" (Belkin & Schofer 2003, 604). A variety of different mechanisms might explain this correlation. Most scholars believe that the first successful coup releases the genie from the bottle, destroying the social and professional norms that might otherwise restrain the military from intervention. The first coup also serves as a practical example, providing a template for other coup makers to follow. In addition, each successful coup damages the integrity of the military, allowing the coup makers to promote themselves and demote others, thus stoking grievances and engendering counter-coups. Although each of these explanations in the literature link past successful coups to future successful coups, they apply equally well to the relationship between past and future coup attempts. The impact should be greater with each successive successful coup, and it should fade over time.

Military hypothesis 3: Coup attempts are more likely in countries that have had a larger number of recent successful coups.

---

[12]I do not test the effects of gross military manpower and budget in addition to these relative measures, because the theory does not make any claims about their effects. I also do not include them as controls, because they are highly correlated with population and total national wealth (GDP rather than GDP per capita) and so add little.

[13]Other scholars disagree with Janowitz concerning the importance of military centrality, most notably Finer (Zimmermann 1983). The empirical findings on this point are also mixed. While Jenkins & Kposowa (1990, 867) finds military centrality measures to be some of the best predictors of successful coups, Collier (2009) argues that military spending (in excess of what is strategically required) reduces the risk of successful coups, but only in highly coup-prone countries.

Whereas the literature posits that past successful coups generate future successful coups, there is little written concerning the implications of past failed coups for civil-military relations. That said, past unsuccessful coups fail to fit the logic of the mechanisms enumerated above: they do not establish the legitimacy of military intervention, provide a template for future successful coups, or create the same sort of institutional grievances. Further, failed coups might serve to cool the ardor of potential coup plotters, as they demonstrate how difficult it is to take over and how high the penalties for failure are. If a past failed coup attempt serves to discourage officers from supporting other coup attempts, this effect should be stronger when there are more failed coups and should decrease over time.

Military hypothesis 4: Coup attempts are less likely in countries that have had a larger number of recent failed coup attempts.

Although this has been an extensive list of hypotheses relating to the macro-structural determinants of coup attempts, there remain a number of other claims that I am unable to test due to a lack of data of sufficient coverage or quality. For example, although one can test (however imperfectly) claims relating to the impact of social divisions on the frequency of coup attempts, one cannot do the same for claims pertaining to the effects of economic inequality. Although scholars suspect that economic crisis may be related to coup attempts, data limitations mean that it is possible to test only the impact of growth on the likelihood of a coup attempt, not inflation or unemployment or real currency fluctuations. Similarly, while we can test the impact of regime type and subtype on the probability of a coup attempt, we cannot examine the impact of government popularity directly.[14]

In addition, although the policy world routinely prescribes increased professionalism as a guaranteed prophylaxis against military intervention, it is not possible to test the relationship between professionalism and coup attempts because the necessary data on professionalism do not exist. Similarly, we have no systematic measurements of the class composition of the officer class, their ideological beliefs, or their opinions concerning incumbent performance, all variables that play an important role in the qualitative literature on military coups.[15]

---

[14]Another example concerns civil society. Although this does not play as prominent a role in most theories of military intervention as some other variables, it is the key factor in Belkin's analysis of coup risk. However, his measure of domestic civil society is actually a count of domestic membership in international non-governmental organizations, collected at four-year intervals. Although it is not clear exactly which organizations he is counting as INGOs, the concept validity of this measure is unclear. For example, INGOs will be a poor measure for the strength of civil society in poor countries where few domestic organizations can afford to branch out overseas, and whatever INGOs are present are likely to be local offices of major foreign organizations, like Save the Children.

[15]Another hypothesis that I do not test concerns the effects of military counter-balancing, the policy of splitting the military into competing factions (such as a presidential guard separate from the regular armed forces) in order to reduce the risk of successful coups (Quinlivan 1999). While Belkin & Schofer (2004, 155) have compiled a measure of counter-balancing, it is limited in its coverage, encompassing 95 countries between 1966 and 1986, which covers only 25% of the country-years in my dataset. In addition, because the data were collected by sampling every fourth year,

Data on Coup Attempts

This section analyzes data from an original dataset covering all coup attempts and their outcomes (successes and failures) for 175 countries between 1950 and 2000, the most extensive data collected on coups to date.[16] During this period, there were 471 coup attempts, of which 238 succeeded and 233 failed. The data analyzed are a fifty-year subset from an original dataset of all coup attempts between 1945 and 2005, gathered by myself and a team of research assistants over four years. Possible coup attempts were identified through a variety of sources, primarily the Keesings World News Archive and the Proquest Historical Newspapers New York Times Archive. These sources were supplemented by various electronic databases, such as Lexis-Nexis, and by annuals, such as *Europa* and *Africa South of the Sahara*. We paid close attention to any country-year or specific incident identified in the lists of successful coups or of coup attempts compiled by Bates (2001), Belkin & Schofer (2003), Ferguson (1987), First (1970), Goemans, Gleditsch & Chiozza (2009), Kennedy (1974), Lunde (1991), Luttwak (1979), McGowan (2003), and O'Kane (1987).

A memo was written about each plausible case, evaluating whether it met the definitional criteria for a coup attempt and, if it did, coding it as either a successful or a failed coup attempt. These cases were then reviewed at least twice, once for consistency of coding and a second time to code the level of the coup makers within the military.

Definitions

For the purposes of this analysis, a **coup attempt** is defined as an **explicit action, involving some portion of the state military, police, or security forces, undertaken with intent to overthrow the government.**

This definition retains most of the aspects commonly found in definitions of coup attempts while excluding a wide range of similar activities, such as conspiracies, mercenary attacks, popular protests, revolutions, civil wars, actions by lone assassins, and mutinies whose goals explicitly excluded taking power (e.g., over unpaid wages). Unlike a civil war, there is no minimum casualty threshold necessary for an event to be considered a coup, and many coups take place bloodlessly. This definition is very close to the standard definition used by McGowan (2003), except that I employ a higher threshold for when assassination attempts are considered coup attempts, more consistent with Goemans and Marinov (2008, 13).

A **coup** attempt is coded as **successful if** it **displaces the government of the country for at least one week and the new government that takes control is substantively different.** For instance, if the president was killed and the vice

---

they were likely to miss cases where counter-balancing institutions prompted a coup that led to the institutions' removal, thus biasing inferences in favor of the effectiveness of counter-balancing in deterring coups.

[16]The full dataset covers all coup attempts between 1945 and 2005, but this study analyzes a five-decade subset to maximize the coverage of independent variables. The 175 countries include all independent countries with population over 100,000, based on the list in Gleditsch & Ward (1999).

president took over, that was not coded as a successful coup.[17] Both the seven-day minimum and the emphasis on displacement of the old government (rather than the seizure of power by the challenger) are consistent with McGowan's definition and standard in most coup data coding.[18]

These data reveal that coup attempts are common. A majority of the countries (55%) experienced at least one coup attempt between 1950 and 2000. At the same time, high numbers of coup attempts were unusual; three-quarters of the countries experienced four or fewer attempts, and only 5% of countries had coup attempts in the double digits. The countries with the highest numbers of coup attempts in the sample were Bolivia, which had twenty-two coup attempts; Argentina, which had eighteen; and Sudan, which had sixteen. In terms of regional distribution of attempts, almost 70% of cases came from Latin America (30%) and Africa (40%). Almost every country in Latin America and Africa experienced at least one coup attempt between 1950 and 2000; the exceptions were Mexico, Belize, Nicaragua, and Costa Rica in Latin America and Tunisia, Tanzania, Namibia, Botswana, and South Africa on the African continent.

Coup attempts were not only prevalent in space but also frequent in time. Between 1950 and 2000, there was both a mean and a median of nine coup attempts per year, with a low of three attempts in 1998 and a high of nineteen attempts in 1975. Although the number of attempts varied greatly from one year to the next, there was a broad trend over time, with the number of coup attempts increasing until around 1970 and then declining. This can be seen in figure 3.1, which shows a smoothed version of both the number of coup attempts per year and their success rate. Lowess smoothing is employed to make the long-term trend over time legible.

The uptick in coup attempts in the first half of the period is partly the result of decolonization, which increased the number of countries in the sample by 75%, thus increasing the number of possible coup attempts in any given year. Even if the number of countries in the sample is controlled for, however, there is still an increase (albeit with a shallower slope) in the frequency of attempts until 1970 and then a decline afterward. This is consistent with the understanding that poor countries are more likely to experience coup attempts but contradicts the narrative that coup attempts were driven by the Cold War and decreased precipitously after it ended.

Analysis of Coup Attempts

The dependent variable for this analysis is the presence of at least one coup attempt in a given country and year. The transformation of the data into binary country-year format has the advantage of ease of analysis. It leads to a loss of information

---

[17]The formal condition is that for a coup attempt to be a success it must not pass power to the allies of the government or the chosen successors of the government—there must be a real change of government power; it is not enough to remove the executive. This is similar to the condition used by Marshall and Marshall (2010) that excludes voluntary transfers of authority.

[18]The one outlier is the Marshall and Marshall dataset, in which "authority must be exercised by new executive for at least one month." (Marshall & Marshall 2010).

Figure 3.1: Coup attempts and success rate Lowess smoothed and mapped over time

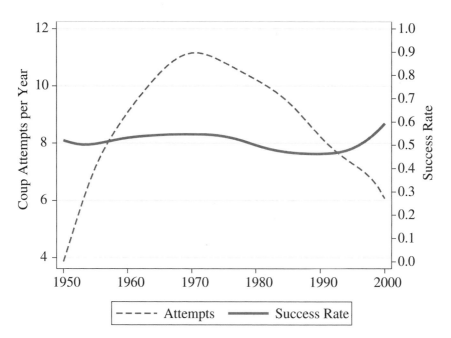

in the sixty-eight times when countries experienced two or more attempts in the same year, but these are less than 1% of the total number of cases.[19]

The results from the analysis are presented in table 3.1. The model includes all variables that were found to be robustly significant and a few that are not but are included because of their theoretical importance.[20]

The presence of such a large number of hypotheses and no strong theory to create a model raises the very real risk of curve fitting. To combat that, robustness was ensured in two ways. Whenever possible, each hypothesis was tested using multiple measures of the same causal factor, and the causal factor was included in the final specification only if most or all measures were consistently significant and had the same sign. For more details, see the appendix, which lists the variables tested for each concept.

---

[19]This transformation is standard; studies of successful coups similarly predict the presence of one or more successful coups in a country in a given year.

[20]There is no control for the number of years that a government or a regime has been in power because the primary reason for government displacement or regime change was successful coups; therefore this variable would be highly collinear with the measure of past successful coup attempts.

Table 3.1: Predicting coup attempts 1950–2000

	Random effects		Fixed effects		Rare events	
Variable	(1)	(2)	(3)	(4)	(5)	(6)
$\log(\text{GDP/cap})_{t-1}$	-0.485^{***}	-0.570^{***}	-0.434^{*}	-0.527^{**}	-0.400^{***}	-0.444^{***}
	(0.121)	(0.127)	(0.238)	(0.237)	(0.110)	(0.102)
Democracy_{t-1}	-0.291^{**}		-0.133		-0.255^{*}	
	(0.139)		(0.166)		(0.149)	
Democracy^2_{t-1}	-0.808^{***}		-0.569^{***}		-0.773^{***}	
	(0.158)		(0.190)		(0.166)	
Mixed democracy$_{t-1}$		0.467		-0.496		0.515
		(0.462)		(0.541)		(0.373)
Presidential democracy$_{t-1}$		0.0503		-0.901^{**}		0.255
		(0.332)		(0.374)		(0.359)
Civilian dictatorship$_{t-1}$		-0.0657		-0.523		-0.0726
		(0.279)		(0.334)		(0.344)
Military dictatorship$_{t-1}$		0.121		-0.650^{**}		0.236
		(0.280)		(0.314)		(0.304)
Monarchy$_{t-1}$		-0.107		-0.0904		-0.219
		(0.399)		(0.547)		(0.357)
Presidential election	0.357^{**}	0.408^{**}	0.299	0.337^{*}	0.359^{*}	0.411^{*}
	(0.182)	(0.183)	(0.183)	(0.184)	(0.205)	(0.211)
Cold War	0.412^{**}	0.390^{**}	0.185	0.142	0.407^{*}	0.385^{*}
	(0.184)	(0.184)	(0.229)	(0.228)	(0.212)	(0.215)
International conflict$_{t-1}$	-0.177	-0.16	-0.235^{*}	-0.237^{*}	-0.127	-0.105
	(0.137)	(0.137)	(0.141)	(0.141)	(0.137)	(0.139)
Domestic conflict$_{t-1}$	0.119^{*}	0.120^{*}	0.0799	0.091	0.138^{**}	0.134^{**}
	(0.0648)	(0.0663)	(0.0725)	(0.0740)	(0.0640)	(0.0650)
$\log(\text{military budget/GDP})_{t-1}$	-0.175^{**}	-0.216^{***}	0.0283	0.0284	-0.202^{***}	-0.246^{***}
	(0.0691)	(0.0692)	(0.0954)	(0.0959)	(0.0562)	(0.0556)
$\log(\text{military size/pop})_{t-1}$	0.153	0.172^{*}	0.161	0.173	0.193^{**}	0.198^{**}
	(0.102)	(0.102)	(0.135)	(0.135)	(0.0834)	(0.0861)
Past successful coups	0.423^{***}	0.377^{***}	0.235^{***}	0.227^{***}	0.522^{***}	0.463^{***}
	(0.0828)	(0.0841)	(0.0805)	(0.0830)	(0.0849)	(0.0850)
Past failed coups	0.254^{***}	0.250^{***}	0.0653	0.0946	0.369^{***}	0.352^{***}
	(0.0762)	(0.0753)	(0.0738)	(0.0737)	(0.0569)	(0.0533)
$\log(\text{population})$	-0.00679	-0.00356	-0.843^{**}	-0.804^{**}	0.0155	0.0115
	(0.0634)	(0.0648)	(0.329)	(0.334)	(0.0596)	(0.0578)
E. Europe/ former USSR	-1.039	0.0707			-0.96	0.14
	(0.636)	(0.614)			(0.594)	(0.674)
North Africa/ Middle East	0.429	1.500^{***}			0.414	1.490^{***}
	(0.504)	(0.491)			(0.428)	(0.540)
Sub-Saharan Africa	0.285	1.338^{**}			0.409	1.432^{**}
	(0.541)	(0.526)			(0.470)	(0.581)

Variable	Random effects (1)	(2)	Fixed effects (3)	(4)	Rare events (5)	(6)
Asia	−0.248	0.743			−0.209	0.796
	(0.518)	(0.509)			(0.447)	(0.580)
Latin Amer/	0.517	1.592***			0.489	1.487***
Caribbean	(0.487)	(0.483)			(0.418)	(0.546)
Observations	5893	5893	3409	3409	5895	5895

Estimates of constant omitted. Standard errors in parentheses. *** $p < 0.01$, ** $p < 0.05$, * $p < 0.1$

In addition, hypotheses were evaluated using multiple estimators. Relationships that were consistently significant in a pooled time-series logit model with random effects were also assessed using logistical regression with fixed effects to see whether the relationship observed was largely driven by cross-sectional correlation. Lastly, the final model was re-estimated using a rare events logit model to address the possibility of bias caused by the relatively small number of positive events (only 6%) in the sample. The fixed effects specification was run only using the subset of countries that experienced at least one coup attempt between 1950 and 2000; as such, it covers only eighty-nine countries and includes only 57% of the observations. Table 3.1 therefore shows the same basic model of the determinants of coup attempts as tested in six slightly varying specifications.

The main finding of this analysis is that there is little support for the conventional wisdom on coups: most hypotheses derived from the literature on successful coup attempts do poorly at predicting the occurrence of coup attempts, even though the logic should be the same. In addition, even those factors that are correlated with coup attempts explain little of the variance observed and therefore do a poor job of predicting when and where coup attempts will occur.

I begin by summarizing the statistical results before moving on to discussing their significance. Of the twenty-one hypotheses, only three find robust support in the data. We can say with some confidence that countries that are poor, neither highly democratic nor undemocratic, and have had recent successful coups are more likely to have a coup attempt in the following year. This is not surprising and is consistent with what we know about successful coup attempts, namely that they are more likely in poor countries with past successful coups (Londregan & Poole 1990). The main contribution of this analysis is to confirm that the effect of democracy is parabolic rather than linear, which means that the countries at the highest risk are anocratic, with both highly dictatorial and highly democratic countries at lower risk. These results were consistent across multiple specifications and multiple measurements of wealth, democracy, and the number of recent successful coups, all three of which are variables consistent with the demand-side account of coup attempts.[21]

---

[21] For example, the effects of national wealth were found for all four proxies of wealth, all three measures of democracy, and all four measures of recent successful coups.

A slightly less robust finding that is somewhat surprising concerns presidential elections. Although the hypothesis predicted that coup attempts would be less likely in the years of a presidential election, the data demonstrate that coup attempts are actually more likely in election years.[22] While this is also a demand-side hypothesis, the reversal in sign completely undercuts the logic involved.

Four additional hypotheses received less consistent support in the data. The Cold War is correlated with a higher risk of a coup attempt, but this relationship is not significant in either fixed effects specification.[23] Domestic conflict is the only variable that had noticeably different effects depending on which measure was used. All measures indicate an increased chance of coup attempts, but not all were consistently significant. The proxy used in the final model is based on the PRIO dataset and covers both low- and high-intensity conflicts. It had the best coverage and contained the most information, but it was not significant in the fixed effects specifications. Measures of civil wars (as opposed to all domestic conflict) had more mixed results. Sambanis's measure of civil wars was significant in fixed effects specifications while Fearon's measures were not.

Lastly, both military spending as a percentage of GDP and past failed coups were significant in the random effects and rare events specifications but not in the fixed effects specification. This seems to indicate that while militaries that are well resourced (relative to national wealth) are less likely to mount a coup attempt, this association is largely cross-sectional and does not indicate that leaders of more coup-prone countries can decrease their risk by increasing military spending. Similarly, while failed coups are associated with an increase in coup attempts (the opposite of what was predicted), this probably indicates that countries with a high number of past coup attempts continue to experience coup attempts in the future, not that failed coups somehow encourage conspirators to try their own hand at coup making.

Among the broad patterns that emerge when considering the hypotheses collectively, one observation is that coup attempts appear to be largely driven by domestic factors. With the exception of the Cold War, which found partial support, the evidence does not support any of the other international variables. Trade openness, foreign patrons, even international conflict (again proxied from the PRIO dataset to include low- and high-intensity conflict) have no consistent effect on the likelihood of a coup attempt. These regressions are not presented here for reasons of space.

Second, while these results demonstrate strong correlations, they reveal little about which mechanisms might be involved. Wealthy countries are less likely to have coup attempts, but there is no additional support for any other economic variable that might provide a mechanism to explain why poverty is associated with

---

[22]This finding is slightly less robust than the first three because there were no alternate measures of the presidential election variable to test, and it is significant in only one of the two fixed effects models in table 3.1.

[23]The fact that the Cold War variable is not significant in the fixed effects model is odd in light of the fact that the Cold War has no cross-sectional variance, so I would expect both random effects and fixed effects estimations to be consistent. Even if true, this result is not highly illuminating, given that the frequency of coup attempts begins to decline around 1970 and shows no significant change at the end of the Cold War.

coup attempts. Strikingly, while poorer countries are more likely to experience coup attempts, neither urbanization, nor economic growth, nor trade openness, nor resource dependence has any impact on the likelihood of attempted military intervention.[24] Similarly, while highly democratic and undemocratic countries are less likely to see coup attempts, type of political regime does not have an impact, giving us little understanding of the mechanisms involved.[25] Lastly, while the Cold War is associated with a greater incidence of coup attempts in some models, superpower alignment does not have an effect on the probability of an attempt, even when interacted with the Cold War variable.

In addition, these results lend little support to the arguments that coup attempts are largely undertaken in response to popular demand. If coup attempts are driven by mass discontent, then low growth and a military government should increase the risk of a coup attempt and elections should decrease the risk. None of these statements is supported by the data. If anything, the fact that coup attempts are more frequent in years of presidential elections suggests that coup attempts are generated by elites (either inside or outside the military) in opposition to the expected decision of the electorate.[26]

The analysis also reveals a second major way in which the conventional understanding is deficient. Even though the model identifies several important variables that are highly correlated with coup attempts, it does a poor job of predicting when and where coups will be attempted. If the random effects specification in column

---

[24]Since these variables were not consistently significant, they were excluded from the final specification for reasons of parsimony and space.

[25]The effect of a military regime is not being drowned out by the control for past coup attempts, even if the past coup attempts variables are excluded, regime subtype has no effect. Similarly, while there is an obvious correlation between presidentialism and presidential elections, dropping the presidential election variable does not increase the significance of presidentialism.

[26]An examination of the cases in which coups were attempted in the same year as a presidential election largely, but not entirely, supports the reading that these coup attempts were anti-democratic. Many seem to have been attempts by military factions to veto the results of the election, such as when leftists had a strong showing in the 1962 presidential election in Peru and a coup was staged to make sure that the American Popular Revolutionary Alliance did not come to power. Similarly, the Nigerian election of 1993 was annulled by a military incumbent that did not wish President-elect Abiola to come to power, and newly elected President Ndadaye of Burundi (a Hutu) was assassinated by Tutsi officers a few months after he was sworn in. Some cases were like the Argentine coup attempt of 1951, when the coup attempt preceded the presidential election but Peron went on to win by a landslide. This is also consistent with the argument, because his clear popular support did nothing to inoculate him against coup attempts. Not all cases fit, however. President Shagari of Nigeria was overthrown in 1983 after he was re-elected in an election widely believed to be fraudulent. Most interesting, however, are cases in which the association between elections and coups is the reverse of what might have been expected. In Bolivia in 1978 and Ghana in 1979, coups were in the same year as presidential elections because the junta called for immediate elections after removing the incumbent. In these cases, coup attempts led to presidential elections rather than being efforts to block them. Still, while such cases weaken the reading of coup attempts as clearly anti-democratic, they do not support the hypothesis that presidential elections reduce the chance of coup attempts. In addition, while I have not coded all the cases, coup attempts that give birth to elections appear to be a distinct minority, especially since a majority of coups in the same year as elections are from Latin America, a region with a tradition of military vetoes of elections.

one is used to generate predicted probabilities for all of the observations in the data (assuming that random effects are zero), the model predicts only a single year when a coup will be attempted, and that prediction is incorrect. In addition, the simulation misclassifies every year when there was at least one coup attempt as years when no attempt was expected.

Part of the problem is that the simulation systematically under-predicts the likelihood of a coup attempt because attempts are uncommon events. Even if one abandons the 50% threshold conventional for classifying a continuous prediction as an incident, there is still only a 25% correlation between the predicted probability of a coup attempt and actual attempts. Although this is a considerable improvement, the model does not do well even at predicting the relative likelihood of an attempt.

There are two possible explanations for the model's limited ability to predict coup attempts. The first is that important variables are omitted. Although this is a very real possibility given the constraints of available data, one would expect that any major omitted variables would be correlated with the regional variables (given the strong inter-regional differences in the likelihood of a coup attempt), yet in the first specification, none of the regional variables is significant and region is not correlated with the residuals.

The other possibility is that, while the model captures much of the systematic variance in coup attempts, by their very nature coup attempts have a strong stochastic component as well. It may be that coup attempts are predictable only to the extent to which coup makers are responsive to broader structural factors such as popular unhappiness with the government, the legitimacy of the incumbent, or perhaps even structural factors related to the presence of logistical factors that either aid or hinder a coup attempt. But coup attempts are also risky conspiracies undertaken by small numbers of people who are trying to avoid detection. Their motivations may be largely idiosyncratic (Decalo 1975) and the timing of their actions may be determined by considerations that we do not observe, such as when the president is out of the country or when a particular officer receives a promotion. Such factors would make it more difficult to completely predict the timing of a coup attempt based on only macro-structural factors.

Each of the hypotheses concerning the causes of coup attempts and the relevant findings is summarized in table 3.2.

Understanding Coup Outcomes

Having established the systematic correlates of coup attempts, we can now turn our attention to the main question of this book, namely why some coup attempts fail and others succeed. That statistical analyses of coups have focused largely on successful coups rather than on coup attempts and coup outcomes is odd for two reasons. First, examining only successful coups is inconsistent with how other conflict events are studied. The scholarship on international and civil wars, for instance, examines both the incidence of war (which is parallel to a coup attempt) and its

Table 3.2: Summary of hypotheses and findings on coup attempts

Variable	Expectation	Proxy	Support
Low economic development	More likely	$\log(\text{GDP/capita})_{t-1}$	**Strong**
Low urbanization	More likely	% urban	None
High trade openness	More likely	Trade openness$_{t-1}$	None
Negative economic growth	More likely	Growth GDP$_{t-1}$	None
Resource dependence	More likely	Oil dependence$_{t-1}$	None
Democracy	Less likely	Democracy$_{t-1}$	None
Anocracy	More likely	Democracy$^2_{t-1}$	**Strong**
Military government	More likely	Military dictatorship$_{t-1}$	None
Presidential democracy	More likely	Pres. democracy$_{t-1}$	None
Presidential election	Less likely	Pres. election	None
High ethnic diversity	More likely	Ethnic heterogeneity$_{t-1}$	None
Few large ethnic groups	More likely	Ethnic heterogeneity$^2_{t-1}$	None
During Cold War	More likely	Cold War	Partial
Superpower ally	Less likely	UN voting$_{t-1}$	None
Former French colony	Less likely	Former French colony	None
International conflict	Less likely	International conflict$_{t-1}$	None
Domestic conflict	More likely	Domestic conflict$_{t-1}$	Partial
Large military	More likely	$\log(\text{soldiers/capita})_{t-1}$	None
High military spending	More likely	$\log(\text{mil. budget/GDP})_{t-1}$	Partial
Recent successful coups	More likely	Past successful coups	**Strong**
Recent failed coup attempts	Less likely	Past failed coups	None

outcome, with each question considered separately and in its own right. It is also puzzling that these studies classify periods in which failed coups occurred the same way they classify periods with no coup attempts, as if a failed military intervention is the same as no military intervention at all. Unlike scholarship on coups, the scholarship on war does not restrict its interest to successful war alone, nor does it treat military defeat as identical to peace.

The argument for considering coup attempts and outcomes separately does not presuppose that there are absolutely no linkages between the incidence of the event and its likely outcome. To the extent that coup makers can be deterred from attempting a coup, the deterrence works precisely by discouraging actors from attempting a challenge that they are unlikely to win or cannot win without paying an undesirable cost. But the presence of such a high failure rate of coup attempts argues that deterrence does not operate as a tight constraint on attempts and suggests that the factors involved in determining attempts and outcomes may be different. Furthermore, deterrence is not an argument for not examining the causes of coup failure; quite the opposite in fact. It is only by examining failed attempts that we can establish the likely mechanisms for deterrence and ascertain how effective it might be.

To combine the analyses of attempts and outcomes into a single regression examining which countries have had successful coups is to assume that the incidence of conflict and its outcomes have the same causes. If the two questions are separated, the analysis does not require such an assumption and in fact reveals whether the assumption can be justified.

The Three Theories of Coup Outcomes

This section discusses the observable implications of the three theories regarding coup outcomes that can be easily tested statistically, starting with the coups as elections approach because it builds nicely upon the results of the earlier analysis.

Coups as Elections

As discussed in the earlier chapters, one approach to modeling the dynamics of a coup attempt is to think of it as an election, a plebiscite on the incumbent, held within the military. According to this perspective, the outcome of a coup attempt is a function of the relative levels of support within the military for the challengers and the government. If support for the coup passes a certain threshold, then the coup succeeds. If the coup is unpopular (or the government is sufficiently popular), the coup is attempted but fails. In this way, a coup attempt is seen as analogous to a vote of no confidence, but one staged by soldiers rather than parliamentarians.

This approach is agnostic to the underlying determinants of military support. The military might be influenced by the legitimacy of the regime, the popularity of the incumbent, class-based disagreements over policy, institutional grievances over pay, or still other factors. Whatever the basis of support, the same process that determines whether coups are attempted should also lead to the success or failure of that attempt.[27]

Coups as elections hypothesis 1: The same factors that predict when a coup is attempted should also predict when an attempt succeeds.

To test the elections theory, I include all of the variables that were associated with coup outcomes in the random effects model, not just the four that found support in both the random and fixed effects specifications. These are GDP/capita,

---

[27]There is an observationally equivalent explanation for why coup attempts and outcomes might share the same causes, but it emphasizes deterrence rather than underlying propensity. It could be that actors know what factors make a successful coup and are much more likely to attempt a coup that will succeed. The problem with this argument is that half of all coups fail and the penalty for failure can be quite high. If coup attempts are strongly shaped by the probability of success, either coup makers are risk-seeking enough to play Russian roulette with half the chambers loaded or they (like most entrepreneurs) substantially overestimate their chance of success.

democracy[2], past successful coups, presidential elections, the Cold War, domestic conflict, the size of the military budget (relative to total national wealth), and past failed coups. This broad range of variables is included so as to make as few assumptions as possible about the mechanisms involved in the coups as elections argument. However, factors that were not associated with coup attempts, such as the level of economic growth, are not considered part of the elections argument with respect to coup outcomes.

Coups as Battles

The other alternative approach views coups as battles whose outcomes are determined by tactical considerations. As discussed in the previous chapter, the major determinants of coup outcomes are therefore the relative military strength of the two sides, secrecy, and speed. Ceteris paribus, we would expect the militarily superior armed faction to prevail, with the likelihood of its victory proportional to its preponderance of force. In addition, some scholars argue that chance can play a critical role in determining the outcome of a coup attempt. For example, Kebschull (1994) argues that the February 1992 coup attempt against President Perez of Venezuela failed because of bad weather over the Atlantic Ocean, making the coup makers sound like the proverbial king whose kingdom was lost for want of a nail.

Even though an explanation that emphasizes the influence of micro-level factors can be very difficult to test cross-nationally, some observable implications associated with this argument can be tested at the macro-level. Even if tactical factors play a dominant role in determining coup outcomes, there may be systematic variance in the ability of incumbents to defend themselves. In particular, military regimes should understand the process of coup making better than civilian regimes, and therefore would be better positioned to resist a coup attempt. Furthermore, military regimes are more likely to have some allies within the armed forces and therefore would be less likely to be left entirely defenseless.

Coups as battles hypothesis 1: Coup attempts against military regimes should be less likely to succeed than attempts against civilian governments.

If coup attempts resemble battles within the state, then attributes of the military are relevant. Militaries that comprise a larger proportion of the national population are more likely to be conscript militaries, making them more diverse and therefore less likely to speak with a single voice as an institution. In addition, they are also more likely to contain loyalist factions that might oppose a coup attempt.

Coups as battles hypothesis 2: Coup attempts by militaries that are large relative to the national population are less likely to succeed.

Similarly, according to this approach, coups should fail more often in countries whose militaries are relatively well resourced. If this money is spread widely within the military, it may buy substantial favor and good will among broad sections of the armed forces, and therefore the military should include many loyalists. If it does not lead to higher salaries for all members of the armed forces, this may be a sign that the money is being spent in a concentrated fashion to buy the support of key factions, thus making resistance to coup attempts more likely by the factions that receive the money. Either way, money spent on the military should buy the incumbent more defenders and therefore make the coup attempt less likely to succeed.

Coups as battles hypothesis 3: Coup attempts by militaries whose budget is large relative to national income are less likely to succeed.

If coups are like battles, then secrecy is important to coup attempts, and one of the key challenges for coup makers is how to move troops into position without arousing suspicion (Farcau 1994, Luttwak 1979). For this reason, coup attempts are often staged during military exercises, with the legitimate movement of troops providing cover for challengers. Since periods of domestic conflict involve large numbers of troop movements, this provides cover for challengers as they maneuver supporters into striking position and should make the attempt more likely to succeed.

Coups as battles hypothesis 4: Coup attempts staged during periods of domestic conflict should be more likely to succeed.

Conversely, according to this perspective, one would expect international conflict to hinder conspirators' ability to launch an attack. Moving forces into forward positions and abroad removes them from contention. In addition, domestic forces assigned to protect the capital during such conflicts are on high alert and primed to repulse any attack. Bringing all of these units into the conspiracy increases the risk of discovery, but if this is not done, conspirators may be mistaken for foreign invaders when they strike. Conditions of international conflict are sufficiently inimical to coup success that Belkin and Schofer (2004) argue that weak leaders sometimes initiate armed confrontations with other nations in order to protect themselves from domestic challenges.

Coups as battles hypothesis 5: Coup attempts staged during periods of international conflict should be more likely to succeed.

As mentioned earlier, throughout the period under study, France had both the capacity and the willingness to intervene in the affairs of its former colonies. The prototypical case is France's intervention in 1964 to defeat the coup against President Leon M'ba of Gabon (O'Kane 1987, 85). Although France did not always intervene to foil coup attempts in its former colonies (and sometimes encouraged them), even the possibility of French intervention may have imposed additional constraints on the coup makers and emboldened defenders.

Coups as battles hypothesis 6: Coup attempts staged in former French colonies should be less likely to succeed.

France was not the only country invested in protecting its clients. The superpowers were better placed to stop coups from succeeding than to prevent them, especially if they had military advisors stationed locally. For example, American advisors played a key role in the defeat of the 1960 coup attempt against the emperor of Ethiopia, providing the emperor with prior warning and intelligence, communications technology, and counter-coup operations planning (David 1987, 39-40).

Coups as battles hypothesis 7: Coup attempts staged against close allies of superpowers should be less likely to succeed.

It is worthy of note that the argument that coups are like battles is not necessarily inconsistent with the argument that they are like elections, as both explanations can be valid at once (Kebschull 1994, 571). One interpretation of coup attempts emphasizes tactics, the other strategy. It is possible that successful coup makers have to establish tactical dominance but can only maintain their position if they have broad support. Conversely, it might be possible that coups never get off the ground tactically unless they pass a certain threshold of support within the military first.

Coups as Coordination Games

The third explanation of what happens during a coup attempt posits that coups are best understood as coordination games within the military and that their outcomes are the result not of preferences (as in the elections model) or of strength (as in the battles model) but of information and beliefs.

According to this theory, during a coup attempt, active proponents and defenders are trying to influence the behavior of the vast majority of the military who are undecided but whose support or inaction could swing the outcome either way. These actors behave strategically, acting according to what they believe others are doing, even if that is not their preferred outcome, so as to avoid fratricidal conflict and the possibility of a civil war.

In this scenario, the coup is won by whichever side is best able to manipulate the beliefs of other actors, convincing them that the side has wide support and their victory is inevitable. When this is done successfully, these beliefs become self-fulfilling (i.e., one side becomes widely supported because everybody believes it is widely supported) and a tipping point is reached. At the end, military supporters of the losing side will choose either to surrender and face the penalty or to run away rather than fight to the last man.

Although many of the observable implications of this theory of coups are at the micro level, two can be tested with the available data. The first involves the claim that the events of recent past coup attempts shape military actors' initial expectations for what will occur in the present coup attempt. Translating this idea into a quantitative hypothesis, however, is tricky, because what actors learn from past coup attempts and the weight they assign to precedent is embedded in local context.[28] In particular, the precedent set by a recent successful coup attempt is

---

[28]In laboratory experiments, actors play the same game repeatedly, so it is easy for precedent to clearly inform expectations. In the real world, the game changes as a result of every past coup attempt, and therefore it is more difficult to understand how players will understand the impact of history

unclear. If a coup succeeds and the last challenger is now the incumbent, that could generate expectations in favor of the incumbent or in favor of challengers more generally, depending on the context. Past failed coups, however, should more clearly shape the expectations of players because they alter the world less, and therefore send a clearer signal to actors in the present. In fact, recent failed coups may have been against the incumbent government, leading to clear expectations that members of the military will act strongly to support the incumbent, just as they did last time.[29] Given that, in the aggregate, the impact of past failed coups on expectations is clearer, the quantitative hypothesis focuses on recent failed coups alone.

Coups as coordination game hypothesis 1: The greater the number of recent failed coups, the less likely a coup attempt is to succeed.

The second hypothesis is based on the importance of institutional factors. Coup makers from the top, middle, and bottom of the military hierarchy possess very different resources with which to make a coup, and coups begun in each level have different patterns of coup dynamics and likelihoods of success. As discussed earlier, the likelihood of success corresponds to the organizational position of the coup makers, with coups from the top being most likely to succeed and those from the bottom the least likely to succeed.

Coups as coordination game hypothesis 2: The lower the rank of the coup makers, the less likely a coup attempt is to succeed.

Once again, this analysis is unable to test all factors that are theoretically relevant because of the limited availability of data for such a wide range of countries and years. For example, it would have been useful to ascertain whether coups are more likely to succeed in countries where the government holds a monopoly on broadcast mass media. Unfortunately, however, no such data on media liberalization exists.

Data on Coup Outcomes

The coups that occurred between 1950 and 2000 were almost evenly split in terms of outcomes, with 233 failures and 238 successes. Both the mean and the median success rates by country are roughly 50%, although they vary in almost a uniform distribution (with only a slight peak at the mean) between 100% failure in some countries (such as Zambia, Zimbabwe, and Kenya) and 100% success in others (such as Pakistan, Cuba, Colombia, and Mali).

As is clear in figure 3.1, while the global success rate varies highly by year, the Lowess smoothed annual global success rate is slightly above 50% for 1950-1980 and slightly below 50% for 1980–2000. Although the number of coup attempts has

---

[29]Failed coup attempts do cause some changes, but mainly in ways that strengthen expectations in favor of the incumbent. For example, a failed coup may lead to the removal of officers who failed to support the government, strengthening expectations that officers currently in critical positions will act to defend the government.

Table 3.3: The regional distribution of coup attempts and outcomes

Region	Successful coups	Failed coups	Success rate
E. Europe / Former USSR	6	4	60%
Western Democracies	4	8	33%
Asia	35	26	57%
North Africa / Middle East	30	34	47%
Latin America / Caribbean	75	64	54%
Sub-Saharan Africa	88	97	48%

declined considerably, the success rate has remained fairly steady. The uptick in success rate is an artifact of Lowess smoothing over that period; if the curve is extended to 2005, the success rate remains more stable.

Table 3.3 demonstrates that regions are all relatively similar in their success rates, with most regions having a close to even split between successful and failed coups. The two regions with the most cases, Latin America and Africa, have success rates of 54% and 48%, respectively. The regions with the highest and lowest success rates are East and West Europe, respectively, but there have been few coup attempts in either, so these cases are likely to be idiosyncratic and do not affect the overall dataset.

Analyzing coup outcomes requires the inclusion of an additional variable to capture the level of origin of the coup attempt. This variable is coded based on the ranks of the officers involved: coups led by officers ranked captain or below (in the army system) are coded as coups from the bottom, coups led by majors to colonels are coups from the middle, and those led by generals or above are coups from the top.[30] Where the identity of the challengers was not known, or in the rare case of a mixed-level coup, the rank was coded as unknown and the case was omitted from the analysis. We were able to code the level of the coup attempt for 75% of the 471 coup attempts in the sample, an astonishingly high rate considering the wide range of incidents included. The level of the coup attempt has a 28% correlation with the success rate, which is shown in table 3.4. This is consistent with the argument in coups as coordination game hypothesis 2, that the likelihood of coup success is positively correlated with the level of the coup attempt.

---

[30]This measure of level does not capture precisely the concept in the theory, since the theory looks at de facto position while the coding measures only literal rank. For example, a colonel commanding the armed forces would be coded as an officer in the middle whereas the theory would treat him as an officer at the top. Cases are coded literally to reduce subjectivity in case coding and therefore to reduce the amount of variance involved in coding cases. Since the systematic measurement error will result in cases being rated as coming from a lower level than they actually are, this should lead to an underestimate of the effects of rank, making it harder to confirm my theory.

Table 3.4: Coup outcomes and success rate by coup level

Rank	Coup attempts	Successful coups	Success rate
Bottom	57	18	32%
Middle	122	58	48%
Top	174	118	68%
Uncodable	118	44	37%

Analysis of Coup Outcomes

In table 3.5, I assess the determinants of coup outcomes, given that a coup has been attempted. The same basic model (in its two variants, depending on which measures of regime are used) is investigated using two different estimators (logit with robust standard errors clustered by country and random effects logit) resulting in four specifications. The four regressions are all consistent, with no important differences between them.[31]

Strikingly, these regressions show no overlap between the reasons for coup attempts and those associated with coup outcomes. Only one variable is significant in both sets of regressions, but it switches directions: past failed coups are positively associated with coup attempts (although not in the fixed effects model of coup attempts) but negatively associated with coup outcomes. This contradicts the idea that coup attempts and outcomes are simply expressions of the same latent variable at different levels, as the coups as elections theory assumes. This should not come as a huge surprise, however, since the data already show us that the macro-political context does not determine the outcome of a coup attempt. In fact, when there are multiple coup attempts in a year, the attempts have different outcomes almost one-quarter of the time.

In addition, all the factors that predict the outcome of a coup attempt are internal to the military and include none of the domestic or international factors that might have been expected to be relevant if competing approaches were correct. There is no evidence that the success of an attempt requires broad popular support or that a coup attempt, once staged, cannot succeed in a particular type of country or another. In particular, there is no impact of GDP/capita, democracy, international and domestic conflict, the Cold War, the percentage of resources used by the military, past successful coups, or the region of the world on the outcome of a coup attempt. This substantially undermines the conventional wisdom about coups and demonstrates that our understanding of the determinants of successful coups reflects factors associated with coup attempts, not outcomes.

---

[31]The unit of analysis is now each coup attempt rather than each country-year that a country was in existence. This better captures the quantity in question and avoids awkward decisions concerning how to code the large number of country-years that had multiple coups with different outcomes.

Table 3.5: Predicting coup outcomes 1950–2000

Variable	Logit w/ robust standard errors (1)	(2)	Random effects logit (3)	(4)
$\log(\text{GDP/cap})_{t-1}$	−0.342	−0.371	−0.342	−0.371
	(0.213)	(0.227)	(0.247)	(0.251)
Democracy$_{t-1}$	0.191		0.191	
	(0.261)		(0.303)	
Democracy$^2_{t-1}$	−0.252		−0.252	
	(0.351)		(0.344)	
Mixed		−0.186		−0.186
democracy$_{t-1}$		(0.708)		(1.134)
Presidential		−0.223		−0.223
democracy$_{t-1}$		(0.545)		(0.653)
Civilian		−0.410		−0.410
dictatorship$_{t-1}$		(0.454)		(0.560)
Military		−0.566		−0.566
dictatorship$_{t-1}$		(0.468)		(0.543)
Monarchy$_{t-1}$		0.0688		0.0688
		(0.942)		(0.837)
Presidential election	0.426	0.510	0.426	0.510
	(0.454)	(0.474)	(0.408)	(0.411)
Cold War	0.571	0.487	0.571	0.487
	(0.442)	(0.426)	(0.445)	(0.434)
Former French	0.0854	0.126	0.0854	0.126
colony	(0.360)	(0.404)	(0.336)	(0.344)
Strongly aligned w/	−0.271	−0.245	−0.271	−0.245
superpower$_{t-1}$	(0.327)	(0.341)	(0.371)	(0.372)
International	−0.0235	−0.0278	−0.0235	−0.0278
conflict$_{t-1}$	(0.176)	(0.177)	(0.301)	(0.302)
Domestic conflict$_{t-1}$	0.0330	−0.00189	0.0330	−0.00189
	(0.120)	(0.122)	(0.128)	(0.131)
$\log$(military	−0.0696	−0.0784	−0.0696	−0.0784
budget/GDP)$_{t-1}$	(0.153)	(0.153)	(0.153)	(0.154)
$\log$(military	0.0177	0.0380	0.0177	0.0380
size/pop)$_{t-1}$	(0.229)	(0.234)	(0.237)	(0.239)
Past successful	−0.227	−0.215	−0.227	−0.215
coups	(0.159)	(0.168)	(0.152)	(0.157)
Past failed coups	−0.284***	−0.269***	−0.284**	−0.269*
	(0.102)	(0.103)	(0.141)	(0.143)
Coup from top	1.099***	1.063***	1.099***	1.063***
	(0.320)	(0.335)	(0.285)	(0.291)
Coup from bottom	−0.740**	−0.706**	−0.740*	−0.706*
	(0.374)	(0.357)	(0.409)	(0.409)

(continued)

Table 3.5: *(continued)*

Variable	Logit w/ robust standard errors (1)	(2)	Random effects logit (3)	(4)
log(population)	−0.193	−0.192	−0.193	−0.192
	(0.126)	(0.128)	(0.125)	(0.128)
E. Europe/			20.00	20.11
former USSR			(14924)	(14927)
North Africa/	−0.108	−0.162	−0.108	−0.162
Middle East	(0.468)	(0.489)	(0.907)	(0.931)
Sub-Saharan Africa	0.132	0.198	0.132	0.198
	(0.672)	(0.720)	(1.039)	(1.067)
Asia	0.0499	0.269	0.0499	0.269
	(0.655)	(0.663)	(0.969)	(0.981)
Latin Amer/	0.0588	0.253	0.0588	0.253
Caribbean	(0.456)	(0.542)	(0.900)	(0.953)
Observations	316	315	317	316

Estimates of constant omitted. Standard errors in parentheses. *** $p < 0.01$,
** $p < 0.05$, * $p < 0.1$

For example, while coup attempts are less likely in highly undemocratic or highly democratic states, the level of democracy does not predict well the outcome of a coup attempt. Highly democratic states have few successful coups because they have few coup attempts, period. Similarly, among countries that have experienced coup attempts, the level of development is not highly correlated with the outcome of the coup. Even at the level of simple correlation, there is little relationship between development and coup outcomes, and development is not a statistically significant predictor of outcome in a bivariate regression. There is no evidence that coup attempts in poor countries are any more likely to succeed than coup attempts in rich countries.[32]

These results do not demonstrate conclusively that the coups as elections and coups as battles theories are entirely wrong, simply that the macro-level correlates tested do not find any support in these simple tests. Especially with respect to the coups as battles theory, there is a poor fit between the predictions of the theory and the cross-national proxies available. The challenge to the coups as elections theory is stronger, though, because the proxies used in this regression are fairly conventional, with democracy commonly used in comparative politics as an indirect measure of regime legitimacy.

Consistent with the theory of coups as coordination games, the two significant predictors of coup outcome are history and coup level; attempts coming after pre-

---

[32]As before, there is no control for the number of years that a government or a regime has been in power, because this variable would be highly collinear with the measure of past successful coup attempts.

vious failed coups and attempts from lower levels of the military are both less likely to succeed.[33] The impact of these variables is robust to basic outlier testing, which is a concern because the distribution of coup attempts is highly skewed. If the regressions in table 3.5 are repeated without Bolivia's twenty-two coup attempts, Argentina's eighteen attempts, or Sudan's sixteen attempts, the direction and significance of the coup history and level variables remain exactly the same. In addition, the direction and significance of almost all of the other variables also remain the same in these twelve different specifications.[34]

That past failed coups decrease the chance of success without also decreasing the chance of an attempt (and in fact are even associated with higher numbers of attempts in a country) is striking, because it indicates a failure of deterrence. There are three possible explanations for this seeming disjuncture. The first is that some countries may have such endemic tensions within the military that some factions may launch pre-emptive coup attempts even when they have a low chance of success. Second, any coup attempt reveals information that may be of use to other groups that are already conspiring, so even a failed coup may encourage another group to attack. But even if either of these is true, it is also very likely that the challengers were overly optimistic about their chances of success, much as entrepreneurs tend to be (de Meza & Southey 1996).

Why might coup makers be over-confident? Over-confidence is one of the best documented of all psychological distortions; multiple studies show that most people are sure they are above average both in their personal qualities and their ability to succeed. According to Johnson (2004), "Studies typically report that 67–96% of people rate their own qualities as better than those of their peers," and most overestimate their control over situations. Some scholars argue that over-optimism is rampant in the run-up to international war, with antagonists holding overly rosy beliefs about their relative power, which leads to challengers' winning less frequently and at a higher price than internal pre-war assessments would indicate (Johnson 2004, chap. 1). Such over-confidence can produce a blindness both to the likelihood of failure and to its attendant costs.[35]

---

[33]That the number of recent past successes is negatively associated with present victory suggests that these measures of coup history are *not* simply picking up the effect of time-invariant structural variables. If some countries were, by their nature, highly prone to successful coups, then the past successful coups would be positively associated with future ones, and the variable would be above conventional levels of significance. That the coefficient for past successful coups is both negative and not statistically significant argues against such a reading.

[34]These regressions are omitted for reasons of space. With outliers excluded, the effect of economic development becomes slightly larger, and therefore passes the lowest conventional threshold for significance, in four out of the twelve regressions. In particular, if the logit regressions in columns 1 and 2 of table 3.5 are repeated without the Bolivian cases, or without the Argentine cases, then log(GDP/capita) is negatively associated with coup success (coups succeed more in poorer countries) at the 10% significance level. Given the number of cases excluded, however, it is surprising that this is the only change in findings observed.

[35]The fact that challengers show irrational optimism about their own chances does not undermine the appropriateness of the coordination model of coup attempts. For one thing, coordination does not require a high level of rational calculation, and the impulse to coordinate can be explained

That said, the penalty for ignoring the effect of past failed coups is not catastrophic. When outcomes are simulated, with all other variables held at their means, each additional failed coup in the prior five years is associated with a 6% lower chance of coup success. Yet, given that most countries had fewer than two failed coups in the previous five years, changing the number of past failed coups from the 25th percentile to the 75th percentile lowers the success rate of a coup attempt only from 59% to 53%.

Coup levels also have both a statistically significant and substantively significant association with the probability of coup success.[36] With all other variables at their mean, coups from the bottom are predicted to succeed 28% of the time, coups from the middle 42% of the time, and coups from the top 68% of the time. This is close to what we see when we examine the simple correlation between coup level and outcome, although the simulated outcomes based on earlier analysis provide slightly lower estimates of coup success for coups from the middle and bottom. The simulated outcomes are displayed in figure 3.2. The graph shows that the simple correlations between coup level and the probability of success in table 3.4 are within the error bounds of the predictions made by the more complicated models. Any statement of the relationship between coup level and coup outcome is conditional on a coup's being attempted in the first place.

This simulation of coup outcomes correctly predicts roughly 70% of coup outcomes, doing a bit better at predicting successful coups (76% of actual successes correctly classified) than failed coups (60% of actual failures correctly classified).[37] This performance is a considerable improvement over simply guessing the modal category, which would correctly predict only 50% of outcomes.

Unexpectedly, the simulation predicts coups from the middle better than coups from the top, correctly predicting the outcomes of 76% of coups from the middle

---

by psychological factors as well as rationalistic ones. For another, while challengers may be overly optimistic about their chances, this does not mean that the average member of the military is so biased, and it is the actions of the vast middle of the military that swing the outcome toward one side or the other. Lastly, if the presence of over-confidence in any of the actors undermines the use of rational models, then we cannot use rational frameworks to explain war, business, or sports.

[36]The fact that cases that were unable to be coded by level were more likely to be failures (62% of cases with no level coded were failures as opposed to 50% overall) raises initial concerns about missing data bias. To see whether this might be a serious problem, I re-ran the regression with an additional dummy to indicate when the level of the coup attempt was unknown, therefore including cases that had been previously dropped. The coefficient for missing levels was not statistically significant, arguing that the missing cases do not behave differently from coup attempts in the omitted category, coups from the middle. This is consistent with my prior expectation that such cases are likely to be from the middle or bottom, since coup makers at these levels are less legible to the outside world when they fail. In addition, the effect of the other variables remained consistent, arguing that these findings are not driven by the cases that were dropped.

[37]This could be because there are more systematic correlates of success than failure, or perhaps because more failed coups than successful coups were dropped from the analysis and so there is more uncertainty about their correlates.

Figure 3.2: Effect of coup level on the probability that a coup attempt will succeed

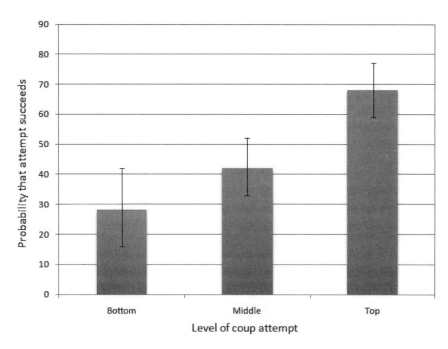

compared to 66% of coups from the top. Coups from the bottom are correctly predicted 61% of the time, but the imprecision is unsurprising, given that there are relatively few cases.[38]

As before, each of the hypotheses concerning the causes of coup outcomes and the relevant findings are summarized in table 3.6.

Understanding Coup Levels

A question that remains is whether the level of the coup attempt is an intermediate variable that is explainable by structural variables and therefore is masking the effect of these more fundamental causes on the likelihood of coup success. There are initial reasons to believe this might be true. For example, coups from the bottom are not evenly distributed among the full population of attempts, as two-thirds of coups from the bottom were in Africa, a sixth were in Latin America, and few were else-

---

[38]This is roughly the same as predicting the modal category for coups from the top and slightly worse than predicting the modal category for coups from the bottom, but it is much better than predicting the modal category for coups from the middle.

Table 3.6: Summary of hypotheses and findings on coup outcomes

Theory	Variable	Expectation	Proxy	Support
Elections	Low economic development	Success	$\log(\text{GDP/capita})_{t-1}$	None
Elections	Anocracy	Success	Democracy^2_{t-1}	None
Elections	Recent successful coups	Success	Past successful coups	None
Elections	During Cold War	Success	Cold War	None
Elections	Domestic conflict	Success	Domestic conflict$_{t-1}$	None
Elections	High military spending	Success	$\log(\text{mil. budget/GDP})_{t-1}$	None
Battles	Military government	Success	Military dictatorship$_{t-1}$	None
Battles	Large military	Success	$\log(\text{soldiers/capita})_{t-1}$	None
Battles	High military spending	Success	$\log(\text{mil. budget/GDP})_{t-1}$	None
Battles	Domestic conflict	Success	Domestic conflict$_{t-1}$	None
Battles	International conflict	Failure	International conflict$_{t-1}$	None
Battles	Former French colony	Failure	Former French colony	None
Battles	Superpower ally	Failure	UN voting	None
Coordination	Recent failed coups	Failure	Past failed coups	**Strong**
Coordination	Higher coup level	Success	Coups from top/bottom	**Strong**

where. Similarly, military governments were more associated with coups from the middle than with coups from the top, which is logical, given that military governments are likely to have co-opted the top brass, giving them fewer reasons to rebel while increasing resentment among officers from the middle who feel locked out.

To test for the possibility that coup levels are merely intermediate variables that can be explained by other theoretically interesting factors, I estimated four variants of the same basic model to predict the level of the coup attempt, as shown in table 3.7. The dependent variable in these regressions is a categorical variable

Table 3.7: Predicting the level of coup attempts 1950–2000

Variable	(1)	(2)	(3)	(4)
$\log(\text{GDP/cap})_{t-1}$	−0.232	−0.291	−0.193	−0.247
	(0.295)	(0.285)	(0.295)	(0.285)
Democracy$_{t-1}$	0.028		0.021	
	(0.263)		(0.266)	
Democracy$^2_{t-1}$	0.590		0.583	
	(0.380)		(0.378)	
Mixed democracy$_{t-1}$		−1.382**		−1.377**
		(0.632)		(0.627)
Presidential democracy$_{t-1}$		−2.248***		−2.258***
		(0.649)		(0.652)
Civilian dictatorship$_{t-1}$		−1.089*		−1.073*
		(0.590)		(0.599)
Military dictatorship$_{t-1}$		−1.027*		−1.026*
		(0.581)		(0.589)
Monarchy$_{t-1}$		0.511		0.555
		(0.783)		(0.786)
Presidential election	0.546	0.397	0.559	0.415
	(0.433)	(0.446)	(0.428)	(0.437)
Cold War	−0.241	−0.0841	−0.194	−0.0399
	(0.385)	(0.419)	(0.389)	(0.421)
Former French colony	0.0854	0.126	0.0854	0.126
	(0.360)	(0.404)	(0.336)	(0.344)
Strongly aligned w/	0.0293	0.132	0.0371	0.145
superpower$_{t-1}$	(0.359)	(0.376)	(0.354)	(0.366)
International conflict$_{t-1}$	0.173	0.0757	0.165	0.0702
	(0.341)	(0.403)	(0.345)	(0.410)
Domestic conflict$_{t-1}$	0.111	0.137	0.102	0.126
	(0.123)	(0.142)	(0.123)	(0.143)
$\log(\text{military budget/GDP})_{t-1}$	−0.118	−0.0609	−0.124	−0.0676
	(0.207)	(0.215)	(0.206)	(0.216)
$\log(\text{military size/pop})_{t-1}$	0.175	0.223	−0.220	−0.231
	(0.325)	(0.330)	(0.341)	(0.341)
Past successful coups	−0.174	−0.134	−0.176	−0.133
	(0.136)	(0.140)	(0.136)	(0.140)
Past failed coups	−0.141	−0.0578	−0.145	−0.0596
	(0.116)	(0.0996)	(0.115)	(0.0990)
$\log(\text{population})$	0.400***	0.468***		
	(0.127)	(0.130)		
$\log(\text{military size})$			0.439***	0.508***
			(0.125)	(0.130)

(continued)

Table 3.7: *(continued)*

Variable	(1)	(2)	(3)	(4)
E. Europe/former USSR	32.81***	29.84***	32.81***	33.85***
	(1.823)	(1.487)	(1.790)	(1.464)
North Africa/Middle East	0.471	0.240	0.501	0.279
	(1.566)	(1.354)	(1.531)	(1.325)
Sub-Saharan Africa	0.0155	0.264	0.0984	0.367
	(1.651)	(1.469)	(1.624)	(1.445)
Asia	0.978	0.963	1.009	1.011
	(1.573)	(1.406)	(1.544)	(1.386)
Latin Amer/Caribbean	1.157	1.830	1.224	1.917
	(1.584)	(1.418)	(1.551)	(1.393)
Observations	316	315	317	316

Estimates of constant omitted. Standard errors in parentheses.
Ordered logit used for all four models. *** $p < 0.01$, ** $p < 0.05$, * $p < 0.1$

indicating the level of the coup attempt, with higher values indicating higher values of the coup level, and each model is estimated using ordered logistical regression. The independent variables in these regressions are the same as in the models of coup outcomes, because we are concerned with the possibility that these variables' effect is being masked by coup level.

Surprisingly, the main predictor of coup level is population size. Coups from the top were more likely in populous countries and coups from the bottom more likely in countries with small population sizes.[39]

Why is country population correlated with coup level? More populous countries have larger militaries, and it is likely that coup level is heavily influenced by the size of the military, with coups from the top being more likely in large and highly complex militaries and coups from the bottom more likely in fairly small militaries where mutinies are more likely to hatch. In fact, there is an 80% correlation between country population and military size, so either country size or military size is a positive and significant predictor of coup level.

However, observing that military size is correlated with coup level does not help us better understand the determinants of coup outcomes. When military size is used in place of coup level (population size must also be excluded) in the analysis of coup outcomes shown in table 3.5, the military size variable is not significant and the percentage of correctly predicted cases drops roughly 7 points to 63%. The bottom line is that understanding the background conditions amenable to coup attempts from different levels of the armed forces does not really change our understanding of the factors that determine coup outcomes.

---

[39] There is one additional finding, but it is odd. Coups from the top are more likely in parliamentary democracies, which is the excluded category, than any other regime subtype whether democratic or dictatorial.

Limitations

As with all cross-national studies, the data are subject to important limitations, including a gap between the proxies and the concepts they are attempting to represent. This limits the ability to test all three theories comprehensively at the cross-national level, and it is the greatest hindrance to assessing the theory that coups are like battles. As a result, the statistical results in this chapter, while thought-provoking, cannot be seen as conclusive and are best understood as complements to the qualitative evidence provided in the case chapters that follow.

In addition, this study should not be understood as providing reliable guidance into the likely outcome of a hypothetical coup attempt in a country far outside the sample, such as Iceland. The analysis of coup outcomes is based on the universe of countries that have had coups. Because countries that have had coup attempts are systematically different from countries that have not, the analysis of the correlates of coup success will have limited external validity and should not be assumed to be valid in all countries. For similar reasons, the analysis of coup outcomes also provides little guidance when trying to predict the outcome of a hypothetical coup attempt in a very different time period, say the 1850s.[40]

That the universe of cases being analyzed is non-random does not automatically lead to selection bias. Instead, selection bias emerges in statistical analysis as a result of what are essentially omitted variables: if sources of unobserved heterogeneity affect both the likelihood of selection (i.e., the chance of a coup attempt) and the likelihood of an outcome (i.e., coup success), the error terms of both analyses will be correlated and observed correlations may not reflect true causal relationships. Such unobserved heterogeneity as exists would limit the internal validity of the study.[41]

An example of how selection bias may produce spurious inferences concerns the relationship between the selectivity of a college and the lifetime earnings of its graduates. Students who go to more selective colleges earn more, but can colleges legitimately take credit for making their graduates richer? According to some economists, this relationship is actually driven by the fact that high-achieving students tend to cluster in more competitive colleges and that if a student chose to turn down MIT and go to another college, the student would earn just as much over his or her lifetime (Dale & Krueger 2011). According to this argument, unobserved student characteristics (such as ambition) determine both college placement and long-term earnings, making them appear to be causally linked.[42] Unobserved het-

---

[40]In addition, the analysis of coup outcomes does not tell us how likely it is that a coup from the middle, for example, will succeed; instead it tells us how likely a coup from the middle is to succeed in a country similar to those studied conditional upon there being a coup attempt at all.

[41]Selection effects decrease the magnitude of a true effect when the cases are selected on the dependent variable (King, Keohane & Verba 1994, 130). When the selection process is separate, however, the direction of its effects is unclear.

[42]This argument is offered only as an example; these findings remain disputed by economists. In addition, since Dale and Krueger are working with data from only a very small non-random subset of colleges (four public universities, four historically black colleges, eleven liberal arts colleges, and fifteen private universities), this research is itself open to charges of selection bias.

erogeneity not only produces spurious relationships but can also have the opposite effect and obscure causal relationships in the data.

It is very difficult to avoid the potential for such bias in observational data, and it is obviously impossible to somehow generate a random selection of coup attempts to avoid inferential complications when analyzing the determinants of coup outcomes. In fact, almost any quantity of interest to political science is the result of prior non-random selection.[43] For those extremely concerned about the impact of unobserved heterogeneity in the data, virtually all of observational social science has the potential for confounding selection effects.

There are statistical methods designed to reduce potential selection bias from unknown sources of heterogeneity; James Heckman won the Nobel Prize in Economics in 2000 for this work. To remove the potential of selection bias, one would jointly estimate both the selection equation (the probability of a coup attempt) and the outcome equation (the probability of coup success). However, this requires a model that both predicts selection well (because the residuals are used as an input in the second stage equation) and produces unbiased results. Neither condition is clearly true here. The model for when coups are attempted predicts only a small number of cases correctly and is itself likely to be biased, because the coups that are attempted are themselves a non-random subset of all conspiracies. Nor is it advisable to try to build a chain of models to cover the entire process of coup making from motive to conspiracy to coup attempt to coup outcome without having a good theoretical understanding of each phase of the process.[44]

The admonition that correlation does not indicate causation (and that not all causation is captured in observed correlations) is always useful to remember. Given that neither randomized experiments in coup making nor Heckman-type statistical solutions are possible in the study of coup outcomes, I instead offer further additional evidence of causal mechanisms using process-tracing in the eight cases presented in the next four chapters of this book.

Conclusion

The analysis of this original dataset supports two of the major contentions of the book: that coup attempts are best understood as coordination games within the military and that it is fruitful to examine the incidence of coup attempts and their outcomes separately.

---

[43]Likely voters, regime type, militarized disputes, economic policies, and even states are all the result of prior non-random processes of selection. For example, likely voters are a non-random subset of registered voters, who are themselves a non-random subset of all voters, who are themselves a non-random subset of possible citizens.

[44]In addition, there are technical obstacles to implementing a Heckman type correction, including the strong assumptions necessary about the joint distribution of the errors that, if violated, cause other problems. There is also the problem that the dependent variables of the two equations do not line up perfectly: the first predicts the probability of at least one attempt a year, and the second predicts the outcome for each of these attempts.

Coup attempts and coup outcomes have disjoint predictors. Looking at the most robust correlates of attempts, military intervention is most likely to occur in countries that are poor, anocratic, have a history of past successful coup attempts, and have a presidential election scheduled in the same year. On a cross-sectional level, coup attempts are also positively associated with the Cold War, domestic conflict, and (oddly) with previous failed coup attempts. Coup attempts are negatively associated with relatively well-resourced militaries. None of these factors, however, predicts the success of a coup attempt once it begins. At that point, what best predicts coup outcomes is the coup makers' level within the military and the country's history of past failed coups.

The finding that the conditions associated with coup attempts are not consistent with successful attempts is revealing but not surprising. It is not surprising because it is already clear in the aggregate data that half of all coup attempts fail, which would clearly not be the case if coup attempts were always staged at the most propitious time. Given the strong incentives for conspirators to succeed, this in turn suggests that challengers are imperfectly able to anticipate when best to attack, are over-confident, or both. Each reading is consistent with the argument that coups are like coordination games within the military because such situations contain a fundamental indeterminacy that makes it difficult for players to predict the outcome of the game beforehand. This indeterminacy cuts in both directions: it is hard for challengers to guarantee success, but at the same time, success always remains possible even if implausible. The latter characteristic feeds over-confidence; very implausible coup attempts sometimes succeed, encouraging the ambition of coup makers who are convinced that they, too, can beat the odds.

This fundamental indeterminacy does not mean that we cannot use our understanding of coup attempts to predict where and when there will be a successful coup, as the question is traditionally framed. The model for attempts can be applied to the traditional question effectively, with more or less the same variables proving significant and consistent for the random effects model. But these factors predict attempts rather than success, and interpreting them as factors that lead to only successful coups is committing the kind of mistake involved in selection on the dependent variable. The traditional approach also would not discover the importance of the institutional factors associated with when attempts fail. As a result, it would miss the level at which deterrence seems to operate, namely that there are more attempts from the kinds of coup makers who have a greater chance of success.

One important area of similarity between the analysis of coup attempts and of coup outcomes is that international factors do not play an important role in either. Contrary to conventional wisdom, coup attempts and successful coups do not seem to have been the result of the manipulation of weak states by hegemonic powers or the result of uncertainty generated by large trade shocks. Trade openness, international war, closeness to superpowers, and even former French colonial status are all statistically insignificant (or not consistently significant in the case of international war). Only the Cold War is associated with attempt incidence (and not in the fixed effects model), yet the end of the Cold War did not lead to a stronger decline in coup attempts than happened in the previous decade.

The other area of similarity between the causes of coup attempts and the determinants of coup outcomes is that neither is related to factors that could be understood as indicating a popular demand for change in government. Rather, the data indicate that the factors that determine coup outcomes are purely elite, the result of the institutional position of the coup makers and the history of past military interventions. None of the proxies that might be associated with popular opinion, such as regime type, have an effect. Although the macro-political characteristics of the state do have an effect on the likelihood of coup attempts, none of the variables that might be associated with popular discontent, such as regime subtype, economic growth, or presidential elections, have the appropriate impact. In fact, attempts are more likely during election years, which argues that coups may be staged to thwart the popular will rather than to serve it.

Still, both of these are negative results, and there are limitations to the implications of such results when there is no agreement on the appropriate variables to include in the model and the correct measures thereof. Although there is no evidence that either mass or international factors drive the incidence of coup attempts or their outcomes in this analysis, this is a limited conclusion.

Another finding is that we are better able to predict which coup attempts succeed than when and where a coup attempt will occur. This is in contradiction to the existing literature, which emphasizes the role of systematic factors when explaining the motive to mount a coup and the importance of both chance and tactical factors when describing the process of executing the coup attempt. These differences in our ability to predict are undoubtedly due in part to the distribution of positive and negative cases being highly skewed in the case of attempts and evenly balanced in the case of outcomes. They nonetheless raise the plausibility of a counter-narrative, one in which coups are attempted for highly idiosyncratic personal reasons and succeed or fail due largely to systematic institutional ones.

Last, these results argue in favor of "bringing the military back" into the center of the study of military intervention. Although there have always been scholars who have taken the characteristics of the military seriously, military actors are ignored too frequently, treated as if their actions were the necessary product of bigger forces of history. For example, Acemoglu and Robinson's account of regime change places military coups as the central mechanism in the grand battle between elites and masses over redistributive policy, yet it assumes that the military automatically mirrors the desires of the elites and therefore can be omitted from analytic consideration (Acemoglu & Robinson 2006). Although some findings of my analysis are consistent with their account, the broader thrust of the results argues against it. At the very least, it would seem prudent to seriously test such assumptions about the role of the military rather than unquestioningly allowing them to dictate the direction of scholarly inquiry into military intervention and democratization.

Chapter 4

Coups from the Top of the Military

A Theory of Coups from the Top

Coups from the top ranks of the armed forces are distinctive in that conspirators at that level have the greatest amount of "soft power." Because of their position at the apex of the military, senior officers have prerogatives that enable them to gather information about what is happening within the armed forces, to preferentially disseminate information favorable to their point of view and, most important, to shape the expectations of military actors even before a coup attempt begins. This grants challengers at the top the ability to "make a fact" in ways not available to members of the military in the middle or bottom ranks, and therefore coups from the top succeed 68% of the time, far more than any other kind of coup attempt.

Because challengers at the top have different avenues available to them for coup making, I find that coups from the top have distinct dynamics as well. Such attempts are likely to be shorter and less bloody than coups fomented by challengers from lower levels of the military.

This section of the chapter discusses the ways in which senior officers plan and execute their coup attempts, detailing how various coup attempts are executed through meetings, proclamations, or force. Each of the two subsequent main sections then presents the case of a coup from the top in Ghana and compares the power of competing explanations in predicting and understanding the mechanisms that contributed to their success. An additional coup from the top, one in the former USSR, is presented in chapter 7.

Conspiracy

Challengers at the top have several advantages that come into play even before the coup attempt begins. First, they have an easier time avoiding detection because they can meet in groups to discuss matters of national policy as part of their professional duties. This provides cover for behavior that might be considered suspicious in lower-ranking officers. In addition, because senior officers are likely to know each other well, their conspiracy builds on existing bonds of trust and they can avoid the risks inherent in bringing a stranger into a plot. Even within a large military, these horizontal connections can span multiple branches of the armed services or specialties within the army, making it easier for challengers to build broad coalitions in support of their objective.

Senior officers are also better able to assess the obstacles they may face while mounting a coup. Because of their position, they may have access to restricted information on the preferences, tactical readiness, and beliefs of other key officers. Senior officers can also commission studies of sentiment within the military, as Admiral Gruber did in Venezuela prior to launching a coup attempt in November 1992 (Gott 2005, 73). Such strategic information is valuable because it allows the challengers to anticipate and address potential problems before the coup attempt begins. However, although such information is helpful, it is not necessary for success, as even those opposed to a coup will be willing to support it if they believe (and meta-believe) that everybody else will do so as well.

Most important, senior officers can use their bureaucratic prerogatives to lay considerable groundwork for a coup before they strike. They can begin to shape expectations ahead of time by telling officers that government policies are highly unpopular within the armed forces or that the military is riddled with coup plots, priming officers in key commands to believe that the coup will succeed, that victory is a fait accompli, and that resisting the coup attempt is futile.

These advantages give coups from the top a good deal of initial credibility. Generals are seen by other members of the military as being better informed about the likelihood that a coup will succeed and better able to make sure that conditions are right when they do move. Their credibility is further enhanced because the top brass tend to be risk averse, with a considerable amount to lose. In peace time, officers who ascend the ranks tend to be bureaucrats with stable, reliable temperaments, not risk-seeking cowboys. This is especially true in countries that are coup prone, as both military and civil leaders are aware of the threat of disruption posed by erratic and ambitious officers.

Senior military officers will also have the easiest time building coalitions with civilian leaders. Because of their position in government and society, they are more likely to come into contact with civilian figures of authority and can meet with them without arousing suspicion. However, I argue that such support is mainly of help after the coup succeeds, when civilian actors can help lend legitimacy to the new government. It does not affect the likelihood of success of the coup attempt itself, since such endorsements rarely have an impact on the calculus of coordination.

Execution

Challengers from the top, unlike those from the middle or bottom, can follow a number of templates when making a coup. From the data I have gathered, three different strategies have been used to make a fact: coup attempts that take place during a meeting, coup attempts by proclamation, and coup attempts that use force. In all three of these scenarios, however, senior officers must grapple with a common constraint, namely that hard power is controlled not by officers at the top but by officers in the middle of the organization, allowing those at the top at best contingent command over fighting units during a coup attempt.

Although the military operates on principles of hierarchical command, it is wrong to assume that generals have the unconditional obedience of all those technically subordinate to them. This point was made repeatedly by my respondents, and its truth can be seen with a simple thought experiment. Imagine that every order given by an officer was automatically obeyed by those under his command. In that case, we should only see coup attempts coming from the very top of the military hierarchy, and each of these attempts would be virtually guaranteed to succeed, since they would never encounter any resistance from within the armed forces. Yet this is obviously not the case.

Even in normal times, higher-ranking officers have only indirect command over fighting units and thus must rely on the cooperation of mid-level officers to accurately transmit and execute their orders. That is, higher-ranking and mid-ranking officers can be said to stand in what economists term a principal-agent relationship to each other. During times of peace or international conflict, the cooperation of mid-level officers is fairly automatic because of strong norms of military obedience and because of organizational sanctions for disobeying an order from a superior officer. Although mid-level officers may argue with their superiors, counseling them on the wisdom and practicability of what they are asking, or even shirk when it comes to implementing an order, open disobedience is very rare within the military, especially during times of international conflict.

During a coup attempt, however, obedience to hierarchical command is far more conditional. Norms do not constrain officers to obey orders given during a coup attempt. Military actors have not only a duty to obey an order from their superior but also obligations to the constitution, civil authorities, and the populace. Because almost all coup attempts involve a violation of the chain of command at some level, coup makers also lack moral authority to demand obedience from their subordinates when they themselves are being disobedient.[1]

More important, the monitoring and sanctions that normally reinforce norms of obedience are also in abeyance during a coup attempt, and it is often unclear to officers whether the penalties for obeying or disobeying orders given by a higher-ranking challenger will be worse. In a coup attempt, mid-level officers are more interested in avoiding a civil war and supporting the winner than in unconditionally following orders given by officers who may find themselves in jail the next day. Because of these factors, a rebelling senior officer may find that his subordinates ignore his orders or even overtly turn against him. As a result, generals do not automatically have hard power at their disposal but must rely on the conditional cooperation of the officers in direct command of fighting units.

---

[1]The only type of coup attempt that does not involve some form of violation of norms of hierarchical authority is an *autogolpe*, a coup mounted by the president himself. Even a coup mounted by the head of the armed forces violates the chain of command in most countries.

Meeting

Because coups are coordination games, officers at the top have a highly effective tactic available to them that is usually off limits to challengers at other levels: the ability to stage a coup during a meeting. While the military's endless meetings are usually seen as a symptom of deep-rooted inertia, a meeting can also be used to produce regime change. In particular, senior officers have the ability to call a meeting of key unit commanders and then use that meeting to create self-fulfilling beliefs about the overthrow of the government. Such meetings are powerful because they create public information quickly and effectively in a stage-managed environment, allowing the challengers to most effectively make a fact around their success. (Once again, public information refers to information which is public or common knowledge to those present at the meeting rather than information which is known to the public at large.)

For most of history, face-to-face meetings have been the primary method for creating public information and shaping expectations (Chwe 2001, 30). While a meeting incorporates a smaller number of people than a media broadcast, it has certain distinct advantages. As with a broadcast, anything said by the challengers in a meeting becomes common knowledge to everybody present. In addition, meetings have the benefit that responses to the challenger also become common knowledge. This considerably speeds up the process of making a fact, since each actor will be able to see the responses of all the others immediately. The appearance of widespread support for the coup attempt (whether real or manufactured) then locks in the cooperation of each player, making it difficult for them to dissent once they have left the meeting, for fear that they will be alone in their of opposition.

The pretext for convening the meeting is irrelevant here, as all that matters is how the meeting is organized and run. Coup makers can bring together military members with the nominal purpose of gathering their opinions, when their actual purpose is to make it appear that there is a consensus supporting a change in government. In his Nobel Prize–winning work, Kenneth Arrow demonstrated that, under the right circumstances, the person controlling the agenda of a deliberation can determine the outcome chosen, even in a fairly open and democratic voting system. In a similar vein, high-ranking challengers can use bureaucratic procedure to control what information is presented to the participants, who gets to speak and in what order, what questions come up for a vote, and how views are to be aggregated. They can do this because they outrank those present at the meeting, thus giving them substantial control of everything that happens in the room. This soft power associated with bureaucratic control can therefore effectively shape the beliefs and expectations of those in the room, making it seem to them that the success of the coup is a fait accompli and opposition is doomed to failure.

Game theorists would argue that the most effective way for generals to produce the outcome they want is to change the nature of the game. (See, for instance, Thomas Schelling's discussion of "strategic moves" in his seminal book, *The Strategy of Conflict* [1960].) Coordination during a coup attempt is difficult, because it is done "simultaneously"—that is, each actor must try to decide whether all the other actors will back the coup or the incumbent without being able to communicate with the other actors or observe their decisions. Although it is difficult to accomplish under most circumstances, coup makers benefit if they can change the nature of the game, forcing actors to declare whether they support the coup one at a time. If each actor's declaration is rendered both public and irreversible, it transforms the game from a simultaneous game to a sequential game with first mover advantage. Coup makers can then either act first themselves or have a proxy act first, ensuring their desired outcome either way.[2]

In theory, if the first actor declares his support for the coup, everybody else present should back the coup as well, as the two-player model of a coup attempt, presented in figure 4.1, reveals. If the first player supports the coup, this leaves the pro-government player with a choice between backing the coup as well or backing the government. A split would produce a fratricidal struggle and a possible civil war. Since coordinating around either outcome is preferred to any non-coordinated outcome, the pro-government player will support the coup as well. In this example, the final outcome leaves the pro-coup player with the best outcome, designated here with a payoff of nine, and the pro-government player with the second-best outcome, a payoff of one. This equilibrium path is indicated in bold on the game tree. An example of this strategy will be seen in the case of the successful 1978 coup in Ghana discussed later in the chapter.

Not all coup attempts in meetings involve sequentialization, however. Although sequentialization is an extremely powerful tactic, it requires a good deal of planning and effort to choreograph. Evidence indicates that there are other paths to the same manufactured consensus in support of the coup attempt. They usually involve two elements. First, the challengers shape expectations by telling those present that there is widespread unhappiness toward the incumbent within the military, perhaps even claiming that lower-ranking officers are on the verge of mounting a coup that will be highly damaging to military unity unless something is done. Then a carefully managed public vote is taken, one in which the options are carefully framed to tilt the playing field even further in favor of the coup. Regardless of their initial preferences, officers will join what they believe is a bandwagon against the incumbent, and in doing so will make real the claim that there is widespread support for the coup.

---

[2] A sequentialized coordination game resembles an information cascade, in that the choices of the first few actors can determine the behavior of all other actors in the game, with later actors imitating the choices of the earlier ones no matter what their preferences or private information. However, the dynamics underlying the two situations are different, and therefore the conditions that would lead to this sort of imitation are different for a coordination game and an information cascade. A sequentialized coordination game requires that decisions be public, but it should take very few actors (perhaps only one) declaring their support for the coup to cause the rest of the military to follow suit. A cascade, on the other hand, can occur based on private information alone and does not require that actors be trying to coordinate, but it usually involves more actors declaring their support for the coup before others will follow suit. A cascade might occur if actors are interested in choosing the side that could win in a civil war, and they imitate other actors as a way of basing their decision on private information that they do not themselves possess.

Figure 4.1: Sequentialized coup dynamics

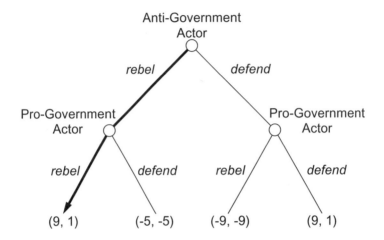

An example of this latter strategy is the overthrow of President Arosemena of Ecuador in 1963, in which the service commanders met and called a general assembly of all officers who could reach the capital by the next morning. Once assembled, the senior officers present denounced the president's drunkenness, argued that his actions increased the communist threat to the country, and warned that inaction would lead to an imminent coup by lower-ranking officers. None of the hundreds of officers present stood up to defend the president or oppose the creation of a military government. This meeting was followed by messages to the military garrisons, an announcement to the nation, and the sending of troops to the presidential palace to arrest Arosemena, who was exiled to Panama (Fitch 1977, 62).

Once expectations have been set in a meeting, history demonstrates that they prove very hard to unravel. In August 1983, the Guatemalan Army High Command mounted a coup attempt against the military dictator, General Rios Montt, with the objective of restoring the country to civilian rule. A meeting of the council of commanders was convened, and even though President Rios Montt showed up unexpectedly, the commanders voted to remove him from office. The president responded by returning to his office and attempting to organize a resistance effort, but despite his connections in the armed forces, nobody came to his aid, and his personal guard were soon defeated (Schirmer 1998, 29). Once the meeting was over, there was little the president could do to overturn the apparent consensus in favor of his removal.

Proclamation

It is not always possible for senior officers to convene a meeting of military commanders, however. In such a case, the next best option for senior officers—especially those from the high command—is to stage a coup by simply declaring one in the name of the armed forces and issuing a public statement that the president is being removed by the military for the sake of the nation.[3] As with a coup from the middle, the key here is to make a fact by publicly claiming that the military as a whole is unified behind the coup attempt, thus creating self-fulfilling expectations of its victory. Officers at the top have a number of advantages in making a fact in this fashion: they can lay the groundwork well, their claim will have a good deal of initial credibility, and they can issue a proclamation without having to assault the broadcasting station first.[4]

It is difficult to resist coups by proclamation, although there is more room to do so than when the coup has been made in a meeting. In a meeting, there is little time between the "broadcast" of the challengers and the reply of those present, both of which are public information among those gathered. With a proclamation, only the broadcast is common knowledge, and the gap between broadcast and reply gives loyalists a chance to disrupt the claims being made by the challengers if they can seize a means of public information and make a counter-claim. Opposing a coup by proclamation is easier in countries with a liberalized domestic media and easy access to international media, since there are more news outlets and it is harder for the challengers to monopolize public information. Of course, it takes more than the president on CNN claiming to still be in charge, as the claims made by the loyalists also have to be believed by key actors within the military.

The most famous example of resistance to a coup attempt by proclamation involves the 1991 Soviet coup, which will be discussed in chapter 7. To oppose this coup by senior members of the party, Boris Yeltsin's supporters in essence waged a counter-coup, using the media to claim that military units were defecting en masse and throwing their support to Yeltsin. Although later official investigation found this claim to be false, concluding that no unit had ever actually refused the junta's orders, Yeltsin managed to convince even junta members that they were losing control, and the coup disbanded.

---

[3] This approach may involve some seizure of symbolic targets. That tactic plays a far more important role in coups from the middle, but it can usually avoid violence. The central mechanism of this type of coup is the announcement.

[4] A coup involving only a private ultimatum to the incumbent telling him to step down is a different tactic. The central mechanism of a coup by proclamation is the manipulation of public information, while a private ultimatum attempts to skip this step, implicitly claiming that the challengers could make a fact easily if they wanted to. This can work if it scares the incumbent sufficiently, but it is risky in that it tips the challengers' hand before they have made a fact. If there is resistance and the incumbent calls the challengers' bluff, the outcome will hinge on how well the coup makers can manipulate expectations once the incumbent knows he is being threatened. For example, in 1970, the armed forces commanders in Argentina issued an ultimatum to fellow junta member President Ongania. The president responded by firing the army commander and holing up in Government House with 1,200 loyal, heavily armed cavalry troops. Ongania did not, however, make any broadcasts, and the challengers had full control of the government radio network. The president surrendered after a series of broadcasts by the challengers in which they claimed they had the support of the infantry, air force, and marines and were prepared to attack (Associated Press 1970).

Force

As noted, coup attempts that use meetings or proclamations as their key tactics use predominantly soft power to make a fact. These tactics are low in both bloodshed and confusion and, when successful, lead to quick coordination. Sometimes, however, generals mount coup attempts that involve the use of hard power. Such coups have some similarity to coups from the middle in that the challengers generally move forces to take control of broadcasting facilities and symbolic sites and thereby make a fact with deeds as well as words. This was the model followed by the Chilean military during their overthrow of Salvador Allende in September 1973: the military seized some radio stations by force and destroyed others to prevent them from being used by loyalists (Scheina 2003, 325).

If coups are coordination games, however, then the overt use of force by challengers of senior rank is a sign of weakness, not strength, as it indicates that the challengers' verbal claim of having the support of the armed forces would not be credible on its own. In such cases, challengers have reasons to expect there might be credible opposition to the coup attempt, and therefore this sort of coup attempt has the potential to be bloodier than other coups from the top.

This method of coup making might be employed if the challenger is a division or corps commander in a large army, making him senior in rank but not at the very apex of the armed forces. Such a challenger would have some hard power but less soft power at his disposal. Because of his position in the hierarchy, his coup attempt would be a challenge not just to the civil authorities but also to his peers and his superiors, so his claim to be in charge might not spur a bandwagon effect unless supported by a demonstration of strength and the creation of facts on the ground.[5] Senior officers from a nation's air force or navy might also use such a tactic, because their claims to be acting on behalf of the entire armed forces would not be as credible without the participation of the army commander, and thus their use of hard power is designed to compensate for their weaknesses in soft power. For example, in June 1955 senior officers in the Argentine navy launched a coup attempt against Juan Peron, sending naval air units to attack the presidential residence during a national holiday, massacring the president's gathered supporters but leaving Peron himself unscathed (Potash 1980, 189).[6] Despite the strong antipathy to Peron within the military at the time, the attack attracted no support from the army and was defeated several hours later.

Lastly, there are other circumstances in which rebelling senior officers are limited in their ability to use soft power and so are obliged to use force to make a coup. This is what happened in 1989 in Paraguay when General Andres Rodriguez used force

---

[5]Commanders at the division or corps level raise questions of taxonomy, since they have some characteristics of more senior officers and some characteristics of officers in the middle. I have decided to keep them in the top for reasons of consistency of coding. Since they constitute roughly 10% of coups from the top, it is unlikely that their presence drives any of the statistical results obtained.

[6]It is unusual to see this sort of attack on civilians during a coup attempt, but this is not inconsistent with the theory proposed. What matters for the theory is low military casualties, since it is bloodshed within the armed forces that might push the conflict into civil war.

to seize control from his father-in-law, President Stroessner. Stroessner, who had come to power via a coup himself, had tried to coup-proof the military by directly exercising control over such matters as troop movements and all officer promotions and by creating a carefully screened 1,500-man presidential guard (Sondrol 1992, 107). As a result of the president's personalistic control of the military, General Rodriguez's nominal position as second-in-command of the Paraguayan armed forces did not give him much soft power, and any claims he might have made of having the backing of the entire military would have been doubted. Instead, Rodriguez had to behave much like a colonel, using the forces under his command to seize control of broadcasting facilities and make a fact by force.

Not only does the use of force by senior officers reveal that they have a relatively weak hand to play, it is a more risky approach than the use of soft power, I argue. Coup attempts that rely on hard power have a greater tactical dimension and therefore a greater number of ways in which something can go wrong. While a meeting in a fairly controlled environment is over quickly, the capture of targets takes longer and more can go wrong. While the theory leads us to believe that forceful coup attempts by senior military officers are still more likely to succeed than coups from the middle, they are still the riskiest method of executing a coup from the top.

In addition, the mobilization of forces around tactical objectives exposes another weakness of officers at the top, namely that they do not have forces of their own to command and may therefore face defection from troops within their own chain of command. Officers at the top have to make a fact even for their own supporters or they may find their strength ebbing away.

The defection of subordinates is a stark illustration of the contingency of command and of the risks involved when senior officers take obedience for granted. For example, in December 1967, the king of Greece mounted a counter-coup against the junta that had taken power in the spring of that year. The king's coup attempt failed because he assumed that orders issued by his supporters, the commanders of the Third Corps and Armored Division, would be carried out, when in fact those generals were stopped and detained by their own subordinates.[7]

One of the most dramatic examples of the contingency of command concerns a failed coup in Ethiopia in May of 1989. General Demissie Bulto was in charge of the Ethiopian Second Army, so he had 150,000 troops (half the entire army) under his control. General Bulto had joined forces with two other senior officers, the armed forces chief of staff and the air force commander, to mount a coup against the military junta ruling the country. Nonetheless, Bulto was opposed both within and outside his command, and the coup failed. In this case, Bulto's nominal command, his personal popularity as a war hero, and his goal of withdrawing from an unpopular civil war were still not enough to ensure the obedience of his subordinates. Hard power can quickly evaporate during a coup attempt unless challengers create self-fulfilling expectations around their victory.

---

[7] *Keesing's Record of World Events*, Volume 14, January, 1968. Greece, p. 22454

As these two cases suggest, the path to *defeating* coups from the top that use force is to win the battle of information and expectations. This gambit does require enough tactical strength on the part of coup opponents to gain access to public information, and preferably to hold on to some of the important symbolic targets, but once opponents are able to shape expectations in their favor, men and guns will follow. This strategy works against coup makers of all ranks and sizes, since the effective use of soft power will allow counter-coup forces to steal their strength. Evidence demonstrates that officers in the middle will join the bandwagon of whichever side they think will gain the support of the others and therefore win, and they will have little hesitation over ignoring orders from a superior officer, even if that officer and his cause are highly popular.

The Case of Ghana, 1975

Ghana's first coup attempt from the top took place early in October of 1975.[8] This was an *autogolpe*, a coup by the president himself, General Acheampong, against the other members of the ruling National Redemption Council (NRC) junta. As we shall see, although the success of this coup attempt is consistent with all three explanations for coup outcomes, the dynamics of the event are most consistent with the theory that coup attempts are coordination games: the coup was staged through a series of meetings that gave the coup makers control over public information and allowed them to make a fact; both sides made efforts to reduce casualties; and the characteristics of the coup attempt were largely shaped by the rank of the coup makers.

Background

The main motivation for the 1975 coup attempt was President Acheampong's desire to consolidate power by displacing the other members of ruling military junta. At the time, Ghana was governed by the NRC, which included the four officers who had overthrown the Second Republic in 1972: Acheampong, a former colonel who had promoted himself to general and taken the title of president after the coup, along with Major Agbo, Major Baah, and Major Selormey.[9] The *autogolpe* was in-

---

[8]The exact date is not clear, but the best estimate is in the first week of October, possibly October 2. Nugent simply cites October 1975 (Nugent 1996, ix), as does Chazan (Chazan 1983, 238), while Aboagye gets the date completely wrong, putting it in 1977 (Aboagye 1999, 101). The official decree announcing the regime change was issued on October 29th, but this was clearly after the fact (Petchenkine 1993, 62). Major Agbo insists that the event took place during the first week of October, most likely on October 2.

[9]In fact, Acheampong was promoted to colonel just two days before the original coup, in an effort to secure his loyalty, leading to jokes that the Second Republic might have survived if only the promotion had come through earlier. The point is that the big difference in rank between Acheampong and the majors was a relatively recent artifact; when they were conspiring, Acheampong was still a lieutenant colonel, the next rank above that of major.

tended to sideline the three mid-ranking officers and replace them with more-senior military men, who better represented the organizational hierarchy and were personally beholden to Acheampong.

The incumbent government was very popular in 1975, having presided over a period of record-making economic growth. In this, the junta stood in stark contrast to its democratic predecessor, which had struggled with a sharp decline in Ghana's main export commodities that had led to decreased government revenues, a highly unpopular austerity budget suggested by the International Monetary Fund (IMF), and Ghana's first-ever currency devaluation (Herbst 1993, 23). When the NRC junta took power, they benefited from an upswing of commodity prices that allowed them to disburse considerable amounts of patronage and revalue the currency, pleasing key urban constituencies, who consumed the lion's share of imports. Two years of good rains had made a success of the government's efforts to increase domestic food production (named Operation Feed Yourself, in classic military style), driving down food prices and giving the junta a reputation for effective and pragmatic governance. The junta's decision to repudiate Ghana's international debt also restored pride among the citizens of a country that had been humiliated by the IMF. Although none of these policies was sustainable in the long term, it seemed that the junta's can-do attitude and lack of corruption had reversed Ghana's economic slide and had put the country back on an upward trajectory.

The coup attempt, therefore, did not emerge from any sense of mass discontent with the junta but was rooted in General Acheampong's ambition and insecurity. The president had always been afraid he would be displaced by a coup, removed from power in the same way he had gained it.[10] One of his worries was that members of either of the two previous democratic governments (both of which had been overthrown by coups) might try to recapture power in alliance with sympathetic officers. The previous incumbent, Prime Minister Busia, retained the support of neighboring Ivory Coast, and the junta had already uncovered one plot designed to restore him to office (Petchenkine 1993, 61).[11]

The president was also concerned about ethnic tensions within the military, in particular between officers from the Akan and Ewe ethnic groups. Acheampong was a member of the numerically dominant Akan ethnic group and was attempting to reduce what he perceived as Ewe over-representation in the armed forces. Given that both of Ghana's successful coups (including the one that had brought Acheampong to power) had involved prominent Ewe conspirators, Acheampong had reason to fear a challenge by Ewe officers.

Another potential source of trouble came from generational tensions within the military and the increasing discontent of some junior officers.[12] Ghana had experienced a coup attempt by junior officers acting against a military government in 1967 that had come very close to succeeding. With the recent success of a coup

---

[10]Interview with General (retired) Laurence Okai. August 30, 2000. Accra, Ghana.

[11]Interview with Colonel (retired) Michael Gbagonah. May 29, 2000. Accra, Ghana.

[12]Interview with General (retired) Laurence Okai. June 16, 2000. Accra, Ghana.

by mid-level officers in Nigeria, General Acheampong was alert to the chance of a similar challenge against his own government.[13]

Lastly, Acheampong was worried about the organizational tensions produced by the presence of three mid-ranking officers in the ruling junta. As members of the executive, they were at the top of the military hierarchy, in stark contradiction to their stated rank. These tensions were exemplified when one of the majors referred to a senior officer by his first name and was rebuked by Acheampong for being disrespectful.[14] This story became widely known and was reported to me repeatedly as an example of the difficulties engendered by the dual roles of the majors.[15] These tensions went beyond those of protocol and etiquette, however. As members of the executive, the majors could legitimately exercise control over decisions concerning the careers of their seniors, especially on matters of promotion, which, since they were still in uniform, was considered improper.[16] As a result of these problems, the heads of the military services began to regularly complain to the head of the armed forces, General Okai, that their authority was being undermined.[17]

Acheampong thus saw multiple reasons to mount a coup against his fellow junta members. The removal of the majors would resolve the concerns of more-senior officers, and a new regime would provide new opportunities to distribute patronage to junior officers. Since two of the three majors also were Ewe, their removal would eliminate a perceived point of vulnerability. Last, a coup would allow Acheampong to consolidate his grip on power by directly establishing his primacy. As the last remaining member of the original conspiratorial group, he could claim full credit for the removal of the unpopular democratic Second Republic that had preceded him. Although the population seemed quite content with the NRC government, General Acheampong had strong incentives to replace it with a different junta.

---

[13]Interview with General (retired) Laurence Okai. August 30, 2000. Accra, Ghana.

[14]Interview with General Edwin Sam. July 9, 2000. Accra, Ghana.

[15]Interviews by the author in Accra, Ghana, with AVM (retired) Odaate Barnor on July 29, 2000, General (retired) Edwin Sam on July 9, 2000, and Colonel (retired) Kofi Jackson, July 25, 2000. There was also the problem of who should salute whom: should the majors be saluted by higher ranking officers because of their position in the government, and were the generals owed salutes from the majors by virtue of their ranks? Interview with General (retired) Laurence Okai. July 16, 2000. Accra, Ghana.

[16]Interview with General Edwin Sam. July 9, 2000. Accra, Ghana.

[17]Oddly, concerns about the subversion of hierarchy were not as much of an issue for Acheampong, even though he was essentially a lieutenant colonel when he assumed power. The reasons for this are three. First, Acheampong was one of the older officers, having joined the army under the British. Second, before his coup, Acheampong had been promoted to a position where he commanded all the army units in the southern half of the country and therefore had reached a position of substantial seniority. Last, Acheampong had systematically sidelined officers who were above him in the hierarchy, often shipping them off as ambassadors or military attaches. Even though this issue was less acute for Acheampong, he was very diligent in removing potential sources of conflict. Of course, Acheampong, alone of the four conspirators, had promoted himself to general. The three majors retained their pre-coup ranks.

Conspiracy

Acheampong's ally in this coup was the head of Ghana's military, General Okai.[18] A few months prior to the coup, Acheampong had given General Okai the green light to secretly develop a blueprint for a new government. Okai proposed a new governing council, called the Supreme Military Council (SMC), to be superimposed upon the existing junta, thus demoting the majors and removing them from governance. The SMC would represent the military hierarchy and include General Acheampong, General Okai, the heads of the army, air force, navy, and border guards, and the inspector general of police. Executive power would nominally reside with the SMC, but in truth Acheampong would be fully in control.

The conspirators knew that this reorganization of the government would not be easily accepted by the members of the junta who were being demoted. Indeed, according to Major Agbo, if (as happened) Acheampong had told them to step down without being willing to leave office himself, "We would have removed him. Damn the consequences. We would have removed him!"[19] In other words, the majors claimed they were willing to resist and had the capacity to do so. To avoid premature disclosure, Okai kept the plan locked in a safe until the day of the meeting. The two generals saw the majors as potential adversaries and wanted to minimize the chance of bloodshed that might be involved in their removal.

Before the coup attempt, Acheampong quietly used the prerogatives of his position to smooth the path to success. Before moving forward, for instance, Acheampong used the military intelligence (MI) wing of the Ghana armed forces to investigate which officers were unhappy with the majors' behavior and which might support the majors if he tried to remove them.[20] Based on the information he thus received, he decided to proceed with his plan.[21]

Having thus tested the waters, Acheampong spoke to key officers in private to further lay the groundwork for the coup. In these conversations, he raised the issues of deterioration of discipline within the Ghanaian armed forces and a coup by junior officers that had ocurred in Nigeria in July.[22] These private meetings allowed Acheampong to make the case that the majors were having a pernicious effect on the military as an institution, framing this issue as one of professionalism rather than of personal ambition. In these interactions, Acheapong also had the opportunity to assess the strength of support among those officers who agreed with him and to convince any who were wavering or opposed. Most important, he could present his concerns with the majors' behavior as being widely shared among other

---

[18]Except for the remark attributed to Agbo, all of the other information in this account comes from my conversations with General Okai.

[19]Interview with Colonel (retired) Kodzo Barney Agbo. August 30, 2000. Accra, Ghana.

[20]Although military intelligence is traditionally used by countries to monitor external threats, Ghana faced no credible threat of invasion by any of its neighbors, and the primary function of military intelligence had become the internal surveillance of the armed forces for signs of sedition.

[21]Interview with General (retired) Laurence Okai. August 30, 2000. Accra, Ghana.

[22]Interview with General (retired) Laurence Okai. August 30, 2000. Accra, Ghana.

officers, thus encouraging officers to fall in line and priming them to agree to the majors' removal later.

Acheampong's extensive preparations provide a vivid testament to the contingency of power within the military. Even though these two generals sat at the apex of the Ghanaian armed forces, they did not take the unconditional obedience or support of their subordinates in the armed forces for granted. Instead they moved in secrecy, first probing, then persuading, and all the time concealing their eventual goal: the removal of the three junior members of the junta.

Meeting

The removal of the majors took place over two meetings, the first of which was held in the offices of the president in Christianborg Castle.[23] The meeting was orchestrated to symbolically demonstrate the majors' exclusion from power in a number of different ways. It began without the majors' being present, as they had been told to remain in a waiting room until they were invited in.[24] When the majors were summoned, they were seated facing the other officers in the room, as if they were on trial.[25] Other officers were already present, including a majority of those to be sworn into secondary positions in the new government and possibly some of the officers responsible for units near the capital.[26]

As soon as the majors were seated, Acheapong announced that they had been removed from the junta. He did so by disclosing the creation of the Supreme Military Council as the new ruling body, saying that the majors would stay on in the NRC, which would no longer have executive functions. According to one witness, "This was done, he said, to make the hierarchy of the Armed Forces coincide with that of the government. The new changes would, among other things, streamline the command structure and promote discipline" (Jackson 1999, 24-25).

The announcement of the organizational changes led to a heated disagreement between the majors, on one side, and Acheampong, Okai, and the service chiefs on the other. The argument in favor of the change in government was two-fold: it would

---

[23]There is some disagreement about exactly which body was holding a meeting. This narrative relies most heavily upon Okai's testimony. According to Colonel Jackson, this was a meeting of the Military Advisory Council (MAC)—i.e., all of the unit commanders around the country—but his account is contradicted by both Agbo and Okai. Okai goes further and argues that the MAC was not created until after the SMC. Agbo's recollection is close to that of Okai, with one minor difference. Agbo claims simply that they were summoned to the castle without any reference as to the pretext, whereas Okai claims that the majors were invited for a regularly scheduled meeting of the executive council. This has relevance for how many people were in attendance, as well as who they were.

[24]Interview with Colonel (retired) Kodzo Barney Agbo. August 30, 2000. Accra, Ghana.

[25]Interview with Colonel (retired) Kodzo Barney Agbo. August 30, 2000. Accra, Ghana.

[26]Jackson was present because he was to be sworn into the SMC. Since he was given no advance warning of this fact, he may have been purposefully misled about the meeting. Okai originally said that brigade commanders and local unit commanders attended the meeting before more firmly stating that it included simply the NRC executive council and that he met with the others later. Agbo, on the other hand, remembers the local brigade commander (who later died in another coup) as being present.

restore hierarchical order to the military, and it had widespread support within the armed forces (Jackson 1999, 25).

The majors were in a much weaker position and could only argue that they had a moral right to be part of the ruling council. They complained that the decision was unfair and constituted a betrayal; having originally risked their lives for the coup, they argued, they were entitled to a seat in the executive.[27] They first tried to compromise, saying that they were willing to accept the inclusion of the service chiefs in the junta as long as they remained members as well. Acheampong would not budge, however, and was supported by the other officers (Jackson 1999, 25). After much arguing, the majors withdrew to one of their offices to caucus, after which they wrote their letters of resignation from the executive council.[28] The new members of the junta were sworn in, and the change in government was made official. The new junta then shuffled the assignments of the officers in charge at the regional level, discharging those appointed during the NRC and putting younger officers in their stead. These officers would owe their appointment to the president and should presumably be more loyal.

The process of removing the majors was then completed with one more meeting, this one involving all the senior officers of the armed forces, who had been assembled at the national military headquarters.[29] General Okai addressed them for around thirty minutes, explaining the changes in governmental structure and fielding questions. They were asked if they had any comments, but none expressed any disagreement.[30] Except for the larger audience, this second meeting served as a recapitulation of the first, with General Okai describing the new junta and asking if anybody objected. Nobody challenged him, producing the appearance of unanimity behind the change.

Analysis

Although all three of the theoretical approaches analyzed in this study predict the success of the coup, only the coordination games approach explains the dynamics that occurred within it.

Coups as Battles

From a tactical perspective, it is unsurprising that this coup succeeded. Although there was no overt fighting, it is likely that the victors would have prevailed in a battle. The coup-making side included the two generals at the top of the military hierarchy, both the head of the armed forces and the president, and the theory that coups are like battles presumes that formal command translates into military

---

[27]Interview with General (retired) Laurence Okai. August 30, 2000. Accra, Ghana.

[28]Interview with General (retired) Laurence Okai. August 9, 2001. Accra, Ghana.

[29]Once again, the exact date of this meeting is unclear, although it may have been as soon as the next day.

[30]Interview with General (retired) Laurence Okai. August 9, 2001. Accra, Ghana.

power. In addition, the president had remained close to his former unit, the main capital infantry battalion, having chosen to remain in the housing assigned to its commanding officer instead of moving to the official residence designated for the head of state. This gave Acheampong both formal and informal command over one of the most powerful units in the country. It is less clear how much force the majors could have brought to bear if they had chosen to fight back, since their allies never identified themselves, but it likely would have been less than what their adversaries could have brought to bear.

It is difficult to judge the fit of the other battle-related hypotheses, because Acheampong took over without firing a shot or even demonstrating his military dominance. While the coup makers did not seize tactically important targets, it appears they did not need to, as they were already in control of both the state and the armed forces.

That said, the coup makers displayed a relaxed attitude toward the majors after the meetings, and that is somewhat inconsistent with the spirit of the argument. The two generals did not have a contingency plan to deal with the possibility that the majors might try to resist their removal by force, and even allowed them to return to their old units as regular officers rather than detaining them or sending them into exile. If the generals were concerned about resistance before the meetings, then, from a purely tactical perspective, they should have been equally concerned afterward and at least taken basic precautions to prevent a counter-coup.

Coups as Elections

The success of this coup attempt is also consistent with the argument that coups are like elections, since it is likely that the winning side commanded a plurality of support within the officer corps. It strains credulity, however, to argue that support for the removal of the majors was unanimous. If the majors had been completely without supporters, Acheampong could have simply asked for a show of hands at the beginning of the meeting. The fact that he did not proceed in such a fashion, combined with General Okai's belief that the majors were not entirely friendless, offers circumstantial evidence that events did not reflect the true preferences of all officers.[31] While the dynamics of this coup attempt look more like an election than a battle, neither theory is fully consistent with behavior observed during the coup.

Coups as Coordination Games

Of the three theories, the one that best fits the described events is the argument that coups are like coordination games. Rather than organize their coup attempt in ways that looked like a battle or an election, Generals Acheampong and Okai instead quietly used their institutional prerogatives to lay the groundwork, then

---

[31] Evidence on the theory's third claim is mixed. On the one hand, Acheampong did not make an appeal for support in either meeting, as might have been expected. On the other hand, he may not have needed to, since he was able to lobby members of the military privately beforehand.

executed the coup via two meetings in which they made the change in government appear a fait accompli, backed by a unanimous consensus of those in command. This maximized their chance of success and minimized the risk of bloodshed.

Consistent with this theory, the winning side had the highest rank and full control over the two meetings that served as the means for generating public information within the group. Both meetings started with a broadcast asserting the creation of a new government, presented simply as a fait accompli. The subordinate status of the majors was emphasized quite clearly in the first meeting, and although they were allowed to speak, they did not use this opportunity to make a counter-broadcast and manipulate expectations to make it appear they had widespread support. To the contrary, the majors showed their weakness in the meeting by bargaining and making moral arguments, implicitly revealing that they could not stop their removal. In the second meeting, General Acheampong did ask if anybody objected, but this was a rhetorical device designed to underscore the lack of opposition. Given the apparent unanimity of opinion, even if some of those present were privately opposed to the new government, they would have been unwilling to voice their disagreement openly. Furthermore, the face-to-face arrangement of each meeting ensured higher-order knowledge of this unanimity among those attending.

The coup transpired bloodlessly, with the generals organizing events so as to reduce the chance of fighting and the majors accepting their removal instead of fighting back. That the government would change without violence was far from a foregone conclusion, which is why the conspirators moved so surreptitiously until their trap was ready to be sprung. According to sources on both sides, the majors still had allies in their own units, and officers from the Ewe ethnic group had reasons to oppose the change, because it would reduce their representation within the junta. Once the second meeting was over, however, the majors had been rendered harmless. Acheampong had already created the public impression that most officers supported the coup attempt, and had done so in way that would have been very hard to counter. This not only stopped an immediate response by the majors but also made it hard to organize a counter-conspiracy afterward. Even the majors joined the bandwagon, accepting their defeat.[32] As noted, General Okai was so certain that the majors would be defeated after the meeting that he lacked a contingency plan to deal with a counter-coup.[33]

As predicted by this theoretical explanation, the challengers employed resources associated with their position in the military to organize and execute this coup. Acheampong used military intelligence to gauge preliminary support for removing the majors, employed his control of previous meetings to repeatedly undermine the majors by linking them to issues of indiscipline, and directly lobbied individual officers. While these lobbying activities took place in private conversations intended to change preferences, the fact that he could do such a thing was public knowledge

---

[32]Major Agbo insisted that they could have regained power, but that they did not believe it would be worth the risk of widespread bloodshed that would have been involved. Interview with Colonel (retired) Kodzo Barney Agbo. July 27, 2000.

[33]Interview with General (retired) Laurence Okai. August 30, 2000. Accra, Ghana.

and increased the credibility of the coup attempt. In other words, it was common knowledge that Acheampong had the ability to assess the situation and therefore was unlikely to move forward unless he thought he could succeed. More important, the coup makers were able to arrange and control two meetings in which they generated public knowledge of their claim to have taken over. In short, their ability to use the soft power associated with their position made the coup attempt fast, bloodless, and successful.

President Acheampong's decision to stage the coup through meetings is significant, especially because he was likely to prevail no matter how he proceeded. He might have chosen to change the structure of the government, for instance, by promulgating a new decree, perhaps arresting the majors before he did so. Generals Acheampong and Okai had the official standing to issue such orders, and their careful work ensured that key officers would at least passively support such a change. However, the risks involved in a change of government by fiat were higher than those involved in a meeting. For example, if the majors had escaped arrest, there might well have been a confrontation and possibly bloodshed, especially if other officers from the same ethnic group felt they were being threatened. The use of meetings was safer and more effective than tactics for coup making that used more force.

It should also be noted, however, that two aspects of the theory are less directly supported in this account. First, the coup attempt succeeded without the seizure of any symbolic targets, most likely because the instigators did not need to use hard power to confirm their claim to be in control when the meetings would do. In addition, both meetings took place in locations of symbolic importance, so there was no need to seize additional targets to make this point. Second, the history of past coup attempts in the country did not play an overt role in this coup attempt. Participants do not seem to have looked to precedent to shape their initial expectations, perhaps because Generals Acheampong and Okai did such a good job of laying the groundwork for this coup and because the coup attempt went so smoothly that initial expectations were less important. That said, the success of this coup attempt is not inconsistent with the claim that past successes breed future successes, given that both the most recent previous coup attempt as well as two out of three of all past coup attempts had succeeded.

Ghana, 1978

Ghana's second coup attempt from the top came three years later, in 1978. This time, the top brass wished to remove General Acheampong from power, but the president was extremely vigilant and had taken a number of precautions to make it difficult for anyone to organize a coup attempt against him. Despite the fact that the conspirators represented the entire command structure of the Ghanaian military, they were stymied until Acheampong accidentally gave them a pretext to call together the mid-level commanders on official business. The challengers seized this opportunity and, using a strategy of sequentialization, were able to create the appearance of unanimous support of the coup, thus forcing the president to step down. This case illustrates both the capacities and limitations associated with senior rank when it comes to coup making.

Background

By 1978, the Supreme Military Council junta installed by Acheampong and Okai's coup had lost legitimacy within Ghana. After several years of negative economic growth and high inflation, the urban middle class had taken to the streets, demanding a return to democracy. A growing segment of the officer corps also wanted to see a return to civilian rule, believing that military governance had damaged the institutional integrity of the armed forces. President Acheampong had no interest in giving up power, however, and dealt ruthlessly with all threats, perceived or real, to his continued rule.

Ghana's economy had serious structural problems that were largely the result of years of economic mismanagement. In pursuit of greater patronage, the junta had greatly expanded its involvement in the economy, creating new state-owned enterprises, increasing government representation on the boards of private companies, and expropriating the operations of some foreign companies. While this strategy had political benefits, it was costly, in that it increased corruption and decreased efficiency and was difficult to sustain at a time when revenues were down. For example, government revenue was low because cocoa production, traditionally one of the engines of the economy, had decreased, even though world prices were at record high levels. The problem was that the government insisted that farmers sell their cocoa crop to the government, which then operated as a middle man to international buyers, and gave the farmers a price far lower than the market price (Bates 2005). Farmers rationally responded to this negative incentive by planting less cocoa and smuggling much of what they did produce to neighboring countries, where its sale did not produce any income for the state.[34] To meet fiscal shortfalls, the government printed more money, increasing the money supply by 44% in 1976 alone (Oquaye 1980, 28). Inflation, already high, had climbed above 100% in 1977 (Frimpong-Ansah 1991, 169).

The government response to this inflation was not to reduce spending but to impose price controls, which simply produced shortages of both food and manufactured goods. Domestic foods were in short supply because it was not profitable for farmers to produce and sell crops at official prices.[35] Industrial production suffered because state-owned enterprises were run inefficiently by politically connected officers and civilians, failing to produce adequate goods for the domestic market.

---

[34]In 1977, 45,000 tons of cocoa was smuggled into the Ivory Coast (Okeke 1982, 17).

[35]Ghana, not self-sufficient in food production under normal circumstances, had suffered a harsh regional drought in 1975-76 that was compounded by the government's steadfast refusal to admit that there was a problem. This drove actual food prices up to five or six times their previous levels (Okeke 1982, 17-18).

There was a shortage of imported goods as well, because of a shortage of foreign currency, and this led to rationing of goods, including infant formula, milk, laundry detergent, soap, matches, toilet paper, toothpaste, corn, rice, flour, and sugar. The basic necessities of life had become hard to come by.

The predictable response to shortages and fixed prices was extensive black market activity. Shortages had decreased supply, thus increasing the price that people were willing to pay unofficially. As a result, few goods were available at the designated price in an official venue; the shelves of government retail stores were bare. Scarcity increased the black market price of most goods considerably, creating ample opportunities for those with access to these goods to profit handsomely. Meanwhile, the formal economy was in a tailspin and real incomes, especially those of urban middle-class professionals, plummeted.

Ghana's economic decline undermined not only the popularity of the military government but its legitimacy. Although military rule had been justified in terms of its efficiency and moral rectitude, it had fallen demonstrably short on both fronts. For instance, much of the retail black market was controlled by women, a consequence of a long history of small-scale female traders in Ghana, and many Ghanaians believed that these women had traded sexual favors to obtain access to these scarce goods, sometimes directly from the president himself (Oquaye 1980, 17). President Acheampong's sexual improprieties were held directly responsible for corruption and the decline of the economy (78).

Unhappy with the government's performance, the urban middle classes increasingly agitated for a return to civilian rule and democracy. In 1977, the Association of Recognized Professional Bodies (ARPB)—an umbrella organization of professional groups representing lawyers, doctors, teachers, engineers, and financial employees, among others—called a general strike and demanded the immediate dissolution of the military regime. The regime responded harshly, banning the organization and even sending soldiers to occupy a major hospital and harass the physicians. Nonetheless, the government was unable to stop the strike until it promised to set a date to begin a transition to some form of constitutional government and elections.

But what the junta actually proposed was not a return to democracy but a referendum on the formation of a no-party regime they called the Union Government (Unigov for short). Unigov was styled along corporatist lines and was to include representatives from all groups in society, with an especially prominent role for the military and security apparatus.[36] The sitting government threw its full weight into promoting Unigov, creating state-sponsored pro-Unigov groups, monopolizing advertisements on radio and television, and using force to intimidate the opposition (Chazan 1983, 259). Unigov supporters openly portrayed it as a continuation of the current junta, distributing shirts, matches, and goods bearing President Acheampong's image and inscribed with slogans such as "Vote Unigov,

---

[36]In a bizarre twist, Unigov attracted the support of American spiritualist Elizabeth Claire Prophet, who compared the tripartite composition of Unigov to the Holy Trinity, with the army representing the Father, the police the Son, and the people, the Holy Ghost (Oquaye 1980, 86).

Vote Acheampong" (Oquaye 1980, 85). The government spent money on this campaign so freely that the governor of the Bank of Ghana objected, and he was dismissed (88).

Despite government efforts to attract support to Unigov, the opposition coalition continued to grow, largely within the middle class. The lawyers, academics, students, and professionals who made up the original core of the pro-democracy movement were now joined by the churches and a variety of eminent political figures across the ideological spectrum, including a respected former military ruler. Even the engineers, normally the most apolitical of the professional groups, collectively organized a disruption of supplies of water, electricity, and fuel to the country (McGough 2001, 17). Such defiance of the government came at considerable personal risk; the government attempted to block mobilization, denying permits for rallies and sending plainclothes thugs to violently disrupt political gatherings.

The referendum was held on March 30, 1978, to light voter turnout and heavy government fraud. As the balloting was about to start, the government announced that votes would no longer be counted at each polling place but instead transported by the military to regional centers and counted there (Chazan 1983, 261). The electoral commissioner opposed these new procedures and refused to implement them, despite having previously been threatened by the government for his lack of cooperation. As counting was under way, soldiers stormed the electoral commission offices to arrest the commissioner, who fled, leaving the assistant commissioner to continue in his place (Oquaye 1980, 103). A few days later, the government announced that it had won the referendum with 55% of the vote. The opposition promptly went on strike, effectively shutting down the country (97-110). Within the military itself, there was increasing dissatisfaction over the course charted by the junta and the consequent loss of military prestige. Some officers were concerned about the damage the junta had caused to the reputation of the once highly regarded armed forces. Civilians would openly mock soldiers who left base in uniform; all members of the military were widely considered corrupt.[37] Officers also were unhappy about being repeatedly used to put down civilian protest.[38] Increasingly, members of the officer corps saw military rule as corrupting the armed forces and distracting the institution from its primary duty.

Despite this dissatisfaction, it remained difficult to organize a conspiracy to remove President Acheampong from office. Acheampong had allies among officers who were profiting handsomely from military rule. Some officers were drawing their regular military salary, an additional civilian salary for bureaucratic duties (such as running a state-owned enterprise), and making illicit gains from their government positions. Conspiracy was also discouraged by tight government monitoring of the officer corps for signs of dissent. A succession of alleged conspiracies had been foiled and the accused made examples of (Oquaye 1980, 76-77). An officer could lose his job for simply failing to show enough enthusiasm for government positions. As the

---

[37]Interview with Elizabeth Ohene. July 1999. London, England.

[38]Interview with General (retired) Edwin Sam. July 9, 2000. Accra, Ghana.

campaign for Unigov was taking off in 1977, for instance, a couple of senior officers were removed from their posts merely for expressing reservations (88).[39]

To prevent coups, the junta carefully selected officers for key positions. Within the military, the president was believed to be particularly close to the commanders of the two main fighting units in the capital. He had once commanded the capital infantry battalion and remained personally connected to not only the officers but the non-commissioned officers and soldiers of the unit.[40] In addition, the president took the extra precaution of creating a counter-coup force within the police, giving them better-armed armored cars than their military counterparts had.[41]

Conspiracy

Despite all these efforts, a conspiracy to remove the president developed at the very apex of the armed forces. It was led by General Akuffo, head of the Ghanaian armed forces, and it included the heads of the army, navy, air force, and border guards and the chief of staff of the armed forces.[42] In short, the conspirators included almost all of the ruling junta other than General Acheampong himself.

Despite Acheampong's vigilance, he foolishly provided the conspirators with a pretext to both conspire and organize meetings of the command structure. In the aftermath of the disastrous Unigov referendum, the president refused to accept responsibility and instead wrote a letter to General Akuffo, in his capacity as armed forces chief, implicitly blaming the command structure of the armed forces for the loss of military prestige. Akuffo was able to use the letter as a reason to meet with the service commanders, thus enabling them to conspire in the open without raising suspicions. They also enlisted the support of the commander of the army's Southern Brigade, whose responsibility encompassed the capital, to have him sound out some of his subordinates on the issue of military withdrawal from politics.[43]

Using the president's letter as a pretext, General Akuffo next summoned to the capital the Military Advisory Council (MAC), which included all middle- and upper-level officers with command appointments, to discuss the decline in military professionalism. As one of the key conspirators explained, "His letter was the spark. The letter was the excuse and the spark because to get people together to discuss his removal was not that easy ... So the meeting was legitimized."[44] The plotters believed that, once in the meeting, they would be able to manipulate officers into supporting the removal of Acheampong, or at least appearing to support it.[45]

---

[39]These were Rear Admiral Dzang, who was the head of the navy and a member of the Supreme Military Council, and Brigadier Hamidu.

[40]Interview with Colonel (retired) Kwesi Oteng. September 4, 2000. Accra, Ghana.

[41]Interview with Colonel (retired) Harry Ofosu-Apea. August 13, 2001. Accra, Ghana.

[42]The one surviving member of this group is Brigadier Nunoo-Mensah, who was the chief of staff at the time.

[43]Interview with Brigadier (retired) Joseph Odei. September 14, 2000. Accra, Ghana.

[44]Interview with Brigadier (retired) Joseph Nunoo-Mensah. July 20, 2000. Accra, Ghana.

[45]Interview with Brigadier (retired) Joseph Nunoo-Mensah. August 6, 2001. Accra, Ghana

Meetings

The overthrow of President Acheampong commenced on Monday July 3, 1978, with a meeting of the Military Advisory Council in the main conference room of the Ministry of Defense.[46] The meeting was chaired by the head of the navy, Rear Admiral Joy Amedume, who was the only one of the conspirators present. The admiral did not overtly try to persuade the group to support a position but instead proceeded sequentially around the table, requiring each officer present to offer his thoughts.[47] The meeting continued into a second day in an attempt to encourage the president to join them. When it became clear that the president was unlikely to appear, Admiral Amedume wrapped up the discussion. At this point, each of the members of the meeting had expressed support for military withdrawal from the government, although the specifics of how this was to occur had not been discussed.

Next, the conspirators moved to confront the president in one final meeting. The conspirators joined Admiral Amedume and the brigade-level commanders in an unscheduled visit to President Acheampong's office.[48] The president, unaware of what was about to occur, continued to work as normal, making a joke about the invasion of his office. General Akuffo then read a speech informing the president that the armed forces had decided that he should step down.

At first, President Acheampong argued back. He said that he should not be held responsible for corruption and charged that General Akuffo's actions were dangerous and would lead to bloodshed. General Akuffo responded by saying that there was unanimous support within the armed forces for the change in government, demonstrating this by asking a few of the officers present if they agreed.[49] Two of the conspirators, the heads of the army and the border guards, appealed to the president to give in, asserting that intransigence on his part might cause bloodshed, a reframing that shifted the blame for any possible violence to the president.

The conspirators also underlined the president's lack of control with an act of symbolic disrespect. As they talked, Air Force General Bob Kotei crossed his legs, lit up a cigar, and began to smoke, his body language and failure to ask the president for permission to smoke sending a clear signal to everyone gathered.

At the end of the confrontation, the president was made to sign a formal letter of resignation stating the following: "In the interest of national unity, I wish to resign my appointment as the Head of State and Chairman of the SMC, with immediate effect, and wish to be retired from the Armed Forces" (Jackson 1999, 70). After that, President Acheampong was taken away to a secure location, where he was held in isolation. His bodyguards had earlier been quietly disarmed by soldiers from the

---

[46]Interview with Brigadier (retired) Joseph Odei. August 7, 2000. Accra, Ghana.

[47]Interview with Air Vice Marshall (retired) Odaate Barnor. September 14, 2000. Accra, Ghana.

[48]This entire section is taken from the account of former Air Vice Marshall Odaate Barnor, interviewed by the author on September 14, 2000, in Accra, Ghana. Barnor was present at the meeting, and his account is far more detailed than those of the other eyewitnesses.

[49]The officers present had been informed that Acheampong was to be overthrown only when they reached the threshold of his office, which left them no time to back down.

engineering regiment, so there were no problems escorting the president into house arrest. The president's resignation was announced to the nation via radio broadcast, along with news of a new transitional junta to be led by the conspirators.

The only difficulty encountered by the plotters came from the police and was easily dealt with. Inspector General of the Police Ernest Ako, a staunch ally of the president's, had just joined the meeting when General Akuffo informed the president that he was to be replaced, upon which Ako registered his objection to the action and left the room. Although General Akuffo warned the police chief not to resist the change in government, the plotters otherwise made no effort to stop him.[50]

Consolidation

The plotters were confident enough that the coup would be successful that they did little to suppress potential opposition to it. They did not move against either the head of the police or against the police armored car unit that was designed to foil coups. They also foreclosed the possibility of challenge from within the main infantry unit in the capital, the Fifth Infantry Battalion, without using force. As noted earlier, the plotters were concerned about the possibility of disruption from the battalion because of its close relationship to President Acheampong. Because the soldiers were closer to the president than to the official commander of the unit, Colonel Kwesi Oteng, it was unclear whether the Fifth Infantry Battalion would assent to the coup.[51]

To avoid possible resistance among the troops, Colonel Oteng first broke the news to his second-in-command and the top enlisted man in the unit; that both accepted the changes was important, because these were the two individuals who would have assumed leadership roles in any effort to resist Acheampong's removal. The troops were then dismissed and sent home before the soldiers heard the news on the radio, making any incipient mutiny more difficult. Colonel Oteng also hoped that the soldiers' families would exercise a restraining influence on them.[52]

Similarly, the commanding officers who had been present at the meeting of the Military Advisory Council also returned to their home units to explain the change in government and keep an eye on matters.[53] The concern was that officers who had benefited from Acheampong's rule and might now be investigated would have an incentive to conspire against the coup. However, the precautions taken by the coup leaders ensured that the entire coup took place without a single shot being fired.

---

[50]Interview with Brigadier (retired) Joseph Nunoo-Mensah. July 20, 2000. Accra, Ghana.

[51]As a precaution, the engineering regiment was on standby to counter any actions taken by either the infantry or armored battalions. Interview with Brigadier (retired) Joseph Odei. August 7, 2000. Accra, Ghana.

[52]Interview with Colonel (retired) Kwesi Oteng. September 4, 2000. Accra, Ghana.

[53]Interview with Brigadier (retired) Joseph Odei. August 7, 2000. Accra, Ghana.

Analysis

As in the previous example, neither of the conventional theoretical explanations explains the 1978 coup attempt well. It is unclear if the challengers could have won a battle, and their attempt was definitely not staged in such a way that made tactical dominance paramount. Similarly, while Acheampong would probably have lost a referendum within the military on the continuation of military rule, it is extremely unlikely that the challengers had unanimous support within the regular military or that the head of the police was the only member of the security forces who supported the president. Understanding coups as coordination games, however, explains why the Military Advisory Council meeting was pivotal, makes sense of how it was organized, and justifies the plotters' confidence that their manipulation of information and expectations would be sufficient to deter potential opposition.

Coups as Battles

The events of 1978 are not consistent with the vision of coups as small battles: the challengers did not attack at night to maximize the advantage of surprise, did not capture military targets, did not suppress opposition ruthlessly, and did not use force to establish clear military dominance. To the contrary, not a single shot was fired, even when the president's bodyguards were disarmed. The challengers did not move to muscularly discourage potential opposition; instead, the inspector general of the police was allowed to walk away, even though he disagreed with the coup and had control over a powerful potential counter-force.

   Because it is hard to tell how much support Acheampong would have retained if a direct military confrontation had taken place, it is less clear if the theory correctly predicts the outcome of the coup. That said, if the president had retained the support of the main infantry and armored units in the capital and the police, he would have proved very difficult to displace.

Coups as Elections

The coups as elections approach fares better in that it correctly predicts President Acheampong's removal, although it also gets the dynamics of the attempt wrong. Military officers shared civilian concerns about the economy and had additional ones about ongoing damage to the integrity and reputation of the armed forces, so the government would likely have lost a vote of confidence within the military.[54] At the same time, the events of the 1978 coup suggest that the president was not entirely without friends. Even though the more popular side won in this case, actions during the coup attempt did not correspond to the preferences of all the actors. We know, for example, that the police chief remained loyal to the president, yet he did

---

[54]The president had even less support among soldiers than officers. Some officers had benefited from military rule, but enlisted men lived and worked in substandard conditions, with their wages often substantially in arrears.

not "vote" for him, refraining from action beyond his initial objection. It is also implausible that a new military junta, even one described as a caretaker regime, would have received unanimous support among either the populace or the military. Although the president was highly unpopular, his unpopularity alone cannot account for the way the attempt unfolded.

Coups as Coordination Games

The events of 1978 are most consistent with the explanation of coups as coordination games: the pivotal event in the overthrow of the president was a meeting of military commanders, officers with different preferences nevertheless supported a single outcome, and the entire attempt was designed to take place bloodlessly. Unlike the competing hypotheses, this account provides insight into both the outcome and the dynamics of the coup attempt.

The key to the overthrow of the president was the plotters' control over public information, achieved here through a meeting of the Military Advisory Council. Prior to the MAC meeting, the conspirators were in a weak position, afraid of what would happen if their plot was discovered. After the meeting, everybody believed that there was unanimous support for the end of the current government and that therefore any resistance would be futile. This belief was so strong that the coup makers could allow the head of police to freely leave, secure and correct in their expectation that he would not dare to upset the apparent consensus.[55]

To create this consensus of support for ending the current junta, according to one of the architects of the coup plot, "the MAC was manipulated to get ... this backing."[56] The challengers did not enter the decisive meeting thinking they had unanimous support for the coup; they had probed officers ahead of time and remained concerned about officers they believed were close to the president. If they had known ahead of time that they had full support, they could simply have asked for a secret ballot or a show of hands and been done with the meeting quickly.

Instead, the meeting was run in a way consistent with the sequentialization strategy described earlier. Each officer was obliged to state his position, declarations that were both public and irreversible. Since Admiral Amedume had foreknowledge about who was likely to support and who oppose the plan, he would have been able to call upon those supporters first. By so doing, any officer who might have been tempted to oppose military withdrawal would have felt like he was perhaps the only one. As more and more officers voiced support, the remaining officers would have felt increasing pressure to conform, both because of the penalties for backing the losing side and out of a desire not to create a potentially bloody rift in the armed forces. Sequentialization would have allowed Admiral Amedume to

---

[55]It is telling that the only overt dissent came from the head of police, who was not present at the earlier meeting and came without being told that there was unanimous support for the withdrawal. That is, the only objector was an officer whose expectations had not been shaped by the coup makers.

[56]Interview with Brigadier (retired) Joseph Nunoo-Mensah. August 6, 2001. Accra, Ghana.

produce the appearance of consensus without having to convince dissenting officers to change their minds.

There are two other logical explanations for the stated consensus that emerged from the meeting, but neither is likely. The first is that all of the officers in the Military Advisory Council entered the room already in support of military withdrawal from government but the conspirators were unaware of how strong a hand they held. This was unlikely because it would have required that both President Acheampong and the conspirators had done their jobs poorly. It assumes that the president, despite his paranoia and vigilance, had lost the support of every officer with a command appointment in the armed forces yet had not realized it, and that the plotters would not have been able to discover this tectonic shift in preferences during their preparatory work.

The other explanation is that officers entered the room with different opinions but were swayed by what they heard. However, the reasons for supporting military withdrawal from politics were plain for all to see. Ghanaian officers did not live in a bubble; they were not insulated from the state of the economy, and all had civilian friends and family members.[57] Thus, they were painfully aware of the low regard in which most civilians held the military, and it was impossible to avoid the signs of corruption and declining professionalism. No new political or economic information was provided during the meeting that might have convinced loyalist officers to change sides. The only new information imparted concerned the willingness of officers to support military withdrawal, information that would have driven coordination.

Once generated, the consensus was stable. The expectations thus created made it nearly impossible for loyalist officers to organize a counter-coup, since each officer now believed that all the others supported the consensus, and this knowledge was public within the group. Because after the meeting officers dispersed to keep an eye on their units, it would have been difficult for loyalists to conspire without attracting notice.

If coups are like coordination games, then the strength of the expectations created by the meeting explains the plotters' lack of concern with possible resistance to the coup, behavior not so easily explained by the competing approaches. If coups are like battles, then the meeting was irrelevant and the coup makers should have arrested all possible opponents at the first opportunity. If coups are like elections, then a "rigged election" would have done nothing to change preferences, and the plotters would have been no better off after the meeting than they had been before. In such a case, General Akuffo would have been well advised to court or purchase the support of loyalists until he could sideline them.

Also consistent with the theory, the plotters deliberately organized the coup attempt to minimize the chance of bloodshed. Confronting the president during work hours was risky, because the challengers' activities might arouse suspicion; as Acheampong himself noted, their en masse unscheduled arrival in his office was

---

[57]Because of the Ghanaian armed forces were developed largely after independence, none of the officers had grown up on military bases. Often they were the only military members in their family, and all of their childhood friends were civilians.

unusual. The plotters, however, believed that Acheampong and his loyalists would behave more calmly and rationally during the day and that the chance of chaos and accident would have been greater at night. In addition, in his residence at night, the president would have been surrounded by heavily armed soldiers, so it would have taken more force to detain him there.[58]

The concern with avoiding bloodshed was also apparent in the way each side cautioned the other against acting recklessly. First the president warned his challengers that their actions might lead to bloodshed, then the challengers reversed the argument and warned Acheampong that loyalist intransigence would be responsible for any blood that was spilled.

Thus, the dynamics of this coup attempt illustrate nicely the strengths and weaknesses associated with coups from the top. The challengers were weak in that they had no troops of their own and that, despite their positions at the top of the military chain of command, they could not rely on their orders being carried out unconditionally. Therefore, they had to wait until provided with a pretext that would allow them to exercise their soft power via a meeting without arousing suspicion.

On the other hand, once they had obtained proper bureaucratic cover, they were able to probe the feelings of various officers ahead of time, run the meeting so as to manipulate key officers into apparent consensus, and use this to bloodlessly remove the president. Once the meeting was concluded, the overthrow of the president was virtually impossible to stop or reverse.

If this coup had come from the middle or bottom of the hierarchy, or even if these same challengers had tried to use hard power to remove Acheampong, there likely would have been a great deal of bloodshed and a high chance of failure. Despite his unpopularity, Acheampong had a sufficient number of allies to withstand considerable assault, especially since much of the military was in a weakened state of readiness and lacked the fuel, ammunition, and equipment to launch an effective attack. Both the outcome and the dynamics of the coup attempt owe more to the rank of the challengers and the strategies employed than to the unpopularity of the president.

This case provides less support for two other hypotheses associated with coordination. As with the previous example, the plotters did not explicitly invoke history to shape the expectations of military actors, and it is unknown if officers relied on history when considering who would win. Because history shapes initial beliefs, it is difficult to see the impact of history in a situation where the challengers quickly and effectively make a fact. That said, the outcome of this coup attempt is consistent with the claim about the impact of history in coordination games, since this was Ghana's fifth coup attempt and no coup attempt had failed for over a decade. More narrowly, the previous coup attempt was the only other coup from the top and had succeeded. Thus, the case neither supports nor undermines the claim for the impact of history.

Second, no symbolic targets were attacked, although again this does not undermine the broader story of coordination during this coup attempt. The capture of

---

[58]Interview with Brigadier (retired) Joseph Nunoo-Mensah. August 6, 2001. Accra, Ghana.

symbolic targets is an indirect way of signaling strength and shaping expectations. Given that the challengers had manipulated beliefs directly using soft power, attacks on targets would have been superfluous and in fact negative, as they would have warned the president.

Conclusion

Coups from the top are the most frequent type of coup attempt and also the most likely to succeed. The theory here proposed posits that generals are successful at mounting coups because the bureaucratic prerogatives associated with their positions allow them to shape the beliefs and expectations of officers in the rest of the military, most importantly those mid-level officers commanding key units near the capital.

Because generals have no forces of their own, they rely on mid-level officers to execute the orders they give. During coup attempts, however, senior officers cannot rely on the unconditional obedience of their subordinates, because coup making often reduces their moral authority and they can punish disobedience only if the coup succeeds. Therefore, generals, like all other coup makers, must try to "make a fact" and convince other members of the military that their victory is inevitable and resistance is futile. If this works correctly, it creates self-fulfilling expectations in favor of the success of the coup, leading the challengers to victory quickly and bloodlessly.

As we have seen from the examples in this chapter, generals are well placed to conspire. They can use the period before they strike to start identifying potential opponents, to disseminate information favorable to the coup, and even to begin convincing key officers that all the others are likely to support a coup attempt. Since generals have so much to lose and have access to information others do not, a coup from the top is usually viewed as highly credible from the start.

Top officers have three broad strategies for making a fact: they can use a meeting to shape expectations, they can make a proclamation, or they can try to issue orders and use force. Among these options, coup attempts that rely more on soft power than hard power are more likely to succeed. Although both of the coup attempts from the top discussed in this chapter succeeded, chapter 7 discusses an unsuccessful coup attempt from the top that proceeded by proclamation—in the Soviet Union in 1991—which supports the argument in this chapter by demonstrating how a coup from the top can fail when the conspirators lose control over public information and their adversaries manage to make a fact that contradicts the challengers' fact. The difficulties of the third option, force, can be seen in the discussion of coups from the middle in the next chapter. In all of these cases, the competing explanations do a poor job of explaining the dynamics of the coup attempt, even if they correctly predict the outcome.

Chapter 5

Coups from the Middle

A Theory of Coups from the Middle

Coup attempts from the middle are organized and mounted by officers in direct command of fighting units, such as battalions, regiments, and brigades. Such units are large enough to move on their own (unlike a company, which may need outside transportation) but still small enough that the entire unit can fall under the direct command of one officer (unlike a division). These groups also tend to be cohesive, as they train, garrison, and move together but separately from other units (Farcau 1994, 47).

As with coups from the top, the goal of the conspirators at the middle is to manipulate the beliefs of other military actors, primarily the other mid-level actors in command positions, so that they will coordinate in support of the coup. However, the resources that officers in the middle have with which to shape expectations are different. Unlike coup makers from the top, challengers from the middle have little of the soft power that comes from being in a top leadership position. What officers in the middle have instead is hard power, because they are in command of the actual fighting units of the military. When they make a coup, they deploy their units to capture and hold important targets, like the broadcasting facility, the parliament building, and other symbols of state authority. Once the challengers gain access to radio and television, they make a broadcast proclaiming broad support for the coup, warning any loyalists that resistance is futile. In this way, they try to use their hard power to make a fact; they want to convince both uncommitted officers and the regime's defenders that the military has coordinated or will soon coordinate in support of the coup. In addition, by dominating the air waves and holding on to both broadcasting facilities and other symbolic targets over time, they signal that they will prevail if the worst happens and fratricidal conflict develops. This in turn further strengthens expectations in favor of the coup. During this whole process, however, they are not trying to establish tactical dominance over their adversary. To the contrary, they are trying to avoid causing bloodshed and destruction.

The process described here for shaping expectations is more indirect than that used by officers at the top, and therefore it takes longer and has more potential points of failure. For example, challengers can be arrested en route to the radio station, or control of the airwaves can be wrested from them. As a result, the success rate for coups from the middle worldwide was only 48%, as compared to coups from the top, which succeeded 68% of the time.[1]

The rest of this section describes in more detail how challenges from the middle are shaped by the resources and constraints associated with rank and the factors that affect their success or failure. To demonstrate how these dynamics play out in actual coup attempts, the chapter then examines in more depth two of Ghana's three coups from the middle, the first of which failed after a promising start, the second of which succeeded without a hitch.

Conspiracy

When conspirators begin plotting a coup attempt, their primary concern is with avoiding detection. This can be difficult, because military intelligence services, especially those in coup-prone countries, tend to be highly vigilant in their internal surveillance. Empirically speaking, conspiracies therefore evolve where members of the military already trust each other, such as among members of the same training cohort or officers who have served together. Practical matters of trust and opportunity are more paramount than creating a coalition with the optimal amount of firepower.[2] It is always risky to approach an officer who is not a close confidant or friend to discuss treason. Even if the officer approached doesn't report the conversation, there is always the possibility that he is already suspected of potential disloyalty and is being monitored by military intelligence. For this reason, strangers are usually approached about joining the conspiracy only if their participation is vital to the success of the coup, and even then very gingerly. Alternately, especially when the conspirators are young, they may opt to wait until their members are transferred into positions of power. This latter strategy has its own risks, however, since it requires keeping a coalition together over a long time while still avoiding discovery.

As is well understood, not all officers are equally valuable in a coup attempt. Infantry and armored units are more useful than engineering or support regiments, for instance. It is best to have at least some allies stationed near the capital, optimally those guarding key locations such as the broadcasting facility or statehouse. Similarly, some armed services are more suited to coup making than others. It is most important for challengers to have the cooperation of parts of the army and perhaps the motorized police, where they exist (Farcau 1994, 58). The usefulness of the air force and navy are considerably more limited, since their forces are intended primarily to destroy an enemy from a distance, not to capture and hold

---

[1]In both cases, this analysis, provided earlier in chapter 3, is limited to only those cases which could be clearly coded as coming from one level or the other.

[2]A small number of authors have written books that offer recipes for coup making. These authors generally stress the importance of creating the ideally powerful coalition, and in so doing, they downplay the difficulties involved in recruiting and the degree to which coalitions evolve in an ad hoc fashion (Farcau 1994, Ferguson 1987, Hebditch & Connor 2008, Luttwak 1979).

a target (Ferguson 1987, 52). In addition, because coup makers typically try to avoid casualties within the military, the ability to bomb or shell a target is not particularly useful. For this reason, naval involvement is usually in the form of the marines rather than the long guns of a battleship. Air power does have symbolic value, however, since planes flying overhead can be a publicly visible sign of control, and tactically, aircraft can be used for reconnaissance or to strafe a target.

Non-military actors, such as civilian politicians, may also be members of a conspiracy. Sometimes the impetus for a coup comes from civilians, and at other times civilians may be recruited by military actors in anticipation of setting up a post-coup government. If civilians have close personal or familial ties to mid-level officers, they may also play a role in recruitment, but this is less common.

Targets

The main targets during coup attempts from the middle are locations that allow the challengers to manipulate information and expectations. The goal of these actions is not to establish military and political dominance, as if they were an invading army, but rather to make a fact within the armed forces. The challengers do not need to kill, capture, or otherwise overpower their opponents to succeed, but simply to convince other members of the military to bandwagon in their favor.

The most important of these targets are the television and radio broadcast facilities in the capital, since these give challengers control over public information. In many developing countries, especially during the Cold War, the government maintained a monopoly over the broadcast mass media, and so control over the main government broadcasting facility was essential for coup success. In countries in which the media have been liberalized, challengers generally take over one of the biggest media networks (which may be government-owned) and then shut down other facilities or force them to repeat the same message. Either way, the challengers are most likely to succeed if they achieve and maintain a monopoly over public information, as this allows them to make a fact more effectively and in a shorter amount of time. Since many things can go wrong along the way, even when there is only a single national broadcasting building to capture, this is an inherently riskier process than that involved in a coup from the top.

The manipulation of public information also includes the capture of prominent symbolic targets, such as the executive mansion, the parliament house, and the airport. While there may be a tactical reason why some of these targets are worth acquiring, it is their symbolic importance that appears most relevant to the outcome of a coup. For example, in the second case presented in this chapter, the challengers launched their coup attempt when the prime minister was out of the country, yet they still captured the executive offices. Similarly, the airport was an important target in all of Ghana's coups from the middle, largely because of its symbolic importance. Although control over the airport can serve an important tactical function in some countries, in Ghana the airport was seized even though the air force was too small to airlift any significant number of troops and none of the incumbents had international allies who were likely to fly in troops to counter the coup. Nonetheless, during each of Ghana's coups from the middle, the challengers captured and conspicuously occupied the airport, because it symbolized Ghana's aspirations to modernity. As with the capture of the statehouse, the occupation of the airport was noticed by a number of commanders and was part of the effort to herd them into bandwagoning behind the coup attempt. Because these locations are public, their capture reinforced the claim that the government was no longer in charge and allowed the challengers to signal their strength, thereby shaping expectations about which equilibrium was risk-dominant.

However, while these targets are important, they are not attacked with the force and ferocity that the military would use if it were assaulting targets in a foreign capital. Just as the targets are symbolic, designed to signal the strength of the challenger without unleashing it, so too are the attacks on these targets. For example, during the very first coup attempt in Ghana, in 1966, the challengers attacked the presidential residence. While this clash has been reported as a heavy battle, participants claimed that soldiers on both sides were firing in the air, away from each other, rather than directly at each other (Afrifa 1966).[3] Similarly, a coup from the middle is unlikely to feature a sneak attack that totally levels a target held by the incumbent, even though this might give the challengers considerable tactical advantage.[4]

How the Coup Succeeds

Consistent with the conventional wisdom, coups from the middle are generally launched either late at night or in the early hours of the morning (Farcau 1994, 125). This allows the coup makers to move their attempt further along without detection, since few people are out during those hours, especially in the developing world. The response to the coup is also likely to be more sluggish at this time, since unit commanders may be at home and enlisted men dozing at their posts.

The conspirators will attempt to move both speedily and stealthily, because the coup is most vulnerable at this newborn stage, before they have started to shape the expectations of other military actors. For this reason, they want to make sure to seize a broadcasting facility early, pursuing other objectives only as necessary. If possible, they will also try to disable military and civilian communications, perhaps by capturing the headquarters of the signals regiment, capturing the operations room of the army, or by cutting the wires that are used for internal communications. Any of these actions is risky, since it can reveal that a coup is under way, but it also slows the defenders' response considerably and sows confusion in their ranks. More important, it heightens the challengers' claim that the government is not in control.

---

[3]Interview with Colonel (retired) Seth Kwahu. September 4, 2000. Accra, Ghana.

[4]During the Baathist coup in Iraq in February 1963, aircraft supporting the coup did bomb a loyalist air base. However, even in this case, it appears that they destroyed the airplanes stationed at the Rashid military and air base rather than attacking the barracks (*Keesing's Record of World Events*. Volume 9, April 1963, Iraq, p. 19323).

Once the challengers have captured a broadcast facility, they will make a public announcement as soon as possible, claiming that their victory is a fait accompli and that they have the support of the whole armed forces. They will either avoid any mention of resistance to the coup or characterize it as minor and about to collapse. To increase the likelihood of success, the broadcast will be made by a powerful member of the armed forces, such as the commander of one of the major units near the capital, which will increase the credibility of the conspirators' claim to be in control. If the broadcast is made by a more junior officer with a lesser command, their wisest move is to avoid identifying themselves and to claim to be speaking on behalf of a broader and more powerful conspiracy.[5] Challengers then have to hold on to the broadcasting center for some time and also strengthen their claims by capturing symbolic targets.

For challengers, the best-case scenario is one where they are able to get military members to quickly bandwagon in their favor, first inside the capital, then in the country as a whole. If everything goes according to plan, they will gain dominance over public information and the main symbolic targets in the capital with little opposition, giving credence to the claim that their victory is a fait accompli. If the challengers can do that successfully, their manipulation of public information is likely to scare members of the military who are potential defenders of the incumbent into sitting on the fence, surrendering, or even joining the coup attempt. In that case, partisan, ethnic, and even personal factors for supporting the government tend to be swept aside by pressures for institutional and individual self-preservation. Once the capital falls to the challengers, major military bases elsewhere in the country will almost always join as well.[6]

In the ideal situation for coup makers, the bandwagon will sweep through the military in a matter of hours, bringing together a variety of different factions into tacit, if not active, support of the new government. The speed with which the incumbent government crumbles in such cases often leads outside observers to infer that the coup attempt has virtually unanimous support within the military or that all the key actors were bought off beforehand in a pact. This, however, is a misreading of the lack of active opposition to the coup attempt, just as it would be mistaken to infer that an incumbent who does not face coup attempts must have broad support within the military. What it overlooks is that actions during a coup attempt are strategic and do not necessarily reveal the actual preferences of the actors involved.

---

[5]Sometimes the challengers will awaken a senior officer in the middle of the night to make the broadcast, telling him he has been chosen as the savior of his country and that destiny has thrust him into greatness. This is still a coup from the middle as long as the senior officer plays little role in the execution of the coup, because the strengths and weaknesses of the coup will still be those related to the officers prosecuting the coup, not the figurehead.

[6]While it is possible for the government to reassert control after losing the capital, it is fairly difficult, and therefore rare, even when the majority of military force in the country is stationed outside of the capital. One unusual example of a coup that failed even though it had control of the capital is the 1954 failed coup in Ecuador. Although the major garrison in Quito had turned against President Velasco, he was able to obtain the public support of the major units outside the capital, and the government then reestablished control of Quito as well (Fitch 1977, 41-43).

The brief duration of the attack phase in successful coups from the middle also demonstrates that victory does not depend on establishing military dominance over the country, or even over the capital city, since a coup attempt can succeed much faster than even a vastly superior invading army could conquer the country. The coalition invasion of Iraq in 2003, for example, took roughly six weeks, but none of the successful coups in that country took longer than a few days.

It is also difficult to successfully mount a coup attempt when the challengers are outside the capital, and therefore this is attempted less frequently.[7] Principally, it is harder to make a fact from outside the capital: the challengers will not be able to quickly gain a monopoly over public information or control of the symbolic sites in the capital, making it harder to claim that they have already established control. Furthermore, an attack based in a regional center gives the incumbent government more time to formulate a response, again making other units less willing to bandwagon behind the challenger. In general, if units based outside the capital wish to successfully mount a coup, they will need to either move quickly enough to strike the capital before their actions are noticed or have an ally within the capital working in concert with them. A good example of why it is difficult to mount a coup from outside the capital is the 1961 coup attempt in France. This coup had the support of the most powerful units in the French Armed Forces, but they were substantially hindered by the fact that they were in Algeria, not Paris. This gave the government time to make counter-broadcasts that successfully turned the tide. The challengers were defeated before they had time to reach Europe.

How the Coup Fails

A coup attempt from the middle is easiest to stop just as it starts, before the challengers have made a broadcast. They are at their weakest at this stage, as they have not yet begun to shape expectations and have the support of only one another. For example, Hugo Chavez's February 1992 coup attempt in Venezuela failed when it was blocked from taking over broadcast facilities and symbolic targets in the capital, leading other conspirators to withdraw their support. Within six hours, Chavez realized that the coup attempt was hopeless and, as part of his surrender, made a brief broadcast asking coup supporters in provincial centers to surrender without a fight (Gott 2005, 63-67).

If the challengers are able to make a broadcast, the incumbent can still foil the coup by regaining control over the radio station and making a counter-broadcast, removing them from the airwaves and undercutting their claim to be in charge.

---

[7]Before WWII, coups by units based outside the capital were more common, particularly in Spain or Latin America. The challenger would revolt and march on the capital, sequentially gaining adherents or facing defenders along the way. These coup attempts had a different structure because, in the absence of widespread broadcast media, the challengers were unable to make a fact by dominating public information. In addition, the structure of these armed forces was far simpler, with fewer commanders able to weigh in and influence the outcome of the coup attempt. Such coup attempts were rare in the period under study (Farcau 1994, 116).

If the incumbent government can thus make a fact of its own, demonstrating its control of public information and symbolic sites in the capital early in the process, it can halt and even reverse the momentum of the coup attempt.[8]

If defenders cannot stop the coup attempt in its newborn stage, their best strategy is to hold their ground and make it difficult for the challengers to make a fact by contesting control of public information and symbolic locations. This is easier when there are multiple major broadcasting facilities and the government is able to control one of them. Each side will counter the claims of the other, and if the broadcasts are equally credible, uncommitted forces will sit on the fence, looking for additional information before they choose a side or waiting for developments that might convince them to back one side or the other. In a stalemate, officers will be very worried that the situation could degenerate into a civil war and consequently eager to resolve matters one way or the other. If the commander of a large unit is convinced to openly support one side, this can cause a cascade of support as other officers come off the fence to join him. Once there is a shift in expectations, the coup attempt typically unravels very quickly, as everybody rushes to bandwagon behind the government.

During this jockeying period, both domestic and international civilian actors are likely to try to influence events. Most coups are over too quickly for civilians to react, but even when a coup attempt slows down, the theory argues that civilians have an impact only to the extent to which they can influence expectations within the military about military behavior. It is a mistake to think that moral suasion alone will shape the outcome of the coup attempt, as militaries have been known to disregard even longstanding normative commitments. For example, the Ecuadorian military long believed that it lost the 1941 war with Peru, and therefore half of its national territory, because military governments (such as the Ecuadorian incumbent at the time) are inherently bad for national defense (Fitch 1977, 19). Despite this lesson, which had become deeply embedded in the institutional DNA of the Ecuadorian armed forces, a close examination of the 1963 coup attempt by Fitch found that none of the actors involved were concerned with the constitutionality of their actions (63). Incentives by outside actors may have some effect, but only after the coup has been successfully concluded. For example, sanctions against coup makers in Latin America may compel a junta to transfer power to civilians, and thus restore diplomatic recognition and aid, but they will do this only after taking power and holding it for more than a week.

If a coup takes a long time to resolve, all other things being equal, the theory indicates this should be bad for the challengers, as the delay contradicts the challengers' claim that their victory is a fait accompli. A stalemate demonstrates that

---

[8]Such conflict usually occurs within the capital. This is not to say that it is impossible to overturn a coup attempt from outside the capital, just that this rarely happens, even when the bulk of the military's forces are based elsewhere in the country. One of the rare examples of overturning a coup from outside the capital happened in Ecuador in 1954. Even there, however, it took a split among pro-coup forces in the capital combined with the clear support of the most powerful units stationed outside, to defeat the coup attempt (Fitch 1977, 41-43).

the challengers are weak and that the loyalists remain viable. At the same time, a victory for the incumbent after several days is not optimal for the victor; although it is better than failure, it nonetheless shows the government to be weak and may invite future attack.

The other possibility, of course, is that a stalemate continues indefinitely until the two sides fight it out, the worst-case scenario for all members of the military. This describes well what happened in the Dominican Republic in April 1965, when a military junta was challenged by the supporters of the previously displaced president, Juan Bosch. After two days of heavy fighting with high casualties, the military split in two, leading to the Dominican Civil War, the invasion of the Dominican Republic by the United States, and, months later, a peace agreement brokered by the Organization of American States.

As this discussion has shown, in the case of both coups from the top and coups from the middle, the goal of the conspirators is to manipulate the coordination of mid-level officers who control the bulk of the firepower in the armed forces. Yet, soft power is better suited for this task, because it is more direct and easier to control, and the superior ability of senior challengers to deploy soft power is the principal reason why coups from the top are relatively more likely to succeed and to be short and bloodless when they do.

Ghana, 1967

By almost succeeding before collapsing, the 1967 coup attempt in Ghana illuminates the central factors that lead to either success or failure for a military takeover. As a result, this single coup provides a high degree of within-case variation while still holding background conditions constant.

At the center of this coup attempt was an outrageous bluff by a very junior officer who was temporarily in charge of a small but moderately powerful military unit.[9] When mounting the coup, this officer, one Lieutenant Arthur, claimed that his actions were part of a far larger plot involving more-powerful officers and units, and in fact he tried to persuade key officers from the middle to join the coup as future leaders of the junta. As we shall see, he was initially convincing because his actions closely resembled those of the conspirators in the coup that just a year earlier had succeeded in overthrowing former president Nkrumah, taking over the same important symbolic locations and making a similar radio broadcast. This strategy worked at first, convincing officers that the 1967 coup attempt would succeed just as the 1966 one had and that they therefore should not resist (Petchenkine 1993, 42).

Thus unopposed, the coup makers had come very close to seizing the reins of power when their bluff was called by a small group of pro-government officers, and a loyalist radio broadcast was made. As soon as the true nature of the coup attempt was publicly revealed, it collapsed. All that had changed was the information

---

[9]This coup attempt is classified as a coup from the middle because of the officer's temporary command over a fighting unit, rather than his rank.

publicly available about the coup makers and hence the expectations that officers held about each other. The military strength of the two sides had not changed, nor the feelings of military men toward the government. In short, the coup succeeded as long as key members of the military believed it would succeed, and it failed when they believed it would fail.

Background

The 1967 coup attempt was the second coup attempt in Ghana and the first against a military government. Its target was the National Liberation Council (NLC) junta that had taken power following the overthrow of Ghana's first president, Kwame Nkrumah, slightly more than a year earlier. Nkrumah had been the leader of the independence movement in the country, was a socialist, and was one of the key figures in the international non-aligned movement. He had been elected prime minister at independence in 1957, then president in 1960. However, his rule had grown increasingly despotic as Ghana became a one-party state and his political opponents were put in jail without trial. When he was removed in 1966 during a coup from the middle that incorporated a wide coalition of officers, the military declared that they had liberated the country, and they promised a quick return to multi-party civilian democracy.

In many ways, the NLC junta was an accidental government. The conspirators originally had planned to transfer power back to civilians in short order and had appointed a constitutional commission to prepare for the transition. Once they assumed power, however, the junta claimed that the civilian opposition was too weak and disorganized to run the government and overcome the pernicious legacy of "Nkrumahism" within the state. They therefore set themselves up as an interim military government.

The junta engaged in a number of strategies to build legitimacy. It did not attempt to rule the country directly through the military but instead developed a partnership with the civil service and formed alliances with Nkrumah's political rivals and Ghanaian traditional rulers, seeking to build the junta's authority by linking it to older, more conservative political forces. More broadly, the NLC strove to strike a note of apolitical, technocratic competence, validating the junta in terms of its efficiency and lack of corruption. They banned partisan politics and announced from the beginning that they had no intention of staying in office indefinitely. Yet, it was impossible for the junta to effectively insulate themselves from political pressures, and soon splits developed between the army and the police, between those who were part of the core group of original conspirators and those who joined later, and between members of different ethnicities.

The junta also adopted a pro-Western, center-right economic policy. Ideologically opposed to Nkrumah's policies of state-led economic development and facing the country's depleted foreign currency reserves, they reached out to the West for economic assistance, adopted the required austerity budget, and canceled many of Nkrumah's large-scale development projects. As a result of these measures, the

economic health of the country improved in a number of respects from what it had
been under Nkrumah (Petchenkine 1993, 40).

Confident in their domestic appeal, the NLC believed that the main threat to
their government came from Nkrumah, in exile in Guinea; he was known to be
conspiring to make a return (Petchenkine 1993, 41). In January and February of
1967, a plot was allegedly uncovered and Nkrumah's former assistant Moses Boye
was arrested and dragged through the streets in a cage. Nkrumah himself was
"Wanted Dead or Alive," and a price of 10,000 pounds sterling was placed on his
head (Nkrumah 1990, 105).

Yet the NLC paid little attention to the possibility of discontent within the
military, thinking they had won over most of its members. The junta had been
quite generous to the military, having granted across-the-board raises to all the
armed forces and rapid promotions to those who had played key roles in the coup
against Nkrumah. Even those soldiers who had been part of Nkrumah's presidential
guard had been absorbed back into the main body of the armed forces without any
trouble. The leaders of the junta, believing that they represented the military as
an institution, could not conceive that any trouble might be brewing there. In fact,
when presented with evidence that some within the military were plotting against
the government, the head of the armed forces, General Kotoka, was dismissive,
responding that the officers in question were loyal, and he took no action against
them.[10] While internal investigation after the coup attempt uncovered a number of
matters about which officers were dissatisfied, it is not clear whether any of these
dissatisfactions were actually linked to the coup attempt or were uncovered just
with the benefit of hindsight.[11]

Conspiracy

The unlikely center of the 1967 coup attempt was a twenty-seven-year-old lieutenant
with temporary command of an armored squadron a hundred miles from Accra.
Lieutenant Arthur was not on anybody's radar as a possible threat. He had been a
commissioned officer for only three years and was assigned to a small armored group
(Reconnaissance Squadron B) based in a provincial capital near the border with
Togo. Arthur had command of this squadron only briefly, filling the gap between the
departure of the unit's commanding officer for the United Kingdom for staff training
and the scheduled arrival of his replacement.[12] As a result, this plot was not the

---

[10]While it is unclear whether the intercepted communications presented as evidence were related to the 1967 coup attempt, General Kotoka's actions demonstrate how secure the junta
felt. Interview with Colonel (retired) Michael Gbagonah. May 29, 2000. Accra, Ghana

[11]Self-examination after the coup attempt uncovered persistent rumors that junta members
were corrupt and benefiting personally from their positions in government (Hutchful 1973, 309)
There were also feelings of estrangement between the officer corps and the junta. Some officers
were frustrated with the slow pace of reforms, believing that the junta relied too much on civilians
and was too responsive to politics; and, since the junta rarely briefed officers or sought their advice
on matters of state, they did not perceive it as a "true" military government (311).

[12]Interview with Colonel (retired) Harry Ofosu-Apea. August 13, 2001. Accra, Ghana.

result of careful deliberation or planning. Instead, it appears that Lieutenant Arthur decided to overthrow the government less than a week before he made the attempt.[13]

Aware that he had only a limited window of opportunity to stage a coup, Lieutenant Arthur "found it absolutely essential to have this thing carried out by all means before 21 April 1967."[14] Once the new captain in charge of the regiment showed up, Arthur would be simply a lieutenant again, with all of the limitations incumbent upon his rank.

According to his official statements, Arthur's motivation for the coup attempt was his belief that the junta had betrayed the trust of the Ghanaian people, that it was no better than the dictatorship it had overthrown, and that members of the NLC were corrupt and enriching themselves at public expense.[15] More important to Arthur, however, were a number of personal and professional grievances with the junta (Hutchful 1973, 311). Arthur was especially unhappy about how the junta had rewarded its allies with promotions; some of the key figures behind the overthrow of Nkrumah had been promoted as often as four times in the fourteen months the junta had been in power (Baynham 1988, 249). He also felt that the military had become so top heavy as to deny younger officers any reasonable chance at advancement and that the promotion exams were stacked, making it impossible for anybody to pass. While Arthur felt these grievances personally, he believed they would be widely shared within the military.[16] Lastly, he appears to have been motivated by a desire for personal glory, by the chance to make history. In his later written statement, he said, "Not in the history of military coups have I heard that a lieutenant had staged one."[17] It has been suggested that Arthur was also politically motivated, either by a desire to restore Nkrumah or by ethnic animus; however, there is little evidence in favor of either claim.[18]

The other two officers charged in the coup attempt were also young. Lieutenant Yeboah was twenty-eight and had been commissioned at the same time as Arthur, while Second Lieutenant Osei-Poku was twenty-two and had been an officer for only six months (Baynham 1988, 241). Both plausibly claimed that they had not conspired with Arthur to overthrow the government but participated only because Arthur was their commanding officer. Their active cooperation, however, was critical to the coup attempt.

---

[13]"Counter Coup Was Not Foreign Inspired—Says Arthur," *Daily Graphic*, May 2, 1967, 8.

[14]"Counter Coup Was Not Foreign Inspired—Says Arthur," *Daily Graphic*, May 2, 1967, 8.

[15]"Arthur: I Staged Coup to Create History," *Ghanaian Times*, May 3, 1967, 5.

[16]"I know the penalty is death—Arthur," *Daily Graphic*, May 4, 1967, 10.

[17]"Arthur: I Staged Coup to Create History," *Ghanaian Times*, May 3, 1967, 5.

[18]Although Nkrumah did publicly endorse this coup attempt after the fact and the earliest arrests and trials after the coup attempt were of Nkrumah supporters (Nkrumah 1990, 107), Arthur himself denied any connection to Nkrumah during his trial."Counter Coup Was Not Foreign Inspired—Says Arthur," *Daily Graphic*, May 2, 1967, 1. The ethnic charge is a bit more complicated, in part because members of the junta were concerned that the coup would be seen in ethnic terms, in particular as a coup by members of the Akan ethnic group against members of the Ga and Ewe ethnic groups who were disproportionately represented in the military junta. That said, there is no direct evidence that Arthur was animated by ethnic animus; in fact, the one junta member he singled out as corrupt was also an Akan.

The squadron itself had around 120 men who could be fielded for battle, plus support elements. It had nine light armored cars (Ferret scout cars), two heavier armored cars (Saladins), two armored personnel carriers, and four large trucks (Ziorklui 1988, 100). Because armored units are designed for reconnaissance and combat, they are primarily offensive and not well equipped for holding targets once captured. While the squadron included a few foot soldiers who could be deployed to help hold targets, the relatively small size of the force meant that Arthur had to focus his efforts on assaulting a small number of highly important sites.

Arthur's plan was to capture the airport, the radio station, the residence of the executive, and the army headquarters building.[19] This script did not involve attacking and neutralizing any of the other units based in the capital. Instead, he believed that the situation was ripe for a coup and that taking control of these few and largely symbolic targets would be sufficient to get the other units in the capital to fall in line. According to Lieutenant Arthur, he "asked Lt. Swatson whether ... anybody who tried to stage a coup in Ghana would be successful?" ... Swatson's reply was, "Yes, because with the present tension in the Army, you only need to have somebody to start and the rest would just join."[20]

Organizational factors also played a role in shaping the plot. Although this coup attempt was a coup from the middle because Arthur was operating as a commander of a significant fighting unit, he was still constrained in multiple ways by his low rank. The execution of the coup attempt was rushed because his command was only temporary, and after the new commander arrived to take control, Arthur would only be able to mount a coup from the bottom.

Furthermore, Arthur's low position within the military limited his credibility. Because he was only a lieutenant, during the coup attempt Arthur consistently claimed that he was following the orders of more powerful senior officers and that his actions were just one piece of a larger attack. This bluff was central to his plan, since it made the challengers appear stronger militarily and therefore more likely to win. This subterfuge also made it possible for higher-ranking officers to support the coup attempt, something they would not have done for a coup by a lieutenant, in part because of the expectation that other mid-level officers also would not support a coup by a junior officer.

Even within his own squadron, Lieutenant Arthur claimed to be acting under the direct orders of his commanding officer as part of a larger conspiracy. Arthur could not even rely on the unquestioning obedience of the men under his own command; they, too, had to be convinced that they were part of a broader initiative that was likely to succeed.

Arthur's claims were credible because they invoked memories of the 1966 coup against Nkrumah. In that coup, officers ordered their units to move (and the enlisted men complied) after having been told that they were part of a larger conspiracy, but without any direct evidence of it. Thus, Arthur was able to leverage memories

---

[19] "Arthur: I Staged Coup to Create History," *Ghanaian Times*, May 3, 1967, 7.

[20] "Arthur: I Staged Coup to Create History," *Ghanaian Times*, May 3, 1967, 7.

of the coup fourteen months earlier to increase his credibility inside and outside of his squadron and therefore increase the likelihood of his success.

Attack

The initial stage of the coup attempt was surprisingly successful. The unit deployed from its base and was able to capture each of its major targets, despite its small size and the distance it had to travel.

The attack was staged under the cover of anti-smuggling operations in which the squadron was taking part. Instead of dismissing the troops when they returned from the anti-smuggling exercise in the afternoon, Arthur kept them assembled and announced that they had another anti-smuggling mission to complete, one whose success would depend on maintaining complete secrecy.[21]

The unit departed around 11 p.m. on the night of April 16.[22] After several minor transportation problems, they reassembled around 2:30 a.m. in the Shai Hills area, about twenty miles from Accra. Only at this point did Arthur inform the squadron that they were involved in a military coup and hand out assignments for the capture of the airport, army headquarters, radio station, and the chief executive's residence, telling them that they would be assisted by friendly forces as soon as they took their targets.

Even though Arthur was in charge of the squadron, his orders did not go unquestioned. Before the different groups departed, Arthur was pulled aside by another officer, Lieutenant Moses Yeboah, who, in front of the most senior members of the unit, Second Lieutenant Osei-Poku and two senior non-commissioned officers, asked him who was behind the coup. According to Yeboah's testimony, Arthur responded evasively, saying simply "some big men" and under further questioning that the entire army was supporting the coup. Yeboah persisted, asking, "Quite naturally, not everybody will support every coup but what I wanted to know finally was who gave you these orders?" to which Arthur finally responded with a name—the commander of the armored regiment (who was also next in the chain of command), Major Achaab.[23] Arthur pleaded ignorance regarding the larger picture, saying that although he had not been fully informed by Achaab, he knew that there were friendly forces in Accra.

It is telling that Arthur responded to Yeboah's challenge by asserting that they were part of a larger group rather than by asserting his authority as squadron commander or by trying to win Yeboah over with promises of glory. Conversely, according to his recounting of events, Yeboah was not satisfied until he believed that he was coordinating with other units, nor was he concerned with the policy implications of the coup attempt. In fact, Yeboah seemed just as likely to stop the coup attempt as participate in it, depending on the circumstances.

---

[21] "Counter Coup Was Not Foreign Inspired—Says Arthur," *Daily Graphic*, May 2, 1967, 8.

[22] Yeboah's account has the departure time as 11:30. ("Who Are Behind Coup?" *Daily Graphic*, May 3, 1967, 3), while Arthur's account has it at 10:40 p.m. ("I Told My Men Of Coup—Arthur," *Daily Graphic*, May 3, 1967, 4).

[23] "How I killed Kotoka—Yeboah's Statement Tells The Story," *Daily Graphic*, May 3 1967, 1.

After some final instructions concerning the rules of engagement, Arthur's troops departed at around 3:15 a.m. The squadron split into four groups, each assigned to a designated target, and began the attack. Two sergeants easily captured the airport, blocking the runway so no flights could land or take off. The airport was conspicuously occupied by an entire platoon of soldiers, a substantial amount of Arthur's manpower, even though it could have been put out of commission with only a handful of men.

Second Lieutenant Osei-Poku was dispatched with another platoon to capture the residence of the junta chairman, General Ankrah. This was Christianborg Castle, a colonial trading fort perched on a rocky outcropping by the ocean, which had once been the residence of the colonial governor. The attack began around 4:15 a.m. and met resistance from the guards, who refused to surrender. This was the heaviest resistance that the coup makers were to encounter during the coup attempt, most likely because the attackers had refused to identify themselves, leading the guards to incorrectly assume they were under attack by the Guinean Army trying to return the deposed and exiled Nkrumah to power.[24]

The coup makers gradually pushed their way inward from the outer perimeter of the castle. Despite the vigor of the defense, Osei-Poku had ordered his men to mainly fire in the air to scare rather than hurt those within the castle.[25] After ten or fifteen minutes of firing, the defenders at the first gate withdrew, and the attackers exploded the gate with a charge fired from their large armored car. The attackers advanced, sending a smaller armored car through the first gate and meeting additional resistance at the second gate. General Ankrah escaped into the sea, with many of the guards following after him.[26] The head of the junta then swam a bit up the coast and took refuge at a police station, where he waited out the rest of the coup. Despite being the president of Ghana, General Ankrah made no effort to organize resistance, apparently believing that the government had been overthrown.

Osei-Poku, believing that Ankrah was still in residence but without sufficient manpower to retrieve him, waited until the firing stopped and called for those inside to surrender. After rounding up those who came out (mainly civilians who worked there), Osei-Poku waited for the support that Arthur had promised would come.

Lieutenant Yeboah was assigned to capture Flagstaff House, a building that had been the home of Ghana's first president and was now part of a complex of buildings which housed the headquarters of the army and the residence of the head of the armed forces, Lieutenant General Kotoka. Lieutenant Yeboah was dispatched to "surround and capture the whole area and see to it that nobody entered or came out," with specific orders to capture General Kotoka (Ziorklui 1988, 88).

---

[24]Captain Sowu of the armored unit believed that this was an attack from Guinea when he heard the shots. See "Sowu: I thought it was an invasion," *Daily Graphic*, May 3, 1967, 16.

[25]"Osei-Poku: I Have Broken Military Law," *Daily Graphic*, May 5, 1967, 1.

[26]According to Colonel Coker-Appiah, Ankrah most likely departed through the castle's slave gate, an aperture in the castle on the ocean side through which slaves were loaded onto ships. Ankrah's departure was clearly a source of embarrassment for him; in the next day's news report he is quoted as saying "How I left the castle is left to myself" ("Attempted Coup Is Crushed," *Daily Graphic*, April 18, 1967, 1).

While he succeeded in his task, this attack caused the first deaths of the coup attempt.

Flagstaff House was attacked by a force comprising one heavy armored vehicle, three lighter armored vehicles, one armored personnel carrier, and one large truck full of soldiers (Ziorklui 1988, 106). This was a substantial percentage of the squadron's forces and illustrates the relative importance of the target. Like the castle, Flagstaff House was surrounded by a series of gates for security. The guards at the first gate were surprised by two soldiers on foot and forced to unlock the gate, and the second and third gates were simply pushed open by the heavy armored vehicle. All the soldiers captured along the way were taken into custody by the attackers. Among the captives were General Kotoka, his aide-de-camp, and his valet. All three men were taken to the airport, where they were shot, either because General Kotoka resisted his abduction or because of a personal grudge held by Lieutenant Yeboah against the general. Although the circumstances remain unclear, the fact that all three men were taken together argues in favor of the former explanation.[27]

Arthur himself went straight to Burma Camp, home to the key military units in the capital, including the armored regiment that was the mother unit of Arthur's squadron and the infantry unit that was tasked with protecting the capital. Arthur's main goal there was to convince his commanding officer, Major Achaab, to join the coup attempt. The success of the coup attempt required that he gain the support of at least one of the commanding officers based in the capital, so that the attempt would be credible to the other officers. It would be impossible if his commanding officer opposed it.

First, however, Arthur took action to make it difficult for the government to organize a response. Arriving at 4:15 a.m., by 4:40 he and two soldiers had cut the internal phone lines and arrested the soldiers manning the telephone exchange. After that, he went to the main operations room and took control. This was so unexpected that the officer on duty mistook Arthur's actions for a readiness drill and even asked Arthur for a signed receipt to certify that Arthur had officially taken control.[28]

Next, Arthur went to the house of his commanding officer, where he woke Achaab and informed him that a coup was in progress and that he, Major Achaab, had been named one of the three members of the new junta. Arthur refused to discuss the matter further, however, until they were alone so that Arthur's soldiers would not realize he had been lying about Achaab's involvement (Ziorklui 1988, 89-91). For his part, Major Achaab cagily attempted to straddle the fence, going along with Arthur without either opposing or too overtly supporting him. When the two were en route to regimental headquarters, Arthur admitted that he was the organizer of the coup attempt, telling his commanding officer that he had brought his entire squadron to the capital, where he had captured the airport, castle, Flagstaff House, and radio station but now needed Achaab to order ammunition and reinforcements for his troops. Arthur had intended to ask Major Achaab

---

[27] "Yeboah killed Kotoka—Owusu," *Daily Graphic*, April 29, 1967, 3.

[28] Interview with Colonel (retired) Seth Kwahu. September 4, 2000. Accra, Ghana.

to convince the commander of the main infantry unit in the capital to also join the coup but was unable to raise the topic before they encountered the regimental quartermaster.

In what followed, Arthur found himself repeatedly frustrated by his rank and the fact that he had only acting command over his unit. These impediments threatened to derail the coup attempt. He needed ammunition because the quartermaster at Arthur's home base had refused to provide as much as he had requested without further authorization from somebody of higher rank.[29] Major Achaab, attempting to avoid obviously committing himself to either side, did not order the quartermaster to re-equip Arthur, but instead instructed Arthur to fool the quartermaster, and then he departed. Rather than take the quartermaster captive, as he had originally intended, Arthur first tried trickery, claiming that he had actually come to the capital to foil the coup attempt and urgently needed ammunition. The quartermaster, however, grew suspicious after he was pulled aside for a private conversation with another officer; and despite Arthur's insistence on the urgency of the situation, the quartermaster, who outranked him, insisted on first stopping at his office. When they arrived at the office, the quartermaster called a few soldiers over, accused Arthur of treason, wrestled Arthur's rifle away, and began to hit Arthur with it. Arthur got free and obtained another weapon from one of his own soldiers nearby, and the two confronted each other once more, though neither pointed his gun at the other. But when the quartermaster kept approaching despite Arthur's warning that he would shoot, Arthur fired two rounds, shooting him dead (Ziorklui 1988, 92). He then drove off toward the radio station without having gained the ammunition he had sought. It was 5:40 a.m.

The radio station, like the airport, had fallen to the coup makers without any significant resistance. Arthur arrived at the broadcasting studios just five minutes before the 6 a.m. news broadcast, canceled the morning news, and ordered the following announcement made instead:

> Today a group of Army Officers have overthrown the NLC regime. The NLC is dissolved and a new military junta is formed. The junta comprises Lt-Col Assassie as Head with Major Asante of 3 Bn of Infantry and Major RA Achaab of the Armoured Reconnaissance Regiment as members. All members of the dissolved NLC are to report themselves to the Army Headquarters as soon as possible or they will have themselves to blame. (Ziorklui 1988, 93)

While he was at the broadcasting facilities, Arthur twice had to hide his critical role from the rest of the military. First, he did not go on air himself to make the announcement, because that would have raised too many questions. Then, as he departed the radio station and the men he had posted outside asked what they should do with three officers they had arrested, Arthur said to detain them while he asked Major Achaab for instructions.

---

[29] "Counter Coup Was Not Foreign Inspired—Says Arthur," *Daily Graphic*, May 2, 1967, 8.

Response

There was virtually no substantive resistance to the coup attempt from any of the major military centers of power. The challengers appeared credible, having successfully captured the symbols of state authority and made a radio broadcast. As a result, rather than organizing resistance, senior officers hid and ran. Nor was there initial opposition from the mid-level commanders in the capital, whether because of a lack of direction from the top, a belief that the coup seemed likely to succeed, or both.

The coup attempt caught the government entirely by surprise. As mentioned earlier, the junta believed that members of the military were generally happy and therefore did not anticipate any internal attacks.[30] In addition, troop movements were common and not closely scrutinized, so the movements of Arthur's troops did not cause any alarm.[31] For these reasons, Arthur and his men were able to reach Accra and to mount their attack without detection.

The earliest alert was sounded by Captain Seth Kwahu, the officer Arthur had ousted from the operations room earlier in the morning. Kwahu was an unlikely defender of the government, as he was a personal friend of Arthur's and had previously been a member of Nkrumah's presidential guard and so had no reason to be sympathetic to the current junta. Nonetheless, Captain Kwahu immediately drove to inform first Colonel Alphonse Kattah and then the army commander, General Bruce, of the coup attempt.[32] From there, he moved to the infantry and armored units in the capital to tell the guards on duty there to sound the alarm, to the officers' mess to wake the officers living there and tell them to report to their units, and again to the main armored and infantry units.[33] Once the attack got under way, the noise of the attack and movements of the armored cars made some additional members of the military aware that something unusual was going on, and of course the radio broadcast just after 6 a.m. alerted the military as a whole that a coup attempt was under way.

For most officers, the coup attempt threw their world into confusion. The state of ignorance concerning the attempt was quite extensive. Most officers had no idea who the coup makers were, how strong they were, and which units had allied with either side. Arthur's radio announcement provided little information concerning the coup attempt other than the identity of the new junta to be installed. As one officer from the armored regiment remarked to me, it is hard to foil a coup if you don't even know whom you are fighting against.[34] Not knowing what to do, they did nothing.

---

[30] Interview with Air Vice Marshall (retired) Michael Otu. July 24, 2000. Accra, Ghana.

[31] Interview with Lieutenant General (retired) Arnold Quainoo. August 8, 2000. Accra, Ghana.

[32] Colonel Kattah had been one of the key actors in the coup that brought the incumbent military government to power. While he was not in the junta himself, nor did he hold a command position, he maintained a good deal of informal influence within the armed forces. He also had a reputation for toughness and resourcefulness, which may explain why Captain Kwahu informed Colonel Kattah before talking to the army commander.

[33] Interview with Colonel (retired) Seth Kwahu. September 4, 2000. Accra, Ghana

[34] Interview with Colonel (retired) Harry Ofosu-Apea. August 13, 2001. Accra, Ghana.

Even those who might have wished to act were paralyzed by the "fog of coup," and this confusion worked to the coup makers' advantage in a number of ways. On a tactical level, confusion enabled the coup makers' movements. Until the very end of the coup attempt, Arthur had complete freedom and was able to roam in and out of Burma Camp without challenge, even though he had killed the regiment's quartermaster in front of several of witnesses. More profoundly, this confusion provided a useful backdrop against which the coup makers could make their fact. The confusion itself was clear evidence that the government was not in charge. Officers knew little other than what the coup makers claimed in their broadcasts and what they could verify by driving to major symbolic sites. While the coup makers' claims to being in control were not totally convincing, given that they had not yet identified themselves, these claims were plausible and consistent with the successful coup the year before. The only public information was dominated by the challengers, and this shaped the beliefs of the officer corps accordingly.

In addition, the senior officers of the armed forces were either unable or unwilling to dispel this confusion. The head of the armed forces, General Kotoka, had been kidnapped and shot. The president of the junta, General Ankrah, was hiding in a police station. The head of the army, Major General Bruce, was safe but too concerned for his own safety (even though he was unaware of General Kotoka's fate) to do much other than increase the guard at his official residence. (Even at the end, after the coup attempt had been foiled, General Bruce was too afraid and distrustful to come out until provided with an armed escort.)[35] The head of the navy, Admiral Hansen, fled with his family until the fighting was over. The officer best positioned tactically to deal with the coup was the commander of the First Brigade, Brigadier Crabbe, who was based in Accra and had responsibility over most of the army units in the southern half of the country, but he also hid until the smoke cleared. (Both Hansen and Crabbe were removed from their posts soon after the coup attempt.) Lastly, the head of the air force, Air Marshall Michael Otu, did not run but played no role in the response, either.

All of these officers owed their positions to the military junta and were supporters of the current military government. The failure of the head of the army and the commander of the first brigade to act demonstrates that they believed the coup would succeed. By failing to act against the coup attempt, they crippled the government's response and brought it closer to success. Being risk averse was a trait that made them reliable as senior commanders unlikely to mount a coup themselves, but also unhelpful in the face of an attack.

The one senior officer who acted in response to the coup was Major General Albert K. Ocran, a junta member who had no current command appointment, although he had been commander of the First Infantry Brigade. General Ocran was awakened at 4:15 by a phone call from General Ankrah, the junta president, who was under attack in the castle (Ocran 1977, 118). General Ocran drove from unit to unit in the capital, putting himself in full view personally to show that he was still

---

[35] Interview with Brigadier (retired) Alphonse Kattah. September 2, 2000. Accra, Ghana.

in authority."[36] Ocran believed that his presence had helped undermine the challengers' claim to be in charge and thus slowed the coup's momentum. He recounted that it was "as a result of my presence and my taking control that nothing happened."[37] This claim by Ocran is likely overblown. Although he may have sown some doubt, his appeals for active assistance were rejected by other officers (Hutchful 1973, 369).

Most of the officers commanding fighting units around the capital had also been appointed by and were supporters of the junta. Nonetheless, they did not know how to respond and were afraid that jumping in without either authorization or sufficient knowledge would cause substantial chaos or worse; therefore they remained in a holding pattern, awaiting orders. As with the top brass, some of these officers believed that the coup would succeed and therefore saw little reason to oppose it, even though they did not support it. Although any of the four powerful battalions based in or near Accra could have stopped the coup with a fraction of the force at their disposal, none of them acted to defend the government when they first learned it was under attack.

The most striking example of a refusal to actively defend the government was that of the Fourth Infantry Battalion, based sixteen miles outside the capital, whose commanding officer, Lieutenant Colonel Ashitey, was a close personal friend of the head of the armed forces, General Kotoka. Lt. Colonel Ashitey believed that the coup attempt would succeed. He had compared the process of coups in Ghana to a pendulum which, having swung one way to bring the junta to power, was now swinging in the opposite direction.[38] For this reason, he ordered his men to "sit on the fence," even when General Ocran asked him for assistance (Hutchful 1973, 369). Ashitey's decision to stay out of the coup was not popular among his subordinates, who protested his decision quite vigorously but still abided by it.

The three major units in the capital itself all similarly failed to defend the government. The engineering regiment had almost a thousand soldiers, making it likely the largest unit in the capital, and yet it did nothing, even though it had played a critical role in the coup that had recently brought the junta to power and its members were disproportionately drawn from the Ewe ethnic group, which made them ethnic kin to General Kotoka. Neither the armored regiment nor the main infantry battalion based in the capital acted, either, even though their main job was to defend Accra from attack.

In short, when the coup makers appeared to be winning, seemingly an unstoppable force, there was no opposition from either key top- or middle-ranking officers. This very public lack of opposition in turn increased the credibility of the coup makers' claim to be in charge.

---

[36] Interview with Major General (retired) Albert K. Ocran. August 11, 2001. Accra, Ghana.

[37] Interview with Major General (retired) Albert K. Ocran. August 11, 2001. Accra, Ghana.

[38] Interview with Brigadier (retired) Alphonse Kattah. June 19, 2000. Accra, Ghana.

Authority Vacuum

At this point, the coup makers had achieved each of their tactical objectives and had virtually the entire Ghanaian military running scared. Yet, while Arthur had succeeded in creating a vacuum of authority, he was still unable to fill it. He could not simply reveal himself as the architect of the coup. Arthur's successes had come, thus far, by pretending to be part of a larger coup attempt. Thus, he needed to publicly produce a strong junta to fully convince members of the military that the coup's success was ensured. Preferably, this would be the junta that he announced in his broadcast, although any variant that also included strong officers would have sufficed. In addition, although he may not have known it at the time, Arthur's troops were also starting to flag. They had little ammunition and were getting listless waiting for the promised reinforcements from other units that had not arrived.[39] As a result, Arthur's ability to use force to shape expectations had declined considerably.

The junta that Arthur had previously announced consisted of three members: Major Asante of the Third Infantry Battalion, Lieutenant Colonel Assassie of the paratroop regiment, and Major Achaab of the armored regiment.[40] Major Asante is not mentioned either by witnesses or in the trial transcripts and so does not appear to have played any role in the coup attempt. Major Achaab continued his policy of almost aggressive neutrality, doing nothing to either overtly aid Arthur or stop him, even after he learned that Arthur had acted alone and after Arthur shot the unit quartermaster.[41]

The only junta member who appeared eager to accept the appointment was Lieutenant Colonel Assassie, whose forces were based in the far north of the country but who was personally present in the capital for a promotion exam. After the radio broadcast, Assassie went to the radio station, where he met Arthur and was escorted to the headquarters of the armored regiment. According to witnesses, Assassie was actively discouraging resistance to the coup and acting as if he had taken over, giving orders and accepting salutes.[42] Assassie's enthusiastic acceptance of his designation as a member of the new ruling council continued even once he found out that Arthur was the sole mover behind the coup attempt.

Lieutenant Colonel Assassie also met with Major Achaab to discuss the state of affairs thus far. According to later accounts, they decided to call a meeting of "all commanders in Accra" to "have matters straightened out."[43] First, though, Assassie suggested that they talk to the head of the infantry unit in the capital, Major Baidoo, to make sure that he was also on board. It is likely they interpreted Major Baidoo's

---

[39] "We Met Resistance At The Castle—Osei-Poku," *Daily Graphic*, May 2, 1967, 3.

[40] Arthur claims he chose Asante and Assassie because he thought they would make good junta members, and that Major Achaab was included to gain his support. "Counter Coup Was Not Foreign Inspired—Says Arthur," *Daily Graphic*, May 2, 1967, 8. Other officers have accused the three putative junta members of having been part of the conspiracy from the start, but they were never tried for any offenses and did not act as if they had foreknowledge of events.

[41] "Sowu: I thought it was an invasion," *Daily Graphic*, May 3, 1967, 3.

[42] Interview with General (retired) Laurence Okai. July 18, 2000. Accra, Ghana.

[43] "I Told My Men Of Coup—Arthur," *Daily Graphic*, May 3, 1967, 6.

inaction as tacit support for the coup attempt and hoped that with his endorsement, the new junta would be able to present the coup's success as a fait accompli. These officers, plus a few captains and lieutenants, set off for the infantry unit.

The Tide Turns

The decision of Assassie and Achaab to talk to Major Baidoo set off an unexpected series of events that culminated in the collapse of the coup attempt. When Lieutenant Arthur, Major Achaab, and Lieutenant Colonel Assassie and their entourage arrived at the infantry unit, they were surprised to be told that they were under arrest. It appears that Major Baidoo had remained loyal to the incumbent government (perhaps due to the appeals of General Ocran) and was willing to arrest his adversaries when they delivered themselves to his gate unarmed. Assassie, however, refused to accept his arrest, saying that he was there to talk, not fight, and arguing that many of the men in Baidoo's unit who had once been under his own command would be unwilling to follow this order.[44] Instead of being locked up, the men were taken into a meeting room, where they were confronted by at least six pro-government officers who had assembled at Baidoo's unit.[45] Among these was Colonel Kattah, who had spent the morning performing reconnaissance and who had just arrived from talking to officers in Major Achaab's armored regiment and was aware that they had not committed their forces to the coup attempt. The pro-government officers quickly called the coup makers' bluff, demanding to know what was going on. When directly asked, Lieutenant Arthur admitted that he was responsible for the radio broadcast, thus damaging the coup's credibility.[46]

After this point, the coup attempt quickly unraveled. Even though Assassie knew that Arthur had been responsible for the announcement and attack, he now distanced himself from the coup, claiming that he had not been involved until he heard his name on the radio and was just trying to sort matters out.[47] When it thus became clear that neither of the officers named to the junta had actually committed their troops to it, the coup attempt went from the cusp of success to clear failure. It was obvious to all involved that the pro-government officers would prevail, and Arthur was persuaded to give himself up (Baynham 1988, 241). Baidoo put all three men under arrest, this time in a more serious fashion, and they cooperated with the loyalists.

Concurrent with this meeting, a loyalist captain from the armored regiment independently took an armored car to the radio station, which probably was entirely unguarded. At either 10 or 11 a.m., he announced that the coup had been foiled.[48]

---

[44] "I Told My Men Of Coup—Arthur," *Daily Graphic*, May 3, 1967, 6.

[45] The official account lists six officers; Kattah mentioned the names of a few who were not on that list.

[46] "I Told My Men Of Coup — Arthur," *Daily Graphic*, May 3, 1967, 6. During the previous coup attempt, the announcement had been made by one of the brigade commanders, so Arthur's confession immediately made it clear that something was wrong.

[47] "I Told My Men Of Coup—Arthur," *Daily Graphic*, May 3, 1967, 6.

[48] "How I killed Kotoka — Yeboah's Statement Tells The Story," *Daily Graphic*, May 3, 1967, 3.

Although his announcement was prescient, it seems to have been pure assertion. The captain had not been present at the meeting, so he did not know its outcome. He also could see that the coup makers were still in charge of the castle and of Flagstaff House and thus that the coup had not yet actually been foiled.[49] At the same time, he also knew that Arthur had acted alone, having been present when Arthur told Assassie and Achaab what was really going on, and he would have understood that the coup attempt was pure bluff.[50]

Consolidation

With the surrender of Arthur and his would-be junta members, all that was left to quell the coup was to organize the pullback of rebelling soldiers from the positions they held in the capital. Kattah took control of the Accra armored regiment, assembling them and addressing them directly. Next, he worked with Major Achaab to order Lieutenants Yeboah and Osei-Poku to withdraw their men from the locations they had captured. Having the coup-making officers give the order to withdraw minimized the possibility of bloodshed. It was easy to gain the cooperation of the two young officers in Arthur's unit because both had sought out senior military officers even before they knew the coup was over. Because Lieutenant Yeboah had been told that the coup involved Major Achaab, he had reported to the headquarters of the armored regiment on his own initiative. Yeboah was confused by the orders to withdraw his men, but he cooperated fully. Lieutenant Osei-Poku, the officer in charge of the forces at the castle, had grown tired of waiting for the reinforcements that Arthur had promised. When his former instructor from the military academy showed up, the two of them left together to figure out what was going on, leaving some soldiers behind at the castle. Hearing that Major Achaab had ordered all armored units withdrawn, Osei-Poku cooperated fully.[51] At both the airport and radio station, soldiers had dispersed on their own, most likely because they were tired of waiting for promised reinforcements.

As part of the final mopping up, Kattah made a radio broadcast confirming that the coup had failed and ordering all units back to their bases.[52] This was followed later in the day by an official statement by the vice-chairman of the junta and a press conference by General Ankrah, the head of the junta.

Analysis

As noted earlier, although all three theories correctly predict the failure of Arthur's coup, the competing explanations fall short in explaining what happened during the coup attempt and how Arthur came so close to victory. Although the stronger side won, the challengers did not try to establish military dominance, and the intensity

---

[49] "Sowu: I thought it was an invasion," *Daily Graphic*, May 3, 1967, 3.

[50] "I Told My Men Of Coup—Arthur," *Daily Graphic*, May 3, 1967, 6.

[51] "I could not capture the Castle and kill Gen. Ankrah—Poku," *Ghanaian Times*, May 3, 1967, 8.

[52] Interview with Colonel (retired) Harry Ofosu-Apea. August 13, 2001. Accra, Ghana.

of fighting was low. Although the more popular side won, preferences do a very poor job of predicting individuals' actions during the coup attempt. Despite the coup's having almost no supporters, almost none of the pro-government officers acted to protect the junta during most of the attempt. Even close friends of the junta members sat on the fence.

Only the theory of coups as coordination games goes beyond correctly predicting the outcome to explaining the trajectory of the entire attempt. This attempt is unusual in that the challengers experienced a significant reversal of fortune, going from the verge of success to total failure as the public information available about the coup shifted. The coup attempt started with expectations strongly favoring its success, as a result of the success of the prior coup attempt and the capture of key symbolic targets, including the radio station. These expectations were undermined when the challengers lost control of public information, both during an impromptu meeting and through a competing radio broadcast. Throughout the coup attempt, officers were clearly bandwagoning, supporting or refusing to oppose the coup attempt when it seemed likely to succeed and turning against it when it seemed likely to fail. This bandwagoning included even personal friends of the current junta and members of the proposed replacement junta.

Coups as Battles

The challengers indeed had little military force at their disposal and were grossly outmatched by pro-government officers, like Major Baidoo, commander of the main infantry unit in the capital. For example, at the end of the coup, the soldiers who had captured the castle were found with only seventeen pistols, ten of which they had taken from the castle itself.[53] In addition, the attackers were short on ammunition for both mounted cannon and small arms. From the perspective of coups as battles, this coup attempt was a minor threat at best and should never have come close to succeeding at all.

Although the theory correctly predicts the failure of the coup, it does much worse at explaining its conduct. Few of the targets of the 1967 coup attempt were of strictly military importance. While the coup makers attacked largely symbolic targets—such as the airport, the radio station, and the residence of the executive— they did not attack any of the major units stationed around the capital. They did not even attack the armory, despite their shortage of ammunition. The only two targets that had a military rationale were the armed forces operations room and the army headquarters building (Flagstaff House), which was also where General Kotoka lived. A coup attempt designed to establish clear military dominance would have targeted loyalist officers, such as Lieutenant Colonel Ashitey, from the start.

Similarly, this theory predicts that any resistance would be dealt with harshly, but that was not the case. The main armed confrontation between the two sides was at the residence of the executive, Christianborg Castle. Here, even though Arthur had given Osei-Poku authorization to use deadly force, Osei-Poku ordered

---

[53] "I Was Shocked—Osei-Poku," *Daily Graphic*, May 2, 1967, 3.

his men to mainly fire in the air; as a result, most of the castle's defenders escaped, and only one person on each side was injured.[54]

Coups as Elections

The theory that coups are like elections also predicts the outcome correctly, but for the wrong reason. In 1967, the junta was still fairly popular (or at least not unpopular) among both the populace and military officers. The challengers, on the other hand, were unknowns who did not identify themselves and lacked any political appeal, both inside and outside the military. Not even Arthur's peers and friends were sympathetic to the coup attempt. By this reckoning, there should never have been a coup attempt, and any challenge that was foolishly mounted should have quickly been defeated. However, this approach cannot explain how the coup makers almost succeeded, nor does it illuminate the failure of the government to find defenders until the very end of the attempt.

The theory not only fails to predict the overall trajectory of the coup attempt, it also does not predict the actions of individual officers. Despite a large number of officers who were pro-government, or at least not anti-government, very few came to its defense. Only one member of the junta itself organized resistance to the coup, and he did not even have any troops under his command. None of the service chiefs acted. The army commander did nothing even when he was explicitly asked for orders. The head of the navy took his family and ran. The head of the air force was preparing to perform reconnaissance, but the coup ended before he could get airborne. Even though the engineering regiment and the Fourth Infantry Battalion had played key roles in putting the junta into power, the officers there did nothing to defend it. This is particularly striking in light of the close personal friendship of Lieutenant Colonel Ashitey with the junta's General Kotoka. Even Major Baidoo, the commander of the capital infantry unit, did not send his troops out to fight the coup makers and was at best tentative when the challengers walked, unarmed, through his gate. In this attempt, there was a large gap between the preferences of officers and their actions, one that can best be explained by the fact that officers were hesitant to support the government when they thought it would lose.

Lastly, neither side used the radio to try to woo potential supporters. Although Arthur believed he had legitimate grievances that were widely held by others, he did not use his radio broadcast to try to encourage supporters to join the coup attempt. Conversely, the loyalist radio broadcasts were not designed to exhort passive government supporters to step up and defend the regime.

Coups as Coordination Games

The argument that coup attempts are like coordination games explains not just the failure of the coup attempt but also why it came so close to succeeding and

---

[54]One of the soldiers in the attacking forces died after the coup attempt, and this may be the same soldier who was injured during the attack, but it is not possible to establish this with any certainty.

why it fell apart when it did and in the way it did. The challengers had the upper hand as long as they were able to convince other officers that the coup attempt was an unstoppable force. Officers believed that the coup would succeed, that others believed that the coup would succeed, and that it would be difficult to find other officers willing to oppose the coup. This all changed suddenly as a result of a meeting where the challengers were revealed to be weak and of a radio broadcast that claimed the coup attempt had failed. It is worth noting that neither of the competing approaches can explain why this was the inflection point of the coup attempt, given that nothing changed in terms of either the tactical strength of the two sides or the feelings of officers toward the coup attempt.

Throughout the coup attempt, members of the officer corps clearly and overtly coordinated their responses with those of other actors in the military. The top brass were too scared to defend the government against what they believed would be a successful coup. Pro-government officers, even those who were close friends with junta members, did not rush to the government's aid. For example, Lieutenant Colonel Ashitey refused to support the government because he believed the coup would fail. Even Major Baidoo was unwilling to act resolutely until after Arthur's bluff was exposed. Instead, most did nothing, acquiescing to the coup makers because they did not want to be on the losing side of a coup.[55] However, when it was revealed that the challengers were weaker than they had originally appeared and that they had lost control of the radio station, officers backed the government.

This bandwagoning behavior is most striking in the case of Lieutenant Colonel Assassie and Major Achaab, two of the three officers Arthur had nominated to the junta. As long as the coup attempt was going well, these two officers were willing to comply and assist, but as soon as it looked like the tide was turning, they abandoned Arthur. It was this lack of open support for the coup attempt that probably saved the government; if Major Achaab, the commander of the armored unit, had openly backed the coup makers, the coup undoubtedly would have succeeded.[56]

Central to the coup attempt was the challengers' effort to control two sites involved in the production of public information: the radio station and the meeting of all local commanders that the coup makers wished to convoke. The challengers' initial possession of the radio station helped them generate the expectations that almost led to their victory, and if they had been able to convene a meeting of all local commanders and control what was said in such a meeting, rather than becoming the subjects of an impromptu meeting not of their making, they might well have won.

As the coup attempt went on, however, the challengers lost their advantage in the area of public information. While they had control of the radio station at 6 a.m., they failed to send reinforcements or make further broadcasts, making it possible for an officer in an armored car to easily take control of the radio station at 10 a.m. and claim that the coup had ended. As in the earlier broadcast by the challengers,

---

[55]Interview with Air Vice Marshall (retired) Michael Otu. July 24, 2000. Accra, Ghana with General (retired) Laurence Okai. July 18, 2000. Accra, Ghana.

[56]Interview with Brigadier (retired) Alphonse Kattah. June 19, 2000. Accra, Ghana.

this claim of victory was also premature and consistent with behavior intended to create self-fulfilling expectations.[57]

Consonant with what one expects if coups are coordination games, private information played a very different role from public information during the coup attempt. Although Lieutenant Colonel Assassie and Major Achaab had already learned that Arthur had been the prime mover behind the actions thus far, when this information came out in front of other unit commanders, they quickly backed away from the coup. Similarly, it is likely that Major Baidoo of the capital infantry knew already that the coup was weak, since he had spoken to General Ocran and knew that Ocran had been traveling freely without challenge. However, Baidoo did not take advantage of that information to commit his troops to action and was meek even when Arthur, Assassie, and Achaab walked into his unit unarmed. Even with the deck stacked in his favor, Baidoo still remained concerned with what other units were doing and would not act firmly until the challengers' weakness became public.

Other key aspects of this coup attempt are also consistent with the theory. Even though the challengers had limited men and ammunition, three of the five major targets initially attacked by the coup makers (the airport, the castle, and the radio station) had largely symbolic importance and little tactical importance. What's more, they devoted a substantial amount of their limited resources to visibly occupying these targets. A handful of men could easily have put the airport out of commission, but that was unnecessary, because there was no chance of government reinforcements arriving by air. Similarly, there was no tactical reason to try to capture the castle. If the coup makers were concerned about General Ankrah, they could have cordoned off the building and cut its communications, thus neutralizing him as a factor. Instead, they sent one platoon to each of these targets, what was likely the majority of their forces. This can only be justified on symbolic grounds, as a visible signal of strength. In fact, other officers did notice that these sites were occupied and allowed that to shape their expectations about the likely outcome of the coup.

Throughout the coup attempt, Arthur's actions were interpreted through the lens of what had happened a year before in Ghana's successful first coup attempt. His actions were made more credible by this comparison, as was his repeated claim to be just a small part of a grander coordinated effort involving multiple powerful units, just as in 1966. This precedent, and his deliberate invocation of it, shaped initial expectations within the officer corps and allowed the coup attempt to continue without challenge. Lieutenant Colonel Ashitey overtly made the comparison when he refused Major General Ocran's call to resist, saying he would not fight this coup attempt, because he expected it to succeed, just as the previous one had. That said, the precedent alone was not enough in the face of countervailing public information.

As also predicted by this theory, during the attempt, efforts were made by parties on both sides to reduce the number of potential casualties. When the challengers encountered resistance at the castle (most likely because the guards believed they

---

[57] "Sowu: I thought it was an invasion," *Daily Graphic*, May 3, 1967, 16.

were facing a foreign invasion), the attacking party fired mainly in the air to scare the defenders rather than harm them.[58] By pulling their punches, the attackers at the castle took longer to achieve their objective and used more of their scarce ammunition, thus sacrificing tactical gain. Similarly, when attacking the complex of buildings at Flagstaff House that housed the army headquarters, the challengers could have simply opened fire and demolished the structure from their armored cars. Instead, they proceeded to advance through each gate and capture those inside.

A similar concern for avoiding casualties was clear on the loyalist side. When the commander of the signals regiment, Colonel Gbagonah, assembled his men to guard the headquarters of their regiment, he issued them only empty rifles with bayonets.[59] He thought a show of strength was necessary but was unwilling to authorize actions that might lead to bloodshed. From a tactical perspective, it would have been more effective for him to arm and hide his small number of soldiers, so they could surprise any possible attackers, but, again, he was hesitant to escalate the situation further.[60]

Even when there were deaths, these came at the end of a prolonged struggle rather than as a result of trying to gain tactical advantage. Consider the struggle between Arthur and the quartermaster of the armored unit. The quartermaster disarmed Arthur but did not shoot him, instead trying to subdue him. For his part, Arthur repeatedly warned the quartermaster to back down and only shot him when he insisted on advancing on Arthur. Similarly, the three hostages from Flagstaff House died once the complex was captured, but only after General Kotoka resisted.

Bloodshed was also reduced by the fact that the coup makers did not fight back when arrested. While Arthur did not have an opportunity to resist, the other two lieutenants could have. Yeboah and Osei-Poku both had motive to resist, as they were facing serious penalties for their actions. Yeboah was later executed by firing squad (as was Arthur), and Osei-Poku was sentenced to thirty years in prison. Still, they were cooperative.

Even with these efforts, there were still five deaths during the coup attempt. While substantial, this total is low compared to the number of people who would have died if the challengers had unleashed their strength fully or would have died in a foreign invasion.

Lastly, throughout the attempt, both the dynamics and the outcome of the coup were shaped by the challengers' position within the military hierarchy. Arthur's main asset was his temporary command over his unit, which he used to effectively follow the classic script for a coup from the middle. At the same time, Arthur was limited by his position as a mere lieutenant. This was a coup from the middle by virtue of his temporary command, not his official rank, and this coup attempt

---

[58] "We Met Resistance At The Castle—Osei-Poku," *Daily Graphic*, May 2, 1967, 3.

[59] Interview with Colonel (retired) Michael Gbagonah. May 29, 2000. Accra, Ghana.

[60] These choices did not reflect a lack of bravery or loyalty on the part of Colonel Gbagonah. Unlike some of the senior members of the military, he personally drove around the capital performing reconnaissance and reporting his findings.

demonstrates the tension between the two. Arthur had to lie to everybody and pretend that the coup was being mounted by majors. Even his own men would have balked if they had realized that Arthur was calling all the shots. He was unable to get the ammunition he needed from either of the two quartermasters he asked, and his forces ran low on ammunition as a consequence. The minute it was revealed that the coup was mounted by a lieutenant, it fell apart, even though Arthur had accomplished everything that a major would have. If Arthur had in fact been a major commanding the same unit, he would have had a far better chance of success. Arthur's limitations as a lieutenant demonstrate the resources that come with being a major, lieutenant colonel, or colonel.

Ghana, 1972

Ghana's next coup attempt was a successful coup from the middle in 1972, which overthrew an unpopular democratic government. In many ways it was a textbook coup from the middle, with the conspirators seizing the radio station, airport, prime minister's office, and president's residence. As we shall see, they manipulated other officers' expectations, used public communications to make these expectations common knowledge, and shaped perceptions of risk to make the coup's success appear the less risky outcome. The challengers were so successful at making the coup attempt seem a fait accompli that loyalist officers refused to resist, and in one case even joined an effort to protect the coup against a loyalist counter-coup that was rumored but never materialized. In the end, the incumbent government fell without a shot fired, and the coup ended quickly and bloodlessly.

Background

The 1972 coup attempt targeted the democratic civilian government led by Prime Minister Kofi Busia and the Progress Party (PP). The PP had come to power in 1969 with the creation of Ghana's Second Republic, when the country's first military government (1966-1969) stepped down, making Ghana the first country in Africa to return to civilian rule after a military regime (Lefever 1970, 72).

The Busia administration was a center-right government. The PP was a later incarnation of the original pre-independence political movement in Ghana, the United Gold Coast Congress. Its core supporters were businessmen, professionals, and chiefs, the old elites who had been pushed aside at independence by the socialist first president, Kwame Nkrumah. The party stood for gradual change, private enterprise, and western political liberalism. Their policies were largely consistent with those of the military junta that had preceded them, although different in style. Busia himself was an Oxford-educated professor from an aristocratic family whose style was patrician, not crowd-pleasing.

With the return of democracy, political tensions quickly rose. One major source of political problems for the PP government was the cleavage between the Akan and Ewe ethnic groups.[61] The leaders of the PP were largely from the Akan ethnic group, and the leaders of the main opposition party, the National Alliance of Liberals (NAL), were primarily from the Ewe ethnic group. Voting in the 1969 election largely followed ethnic lines (Petchenkine 1993, 48). There were no Ewe in the new cabinet, and the new government was seen as clearly advancing Akan interests.[62] Soon after assuming office, the government passed an amendment to the new constitution that allowed them to fire any official who had been appointed during military rule. The 568 civil servants they removed came largely from the Ewe and Ga ethnic groups that is, from groups whose members were largely allied to the opposition. Although the government justified this move by pointing out correctly that the military junta had swollen the civil service with patronage appointments, the purge was widely perceived as blatant ethnic discrimination. Opposition anger about this matter increased when the prime minister, refusing to abide by the Supreme Court's decision to reinstate one of the dismissed bureaucrats, made a speech in which he lectured the Supreme Court on constitutional law and accused it of having behaved in a biased and political manner.[63] While there was some merit in this criticism, opponents saw the government's behavior as clearly undemocratic (Petchenkine 1993, 49).

The other major problem faced by the government was the economy. The administration had inherited a large amount of foreign debt and a balance of payments problem.[64] When the price of Ghana's main export, cocoa, plummeted in 1971, Ghana's short-term foreign debt rose to more than half the value of its annual imports (Petchenkine 1993, 52).

The government first tried to address the balance of payments problem through fiscal means, slashing budget expenditures across the board, enacting several new taxes, increasing bank interest rates, raising gasoline prices, and abolishing free medical care (Esseks 1975, 54). These cutbacks were unpopular with urban constituencies who viewed government support as an entitlement. University students, who had clashed with the government previously on other issues, grew irate at the government's plan to replace free higher education with no-interest loans payable over twelve years (Bennett 1975, 303). The confederation of unions mounted a series

---

[61]While ethnicity had been a factor throughout the politics of modern Ghana, tensions between Akans and Ewe had not been salient during the First Republic and only became significant during military rule. This is ironic, since the overthrow of Nkrumah involved a coalition of Akan and Ewe officers.

[62]According to the constitution, any cabinet member had also to be an elected member of parliament. Since there were no Ewes amongst the PP parliamentarians, there could not be an Ewe member of cabinet.

[63]Two of the judges had connections to the plaintiff or other discharged civil servants, yet they refused to recuse themselves. The ruling can legitimately be understood as political and was probably bad law, yet the judiciary refused to hear an appeal.

[64]The foreign debt came largely from Nkrumah's government, but it had been increased by added loans and rescheduled interest under the military junta until it was nearly 400 million pounds sterling. This was not Ghana's first brush with a balance of payments crisis. President Nkrumah's government had faced insolvency because of its trade deficit, just before it was overthrown (Esseks 1975, 37-53).

of strikes before the government unconstitutionally dissolved it, but the strikes continued when sixteen of the seventeen national unions simply formed a new umbrella organization (Petchenkine 1993, 53).

These fiscal measures were insufficient to stop the decline in the real value of the currency. In the last days of December 1971, the government devalued the currency by 48%.[65] For Ghana's elites, used to a standard of living that was heavily reliant on imported goods, this represented as much as a 25% loss in purchasing power (Bennett 1975, 302). Although the government tried to cushion the blow, the devaluation was a blow to national pride and seen as a sign that the government was unable to effectively manage the economy.

The government also managed to alienate many within the military. After being repeatedly praised as national saviors under the military junta, the armed forces were shocked to learn that, under the Second Republic, they were considered just another government bureaucracy and would not receive special deference. As money grew short, the government began to discuss how the military could make itself useful by engaging in national development efforts, further wounding the military's pride (Bennett 1975, 301). Because the government made a conscious effort not to spare any area of expenditure, the military was strongly affected by the budget cuts.[66] The navy and air force were crippled by the cutbacks, and even the army had little money for exercises, training, ammunition, or maintenance. The government's austerity measures reduced officers' take-home pay by increasing rents, and they ended free water and electricity for occupants of military housing. Compounded by the devaluation of the currency, real incomes sank, and many within the military were unhappy with the government.[67]

Lastly, ethnic grievances against the government were also felt within the military, where Ewes believed they were discriminated against by the government. By 1972, only one Ewe officer within the army held a senior position, a sharp decline from the beginning of the NLC junta (Bennett 1975, 304).

Conspiracies

During the Second Republic, there were at least three simultaneous coup plots against Prime Minister Busia. Ironically, despite the salience of ethnicity in all of these conspiracies, it was an over-reliance on ethnic calculus by the incumbent government that contributed to its overthrow. Members of the government failed to take sufficient counter-measures against the plot that succeeded because, although they knew of its existence, they refused to believe that an officer from the same ethnic group as the prime minister and president would be disloyal.

---

[65]This was not the first major devaluation of the cedi, although it is often erroneously called so. In July 1967, the cedi was devalued by 30% by the NLC military junta (Esseks 1975, 45).

[66]As part of Acheampong's justification for his military coup, he said that the military intended to "control rather than be controlled" by the economy (Bennett 1975, 309). Many within the military felt that the military should not have been subject to the same budget cuts as other government organizations.

[67]Interview with Colonel (retired) Seth Kwahu. September 4, 2000. Accra, Ghana.

The conspiracy that the government was most worried about involved Brigadier Kattah, who was from the Ewe ethnic group and had been a key figure in the successful overthrow of President Nkrumah in 1966 and in foiling Ghana's second coup attempt, in 1967. Trying to neutralize Kattah, the government first sent him to India as a defense attache, where it kept him under constant surveillance. Still worried, it brought him back to Ghana to stand trial on fairly minor and possibly trumped-up charges. Upon his return, Brigadier Kattah did in fact begin to plot against the government, although, because he was under close watch, he delegated the recruitment and details to his godson, Major Anthony Selormey of the armored regiment. According to Kattah, Selormey reached out to disgruntled officers around the capital to bring them into the plot.[68]

Kattah's plotting was well known enough that it spurred a counter-conspiracy intended to pre-emptively take power before Kattah could strike. This plot centered around a civilian politician, Imoro Ayanah, from northern Ghana who was concerned that his region would be excluded from power should there be a takeover by the Ewe.[69]

The conspiracy that overthrew the government, however, was one that the administration had failed to take sufficient counter-measures against, having assumed the loyalty of members of their own ethnic group. This plot involved a forty-year-old infantry officer from the Akan ethnic group, Colonel Ignatius Kutu Acheampong, and three majors from the units around the capital, one who was also Akan and two who were from the Ewe ethnic group. Acheampong's disloyalty would not have been a surprise to a neutral observer, as the intelligence community had documented that he had a mistress, was in need of cash, and was known to be holding clandestine meetings with politicians from the opposition (Quantson 2000, 96).[70] Nonetheless, the government's response was to inform the intelligence services that they had no doubts about Acheampong's loyalty and to inform Acheampong that baseless accusations were being raised about him by jealous parties (101). In fact, the government was so sure of Acheampong's loyalty that it promoted him to commander of the First Infantry Brigade, where he was in charge of all the army troops in the southern half of the country, and, just a few days before the coup attempt, raised his rank from lieutenant colonel to colonel.[71]

Acheampong's promotions were a clear sign of ethnic bias within the military. Because the commander of the First Brigade was responsible for coordinating counter-coup activity, this position should have gone only to an officer who was above reproach, which Acheampong clearly was not. Nor was he highly qualified on a professional basis. To the contrary, his peers criticized his performance both as a

---

[68]Interview with Brigadier (retired) Alphonse Kattah. September 2, 2000. Accra, Ghana.

[69]Interview with Colonel (retired) Daniel Prah. August 6, 2001. Accra, Ghana.

[70]Interview with Professor (retired) Ofosu-Amaah. November 24th, 1999. Accra, Ghana. Ofosu-Amaah was the former head of the Bureau of National Investigation (BNI), the analogue of the FBI. Although Ofosu-Amaah's jurisdiction was over civilian crime, in practice it extended to broader conspiracy as well. Also see Quantson (2000, 99), an account written by Ofosu-Amaah's subordinate in the BNI.

[71]Acheampong was supported by one of the prime minister's close advisors, a retired general named Akwasi Afrifa.

desk officer[72] and as a field officer.[73] In fact, Acheampong had twice come close to being expelled from the military, once as a young officer and again in 1971, both times surviving largely by luck.[74] Despite recognizing that Acheampong might have been disgruntled, the government considered him essentially harmless because of his ethnicity and lack of character. (His own friends shared this view and did not take Acheampong seriously when he warned them ahead of time about the coup.)

There are some interesting questions about the possible relationship between Colonel Acheampong's plot and Brigadier Kattah's plot, because both involved Kattah's godson, Major Selormey. In my conversation with him, Kattah alleged that Acheampong essentially hijacked his plot, binding the majors with a powerful oath sworn at a church.[75] Acheampong's version of events was different. He claimed that he had decided to mount a coup years before Kattah began to put his plans into action, in fact only six months into the Second Republic (Quantson 2000, 98).[76] A third perspective comes from the only surviving member of the conspiracy, Major Kodzo Barney Agbo, who claims that the plot originated with the majors, who then brought Acheampong into their effort as a supporting player. The truth of the matter is difficult to ascertain and luckily does not affect our understanding of the coup attempt itself. What is relevant is that this conspiracy was organized and acted out independently of Brigadier Kattah, regardless of whence it sprang.

The conspirators in the Acheampong plot were well placed to mount a coup. Each of the three majors was the second-in-command of one of the key units near the capital: Major Selormey was the second-in-command of the armored regiment, Major Kwame Baah was the second-in-command of the infantry battalion, and Major Agbo was the second-in-command of the infantry battalion in Tema, barely ten miles away from Accra. The coup attempt would start with the majors seizing control over their units, the most dangerous part of the enterprise but one made easier because each of their commanding officers had been freshly installed as part of the recent round of promotions. They would then seize the radio station, the airport, the president's residence, and the prime minister's office in Christiansborg Castle.

They did not expect to encounter any opposition at this stage. The only other unit near the capital was the engineering regiment, whose commanding officer, Major A.K.N. Mallet, had refused to join the coup but had assured the challengers that he would not oppose them, either.[77] In addition, since Acheampong's recent

---

[72]Interview with General (retired) Edwin Sam. 2000. Accra, Ghana.

[73]Interview with Colonel (retired) Victor Coker-Appiah. June, 2000. Accra, Ghana.

[74]The first time, Acheampong was spared because there were few indigenous officers within the armed forces at the time. The second time, the head of the armed forces stepped down in protest against military budget cuts before he had a chance to fire Acheampong. Interview with Air Vice Marshall (retired) Michael Otu. July 24, 2000. Accra, Ghana.

[75]Interview with Brigadier (retired) Alphonse Kattah. September 2, 2000. Accra, Ghana.

[76]To complicate matters yet further, Military Intelligence believed that Acheampong was aware of Ayanah's plans and promised to assist Ayanah in his efforts. Interview with Colonel (retired) Daniel Prah. August 8, 2001. Accra, Ghana

[77]Interview with Colonel (retired) Kodzo Barney Agbo. July 27, 2000. Accra, Ghana. Mallet's story is interesting. Mallet claims that he told Acheampong not to mount the coup, since Mallet supported democratic rule. However, since Mallet was an Ewe and had wrongly been under surveil-

promotion placed him in charge of coordinating counter-coup efforts as head of the First Infantry Brigade, they knew they could at the very least delay a response from units outside the capital.

Because it was important to the conspirators that the coup be executed with "as little bloodshed as possible," they planned to attack when the prime minister was out of the country. According to Agbo, they reasoned, "If he's in town, it creates a bit of a problem because soldiers guarding him [might react and] ... [there] may be some bloodshed." The coup makers were less concerned about Ghana's president, who would remain in the country. The position was largely ceremonial, the president was rather frail, and the president's residence could easily be sealed off, preventing him from becoming a locus of opposition.[78]

Attack

Originally, the plan was to attack during the spring, to give the conspirators more time to bring other commanders into the conspiracy. They also felt that a coup attempt close to Easter, when many in Accra would have traveled to their home towns for the holiday, would reduce the chance of accidental harm to civilians.[79] However, the date for the attack was then moved up to take advantage of the prime minister's trip to the United Kingdom for medical care.[80] Brigadier Kattah had also advanced the date for his own planned attempt, and Colonel Acheampong likely wished to pre-empt him.[81] Once the date was set, Acheampong was not very discreet about his intention to overthrow the government. Two of my respondents indicated that Acheampong had warned them, in vague terms, about an impending coup attempt, although neither had taken him seriously.[82]

On January 11, 1972, the night of the coup attempt, the intelligence services went on alert. They received reports about suspicious activities in the infantry and armored units in the capital and sent two officers to investigate, neither of whom returned.[83] With this, intelligence officials grew concerned and invoked Operation Contamination, the counter-coup contingency plan, which directed Acheampong to send loyal troops to key locations, including the buildings in the national broadcasting complex (Quantson 2000, 94). The troops he was to send were those commanded by the majors.

---

lance himself as a possible coup risk, he saw no reason to stick his neck out to assist the very intelligence agencies that were hounding him. Interview with Colonel (retired) A.K.N Mallet. September 5, 2000. Accra, Ghana.

[78]Interview with Colonel (retired) Kodzo Barney Agbo. July 27, 2000. Accra, Ghana.

[79]Interview with Colonel (retired) Kodzo Barney Agbo. July 27, 2000. Accra, Ghana.

[80]Interview with Colonel (retired) Kodzo, Barney Agbo. July 27, 2000. Accra, Ghana.

[81]Interview with Brigadier (retired) Alphonse Kattah. September 2, 2000. Accra, Ghana.

[82]Interview with General (retired) Laurence Okai. July 25, 2000. Accra, Ghana. The other officer who was informed was Colonel (retired) Michael Gbagonah.

[83]One of these officers was the deputy director of military intelligence for counter intelligence, who made the mistake of going to meet with Acheampong at a location away from military headquarters, to fill him in before investigating what was happening in the units. At the meeting, Acheampong revealed that he was taking over the government and detained the deputy director until the conclusion of the coup. Interview with Colonel (retired) Daniel Prah August 8, 2001 Accra, Ghana.

At some point that night, the majors took control of their units. Major Agbo did this by assembling his entire unit on the parade field and informing them that they were part of a coup attempt involving all the units around the capital. Agbo then gave them a choice: they could participate or, if they objected, they could stand to the side. No one opted out.[84] Major Agbo's actions established his control of the unit by manipulating expectations, mirroring the technique used when making a coup in a meeting. If any of the soldiers present had been opposed to the coup attempt, they would have been unlikely to speak up so publicly, especially given that Agbo had told them that they were part of a larger effort. Once the appearance of unanimous support had been created, Major Agbo was firmly in charge. He then told his men that if either the new commanding officer (who had just taken over command of the battalion eight days before) or the old commanding officer showed up, they should be arrested.

The majors then sent troops to take over the radio station, airport, president's residence, and Christianborg Castle. They succeeded in their task without encountering any resistance. Although the exact timing of these maneuvers is unclear, they most likely took place once the contingency plan was invoked, since the intelligence services did not receive any news of these troop movements during the initial stages of the coup attempt.

Meanwhile, the government was still in the dark concerning what was going on. All they knew was that they had invoked the contingency plan but there had been no further news. At 5 a.m., the capital appeared calm. Among civilians in the security services, there was even speculation that this had been a false alarm and they considered going home and calling it a night. Out of prudence, however, they decided to wait for the 6 a.m. news broadcast, when coups (as well as changes in the cabinet) were traditionally announced (Quantson 2000, 94). They were surprised to then hear Colonel Acheampong's voice on the radio, saying, "Fellow Ghanaians ... we in the Ghana Army have once again taken over the administration in Ghana" (Kirk-Greene 1981, 138).

Response

Within the capital, the only attempted resistance came directly from the head of the armed forces, Major General Addo, who traveled to Tema to personally assert control over the portion of Major Agbo's forces that had remained behind.[85] General Addo tried to appeal to the soldiers' ethnic sentiments, telling them that the coup was being organized by Ewe officers and that they should oppose it. The soldiers rejected both General Addo's reasoning and his authority, however, refusing to act unless they heard from Major Agbo, at which point they arrested the head of the armed forces. This incident demonstrates the extent to which command is contingent during a coup attempt, in this case leaving even the highest ranking

---

[84]Interview with Colonel (retired) Kodzo Barney Agbo. July 27, 2000. Accra, Ghana.

[85]Agbo's unit attracted attention because it was the first to move, a consequence of its being the farthest away from its targets.

military officer helpless to enforce his writ. At some point that night, both the old commanding officer of the battalion and the new commanding officer were also arrested by Agbo's troops.[86]

One possible source of opposition to the coup attempt was the Second Infantry Brigade, which comprised all forces in the northern half of Ghana. The commander of this unit, Colonel Osei-Wusu, and all the officers subordinate to him were known to be government loyalists, and the brigade was headquartered in a city that was the cultural and commercial capital for the Ashanti people, the biggest Akan subgroup. On the day of the coup, Colonel Osei-Wusu was 120 miles north of his base, visiting the Sixth Infantry Battalion. Upon hearing news of the coup attempt, he went back to his headquarters to gather more information rather than striking back immediately, at which time he was arrested by junior officers supporting the coup.[87] The commander of the infantry battalion in the same city was also detained.[88]

Another source of possible resistance in the north was the commander of the Sixth Battalion, Lieutenant Colonel Enoch Donkoh. Colonel Donkoh assembled his men and told them that there had been a coup attempt in the capital and that, while he did not approve, he would not resist; he ordered his men to stay in their barracks until further notice.[89] Even though Donkoh was strongly opposed to the coup (so much so that he became one of the few officers in Ghana to resign his commission rather than serve under a military government), he was unwilling to oppose it or let others in his unit do so.

The last source of possible opposition to the coup attempt in the country was the forces based in the coastal city of Takoradi, 135 miles to the west of Accra. Takoradi houses an unusual concentration of military assets; it is home to an air force base, a naval base, and an infantry battalion. The commander of the air base, who was also the commander of the combined garrison, was Colonel John Barnor.[90] When the coup attempt took place, all three of the Takoradi base commanders plus the head of the air force (who happened to be there on business) put their respective troops on alert and spent the next twenty-four hours conferring to decide how to respond. In the end, they decided not to oppose the coup.

According to Barnor, an important part of their reasoning was that it was hard to oppose a coup once the capital had fallen. Barnor claims that opposition would have been forthcoming if the "center" had held and contingency plans had been invoked,

---

[86]Interview with Colonel (retired) Kodzo Barney Agbo. July 27, 2000. Accra, Ghana.

[87]The officers responsible for the arrests are thought to have been Ewe officers who believed that the coup was bringing Kattah into power, and who acted on their own initiative.

[88]Interview with anonymous officer. July 22, 2000. Accra, Ghana.

[89]Interview with Staff Sergeant (retired) John Apatinga. August 14, 2001. Accra, Ghana.

[90]Barnor is the sole source of information for this account. To avoid confusion, it is worth noting that both Barnor's name and rank change over time. At the time of the coup attempt, the air force was using army ranks, a practice they later stopped. Hence Barnor was Colonel Barnor then, and Air Vice Marshall Barnor when he retired. Besides the type of rank he held, Barnor's first name also changed. He was born John Barnor and later discarded his British first name in favor of his indigenous one. While Barnor in 1972 held the name Colonel John E. Barnor, he is cited as Air Vice Marshall Odaate Barnor, since that was the name he used and rank he held when he was interviewed.

allowing for a coordinated resistance. With Accra falling to the coup makers, however, they believed opposition would just lead to confusion and bloodshed. Barnor also claims that it was difficult to gather information from their location and that it was important to know what was happening in Accra (what he called "the situation on the ground") before reacting. The main thing one wants to avoid during a coup attempt, he noted, "is unnecessary bloodshed and destruction. This is why one waits for a consensus."[91] The officers' broader strategic considerations were reinforced by tactical ones. Busia's budget cuts had led to a shortage of gasoline available for military use, making it more difficult to move a large number of troops to Accra. My impression, however, is that logistical issues were only a minor part of the calculation and that defense of the government was not seriously considered once it was clear that the coup makers had taken the capital.

In fact, not only did the officers in Takoradi assent to the coup, they showed they were willing to defend it against a counter-coup, albeit one which never materialized. After the coup attempt occurred, Colonel Barnor received a phone call informing him, in code, that a counter-coup was being organized by a powerful loyalist retired general, whose troops would travel through Takoradi on their way to the capital.[92] Although these forces never arrived, Barnor reported that he would have defended the newly formed junta against them, even though he was a supporter of multiparty democracy, because he felt it was important to support whoever had control of the capital to avoid a descent into chaos.[93]

Consolidation

After the coup, Acheampong called a meeting of all the officers in Accra in the main auditorium at the headquarters of the armed forces. There he told the assembled officers that he had taken over on behalf of the military as a whole and that they should consider the government as representing them. Furthermore, he announced, anybody who wished to leave the military could do so at that time, without prejudice.[94]

Once again, we see the use of a meeting to shape expectations. Here as well, dissenters were asked to speak up, and when they quite reasonably failed to do so, the assent to the coup of all the officers stationed around the capital became common knowledge. It is likely that Acheampong convened this meeting to demonstrate that the junta had been accepted within the military as the legitimate ruler, since there

---

[91]Interview with Air Vice Marshall (retired) Odaate Barnor. July 24, 2000. Accra, Ghana.

[92]From the beginning, the conspirators were afraid that their coup would face opposition from General Afrifa, a key player in Ghana's first coup, a head of state under the military junta, and now a significant backer of Prime Minister Busia. They expected he would rally troops in the city of Kumasi, part of the Second Infantry Brigade, and march on Accra, much as he had during Ghana's first coup attempt.

[93]Interview with Air Vice Marshall (retired) Odaate Barnor. July 24, 2000. Accra, Ghana.

[94]Interview with General (retired) Laurence Okai. August 9, 2001. Accra, Ghana. Also see Okai, June 16, 2000

were tensions between Acheampong and more-senior military officers, one of whom refused to accept Acheampong's authority right at the start.[95]

Analysis

The success of the 1972 coup attempt was overdetermined and consistent with all three theories. The coup was mounted by a very strong military faction against a government that was unpopular both inside and outside the armed forces. The challengers were also effective at seizing control of the radio station and symbolic targets and using these actions to create self-fulfilling expectations around their success. That the coup succeeded should therefore come as no surprise. Once again, however, of the three theoretical approaches to understanding coups, only the theory of coups as coordination games explains how the coup succeeded.

It is telling that these challengers, so likely to succeed by any measure, closely followed the recipe associated with the coups as coordination games theory. Their adherence to this formula suggests that challengers are still primarily concerned with shaping information and expectations, no matter how much of an advantage they have in military strength and popularity. This theory also explains the alacrity with which the forces in the west of the country flipped sides, supporting the presumed winners to such an extent that they were willing to block potential efforts to restore the democratic incumbent, behavior that cannot be explained by either of the competing theories.

Coups as Battles

Since the challengers had control of the three most powerful battalions in the country, they were clearly militarily stronger than the potential defenders, but they did not wield their power in pursuit of tactical objectives, as the theory of coups as battles would suggest. The primary targets of the coup were the airport, the president's residence, the castle (which housed the prime minister's office), and the radio station. None of these had great tactical value, not even the airport, given that loyalists had no capacity to airlift large numbers of troops.

In addition, neither side tried to use their power to crush their opponents. The challengers did not launch a fierce assault on the areas where government partisans were in control, and government partisans preferred to capitulate rather than resist. The coup attempt was bloodless, even though important officers were divided in their preferences regarding its success.

Coups as Elections

From the perspective of the theory of coups as elections, it is unsurprising that the coup attempt succeeded. The Busia administration had lost a good deal of support, both inside and outside the military, because of the declining economy and the appearance of ethnic bias on the part of the government. Members of the

---

[95]Interview with Colonel (retired) Samuel K. Ofosu-Appiah. August 15, 2001. Accra, Ghana.

military also had institutional grievances concerning budget cuts and a sense that the government did not treat the military with the proper deference and respect. While the government might have been able to survive in a general election, it is unlikely that they could have won a military plebiscite. From this perspective, the end of the Second Republic was only a matter of time.

However, behavior during the coup attempt was not consistent with this theory. Critically, the actions of military players during the coup did not correspond to their individual attitudes toward the government. Although many officers still supported the government, only two (Colonel Donkoh in the north and General Addo in the capital) openly spoke against the coup. Other government supporters, including those in command of units outside the capital, simply acquiesced once Acheampong took over the capital. Thus, Acheampong's success cannot be explained simply by the unpopularity of the administration he overthrew. In addition, although Acheampong did enumerate grievances against the government in his broadcast, he did not use his speech on the radio to appeal for support for the coup attempt. To the contrary, by claiming that the coup had already succeeded, he inhibited sympathetic officers from declaring their support for the coup and finding ways to actively support it.

Coups as Coordination Games

The theory that coups are coordination games is the only approach that explains not only the outcome but the dynamics of the 1972 coup attempt. The success of the coup can be explained in terms of the challengers' success at manipulating expectations so that their victory seemed inevitable. They gained control of the radio station early and never relinquished it, using it to make a fact of the claim that "we in the Ghana Army have once again taken over the administration in Ghana" (Kirk-Greene 1981, 138), even though it falsely implied that the entire army was behind the coup attempt and that the attempt had already succeeded. The broadcast also made use of historical precedent to increase expectations of the coup's success by framing the current coup attempt in terms of the successful overthrow of President Nkrumah in 1966 rather than the failed coup of 1967. Acheampong's emphasis on the similarities between the current attempt and the earlier success is particularly blatant, given that his coup was intended to unravel the political legacy of the previous successful coup, thus underscoring the importance of appearing to have precedent in his favor.[96]

The challengers also supplemented the radio broadcast with the capture of the main symbols of state authority as a further demonstration of their strength and the fact that they were in charge. The next day, they held a meeting of all officers in the capital during which the belief that the coup was unanimously supported in the capital was made common knowledge.

---

[96]Less clear is whether Acheampong's references to the previous successful coup were effective in shaping expectations. The two previous attempts were evenly split between success and failure, so history cast an uncertain shadow. During interviews, respondents did not refer to either previous attempt as helping them decide on a course of action, perhaps because the challengers were so effective at making a fact that this was not necessary.

Outside of the capital, officers acquiesced to the coup as well. In the west, officers believed that it would be hard to organize coordinated opposition to a group that controlled the capital and that defending the government was likely to lead to bloodshed and destruction. The kind of bandwagoning in which even supporters of the incumbent were willing to defend the coup against potential opposition cannot be explained by either the unpopularity of the government or the relative military strength of the challengers.

The challenge was deliberately designed to take place with as little bloodshed as possible, as this theory predicts, and over the course of the coup attempt, there were no casualties or injuries. An important reason why there were no casualties is that pro-government officers did not offer resistance. Only General Addo, the head of the armed forces, stood up against the coup attempt, and he was easily arrested since he had no forces under his direct command. Colonel Osei-Wusu, the commander of the Second Infantry Brigade, chose to delay his response to the coup and gather more information, which gave the coup makers time to arrest him. Colonel Donkoh of the Sixth Infantry Battalion told his men that he did not approve of the coup but would do nothing to organize resistance to it. None of these military actors behaved according to their political preferences, bowing instead to the pressure to coordinate around the presumptive victor.

The dynamics and outcome of this coup attempt were clearly shaped by the resources available to challengers. The particulars of Acheampong's position as an officer in the middle of the hierarchy placed him well to mount a coup attempt. As the commander of the Southern Brigade, his claim to be in charge had considerable credibility, and since Acheampong was in charge of anti-coup operations near the capital, it would be difficult to organize opposition to the coup without him. His actions caught pro-government actors by surprise and allowed the coup makers to rapidly take over the capital.

Yet there were limitations associated with Acheampong's position as well. Because he was a brigade commander, he (much like officers at the top) needed the cooperation of the battalion commanders under him to actually commit troops. In this case, Acheampong did not feel secure about the obedience of the battalion commanders and was unable to hold a meeting to manipulate them, so he needed the majors to help him usurp control over the battalions. Nonetheless, this did not weaken his credibility when he claimed to have taken control, as officers probably assumed the cooperation of his subordinates based on the example of the successful 1966 coup that overthrew Nkrumah.

The majors also benefited somewhat from their position, although less than Acheampong did. They faced some structural impediments, as they had to remove their commanding officers and seize control of their units. Still, they were able to use their considerable power as second-in-command officers both to remove their superiors and to convince their subordinates to cooperate. Agbo, for example, was able to detain his commanding officer and then use his authority to call a meeting of the unit where he made a fact of being in charge.

The presence of these obstacles, even for a challenger with as much hard power as Acheampong had, demonstrates the ways in which soft power is superior to hard power for making a fact. This coup attempt unfolded in a nearly ideal fashion. The challengers were in command of the troops stationed at their primary targets, and thus could seize them without firing a single shot. The ethnic calculus that led the government to rely on Acheampong to coordinate counter-coup activities neatly decapitated local efforts at resistance. The coup succeeded quickly and bloodlessly because of the ease with which the challengers made a fact and others around the country bandwagoned in support. Yet, even in this case, the coup attempt took longer, required more moving parts, and allowed more opportunities for something to go wrong than would a coup from the top with only soft power at its disposal.

Conclusion

As this chapter has shown, conspirators at the middle, like all other challengers, try to shape the beliefs of other members of the military so as to create self-fulfilling expectations behind the success of the coup. To do so, they will try to seize control of broadcasting facilities to publicly claim that the coup is a fait accompli and that resistance will be futile or even dangerous to the fabric of the state. As in the cases presented above, they will also try to support this claim by capturing symbolic locations, thus signaling their strength and making their cause appear the least risky alternative. Recent successful coup attempts will also predispose members of the armed forces to believe that success is likely, thus facilitating bandwagoning behind the coup. Unlike coups from the top, coups from the middle must use force to make a fact. Nonetheless, as both these cases demonstrate, both sides will deliberately try to restrict the opportunities for bloodshed, even at the sacrifice of tactical advantage.

The 1972 coup attempt by Acheampong, Selormey, Baah, and Agbo is a good example of what happens when a coup from the middle is executed well, under favorable conditions. The three majors, taking advantage of the element of surprise, seized control over their units without a hitch, quickly captured the radio station and other symbolic targets, and used a broadcast and a meeting the next day to make a fact. The 1967 coup attempt by Arthur also started out well, with the key targets in the capital similarly captured and a convincing broadcast made by the challengers. Their actions, plus the precedent of a similar successful coup attempt only a year before, meant that even junta members and their close friends initially failed to oppose the coup attempt. Yet, the low rank of the challengers and the fact that Arthur's command was only temporary led in several ways to difficulties in shaping expectations, the challengers' loss of control over public information, and their eventual defeat. Despite their different outcomes, these two cases clearly demonstrate that the process of shaping expectations from the middle of the military hierarchy is more indirect and offers more opportunities for something to go wrong, and therefore why coups from the middle are less likely to succeed than those from the top.

Chapter 6

Coups from the Bottom

A Theory of Coups from the Bottom

The final category is coups from the bottom of the military hierarchy, which encompasses coup attempts organized by enlisted men, non-commissioned officers, or very junior officers. These can be considered mutinies with objectives that go beyond better pay and working conditions to explicitly aim at overthrowing the government. This type of coup attempt is the least likely to succeed, as the challengers are substantially hampered by their low position: they have neither the hard power of colonels nor the soft power of generals, yet they face the greatest obstacles to their success. Unsurprisingly, only 32% of coup attempts from the bottom are successful, in comparison to 68% of those from the top and 48% of those from the middle.

This chapter explains how challengers from the bottom can effectively build expectations favorable to their success, as well as how a coup from the bottom can be foiled. These dynamics are then demonstrated by three examples of coups from the bottom in Ghana, one of which failed and two of which succeeded. The cases form an interesting pseudo-experiment with a large number of relevant background factors held constant and outcomes varying systematically according to the belief in the viability of the attempt and the effectiveness of the coup makers at controlling public information. As in the earlier two types of coups, the outcomes of these three cases were clearly driven by information and expectations, not grievances or initial tactical strength.

Conspiracy

Prospective mutineers are handicapped at each step of their attempt to seize power, starting with their limited ability to conspire. Open discussion of politics in the mess hall or barracks is against the norms of most militaries, and it is not possible for large numbers of soldiers or junior officers to meet for explicitly political purposes without attracting attention. To get around such prohibitions, men will sound each other out privately, in small groups, or during social events such as birthdays, weddings, or christenings where peers might legitimately gather.

Because coups from the bottom often claim legitimacy from mass discontent with the status quo, mutinies are often explained using the metaphor of elections. Such explanations, however, give too much importance to the nature and intensity of the grievances motivating the mutiny and too little to the collective action dynamics involved. Widespread unhappiness with the government is not a sufficient condition for a coup from the bottom to succeed. Even when a majority of soldiers would wish to see the government overthrown, those soldiers will be unwilling to join a mutiny unless they believe that many others will also do so and the coup will therefore succeed.

Civilians will generally play a smaller role in the organization of coups from the bottom than other kinds of coup attempts. The grievances at the heart of a coup from the bottom often have as much to do with military politics as civilian politics, and the mutiny may be framed as a response to a morally bankrupt civilian order. This gap between the civilian and military world can be bridged under special circumstances, such as if a coup plot is embedded in a larger revolutionary conspiracy (especially a Marxist one) uniting both sides under a common ideology. Other times, a civilian revolution either inspires a mutiny or is inspired by one, in which case there will be linkages between leaders but no direct civilian involvement in the mutiny. In this way, mutinies formed an important part of both the February Revolution in Russia 1917 and the Iranian Revolution of 1979. Lastly, civilians who are ex-military officers sometimes return to lead coups that involve their former peers.

Execution

On a tactical level, a mutiny resembles a coup from the middle more than a coup from the top, because mutineers have some hard power but almost no soft power. They have some hard power because soldiers, NCOs, and junior officers are the ones who actually transport troops, fire guns, and maneuver tanks during an assault. The ability of mutineers to wield military force, however, will always be weaker than that of coup makers in the middle. Although lieutenants can command platoons (25-50 men) and captains can command companies (roughly 75-200 men), these are integrated into larger structures rather than being autonomous units that can function independently. As a result, challengers may lack access to transport, be unable to unlock armories, and have a hard time deploying specialized weaponry.

Even when the challengers are able to get the weapons and the transport they need, ad hoc groupings of enlisted men are likely to be weaker than a similarly sized and armed but more hierarchically organized unit. The strength of an armed group is not in the quantity of men or materiel deployed but in the coordinated action of military members. Therefore, the more disorganized the mutiny, the weaker it will be militarily, because it will lack the force multiplier associated with synchronized and practiced action (Biddle 2004, chap. 3).

At the same time, mutineers are entirely unable to use the softer gambits used by challengers from the top: they cannot gather information from military intelligence files, use bureaucratic prerogatives to lay the groundwork for a coup attempt, or call for meetings of the constituencies whose expectations they are trying to mold. Unlike generals, sergeants have little initial credibility, a proclamation made by a bunch of NCOs will not be sufficient in and of itself to make a coup, nor can they order large troop movements or issue ultimatums.[1]

Another obstacle is that mutinies are likely to face active and powerful opposition, because they threaten all those higher in rank. Since the process of mutinying involves a rejection (usually a violent one) of hierarchical obedience, a successful mutiny is a revolutionary act that inverts the rank structure of an organization in which every aspect of life is dominated by hierarchy. For this reason, all officers of higher rank have a strong incentive to resist a mutiny, including using relatively harsh measures to combat such a fundamental challenge to both their privileges and the organizational integrity of the armed forces. If a mutiny goes unchallenged, it is not because the rest of the officer corps is indifferent but because they believe the coup attempt will succeed and they do not want to get in the way.

Typically, a mutiny will be the bloodiest and most chaotic type of coup attempt. Since these challengers are the most likely to be opposed, it is far less likely that a coup attempt from the bottom will occur without a single shot being fired. When force is used, the danger of actual bloodshed is higher than during other kinds of attempts, and ad hoc groupings may not have the precision necessary to use force in a surgical fashion. In addition, because officers are skeptical of the ability of mutineers to organize tactical strength, challengers have to demonstrate their ability to wield armed force in order to establish their credibility. Mutineers also will use more force than other coup makers, because a mutiny, more than any other kind of coup attempt, involves a rending of the fabric of military life, a thoroughgoing rejection of hierarchical command. As in a revolution, symbolic violence against emblems of authority, like officers, can be part of the process of demonstrating that the old order has ended. Because all of these reasons are more true for coups that involve primarily enlisted men, such mutinies will be bloodier than those led by junior officers.

Also, the risk of bloodshed is higher during a mutiny than during other types of coups because the weakness of the challengers leads them to engage in brinksmanship, deliberately increasing the risk of chaos to force the government to capitulate. Although the objective is still not to slaughter the other side, and in fact both sides take pains to avoid bloodshed, during such a clash, more force is used, guns are pointed more directly at opponents, and bullets fly closer to their targets.[2]

---

[1]There are two exceptions to this overall scenario: when uniformed personnel of nominally low rank hold top positions in the military or government, for example in a post-mutiny junta or a revolutionary government. However, these are not real exceptions, because a coup in either scenario would really be a coup from the top. It is the organizational position of the coup makers that is relevant, not the rank they hold. Since the military is a hierarchical organization, rank and functional position rarely diverge so greatly, so these are quite rare counter-examples.

[2]Where the mutiny becomes part of a popular revolution, as in Bolivia in 1946, the death toll can be very high, because the inter-military restraint is gone and because civilians are directly involved. The overthrow of President Villaroel and the capture of the rest of the country may have led to a thousand deaths, largely civilian.

The tactics involved in a successful mutiny usually take more time than coups at other levels. Coups led by low-ranking members of the military involve many more actors, making choices in situations with very high confusion and risk. It can take a while for the coup to spread, for soldiers to come off the fence, for higher-ranking officers to be convinced not to resist. Sergeants usually cannot take over the country in a couple of hours the way generals can.

Targets

To succeed, a mutiny needs to make facts at multiple levels, as they must convince both their peers and their superiors to bandwagon in favor of the coup. As in all coup attempts, control over the broadcasting facilities is vital. But, in addition to the symbolic political targets favored by coups from the middle, coups from the bottom need to visibly signal their strength within military barracks, to convince those enlisted men who may not be aware of what is happening at other sites. This they do by capturing symbols of military authority as well as of civil authority.

This process of making facts must also be repeated on a smaller scale within units. For instance, mutinous soldiers try to convince individual companies to join the coup by telling them that the other companies in the battalion have already switched allegiance. If the challengers succeed at manipulating expectations such that the mutiny spreads within the military, officers who are assigned to suppress it will find their soldiers shirking their duties, openly refusing to follow orders, or even turning against them. Just as generals cannot assume unconditional obedience by mid-level officers during a coup attempt, mid-level officers opposing a coup have no guarantee that enlisted men and junior officers will follow their commands, although the structure and culture of the military makes obedience at this level much more likely.

In addition to directly manipulating expectations by trying to control public information, challengers also use strategies that engage the risk aversion of military players. Mutineers want to convince the defenders of the status quo that if they do not stop resisting the coup attempt they will be swept away by an unstoppable torrent of rage coming from the oppressed and exploited at the bottom of the military, endangering not only their own safety but also the integrity of the institution.

How the Coup Succeeds

For mutineers, the optimal scenario is one in which the uprising spreads like wildfire through the military, resembling a cross between a coup from the middle and a popular revolution. As in other coups, it is vital that the challengers both capture and hold the broadcasting facilities so as to persuade both enlisted men and officers that everybody believes (and meta-believes) that the mutiny is unstoppable and resistance is futile. It is particularly difficult for challengers from the bottom to shape expectations, because each soldier knows that if the insurrection is to stand a chance, a large number of others, not just a few powerful actors, will have to join, and thus he will hesitate unless convinced there truly is a bandwagon under way in support of the coup. In this way, the challenges of collective action in a coup from the bottom add powerfully to the inertia against it.

As a result, a mutiny will initially be more credible if the original number of conspirators is large, if it involves a high percentage of low-level officers, or both, as these factors make it easier to seize targets and demonstrate the viability of the coup. Unless regime loyalists abandon their posts early in the attempt and the mutiny triumphs quickly (which is unlikely), a successful mutiny will have to spread across the armed forces, weakening regime loyalists in the process. Soldiers in units led by loyalist officers may undermine efforts to stop the uprising by shirking their duties, engaging in sabotage, and turning against their officers when mutineers appear at the gates. As the mutiny gains steam and appears more likely to succeed, soldiers may even rise against their officers spontaneously and declare their unit in support of the coup.

By the end of a successful attempt, loyalists will be restricted to small pockets of the military, trying to fight on while the enlisted men under them slip away. At some point, they will decide that they do not want to continue to support a doomed regime, given the possible risk of civil war, and will either surrender or take off their uniforms and walk away from their posts.

How the Coup Fails

Most coups from the bottom fail because of the inherent challenges of making a fact with such limited resources. Even more than coups from the middle, the process of making a coup from the bottom involves many small steps, each of which involves a reasonably high degree of risk. For example, the leaders of the mutiny must try to rally hesitant enlisted men in person by leading from the front, which creates many opportunities for them to be shot or captured.

As with a coup from the middle, it is easiest to stop a mutiny in its most embryonic form, before the mutineers have been able to make a broadcast and get their message out. The initial conspiracy is likely to involve a relatively small number of soldiers so as to avoid detection. Even if the core group is in fact larger, they will be ill-equipped, lacking both transport and arms, as a consequence of the tactical limitations inherent in their rank. They will be far weaker than a similarly sized conventional unit, or even than regular police units who may arrive to investigate.

Although the mutiny will get stronger after its initial broadcast, it can still be easily blocked at this point. The broadcast makes victory possible for the mutineers but, as with a coup from the middle, is not always sufficient for success. Except for the rare coup attempt that starts with a large initial conspiracy, most coup attempts will gain strength only once their message spreads, and units may hesitate even after a broadcast is made, afraid the coup attempt will not succeed and unwilling to cast their lot with a doomed cause. While this is true for all coup attempts, it is especially true for mutinies because of the extent to which each actor is individually weak and therefore exposed to risk. Like a revolution, each coup attempt from the bottom requires the support of many participants to succeed, and therefore the uncertainty for each actor about whether a sufficient number of others will join in is quite great. Both of these issues are easier for coup makers to address in small militaries, which may be why mutinies are more common there.

The fact that enlisted men will hesitate before joining a mutiny, out of concern with its viability, creates additional opportunities for loyalists to foil the coup. As with coups at all levels, if opponents can contest public information and symbolic targets, especially if they can deny the challengers access to public information, they can reverse the momentum of the coup attempt.

This concern about the viability of a mutiny is a real obstacle for challengers. Sometimes challengers from the bottom will choose to hide their rank in the hope they will be mistaken for a higher-ranking opposition faction. For example, when Muammar Gaddafi (then only a junior officer) overthrew King Idriss of Libya, he announced the coup attempt in the name of the entire armed forces, keeping his identity secret until after the coup had succeeded.[3] This is a dangerous game, however, and can backfire if the identity of the challengers is disclosed, as Lieutenant Arthur discovered in Ghana. It is also one that can be played by low-ranking officers but not by enlisted men, since they cannot plausibly mimic a coup from the middle.

Although it becomes harder to stop a mutiny as time passes, foiling the coup remains possible as long as the loyalists retain some control of public information and can contest the claims made by the challengers. The key is to make sure that the mutiny does not spread geographically, surrounding disloyal units with loyal ones, and to then make sure there are not spontaneous outbreaks in other areas by credibly and repeatedly telling the rank and file that the mutiny is contained and has little chance of success. Sometimes the government will defuse the situation by offering the mutineers a chance to surrender without punishment, which can take the air out of the current challenge but risks future conspiracies by setting an adverse precedent and allowing mutinous members to remain in the armed forces.

All the various difficulties inherent in successfully mounting a coup from the bottom mean that mutinies may fail even when the incumbent is intensely disliked and the conspirators are reasonably strong. In November 1960, over 100 leftist junior officers in the Guatemalan armed forces attempted a coup after they had not been paid for two months. There was widespread sympathy for their socialist and nationalist goals, and younger officers felt that the older ones were corrupt and had sold out (Schirmer 1998, 15). However, even though roughly 40% of the officer corps was involved in this uprising, the coup did not succeed. They did not establish a presence in the capital or dominate the airwaves, and President Ydigoras responded by declaring martial law and stating that he would not negotiate with the Marxist rebels. Loyalist troops counter-attacked and the coup attempt failed.

---

[3]In fact, the Libyan crown prince offered the regime's surrender without knowing to whom he was surrendering (Simons 1996, 160–161). It is very possible that both the prince and other officers within the military confused Gaddafi's challenge with an anticipated coup attempt by two powerful colonels.

While the mutiny might have been able to win a referendum against the president, it could not successfully organize a mutiny without making a fact.[4]

Ghana, May 1979

The failed coup attempt of May 15, 1979, was the first of Ghana's several coups to come from the bottom of the military hierarchy. The seven years of military rule that had followed the 1972 coup discussed in the previous chapter had impoverished the country and generated substantial discontent among the rank and file of the armed forces. Ordinary soldiers saw their fortunes sinking along with those of the most of the country, while higher-ranking officers and well-connected civilians raided the state's coffers with seeming impunity. Although the 1978 coup from the top discussed in chapter 4 had promised change, those at the bottom of the hierarchy felt that the situation within the military had not gotten any better.

Despite high levels of grievance and intrigue within the military, the May 15 coup attempt still failed to attract support, even from soldiers who were eager to see the government overthrown. This coup attempt illuminates two different aspects of coups from the bottom: the difficulties inherent in trying to successfully mount a mutiny and the importance of shaping beliefs and expectations even when the incumbent is highly unpopular and there would appear to be a strong demand for a coup.

Background

The target of the coup attempt was the Supreme Military Council II (SMCII) military junta, Ghana's third consecutive military government since the end of democratic rule in 1972. As discussed in chapter 4, the SMCII had come to power a little less than a year earlier, capitalizing on the feeling within the officer corps that military rule had been corrosive to the institution. After displacing General Acheampong from power, however, the SMCII blamed his "incompetent advisors" for what had gone wrong and made no move to criticize the previous government or even distance themselves from its policies (Petchenkine 1993, 78). Although they had originally promised to transfer power to a constitutional government within a year, they soon backtracked and proposed a four-year transition during which parties would remain banned and the military would play a major role. The pro-democracy movement, already mobilized and activated during the previous military government, resumed pressure for genuine multi-party democracy (79). Despite

---

[4]Although most of the junior officers were captured, several escaped, including two who used their training in counter-insurgency and jungle warfare (courtesy of the U.S. government) to build leftist rebels into the guerilla force at the heart of the Guatemalan civil war. President Ydigoras continued to be so strongly disliked within the military that these rebel officers maintained their connections with their cohort for years, showing up at promotion parties, and even buying arms from military sources who hoped the guerillas could force the downfall of the president (Schirmer 1998, 16).

using harsh measures to suppress democratic activists, the junta was unable to crush the movement. After a series of half steps, the SMCII announced that it would hand over power to an elected multi-party democracy by July 1979. On New Year's Day 1979, the ban on political parties was lifted and twenty-nine political parties were formed, six of which survived to campaign in the spring as Ghana prepared to hold its first democratic elections in a decade (82, 85).

A continuing area of contention between civilian groups and the government concerned the junta's unwillingness to investigate or punish members of past military governments for corruption. The government was finally forced to change course after successive disclosures that former president General Acheampong had stolen large sums of public money, and in May Acheampong was stripped of his rank, honors, and pension and confined to his home village (Okeke 1982, 31). To most Ghanaians, however, this administrative punishment was paltry compared to the long list of misdeeds of which the former president was accused, and no other members of any prior military government were investigated, even though it was clear that the ex-president had not acted alone (Oquaye 1980, 124-125).

The government was also unpopular because it had inherited an economy that was in extremely bad shape. Inflation had climbed to the record high figure of 116% in the year before the junta took power and remained quite high afterwards (Frimpong-Ansah 1991, 169). The currency was significantly overvalued, economic growth was negative, and the government had very little revenue. Most consumer goods were imported and in short supply, largely impossible to obtain outside the black market.

Not only was the economy collapsing; it was doing so at a time when Ghana's main commodity exports—cocoa, gold, and timber—were fetching record-high prices on the global market. To the average citizen, this appeared to be clear evidence of corruption and malfeasance at the very top, although it would be more accurate to say that bad policy both damaged the economy directly and engendered corruption that made the situation worse. Ghana had historically required that all domestic cocoa production be sold to the government, but after decades of offering farmers substantially less than market prices for their output, cocoa production declined and much of the remainder was smuggled into neighboring countries, where it fetched higher prices. Government revenue from cocoa declined by up to 30%; gold and diamonds were smuggled out as well (Rimmer 1992, 146).

Because citizens thought corruption was the cause of the economic slowdown, government austerity measures proved wildly unpopular. Unable to obtain outside assistance, the government devalued the currency by 58% in the summer of 1978 (Rimmer 1992, 166). The price of basic necessities shot up, and columnists asked whether Ghanaians were expected to use corn cobs to wipe their behinds instead of the expensive and impossible-to-obtain imported toilet paper (Okeke 1982, 27). Unions took to the street after the government imposed a wage freeze and levied new taxes. In November, when strike activity was at its most intense, 30,000 Ghanaians were on strike, including utility workers, who turned off the electricity, and civil servants, who brought the bureaucracy to a standstill (Petchenkine 1993, 81).

As it had with the democracy movement, the junta first tried and failed to crush the unions by force. They declared a state of emergency on November 6, 1978, allowing anybody to be detained without charge or trial and declaring strikes illegal. When this failed to solve the problem, the junta was forced to the negotiating table. It abandoned many austerity measures and canceled the state of emergency after two months, bringing an end to the general strike (Petchenkine 1993, 81-2). Industrial unrest continued after this point, albeit on a smaller scale. For example, in May, nurses protested that their daily salary was just enough to buy a tin of sardines, and not even enough to buy a bar of soap (Okeke 1982, 25).

It was not just civilians who were upset with the government; soldiers were seething with discontent as well. After years of military government, their working and living conditions were quite poor. They were not paid on time, their housing was dilapidated, their uniforms were "grossly inadequate," and their food was of very poor quality.[5]

These indignities were made worse by the situation of the officer corps, some of whom had grown wealthy from revenues gained outside the military. Soldiers believed that such officers were wealthy because they had stolen from enlisted men, that their own food was poor because officers had siphoned off their rations for sale on the black market, and that they were paid late because their pay packets were being "borrowed" or stolen outright. They accused officers of using soldiers as free labor in private business ventures, thus exploiting their men for private gain.[6] As a result, those in the bottom tier of the military were even more keen than civilians to see an official investigation into military corruption. They also did not want officers who had held official positions at parastatals or within the military government to be allowed to return to active duty without returning any ill-gotten gains.

Soldiers were also unhappy about the way they were treated by civilians. While enlisted men faced many of the same problems as working-class Ghanaians, most of the population saw them as beneficiaries of military power and thus treated them with scorn and derision. Soldiers, on the other hand, saw civilians as the beneficiaries of government corruption and themselves as the victims of it. One widespread but likely apocryphal story demonstrates the helplessness and rage felt by enlisted men. A soldier went to the market, wearing his uniform so he could insist on paying the official price for his purchase rather than the higher black market price. Instead of complying, however, the woman running the stall squatted, urinated in a cup, and dowsed the soldier in urine.[7]

By May, the junta had lost legitimacy among civilians and was resented by the military rank and file. That said, nobody anticipated a coup attempt. With the first round of elections in a decade scheduled for June, there was no appetite among civilians for anything that might derail the scheduled transition from military rule. Senior members of the military did not believe a challenge was likely,

---

[5]The depiction of uniforms as grossly inadequate is a quote from an official report (Hutchful 1998, 222).

[6]Interview with Corporal (retired) Peter Tasiri. August 10, 2001. Accra, Ghana.

[7]Interview with Corporal (retired) Adam Al-Hassan. August 17, 2001. Accra, Ghana.

either. Officers were generally happier with the junta than were enlisted men and so were largely focused on managing the upcoming transition. Although officers knew that conditions for enlisted men were bad, they did not understand how deep the resentment held by soldiers was. As a result, everybody was surprised when Ghana's first attempted mutiny began.[8]

Conspiracy

In 1979, according to one scholar, "the armed forces were pregnant with dissent" and military intelligence was having trouble containing all potential challengers (Hutchful 1998, 223). Although multiple conspiracies were being hatched, the conspiracy that acted first was small and poorly organized, led by a young air force officer, Flight-Lieutenant Jerry John Rawlings. Unusually for an officer, even one of junior rank, Rawlings frequently fraternized with enlisted men and was genuinely popular among them. Chatting with soldiers about their lives, Rawlings would gradually introduce political topics, such as military corruption and its impact on the country, then move from general dissatisfaction with the state of the military and the country to an argument that something needed to change. Ideology was not Rawlings's strong suit, but that made his argument more appealing to his audience.

Rawlings was able to recruit a small number of enlisted men who met with him at a cassava farm on the outskirts of the air force station in the capital. Rawlings assured them they were just part of a larger group and that he was connected to others in the army who felt the same way. The conspirators' original plan was to gain control of a jet fighter, which Rawlings would then pilot, but they were unable to get the cooperation of the soldiers in charge of arming the jets and were unsure about how next to proceed.[9] Nonetheless, they decided to strike anyway, confident that they would soon be joined by large numbers of unhappy enlisted men.

Attack

The coup began on the night of May 14, 1979. At 8 PM, Rawlings met with four other conspirators in a plantain grove near the air force station. The challenge for Rawlings was to mount a coup attempt with no forces under his command and very few enlisted men in his conspiracy. The challengers improvised around two objectives: obtaining firepower and convincing others to join their cause. As we shall see, they did well at the first task, given their constraints, but poorly at the second. The mutiny attracted at best a handful of voluntary recruits over the course of the coup attempt. In fact, not even soldiers who were eager to see a mutiny supported Rawlings, and many responded with intransigence and disruption. As a result, the mutiny was easily put down by loyalist forces from the armored unit.

---

[8]Interview with Brigadier (retired) Joseph Nunoo-Mensah. July 25, 2000. Accra, Ghana.

[9]Interview with Lance Corporal (retired) Ali Yemoh. August 17, 2001. Accra, Ghana.

Since guns and ammunition were tightly controlled, the conspirators were entirely unarmed at the start of the mutiny. The first step of their plan, therefore, was to use guile, theft, and coercion to obtain weapons and armored cars. This was a laborious process that took all night. First, they stole two boxes of ammunition, then waited until 2 a.m. for a senior guard at the air force armory to fall asleep, after which sympathetic guards were able to steal ten rifles and ten submachine guns for them (Okeke 1982, 128). After this, they stole a car (because they lacked any form of transport of their own) and, after some elaborate trickery, were able to commandeer two armored cars and their crews (129), even though the men operating the armored cars were not willing participants and had to be directed at gunpoint.

Next, the mutineers attempted to take control of the armored regiment. Rawlings knew many members of this unit and likely believed they would be sympathetic to his cause.[10] Success at this step would have brought all of the armored cars in the military into the mutiny, making them a formidable force. Members of the armored unit were not eager to join the mutiny, however. When Rawlings arrived in an armored car and told a member of the regiment to sound the alarm so all soldiers would assemble, presumably so he could address them as a group, the soldier claimed that the siren was broken. Rawlings then sent his right-hand man, Newton Gatsiko, back to the air force station to retrieve the siren there.

While Rawlings was able to obtain a siren, he did not get a chance to sound it because he was interrupted by the unit commander, Major Abubakar Sulemana. Major Sulemana had driven to the unit in his personal car, dressed only in a pair of shorts and a sleeveless t-shirt, to find out why the official duty vehicle that Rawlings had seized earlier in the night had not arrived at his house. Although Sulemana had no idea that a mutiny was under way, he noticed that an armored car was not at its assigned location and was beginning to ask the driver why when Rawlings (hitherto unnoticed) suddenly interjected himself into the interrogation from the armored car, grandly informing Major Sulemana that he had taken control of the unit and was placing him under arrest. Major Sulemana responded by quickly driving away. To his surprise, Rawlings, whom he considered a friend, opened fire at his escaping vehicle.[11]

Sulemana drove back to his house to retrieve a side arm, with Rawlings in pursuit. The major beat a hasty retreat by diving out a window at the back of his house, spraining his ankle, then climbed over a fence into a neighboring farm. As he did, he heard the sound of gunfire, although the gunner had intentionally fired high and over the house to avoid casualties. Sulemana limped back to his unit, where he organized a counterattack. To distract the mutineers and buy Sulemana time

---

[10]Under the normal course of events, it would be unusual for an air force officer to know enlisted men in the armored regiment. Rawlings got to know members of this unit because he was an avid horseback rider and the armored regiment had stables, having evolved from the mounted cavalry. Since the Ghanaian army never had a functioning cavalry, the stables were purely a matter of military tradition (Aboagye 1999, 180).

[11]Even after Sulemana had been forced into exile for decades by Rawlings, Sulemana defended Rawlings, explaining his behavior as the result of manipulation by others. Interview with Major (retired) Abubakar Sulemana. August 18, 2001. Accra, Ghana

enough to sneak into his office and get the keys to the unit's armory, one of the unit's officers took an armored car from the garage and drove it through a gate, which scared the mutineers into retreating to the air force station, which was now under their control.

Response

Seizing the initiative, Sulemana sounded the unit's alarm (which appears to have been working after all) to assemble his men, distributing arms and ammunition so they could defend the unit from further attack. He left his subordinates in charge while he returned home to quickly bathe and put on his uniform. As he was about to return, the mutineers attacked the unit but were repulsed. Gunfire was exchanged and a few rebels captured. Sulemana informed the army commander over the telephone that he was not going to wait for a third attack by Rawlings but was moving on the air force station. He organized his men into two troops, supported by four armored cars, and sent his captains to secure the rebels' location.

Over the course of the mutiny, the rebels had captured a number of serving and retired officers and now had at least ten officers held hostage (along with an unknown number of women and children from their families) at the air force base.[12] While the hostage taking had started accidentally, it now provided the mutineers with protection.[13] Rawlings invited the hostages into the courtyard and gave the commander of the air force station a seat atop one of the armored cars, showing him respect but also making him very visible. When Rawlings was asked what he hoped to achieve by his actions, he held forth on the causes of the country's decline, criticizing the actions of the military government and complaining that foreigners (by which he meant Lebanese, Syrian, and Indian residents of Ghana) were stealing the country's wealth.[14]

While Rawlings was lecturing his hostages, forces from the armored regiment arrived and surrounded the air force base. There was a brief clash between the two sides, and then matters were calm until Major Sulemana arrived. The major, still hoping that his friendship with Rawlings would allow him to resolve the incident peacefully, approached the mutineers on foot, using a walking stick and accompanied by only two officers. He informed Rawlings that he was under arrest and that it was up to him whether he came along dead or alive.[15] One of the hostages, a retired officer who had been involved in the very first coup in the country, advised

---

[12] This section is based upon the accounts given by the prosecutor at Rawlings's trial, three of the hostages, and Sulemana. Although I have interviewed Rawlings, our interview did not cover the events described below.

[13] The first hostages were taken by Gatsiko when he went back to the Air Force station to get the siren; later hostages were officers who had come by to investigate when they heard shooting, or officers and former officers whom Gatsiko had stopped at a checkpoint as they drove by. The prosecutor's account lists ten hostages, but there were women and children present as well, since sometimes an entire family was stopped together.

[14] Interview with Colonel (retired) Harry Lawrence Ofosu-Appiah. August 13, 2001. Accra, Ghana.

[15] Interview with Major (retired) Abubakar Sulemana. August 18, 2001. Accra, Ghana.

Rawlings that if he surrendered, he might live to fight another day.[16] Rawlings agreed to surrender peacefully, and his men put down their arms.

Analysis

As these events demonstrate, the theory that coups are like elections does a poor job of predicting both the outcome and the dynamics of the May 1979 coup attempt. If preferences are the most important factor, then Rawlings should have attracted a large number of enlisted men to his cause and succeeded handily. Instead, nobody joined the original conspirators, and the attempt was defeated easily. The theory that coup attempts are like battles, on the other hand, correctly predicts the outcome of the coup attempt but not the events that occurred during it. That weak conspirators failed should be no surprise, but the theory would have expected them to be ruthless in their use of force.

Only the theory of coups as coordination games correctly explains both the outcome and the dynamics of this coup attempt. That Rawlings failed is unsurprising by this theory, given that this was a coup from the bottom, there had been no prior similar attempts in the country, and Rawlings never captured the radio station or any other instrument of public information to make a broadcast. It also explains the challengers' unwillingness to cause substantial casualties, even though this cost them significant tactical advantage.

Coups as Battles

The failure of this coup is consistent with the theory of coups as battles in that the mutineers were at all times weaker than government forces. Rawlings began with just five unarmed men, but even with two armored cars under his control he was still vastly outmatched by the armored regiment. The theory also correctly predicts that the mutineers would restrict their activities to strictly military targets, although, as I later argue, this actually contributed to their defeat.

However, the theory falls short in explaining the conduct of the mutineers during the coup, since they did not ruthlessly crush potential sources of resistance. The armored unit was their main rival, as it possessed the only other armored cars in the capital, and Rawlings caught them entirely unprepared. In a war, a weaker force catching a stronger adversary by surprise would have used the moment to even up the odds. From a tactical standpoint, the rebels also should have unleashed a torrent of gunshots as they withdrew, crippling their opponents.

But instead of a series of pitched battles as the theory would predict, there were just three occasions on which gunshots were fired. The first was when Rawlings pursued Major Sulemana in an armored car, resulting only in a sprained ankle as the major dove to get away. The second was the brief encounter between pro-coup soldiers and soldiers of the armored unit, which also does not seem to have resulted in any casualties. The third was the clash between coup makers and the

---

[16]Interview with Colonel (retired) Victor Coker-Appiah. August 3, 2001. Accra, Ghana.

armored unit soldiers outside the air force base just before Major Sulemana arrived to negotiate a peaceful surrender. None of these is consistent with what would happen, for example, during a foreign invasion.

Coups as Elections

If coup attempts are like elections, then the May 15 coup attempt should have succeeded. While the junta had support among senior and middle-ranking officers (who were definitely against a mutiny), there was a great wellspring of antipathy toward the government among the enlisted men. Had soldiers acted based solely on their preferences, the mutiny would have picked up a large number of recruits easily. Yet the conspiracy picked up no new members other than the soldiers in the armored cars who were conscripted at gunpoint. Even members of other conspiracies, men extremely eager to see the government overthrown, failed to join.[17]

There is ambiguity on one point: since Rawlings was interrupted before he could make a public broadcast (his planned address to the armored regiment), we do not know whether he would have used the opportunity to try to appeal for support.

Coups as Coordination Games

If one understands coup attempts as coordination games, then it is unsurprising that Rawlings's coup attempt failed. With no history of prior successful mutinies in Ghana, initial expectations within the military were stacked against the rebels. Once the coup was under way, the challengers failed to change these expectations by making a public broadcast or capturing symbolic targets. As a result, the mutiny did not attract new members, not even among men who were actively plotting to overthrow the incumbent.[18]

The failure of the mutiny to grow surprised the rebels, who had believed that the enlisted men constituted a dry tinderbox of resentment that would go up in flames with just a small spark (Okeke 1982, 39). However, enlisted men thought the mutiny would fail, believed that other enlisted men felt the same way, and acted accordingly. Instead of being greeted eagerly by the rank and file, the mutineers encountered obstructionism. They had to use coercion to gain control of their two armored cars and to direct the soldiers inside at gunpoint. Similarly, upon arrival at the armored regiment, Rawlings was told, apparently falsely, that the unit's alarm was broken. The unwillingness of soldiers to join, based on their skepticism that the mutiny could succeed, was a rational response to the coup attempt from the bottom. The penalty for supporting a failed mutiny would be high, and each soldier felt that the coup could succeed only if it had widespread participation, something that did not appear to be forthcoming.

Also consistent with the theory, actors on both sides acted to reduce bloodshed, even if this created a tactical disadvantage. The rebels' decision not to open fire at

---

[17]Interview with Corporal (retired) Peter Tasiri. August 10, 2001. Accra, Ghana.

[18]Interview with Corporal (retired) Peter Tasiri. August 10, 2001. Accra, Ghana.

the armored regiment, either upon entry or when exiting, was costly. If they had killed the unit's officers, loyalists would have had a hard time organizing a response to the mutiny. Even when shots were fired, such as at Major Sulemana's house, the gunner intentionally shot high, over the roof of the house.[19] On the loyalist side, Major Sulemana arrived to negotiate at the air base unarmed and on foot, exposing himself to harm in order to de-escalate tensions. The mutineers responded by surrendering rather than fighting to the last man, even though they knew they might be executed.

The dynamics and outcome of the coup attempt were clearly shaped by the fact that it was a mutiny. Unlike during a coup from the middle, the conspirators faced serious logistical difficulties. They had to steal and coerce to get the bare minimum of guns, ammunition, and transportation to start their coup, which caused delay and created numerous points at which their challenge might have been stopped, even purely by chance.

We also see the impact of rank on the dynamics of this coup attempt in terms of the increased threat of violence during the mutiny. Even with deliberate efforts to reduce bloodshed, this was the most violent coup attempt since 1967. Shots were fired at a house on base, women and children were held hostage, and it appears that one mutineer died in the final brief clash at the air force base just before the mutineers surrendered.[20] Because of their weakness, the rebels used tactics that were riskier and exposed more people to the chance of injury or death.

Ghana, June 1979

The second coup from the bottom in Ghana occurred less than a month later. The June 4 coup attempt occurred in much the same context as the one on May 15. The country had experienced no large-scale changes during the intervening three weeks, and campaigning for the multi-party elections had proceeded without problems. Overall, the junta believed that things were moving quite smoothly toward the impending democratic transition.

The trial of the May 15 mutineers had begun and was being held openly, according to standard military procedure. Although such rules had not been followed for most of Acheampong's time in office, there was now a movement within the military to behave in a manner that was more professional, transparent, and accountable.[21] Unexpectedly, the public prosecutor, Mr. G. E. K. Aikins, used his opening remarks to criticize current and past military rule in Ghana. In the process, he painted Rawlings in a flattering light, describing him as an idealist motivated by

---

[19]Interview with Major (retired) Abubakar Sulemana. August 18, 2001. Accra, Ghana.

[20]Kojo Yankah identifies the dead soldier as Leading Aircraftman Osei-Tutu (Yankah 1986, 22). That one mutineer died and one was injured was established by the prosecutor in the trial that followed, but there is no information about how this happened. In fact, two of the hostages claimed that there was no shooting at the base at all, while a third confirms that it happened but claims that it was very brief.

[21]Interview with General (retired) Edwin Sam. June 28, 2000. Accra, Ghana.

nationalism and a concern for the poor, thereby attracting public interest.[22] Before it was interrupted by the June 4 mutiny, the trial went three days. It was front-page news, even though the newspapers were state-owned, and news coverage was uniformly positive toward the coup leaders. With each day, the enlisted men in the gallery grew increasingly vocal in their support for Rawlings, which is ironic in light of how little support he had attracted during his coup attempt. Rawlings now emerged as a positive figure without ever having to say a word. Thus, the critical factor that changed in this brief period was the informational context: enlisted personnel learned how much support there was for a coup, and this knowledge became public, allowing for coordination.

Conspiracy

The June 4 mutiny was the outgrowth of two different groups' clandestine efforts to overthrow the military junta. The better-organized faction was a revolutionary leftist group called the Free Africa Movement or the Young Officer's Club. It had been started by Captain Kojo Boakye-Djan in the early 1970s with the long-term goal of taking power in 1984. Its members were primarily young officers from Boakye-Djan's cohort (Hutchful 1998, 223). It met and recruited members using discussion groups on current affairs as a cover. The group also had a civilian counterpart named the Movement on National Affairs, or MONAS. Their strategy was to inculcate recruits with revolutionary ideology, then, once their members held key positions of power within the military, to make their move much like Portugal's Carnation Revolution.

Boakye-Djan was a close personal friend of Rawlings. The two had been friends since high school, when they attended the nation's most elite boarding school, and Boakye-Djan had been the best man at Rawlings's wedding. Rawlings was far more impatient than Boakye-Djan, however, and had been unwilling to subsume his political ambitions, so he struck first.[23]

The other relevant of plotters group was organized by Corporal Peter Tasiri and was composed entirely of enlisted personnel. This group also drew from its training cohort, in this case an unusually large group of 1,200 enlisted men who had been recruited between 1974 and 1975.[24] Most of these recruits came from the north of

---

[22] It is still unclear why the prosecutor chose to lionize Rawlings in his opening remarks. Some have argued that Aikins was in cahoots with Rawlings, but others claim (more plausibly) that Aikins was a reformer who used his moment in the spotlight to attack the junta. Lawyers had long been at the forefront of the movement to restore civilian rule. It is likely that he saw in this minor trial an opportunity to criticize Ghana's succession of military rulers.

[23] It is believed that Rawlings may also have been a member of Boakye-Djan's conspiracy, at least for a time.

[24] The existence of such a large cohort of enlisted men is verified by Colonel Samuel Ofosu-Apea. According to Ofosu-Apea regular recruitment procedures had been disturbed by the first coup in 1966 and had not been restored, leading to shortfalls in properly trained enlisted men. In 1973, Colonel Ofosu-Apea was authorized to create a new armed forces recruitment center, enlist a large number of men, and train them. This large group of inductees was an effort to catch up with a manpower backlog (interview with Colonel [retired] Samuel Ofosu-Apea. August 15, 2000. Accra, Ghana).

Ghana, and thus were close culturally, even though they were from different ethnic, linguistic, and religious groups.

Corporal Tasiri had a difficult time recruiting them, however, because any group of more than two or three soldiers was considered suspicious. Despite such constraints, he met with several such small groups a day, talked to soldiers who were on guard duty with him, and used pretexts such as family events at relatives' houses to meet with soldiers outside of barracks.[25] Unsurprisingly, his commanding officer in the capital infantry battalion was well aware of these efforts, which allowed him to respond easily when Tasiri decided to strike.[26]

On the evening of June 3, Tasiri met with twenty soldiers at his house and was able to convince eight of them to join him at the plantain groves near the base at 2:00 a.m. to mount some sort of attack. However, word of their conspiracy had leaked, and Tasiri was arrested.[27] Matters might easily have ended at that point except that another person arrested was a young officer, Lieutenant Baah Acheamfour, who was a member of the Free Africa Movement, whose other members decided to move into action before their own plans could be uncovered.[28] (Ironically, Acheamfour was not actually a member of Tasiri's organization at all but was arrested that night because Corporal Tasiri had once tried, but failed, to recruit him.) The Free Africa Movement had reason to be worried, as Captain Boakye-Djan and Corporal Tasiri were both members of the Fifth Infantry Battalion, and so any investigation of those men's conspiracies might uncover traces of their own.

Attack

At 2:00 a.m., the Free Africa Movement began their coup attempt by sending two men to free the recently arrested members of the infantry. In the course of the jailbreak, one of the guards was killed.[29] Soon thereafter, one of these two conspirators also died, in circumstances that remain murky to this day.[30]

The mutiny then spread across the Fifth Infantry Battalion. The unit's enlisted men soon joined the mutiny, although some did so under duress. Corporal Tasiri went building to building, announcing the uprising and coercing those who were reluctant to join.

At this stage, the mutiny was still very weak. Although the mutineers in the infantry were joined by some enlisted men from the air force, they were still small in number. They had some small arms but no heavy weapons and seem to have

---

[25]Interview with Corporal (retired) Peter Tasiri. August 10, 2001. Accra, Ghana.

[26]Interview with Reverend Colonel (retired) Kwesi Oteng. August 14, 2001. Accra, Ghana.

[27]Interview with Corporal (retired) Peter Tasiri. August 10, 2001. Accra, Ghana.

[28]Interview with Kweku Baaku. June 28, 2000. Accra, Ghana. Boakye-Djan claimed that they attacked because Rawlings was due to be executed on June 4th, but this is manifestly false. Interview with Major (retired) Kojo Boakye-Djan. July 2, 1999. Hemmel Hempstead, UK.

[29]Interview with Corporal (retired) Peter Tasiri. August 10, 2001. Accra, Ghana.

[30]Lieutenant Agyeman Bio died at the air force commander's residence where he may have committed suicide. No explanation is given for this puzzling action, but multiple sources state the same claim.

been short of ammunition (Ziorklui 1988, 251). They were able to take guns from soldiers who were on guard duty and supplemented those with what they could take from the armory. Even as the mutiny spread to other units, it remained logistically challenged, since the keys to the ammunition depots were held by officers, many of whom fled, taking their keys with them (250).

The mutiny was also weakened by its lack of central leadership. It was chaotic and disorganized, without anyone to shape its strategy. Neither Captain Boakye-Djan nor Corporal Tasiri (nor Flight-Lieutenant Rawlings later on) was in control, although they may have exercised influence in their immediate area.[31]

At a tactical level, leadership of the coup was assumed largely by a group of elite enlisted men, the graduates of the Junior Leader's Company, or Boys Company, as it was informally known.[32] These were second-generation soldiers who were being groomed to step into senior non-commissioned officer roles. Although they were still young and mostly corporals in rank, they gave the mutiny a modicum of command structure and coherence.[33] For the mutiny to succeed, it had to challenge the authority of the officer corps and weaken ingrained habits of obedience. One way in which they did this was to publicly beat and humiliate captive officers. Since the military still practiced corporal punishment, this was a deliberate inversion of roles and an intentional violation of the taboo against striking an officer. Captives also had their heads shaven, like raw recruits.

Many of the officers captured during the early phase of the mutiny were taken to the guard room of the military intelligence unit, where they were terrorized. Captives were told they were going to die, and mock executions were staged in which an officer would be taken outside and a gun would fired to convince the remaining captives that an execution had taken place. This was extremely convincing, persuading at least one of the officers present that he would not survive.[34]

The military as a whole was caught by surprise. The armed forces had not been put on a state of alert while the trial was going on because military leaders did not anticipate any serious danger.[35] Even the Fifth Infantry Battalion, which was still on alert because they had made arrests earlier that night, was caught off guard by the uprising. Captain Boakye-Djan's actions were particularly unexpected because he was close to the unit commander[36] and may even have been assigned to suppress the mutiny.[37]

Although loyalists were aware of the uprising as soon as it started, they were slow to respond. At the top, the army commander, General Odartey-Wellington, had

---

[31] Questions have been raised about whether Rawlings and Boakye-Djan were present throughout the mutiny. If they were away from the front lines, this would have made it harder for them to exercise control over events.

[32] Interview with Lance Corporal (retired) Rexford Ohemeng. August 13, 2001. Accra, Ghana.

[33] Interview with Lance Corporal (retired) Rexford Ohemeng. August 13, 2001.

[34] Interview with Colonel (retired) Seth Kwahu. September 4, 2000. Accra, Ghana.

[35] Interview with General (retired) Edwin Sam. June 28, 2000. Accra, Ghana.

[36] Interview with Reverend Colonel (retired) Kwesi Oteng. August 14, 2001. Accra, Ghana.

[37] Interview with Major (retired) Abubakar Sulemana. August 18, 2001. Accra, Ghana.

been monitoring events from the army operations room since before 2:00 a.m.[38] His subordinate, Brigadier I. K. Amoah, commander of all the army forces in the south of Ghana, assured the army commander that the situation was under control.[39]

Interviews with those involved revealed that the officer corps did not quite realize the danger they were in, since no mutiny had succeeded before. As one explained, the mutiny was "an experience that was new and unique ... a mutiny and we were the target. The other time[s] the government was the target, this time we were the target."[40] In fact, some officers had trouble even accepting that a mutiny was under way. When the Ministry of Defense operation room was besieged by mutineers using an officer as a shield, some officers inside believed that the hostage must have been leading the attack.[41] They were then surprised when enlisted men inside the ops room switched sides and took them captive.

Despite Rawlings's symbolic importance, nobody attempted to free him until roughly 5:30 a.m., at which point the mutiny was already under way.[42] Rawlings at first balked at leaving his cell, since he did not know the mutinous soldiers who had arrived and was concerned this was a ploy to shoot him while escaping. Once he acceded, however, he ran the approximately 500 meters to the radio station, which was under the control of the mutineers and guarded by enlisted men from the Fifth Infantry who had already joined the mutiny.

Rawlings burst on the air and made two consecutive broadcasts sometime around 6:00 a.m.[43] The core of his remarks was as follows:

> The ranks [enlisted men] have just taken over the destiny of this country. Fellow officers, if we are to avoid any bloodshed, I plead with you not to attempt to stand in their way, because they are full of malice, hatred—hatred we have forced into them through all these years of suppression. They are ready to get it out, the venom that we have created. So for heaven's sake do not stand in their way ... You are either a part of the problem or a part of the solution. There is no middle way ... [Further bloodshed] is not necessary. This country can solve its problems without participating in bloodshed. Further announcements will come later. Meanwhile, citizens can carry on with their normal duties. (Ziorklui 1988, 246-247)

---

[38]Interview with Colonel (retired) E.D.F. Prah. August 13, 2001. Accra, Ghana.

[39]Interview with Colonel (retired) E. D. F. Prah. August 13, 2001. Accra, Ghana.

[40]Interview with Brigadier (retired) Joseph Nunoo-Mensah. July 25, 2000. Accra, Ghana.

[41]Interview with Colonel (retired) Harry Lawrence Ofosu-Appiah. August 13, 2001. Accra, Ghana.

[42]There is some minor disagreement about the exact time that Rawlings was freed from his jail cell. According to Yankah, the mutineers came for Rawlings at 4:00 a.m. (Yankah 1986, 21), but Shillington places the time at 5:30 a.m. (Shillington 1992, 44) and Duodo states that it was 5:45 a.m. (Ziorklui 1988, 244). The later times are more plausible, since Rawlings made a broadcast soon after he was released, and the broadcast was close to 6 a.m.

[43]Two interviewees place the first broadcast at around the same time as the 6:00 a.m. news, while Aboagye puts this broadcast at 7:30 (Aboagye 1999, 102).

Rawlings's claims, which were clearly directed toward the military, and particularly toward officers, were also underscored by the presence of an air force plane flying low and noisily over most of the capital. The mutineers had captured an unarmed training jet, a first in the history of Ghanaian coups.

Response

After Rawlings's broadcast, the army commander no longer accepted that the First Brigade had matters under control. Bypassing his subordinate, he sent Major Sulemana of the armored regiment to suppress the mutiny, just as during the coup attempt a few weeks before. Sulemana assembled his men at the main square of the unit and dispatched six armored cars to quell the disturbance.[44] One group of armored cars was sent to free senior officers who were being held captive by the mutineers and bring them back to the headquarters of the armored regiment.[45] A second group of armored cars was directed to retake the radio station. There they skirmished with a small group of mutineers, traveling in three light transport vehicles, who had just left the target. One truck was captured; Rawlings was in a second one that was hit by gunfire but managed to escape.[46]

Once the armored troops were able to retake the radio station, the army commander made two broadcasts. The first, at 9:00 a.m., was a boilerplate response to a mutiny. General Odartey-Wellington announced that the uprising had been put down, and he attempted to restore military order:

> ... I am hereby offering all officers and men of the Ghana Armed Forces to return to their respective units. Steps are being taken to restore the armed forces to normalcy ... I would like to assure all citizens to go about their normal duties whilst they can be sure that all steps are being taken to ensure that life and property are being protected. I would also like to add that all officers and men, whether they were actively involved in the uprising or not, are to report back to their units whilst steps are being taken to iron out any grievances or any alleged injustices. (Okeke 1982, 43)

However, the rebel plane flying overhead made clear that the government was not in control, and so at around 10:30 a.m., the army commander returned to the radio, this time sounding more conciliatory:

> I have come to the studio once again. This time to make a personal appeal to all members of the Ghana Armed Forces. I urge all ranks who are out to cease firing forthwith. I also urge Flight Lieutenant Rawlings and any following who he has with him to meet me at headquarters ... I give you all the full assurance that there will be no victimization,

---

[44]Interview with Major (retired) Abubakar Sulemana. August 18, 2001. Accra, Ghana.

[45]Interview with Colonel (retired) Harry Lawrence Ofosu-Appiah. August 13, 2001. Accra, Ghana

[46]See Ziorklui (1988, 250) and interview with Corporal (retired) Peter Tasiri on August 10, 2001 in Accra, Ghana.

no arrests of any sort whatsoever. All other personnel are to report to their respective units as previously instructed. All flights of Air Force planes are to cease. I urge you all to cooperate fully to enable speedy normalization of this mission. Thank you. (Okeke 1982, 43)

The government offer to negotiate was sincere, and General Odartey-Wellington was one of the few senior commanders who was respected by the mutineers. However, negotiations never took place, because each attempt to set up a meeting between Rawlings and the army commander was stymied by fear of an ambush. In any case, there was no center of the mutiny for loyalists to negotiate with.

Although the government had not succeeded in crushing the mutiny, the mutineers were struggling. The uprising was disorganized and appeared to have lost ground to various government efforts to suppress it.[47] Their logistical problems were also growing more acute. According to Rawlings, the mutineers were "thinly spread and had ... little ammunition (Ziorklui 1988, 251). On the other hand, the fact that the mutineers were disorganized and had no central leadership also made it very difficult to put down the mutiny once it had spread. Since individual mutineers had a lot to lose by surrendering (despite the army commander's promises), and as long as the likely outcome of the coup remained uncertain, they persevered.

The Tide Turns

The tide gradually turned in favor of the mutineers. Some of their logistical problems were alleviated when the mutiny spread to the First Infantry Battalion, stationed about ten miles from the capital, in the port city of Tema. Captain Henry Smith, one of Boakye-Djan's top men, was stationed at the First Infantry and had built a conspiratorial nucleus there. Not only did the First Infantry Battalion fall, but Captain Smith also was able to open the unit's armory, providing the mutineers with much of the ammunition used during the uprising.[48] This was a blow to the government forces, given that this was the only other infantry unit near the capital and that loyalists were relying upon it to provide reinforcements.

Mutineers also increased their tactical strength when they started to use light artillery. At first there were technical problems because the mutineers were not used to operating the mortar without an officer present and as a result were hitting their own buildings rather than those of their adversaries. After some refinement, however, they improved their aim and began to successfully hit buildings belonging to the armored regiment. This shelling was followed with an infantry attack that captured the armored regiment's headquarters (made easier by the fact that these buildings were largely empty).[49] They also used mortars to fend off an attack by the engineering regiment.[50] The sound of artillery could be heard at a distance and announced to the rest of the base that the mutiny had not yet been defeated.

---

[47]Interview with Kweku Baaku. June 28, 2000. Accra, Ghana.

[48]Interview with Kweku Baaku. August 6, 2001. Accra, Ghana.

[49]Interview with Corporal (retired) Peter Tasiri. August 10, 2001. Accra, Ghana.

[50]Interview with Corporal (retired) Adam Al-Hassan. August 17, 2001. Accra, Ghana.

An even more important advance in tactical capacity came when junior officers joined the coup, increasing the fighting power of the mutiny and simultaneously decreasing the capacity of loyalist forces to contain it. Even though the junior officers who joined the mutiny removed their rank insignia to indicate their solidarity, they still filled leadership roles, coordinating and organizing the insurgency.[51] Despite its tactical advantages, the inclusion of junior officers required a significant shift in thinking by the rebels. The mutiny had begun as the equivalent of a class war between enlisted men and officers, in which even senior non-commissioned officers were sometimes seen as part of the machinery of oppression.[52] In fact, antipathy toward the officer corps was so intense that both Rawlings and Boakye-Djan may indeed have hidden for extended periods during the coup attempt, afraid that they, too, would be attacked, despite their revolutionary credentials (Okeke 1982, 43). Unfortunately, there is little information about how this change occurred, but its effects on the mutiny are clear.[53]

Another key point in the coup attempt came when the rebels once again seized the radio station from loyalist troops, who lacked sufficient infantry to adequately defend it.[54] Because there was no centralized leadership, different ad hoc representatives for the mutiny made on-air announcements throughout the afternoon, asserting that the mutiny had succeeded and directing middle- and top-ranking officers to report to the new authorities for their own protection.[55]

These broadcasts seemingly took a toll on the defenders, whose numbers dwindled. Even within pockets of resistance, soldiers were leaving and their officers were giving up.[56] At some point in the afternoon, the army operations room fell to the mutineers, removing a central point of coordination for loyalists. The soldiers who had been guarding the operation room were exhausted and needed relief, but the expected reinforcements from the First Infantry Battalion never showed up. Reinforcements did eventually arrive from the engineering regiment, but they simply opened the gates when the mutineers arrived. The army operations room thus fell without a shot.[57]

Around 3:00 p.m., the army commander, General Odartey Wellington, was killed in a gun battle outside the police station he had been using as his temporary headquarters. Having lost contact with the brigade headquarters, he had been trying to rally forces on his own. It is unclear how much of an impact his death actually

---

[51]Interview with Corporal (retired) Peter Tasiri. August 10, 2001. Accra, Ghana.

[52]Interview with Corporal (retired) Peter Tasiri. August 10, 2001. Accra, Ghana.

[53]Some sources credit efforts by Rawlings to broaden the mutinous coalition, but this grants Rawlings much greater agency than he seems to have had. Making the matter more confusing, the entrance of junior officers did not happen in a single discrete moment. In some parts of the mutiny, junior officers had long been involved. Junior officers from Boakye-Djan's faction performed critical functions at the very start of the coup and were a part of the mutiny the entire time. Similarly, the plane flying over Accra was piloted by an officer. All we can say is that by the late afternoon, the rebellion seems to have included more junior officers, and this had a significant effect on the trajectory of the coup attempt.

[54]Interview with Major (retired) Abubakar Sulemana. August 18, 2001. Accra, Ghana.

[55]Interview with Captain (retired) James Owoo. August 2, 2001. Accra, Ghana.

[56]Interview with Colonel (retired) Harry Lawrence Ofosu-Appiah. August 13, 2001. Accra, Ghana.

[57]Interview with Colonel (retired) E.D.F. Prah. August 13, 2001. Accra, Ghana.

had at the time. On a tactical level, it may not have reduced loyalist military strength in any significant fashion.[58] Nor does it seem that news of his death spread quickly, so it is unlikely to have been a serious psychological blow to defenders. The mutineers made no mention of it on their radio broadcasts, implying that many participants found out about it only later (Awoonor 1984, 110).

The critical turning point was the decision in the evening of June 4 by the First Infantry Brigade to stop resisting. The armored regiment had regrouped around the headquarters of the brigade to defend it after infantry reinforcements had failed to show up. Around dusk, at roughly 6:00 p.m., rebels approached the headquarters of the First Infantry Brigade in four armed and loaded Pinzgauer light transport vehicles, small trucks that hold roughly ten men each. In response, the head of the armored regiment, Major Sulemana, sought permission to deploy defensively around the perimeter of the headquarters, but this was denied. The head of the brigade told Sulemana that enough blood had been shed already and that government forces should not resist further. Although Major Sulemana argued that surrendering would put his men at risk because of their central role in the resistance to the mutiny, the brigade commander refused to change his position. In the end, Sulemana and two other officers from his unit melted away into the bush, thus ending the last real opposition to the coup.[59]

Consolidation

The government's capitulation to the mutineers was formalized in a radio broadcast later that night. At 8:30 p.m., the head of the Ghanaian armed forces, General Joshua Hamidu, declared a victory for the "revolutionary forces" and announced that the old military establishment had been removed (Aboagye 1999, 103):

> I am happy to announce that the hypocrisy of the Acheampong and Akuffo regimes ... has been brought to an end. All members of the said regime are to report to the air force station or the nearest police station now for their own safety. We wish to assure you that the elections will go on as planned ... It is in the national interest, therefore, that we are pursuing this course. We have suffered for far too long ... May God bless this nation. (Yankah 1986, 23)

With the head of the entire armed forces confirming the success of the coup, there could be no further uncertainty about which side was in charge (Okeke 1982, 44).

Analysis

There are ways in which the June 4 mutiny resembles a battle. This was the most bare-knuckled coup attempt in Ghana's history, and access to both ammunition

---

[58]It is likely that he was traveling with a small group of men, since he had no forces under his direct command and there was a shortage of loyalist forces.

[59]Interview with Major (retired) Abubakar Sulemana. August 18, 2001. Accra, Ghana.

and artillery was critical to the mutineers' ability to fight. That said, tactical factors, taken alone, would have predicted the failure rather than the success of the uprising. The challengers started out far weaker than loyalist forces and remained so for quite some time.

To explain why the mutiny succeeded, commentators usually point to the unhappiness of enlisted men, implicitly arguing that coups are like elections. But this perspective does not explain why so many soldiers hesitated to join the rebellion. If preferences are the most important factor in coup attempts, the mutiny should have succeeded far more quickly and with less difficulty.

Only the theory that coups are coordination games is consistent with both the dynamics and the outcomes of this coup attempt. The trial of Rawlings and his fellow conspirators shaped beliefs within the military in a pro-mutiny direction, making common knowledge of the widespread support for a mutiny among enlisted men. Once the coup attempt started, the mutineers dominated the airwaves, using both radio broadcasts and the sound of a jet flying overhead to influence expectations. The longer the rebels were able to control public information, the more members of the military bandwagoned in their favor. First enlisted men joined, then junior officers, and finally mid-level and senior officers decided to stop fighting rather than tip the country into a bloody conflagration.

Coups as Battles

If coup attempts are understood solely in terms of their tactical dimension, there is no reason why the June 4 coup attempt should have succeeded rather than being quickly and decisively crushed at the start. Yet the problem with this approach is deeper than its failure to explain why the mutiny survived past its infancy. At each successive stage of this coup attempt, it is difficult to understand how the mutiny prevailed in terms of strictly tactical factors alone.

Clearly, the challengers did not have enough power to prevail at the start of the coup attempt. The rebellion was centered in a single company of the Fifth Infantry Battalion, which was commanded by the mutineer Captain Boakye-Djan, and had attracted roughly thirty additional enlisted men from the air force. Even if one assumes that the mutiny would have engulfed the entire battalion, it would still have been no match for the loyalist armored regiment and weaker still than the combined loyalist forces arrayed against it. Although the capital infantry battalion was a formidable force under normal circumstances, it was hampered by significant logistical disadvantages during the coup attempt. Mutineers had mostly small arms at their disposal and only limited ammunition, having been locked out of the ammunition depots by officers who had taken the keys when they retreated (Ziorklui 1988, 250-251). Even the air force fighter plane they controlled was unarmed and thus could be used neither to bomb nor to strafe loyalist forces (Jackson 1999, 94).

In addition, the mutiny was tactically weak because it was disorganized and lacked centralized leadership, so soldiers were unable to act in a coherent fashion.

While they had some tactical leadership in the form of non-commissioned officers who joined the attempt, the absence of officers in the mutiny in its earliest phase meant that the mutineers were not able to fight effectively. As a result, the insurrection in the early stages lost ground to government efforts to suppress it.[60] From a balance of forces perspective, the mutiny was doomed to fail.

Contrary to what this approach would expect, the mutiny did not collapse at this point but persisted and in fact grew stronger. When the mutiny gained tactical advantage against loyalist forces, it was usually due to defections from the government side rather than the defeat of loyalist forces in hard-fought skirmishes. For example, over the course of the mutiny, both the army and defense operation rooms fell, making it more difficult for loyalist forces to coordinate a response. In each case, enlisted men within the operations room switched sides when mutineers arrived at the gates; rebellious forces never had to force their way in.[61] Over time, new forces joined the mutiny, ameliorating its tactical deficits. The rebels were able to replenish their ammunition when the First Infantry Battalion joined the mutiny, granting access to their armory.[62]

The most significant tactical advance came when junior officers began to join the mutiny, coordinating and organizing the mutineers.[63] The defection of junior officers simultaneously strengthened the mutiny and weakened the loyalists' ability to suppress the uprising.[64]

Even after the mutiny became significantly stronger, it continued to gain ground largely by attrition rather than force. Loyalist officers and enlisted men abandoned their posts and simply walked away. Some soldiers stayed and switched sides, but it is likely that government forces lost more men than challengers gained. This dynamic change in the strength of the two sides was critical to the success of the coup, but it is largely external to any tactical model.

Even at the end of the coup, the mutineers had not conclusively defeated loyalist forces. Pro-government forces retained the capacity to resist, and in fact the head of the armored regiment wished to continue doing so but was overruled by his commanding officer. Tactical factors cannot fully explain the mutiny's success at any stage of the event.

The battle theory does better at explaining some aspects of the mutiny's dynamics, in particular the primary targets of the coup attempt and the intensity of the conflict. The coup attempt was fought entirely on military bases, and most of the sites of contention had clear tactical value. The challengers took over every military unit in or near the capital as well as significant locations of command and control. The least tactically valuable target was the radio station, but even this was used to communicate over the chaos and confusion of the mutiny.

---

[60]Interview with Kweku Baaku. June 28, 2000. Accra, Ghana.

[61]Interview with Colonel (retired) E.D.F. Prah. August 13, 2001. Accra, Ghana.

[62]Interview with Kweku Baaku. August 6, 2001. Accra, Ghana.

[63]Interview with Corporal (retired) Peter Tasiri. August 10, 2001. Accra, Ghana.

[64]Interview with Colonel (retired) Kwesi Oteng. August 14, 2001. Accra, Ghana.

Also consistent with the theory, the June 4 coup attempt was one of the most violent and dangerous coups in Ghana's history. Loyalist armored cars opened fire on mutineers in trucks, and mutineers shelled pro-government forces and killed the army commander in a fire fight. Rebel behavior was far from genteel, with rebels making death threats against both enlisted men and officers, although in neither case did the threats escalate to action. This was the first coup attempt in Ghana in which the rebels demonstrated widespread ruthless behavior.

Coups as Elections

The predominant explanation for the June 4 coup attempt is that the uprising occurred and succeeded because of the intense resentment of enlisted men toward the military hierarchy. According to this interpretation, the rage of the common soldier was so intense that it consumed everything in its path, like a wildfire (Okeke 1982, 42), making the mutiny unstoppable and the overthrow of the Supreme Military Council II inevitable. This argument thus implicitly assumes that coups are like elections and that the most important factor in this coup attempt was the sentiment of the common soldier.

But while the argument that coups are like elections does fit the outcome of the June 4, 1979, coup, it does not do as well at explaining the dynamics of the coup attempt. In particular, it fails to explain why so many soldiers initially hesitated to join the mutiny despite their intense antipathy toward the government. If the predictions of this theory were correct, enlisted men who disliked the government should have joined the mutiny en masse as soon as it began. Instead, the evidence demonstrates that the mutiny did not attract large numbers of volunteers until fairly late, maybe twelve or more hours after the uprising began.

Despite the propitious conditions for a mutiny, the challengers had considerable difficulty attracting soldiers to their cause at the start of the coup. The heart of the mutiny was the Fifth Infantry Battalion, where Peter Tasiri was a corporal and where Captain Boakye-Djan commanded D Company. Here, where the groundwork for a mutiny had been best laid, one would have expected enlisted men to flock to the uprising, yet Corporal Tasiri went through the base in the middle of the night forcibly conscripting soldiers. By his own account, he told soldiers that he would kill them and their families if they failed to cooperate, a threat taken seriously enough that some wives pushed their husbands out of the house. Although the mutiny was soon joined by volunteers as well (thirty soldiers from the air force who joined the coup right away, and most likely some members of D Company), volunteers were clearly the exception if the challengers found it necessary to issue death threats to members of their own unit.

This hesitancy on the part of enlisted men to join the mutiny also undermines the argument that the trial of the May 15 mutineers somehow inflamed the rank and file of the military, convincing them to join the uprising. Although it is commonly argued that the trial was a bad idea because it lionized Rawlings and convinced soldiers that a coup attempt was a good idea, this claim rests on the paternalistic assumption that enlisted men had no idea how bad their circumstances were until they were either enlightened or deceived by the trial.[65]

The elections approach also fails to explain the timing with which recruits joined the mutiny, once its ranks began to swell. The mutiny grew only gradually through the late morning and early afternoon. Even then, many enlisted men remained members of loyalist units. For example, the engineering regiment was one of the largest units in the capital and its soldiers remained loyal for roughly eight hours. They joined the mutiny only after they were surrounded by the mutineers, some time around noon. Although they were persuaded to change sides, rather than coerced into doing so, they can hardly be credited with rising up to join the mutiny on their own.[66] Junior officers and other enlisted men likely did not join until late afternoon or early evening, and their decision to do so does not seem to have been the result of a concerted propaganda effort. Instead, the evidence suggests that there was a significant gap between a desire to see the government overthrown and a willingness to engage in doing so. Anti-government preferences were not a sufficient condition for soldiers to join the mutiny.

The elections theory also incorrectly characterizes the content of the various radio broadcasts made. If coups are like elections, then Rawlings's initial broadcast should have been an impassioned appeal to enlisted men to join in the uprising. Instead, he only asked them to elect designated representatives from within each unit to send to a meeting of the new revolutionary council the next day (Ziorklui 1988, 246-247). In fact, Rawlings made no effort at all either to sway hearts and minds or to decrease free-riding among enlisted men. And while we know less about the later broadcasts made by the challengers, there seems to have been little or no attempt to either persuade or mobilize their constituency. The closest that one comes to a broadcast appeal was from the head of the army, General Odartey-Wellington, who let the mutineers know that they would not be prosecuted if they laid down their arms and that he was willing to negotiate with Rawlings.

Coups as Coordination Games

The May and June 1979 coup attempts form an interesting pseudo-experiment because they had different outcomes despite a great number of points of similarity. On a macro-level, both coup attempts took place in the same country (controlling for social and historical factors), both took place against the same government, and both occurred in the same economic climate. On a micro-level, both were mutinies that expressed the same set of broadly held grievances, both were able to achieve a

---

[65]One officer wrote the following in his memoirs: "Rawlings' 'defence' as put up by the prosecution ... was like a seed falling on rich, moist soil that had been ploughed and harrowed to a good tilth. It germinated and blossomed into an uncontrolled venom in the hearts of many ... *When people become aware that they are being cheated, or being unjustifiably deprived, they are not likely to remain indifferent or passive for long.* They are bound to react, and the action of an angry man may not be the most gentle ... From then on, it was clearly evident that a mighty storm was gathering over our nation, Ghana" (italics mine) (Jackson 1999, 85).

[66]Interview with Corporal (retired) Adam Al-Hassan. August 17, 2001. Accra, Ghana.

reasonable amount of military strength before government forces moved to oppose them, and both were opposed primarily by the armored regiment.

From a coordination perspective, however, there were two key differences between the mutinies. The first is that the trial of the May 15 mutineers served to "prime the pump" for the June 4 coup attempt, creating more favorable expectations going into the revolt. The decision to hold the trial openly has been called "the most unfortunate and the most suicidal" choice in Ghanaian history (Quantson 2000, 176-177). Before the May 15 coup attempt, enlisted men would have had little reason to believe that a mutiny could succeed, and the failure of the uprising would have confirmed this opinion. As a result of the trial of Rawlings and his confederates, however, enlisted men had good reason to believe that a mutiny could possibly succeed. Enlisted men on the main military base would have seen antigovernment slogans such as "STOP THE TRIAL OR ELSE ..." and "REVOLUTION OR DEATH" posted on public buildings (Yankah 1986, 18).[67] The audience that attended the trial, most of whom were enlisted men, took advantage of their anonymity in the crowd to applaud the defendants loudly, growing increasingly demonstrative with each day of the trial. On the third day, the presiding officer warned those in the gallery to "desist from any further shouting and clapping" or he would close the trial (19).

The banners and the shouting and clapping could all be seen and heard in public venues, where support for the defendants could become common knowledge. They were then amplified further by the news coverage of the event, which created common knowledge among all members of the military, officers and enlisted men alike. Under normal circumstances, enlisted men were unable to discuss politics even with their friends for fear of being accused of sedition. Bypassing these barriers, the trial created common knowledge of strong anti-incumbent feeling at the bottom of the hierarchy and transformed it into the basis of collective action.

As important as it was, however, the trial demonstrated only that a mutiny was feasible, not that it was inevitable. In game theoretic terms, the trial revealed the existence of a possible equilibrium without creating a focal point around it. It still made sense to join the mutiny only if you believed that enough other soldiers would join the mutiny for it to prevail. Soldiers therefore hesitated at the start of the coup, waiting to see what would happen.

The other major difference between the two attempts is that the May 15 rebels failed to make even a single broadcast, whereas the June 4 challengers had control of the radio for almost the entire duration of the coup, thus allowing them to shape expectations and make the success of the mutiny appear a fait accompli. In their broadcasts, the June challengers very explicitly claimed that they were in control, that their victory was inevitable, and that resistance to the coup attempt was both futile and dangerous. When Rawlings first made these statements in the morning, such claims were premature, although still credible. In the initial broadcast of the

---

[67]The slogans were the work of MONAS, the civilian branch of the Free Africa Movement. However, at the time it was believed that these were spontaneous exclamations of support from within the military.

coup, he said that the enlisted men as a whole had risen up, when in fact only a few were then involved. He proclaimed that "the ranks have just taken over" at a time when they were still disorganized and nowhere near in control (Yankah 1986, 22). He claimed that all attempts to resist were futile and would only unleash total chaos, imploring officers, "For Heaven's sake ... if we are to avoid bloodshed, I plead with you, make no attempt to stand in their way" (Ziorklui 1988, 246-247).

The impact of Rawlings's broadcast was reinforced by the sight and sound of an air force plane flying low over the capital at around the same time (Ziorklui 1988, 245). The jet was noisy, its sound described as "thundering" and "ear-splitting," with a "shrill whine" (Jackson 1999, 94). These flights were not used to strafe or bomb loyalist troops, and the Aeromacchi MB326F jet trainer was in fact unarmed. They did, however, have a clear impact on expectations. Because of the ubiquity of the jet for those in the captial, the flight was just as much a public broadcast as a speech on the radio, and its meaning just as clear. This was the first time that a jet had been used in a coup attempt in Ghana, and the mutineers used it to imply that they were well armed and firmly in charge and that resistance by loyalists could lead to civil war.

The jet flying overhead also undermined the government's claim, broadcast at 9:00 a.m., that it was restoring order. This much was acknowledged in the government's more conciliatory address eighty minutes later, when the army commander asked to meet with Rawlings and ordered the plane to stop flying overhead. This constituted a public admission that the government lacked control and certified the mutineers as a significant threat, not just a ragtag coalition of disaffected soldiers.

Once the mutineers regained control of the radio, they continued with broadcasts that claimed the mutiny had succeeded and that the dwindling resistance was endangering itself. Middle- and top-ranking officers were directed to report to the new authorities for their own protection.[68]

Consistent with this theory, we observe coordination driving behavior at all levels of the armed forces. Although enlisted men were sympathetic to the goals of the mutiny, they remained hesitant to join for some time, and even had to be coerced at the start of the uprising. Once the mutiny began to seem more viable, soldiers were more willing to join but still often waited until the challengers were dominant in the area around them. For example, enlisted men inside the Ministry of Defense operations room switched when rebels appeared in force outside, thus bandwagoning with the locally more powerful side. It was not until later, once the government had been silenced on the radio, that enlisted men joined en masse and even loyal units found that their soldiers were disappearing. One conspirator observed that many soldiers took cover first, waiting to see how the wind was blowing.[69]

The behavior of junior officers during the June coup attempt is also consistent with coordination. It is unlikely that they joined the rebellion out of a sense of soli-

---

[68]Interview with Captain (retired) James Owoo. August 2, 2001. Accra, Ghana.

[69]Interview with Kweku Baaku. June 28, 2000. Accra, Ghana.

darity with enlisted men, since the success of the mutiny endangered their privilege and status. In addition, any actions driven by solidarity should have come early, though we do not see junior officers joining in large groups in the morning, or even after Rawlings's broadcasts. Instead it seems that they waited until after the head of the army made it publicly clear that the government was weak and perhaps even after the mutiny had regained control of the airwaves. Thus, the decision of junior officers to join the mutiny appears to have been driven more by changes in beliefs than changes in tactical advantage on the ground. Ironically, before the involvement of junior officers, the mutiny was weak and struggling to survive and could have been defeated. The belief that the mutiny would prevail was therefore self-fulfilling, as it drove junior officers to join the uprising, which was in turn critical to the coup's success.

Command-level officers also came to the conclusion that the coup was bound to succeed after the mutineers resumed their control of the radio station and after junior officers began to defect. Some officers who had been resisting and were out of communication with the hierarchy simply gave up and let their men leave their units.[70] For command-level officers and above, there was concern about what would happen if they continued to fight. The mutineers' broadcasts at the beginning of the coup warned officers that resistance would lead to a massive bloodbath, deliberately raising the specter of a civil war. While officers did not initially consider such statements credible, this changed later in the day, as did their beliefs about the beliefs of others. Both officers who were making decisions for themselves and those making decisions for larger units concluded that a disadvantageous peace was preferable to a fratricidal conflict.[71]

The June 4 mutiny was violent and chaotic, certainly the most dangerous military uprising in Ghana's history, one in which the potential for a slip into fratricide was clear. At the same time, it was far less bloody than commonly believed, as a result of deliberate efforts by actors on both sides to reduce the number of potential casualties. While there are neither official nor unofficial counts of the number of military personnel killed during the uprising, the conventional wisdom is that the death toll was high, perhaps in the hundreds (Yankah 1986, 26). However, my enumeration of the dead suggests that only between two and six men died as a direct result of the fighting.[72] Even if this estimate is off by a significant number,

---

[70] Interview with Colonel (retired) Harry Lawrence Ofosu-Appiah. August 13, 2001. Accra, Ghana.

[71] Interview with Major (retired) Abubakar Sulemana. August 18, 2001. Accra, Ghana. Interview with Corporal (retired) Stanley Okyere. August 15, 2001. Accra, Ghana.

[72] Written sources mention only three of the dead by name—General Odartey-Wellington, Colonel Enninful (the officer presiding over Rawlings's court martial) and Lieutenant Agyeman Bio—and make no mention of any other unnamed dead. Lieutenant Agyeman Bio is believed to have committed suicide during the coup attempt, under circumstances that remain murky to this day. Interviews mentioned only three other people as possibilities—a guard who was shot during the jail break, an aide to General Odartey-Wellington, and an unnamed soldier from the engineering regiment (interview with Corporal (retired) Adam Al-Hassan. August 17, 2001. Accra, Ghana) who died when their truck was shelled. While there were numerous clashes between the two sides, eyewitnesses claim that most of these ended without bloodshed. The only confrontation that may

say a factor of four, it would still mean that at most twenty-four men died during the coup, or the equivalent of eight days of traffic fatalities in Ghana today. While these deaths are regrettable, given the level of disorganized fighting this is a very low number.

Consistent with the coordination game theory, there is clear evidence that the parties to the conflict avoided using deadly force against their adversaries, despite the very high stakes involved. Both sides took prisoners, even when short-handed, rather than execute those they captured. Captive officers were threatened with mock executions during the coup but never killed. Corporal Tasiri recounts firing at the other side but is adamant that he did so in such a way as not to kill them.[73] Although Tasiri has an incentive to deny having caused any deaths, he has never been accused of having shot somebody. On the loyalist side, the commander of the First Infantry Brigade, Brigadier Amoah, decided to surrender rather than fight to the bloody end, even though costs associated with surrender were likely to be quite high.

The perception that the uprising killed many members of the military is in part a deliberate consequence of the mutineers' brinksmanship.[74] Tactically disadvantaged, the challengers compensated by convincing loyalists that they were willing to plunge the entire country into revolutionary violence rather than lose. In addition, loyalist officers experienced conflict in a far more alarming and immediate fashion than they ever had before. By necessity, the mutineers were disorganized and fighting in an improvised fashion, exposing loyalists to a far more chaotic environment than in prior coups. The immediacy of this violence was heightened by the fact that it was directed personally at officers. They were threatened, beaten, and humiliated, symbolically inverting the command hierarchy and demonstrating to enlisted men that officers no longer possessed authority. Lastly, the perception that the coup was bloody may also have been shaped by the bloodshed which followed the coup, including deaths of many civilians, further harassment and violence against officers, the execution of eight former junta members from various regimes, and the threat to execute two hundred of Ghana's civilian elite.

The rank of the challengers shaped other attributes of the coup attempt beyond its level of violence. For example, unlike senior officers, mutineers could do little to shape expectations prior to the attack. While they did benefit considerably from the effects of the trial of the previous mutineers, the trial was an atypical exogenous

---

have led to deaths is one where loyalist armored cars opened fire on mutineers leaving the radio station, but even in this case there are no references to anybody's dying. While my account of this coup attempt is not comprehensive, neither side has long lists of martyrs whose deaths they commemorate, even though this incident remains highly contentious and politicized to the present time.

[73]Interview with Corporal (retired) Peter Tasiri. August 10, 2001. Accra, Ghana.

[74]There is an argument to be made that mutineers are far more risk acceptant than coup makers at higher ranks. Military promotion systematically selects for reliability and weeds out cowboys. A junior officer like Rawlings, who was a jet pilot, equestrian, and boxer, would never have advanced far in the Ghanaian air force. Conversely, more senior officers organize and execute coup attempts in a far more cautious fashion than do mutineers.

event. This mutiny illustrates a number of obstacles associated with launching a coup attempt from the bottom, even if it did succeed. The mutineers were hampered logistically by their lack of weapons and ammunition. They were also tactically weaker than loyalist forces because they had broken the command structure of their units and therefore had a more difficult time fighting coherently. For these reasons, the mutiny was almost defeated during the early stages of the coup attempt. The challengers were able to surmount both of these obstacles once more junior officers joined the coup; an uprising composed solely of enlisted men would have had a more difficult time prevailing.

Lastly, there are two areas in which the theory matches the evidence less well, although without challenging the overall interpretation of coups as coordination games. First, despite the very recent failure of an almost identical coup attempt, this mutiny started with somewhat favorable initial expectations and went on to succeed. I argue this is due to the idiosyncratic impact of the trial, which superseded any precedent that may have been created by the failure of the May mutiny. Second, there were no attacks on symbolic political targets except the radio. This may have been due to the fact that the incumbents ruled entirely from the military base, which is unusual even for a junta, so there were no seats of state authority in the civilian part of the capital that the coup makers could have targeted.

Ghana, 1981

Two and a half years later, on December 31, 1981, Ghana experienced its third coup from the bottom. In this attempt, Rawlings struck again, using almost the same strategy as he had in his first and unsuccessful attempt on May 15, 1979, although this time he captured the radio station and declared a revolution. That this seemingly improbable attempt proved successful was once again due to missteps by the incumbent government that had a significant effect on expectations within the military. For months before the coup attempt, the president had been publicly warning about the threat posed by Rawlings and begging enlisted men to remain loyal. Based on these broadcasts and their experience with the prior successful coup attempt, most officers believed that enlisted men would rally around Rawlings and that such an uprising could not be stopped, once started.

As we shall see, this case throws all three theories of coup dynamics and outcomes into sharp relief. Rawlings did not win because he possessed a superior strategy or dominant force. Similar strategies had failed in 1967 and in May 1979; both Rawlings's supporters and his detractors admit that he would have been fairly easy to stop. Nor did he win because the coup attempt was popular. Although the incumbent democratic government was highly unpopular, having presided over Ghana's worst economic conditions to date, neither civilians nor members of the military were enthusiastic about another coup. Instead, the coup succeeded because the officers believed that it would and therefore did not resist. Again, enlisted men waited a while before supporting the coup, and then did so only after resistance had ceased. Beliefs mattered in this case far more than tactical strength or popularity.

Background

After the June 4, 1979, coup, Ghana was ruled first by a revolutionary military junta, then by a civilian democratic government. The restoration of civilian rule marked the beginning of Ghana's ill-fated Third Republic. Although the new democracy had started with more popularity and legitimacy than any government in a decade, it quickly squandered all its good will and showed itself to be highly dysfunctional. Parliament was deadlocked in squabbles, the economy collapsed once more, and the bureaucratic apparatus of the state became sclerotic and ground to a complete halt. In addition to all its other problems, the Third Republic inherited severely disturbed civil-military relations in the wake of the June 4 mutiny. The new president ineptly tried to appeal directly to the enlisted men and win them over to the new government, merely succeeding in undermining efforts to restore hierarchical control within the military. Most important, Rawlings had refused to fade gently away and began to plot a return to power, and the government set up conditions for his success by building up his threat and mystique by its overt wariness of him.

To understand the circumstances of the 1981 coup attempt, one must begin with the consequences of the June 1979 coup attempt. The mutiny had unleashed a tremendous flow of class resentment by soldiers toward the establishment, both military and civilian. The new junta, the Armed Forces Revolutionary Council (AFRC), had only a tenuous grasp on power and thus tried to shape events via persuasion and co-optation of key factions. Although the junta kept changing in size and composition, it had roughly fifteen members, none higher in rank than major, and always included at least one private. Jerry Rawlings was the chairman, Captain Kojo Boakye-Djan was the official spokesman, and Corporal Tasiri was a junta member.

Discipline had completely disintegrated within the armed forces, resulting in chaos within the barracks and on the streets as enlisted men meted out revolutionary justice on their own initiative. Soldiers engaged in revolutionary redistribution, looting shops and businesses (Shillington 1992, 48). Tribunals and people's courts sprang up to try those accused of corruption, and wealth was considered prima facie evidence of wrongdoing. Official investigations of members of the private sector, heads of parastatal corporations, and bureaucrats claimed to have recovered unpaid taxes and fees worth almost three million dollars, a significant amount for a poor African country in 1979, although it is less clear if this money was actually collected by the state (Oquaye 1980, 146). To many Ghanaians, it seemed as if justice was finally being done.

Bloodlust was high after the coup, and there was a strong expectation among many that there would be executions. Six stakes went up at the firing range even before any judicial proceedings were started, and students marched carrying signs that read "Let the blood flow" (Shillington 1992, 52). A list of 207 prominent men to be executed had been compiled anonymously and was circulating among soldiers (51). The names on the list constituted a virtual "Who's Who" of the

Ghanaian elite, including officers, politicians, lawyers, businessmen, and luminaries (Yankah 1986, 183). In the end, eight former officers were executed for the crime of engaging in previous coups d'etat, including three former heads of state and several past junta members. Members of the AFRC felt that by allowing these executions, they were saving the lives of the others on the list (Yankah 1986, 182-183).

Despite all the chaos and upheaval, elections took place on the scheduled date, June 18, only two weeks after the June 4 mutiny and just two days after Acheampong and a second general were executed. Turnout was a record low of 35%, for many voters were suspicious about whether the election would be run fairly (Petchenkine 1993, 91). After just 112 days, the AFRC stepped down and handed power over to a duly elected government, enhancing the junta's reputation by keeping its promise to be no more than an interim administration.

A center-left Nkrumahist party, the People's National Party (PNP), had emerged the victor in both the parliamentary and presidential elections. It controlled a one-vote majority in the legislature, and its candidate, Dr. Hilla Limann, won the second round of the presidential election (Petchenkine 1993, 91).[75] Dr. Limann was an accidental candidate, a last-minute replacement for his uncle, who had been disqualified under an old law forbidding members of Nkrumah's socialist government from running for office. Limann was also the first head of state from the north of Ghana, a region that was poorer, less populated, and less influential than the south. An outsider in multiple ways, Limann had no political base of his own, within his party or among the capital elites.

The new government had only a brief honeymoon period before it found itself beset with problems. Budgetary austerity measures provoked rising levels of labor unrest. In 1980 alone, 70,000 workers went on strike, even more than had gone on strike against General Akuffo in 1978 (Petchenkine 1993, 103). Several students were injured and one died in anti-government protests, leading to the closure of the university system in the spring of 1980 (Chazan 1983, 315). Unprecedented ethnic violence broke out in the north of Ghana in 1981, and 3,000 people died (Petchenkine 1993, 105). The government was impotent in the face of spreading civic disorder (Petchenkine 1993, 103).

The challenges of governing were made worse by parliament's paralysis. Until this parliament convened, it had been almost a decade since one had been in session, and because 80% of the ruling party MPs were new to politics, parliament spent a lot of time dealing with procedural issues (Petchenkine 1993, 92). Although they were able to raise their own wages to forty-five times the minimum wage in September 1980 (Chazan 1983, 308), the legislators showed little interest in tackling any of the thornier issues on their agenda. The ruling party, despite having a majority of seats, was barely able to pass a budget (Petchenkine 1993, 110-112).

---

[75]Limann had a Ph.D. in political science from the University of Paris. This continued a trend of well-educated Ghanaians being elected during democratic governments. Busia, the prime minister during the Second Republic, also had a doctorate, and Nkrumah had done the course work for his Ph.D. but left the program afterwards.

Then, in November 1981, the ruling party fell apart, beset by scandal. The party chairman, the general secretary, and the chairman of the Propaganda Committee were accused of having received millions of dollars in kickbacks from a multinational company. The party chairman refused to step down quietly and leveled counter-allegations at his accusers within the party. The party, barely a coherent organization to begin with, splintered into factions (Petchenkine 1993, 115-116). By the end of 1981, President Limann had little control of his party, the parliament, or the government apparatus. The state was rudderless.

Further complicating matters for the government was the fact that it had no money, having inherited an economy that was in far worse shape than anyone had realized. Not only was Limann unable to turn the economy around, but matters steadily became even worse during his presidency until the formal economy became totally dysfunctional. As revenues plummeted, the government could barely function, let alone provide patronage to those who expected it. At the same time, there was little understanding among either citizens or elites of the structural nature of Ghana's economic problems and therefore no support for any of the serious policy changes necessary.

Domestic production decreased significantly in every sector of the economy during the Third Republic. Between 1979 and 1981, Ghana's GDP decreased by 8.7% (Petchenkine 1993, 102). Industry operated at only 10-15% of capacity (100,102). Cocoa production, a mainstay of the economy, reached its lowest level since independence, and since world prices were also declining, income from cocoa dropped even further (Chazan 1983, 313).

As the formal economy shrank, tax revenues dwindled. Annual deficits increased by a staggering 300% between the first and second fiscal years of the new democratic government. By the end of the second year alone, annual government expenditures constituted more than twice its collected revenues (Petchenkine 1993, 110-111). The government requested a one billion dollar loan from the International Monetary Fund but was told that a drastic reduction in the value of the currency, greater than tenfold, would be required first (Chazan 1983, 312). Limann balked, claiming that past devaluations had led to military coups (Yeebo 1991, 33). Instead, the government simply printed more money (Petchenkine 1993, 101). By 1981, inflation had reached 116% (World Bank 2004). The cumulative effect of years of inflation was to eviscerate the purchasing capacity of the average Ghanaian. Food prices had shot up to more than twelve times what they had been in 1977 (Petchenkine 1993, 101), while real income was a third less than it had been a decade before (Herbst 1993, 27). By spring of that year, the daily minimum wage could barely buy a loaf of bread (Petchenkine 1993, 103).

A final area of concern, unsurprisingly, was civil-military relations. The Limann government had admittedly inherited an extremely fraught situation, but once again it made matters worse through its own actions. Although civilian rule had been restored, enlisted men remained restive and continued to assert themselves, in one case clashing violently with the police (Petchenkine 1993, 96). In some units, officers had been able to reassert conventional military discipline, but in others officers feared for their safety and simply avoided conflict. Soldiers who had taken an active part in the mutiny and then returned to their posts felt that they were being persecuted by officers, and so were unhappy as well.

The president destabilized the situation further by trying to bypass the officer corps and appeal directly to soldiers, many of whom also came from the north of the country, on the basis of regional solidarity. This tactic antagonized many officers, who felt that Limann should be trying to restore hierarchical control within the military instead of circumventing and weakening it. President Limann, however, had little respect for the officer corps and blamed them for the problems within the military. He also wrongly believed that he was popular among soldiers (Hutchful 1997, 555). In fact, when the coup attempt came, not even the northern soldiers selected to be part of a special counter-coup group within the military remained loyal to him.

Conspiracy

The specter of another Rawlings coup loomed over the Third Republic from its inception. Rawlings was not a supporter of multi-party democracy, believing that a radical populist state would be better (Shillington 1992, 82). His public remarks at the official transition contained a thinly veiled threat: "We know you will deliver the goods. That is why we have turned a deaf ear to those who have entreated us to stay on a little longer, because our job is not complete. We have every confidence that we shall never regret our decision to go back to barracks" (Shillington 1992, 62).

Rawlings immediately became a thorn in the side of the new government. While most members of the AFRC junta were convinced to leave the country, Rawlings refused either to leave or to join the government as part of the advisory Council of State. Instead, he insisted on rejoining the armed forces at his old rank, despite having just functioned as a member of the executive for three months, deciding the fates of officers senior to him in rank. After two months, however, Rawlings was ejected from the military and banned from the barracks. He then became head of the June Fourth Movement, a Marxist organization that had grown out of campus radical groups, which he (not a Marxist himself) used to screen his activities from surveillance by intelligence groups (Nugent 1996, 33).

Although Rawlings had been a popular figure and the incumbent government was widely despised, he attracted few civilian followers outside of young radicals. The middle class had no appetite for further instability, and the working class was too busy trying to stay alive. The core of Rawlings's support came from radical soldiers who had been expelled from the armed forces after the transition, although he did not try to bring these veterans into a political organization.

That Rawlings was plotting a coup was well known to the government and discussed regularly in cabinet meetings.[76] Military intelligence followed Rawlings and his closest ally everywhere they went, playing out an elaborate cat and mouse

---

[76]Interview with KSP Jantuah, former minister of the interior under Limann. December 3, 1999. Accra, Ghana.

game that sometimes verged on slapstick. Members of the government made repeated public statements accusing Rawlings of engaging in seditious activities and pleading with members of the armed forces to remain loyal (Chazan 1983, 318). Rawlings accused the security services of kidnapping him, threatening him, and plotting against his life (Ray 1986, 25). Still, he was never arrested, charged, or made to disappear by the government. There is evidence that military intelligence officers were so frustrated with this government inaction that they contemplated mounting a coup themselves so as to be able to stop Rawlings (Yeebo 1991, 45).

It is unclear why the government did not act to decisively stop Rawlings at this stage. The usual explanation is that both civilian and military officials wanted to gather enough proof to successfully prosecute Rawlings (Hutchful 1997, 555), while others claim that the government had enough evidence to arrest Rawlings but was too inept and afraid to act.[77] In any case, civilian and military intelligence bickered over how best to address the threat, more concerned with protecting their turf than protecting the state (Hutchful 1997, 550, 557).

Foolishly, President Limann repeatedly undertook actions and made statements that made him seem feeble and made a coup by Rawlings appear both imminent and unstoppable. After just two months in office, President Limann, keenly aware that all of Ghana's previous civilian governments had been overthrown by military coups, moved to replace the top members of the military, intelligence, and police hierarchies who had been appointed during the AFRC, because he did not trust them. When these decisions proved controversial, Limann openly threatened to resign if the public did not accept his decision (Petchenkine 1993, 96). From 1980 onward, the government grew increasingly desperate. In a series of public statements, various members of the government raged against coup plotters, pleaded for members of the military to stay loyal, and leveled accusations of sedition against Rawlings (Hutchful 1998, 236). But, because the government failed to follow up their accusations with either legal charges or direct action, they simply magnified the Rawlings mystique, elevating him to a powerful, Rasputin-like figure (Chazan 1983, 318).

The original date set for the coup attempt was December 24th, presumably because the military would be at low readiness on Christmas Eve. When the government refused to pre-emptively arrest Rawlings, the officer who discovered the plot, Colonel Samuel Ofosu-Apea, acted to scuttle it anyway, believing that he would be assassinated the night before the scheduled coup attempt to facilitate it. Colonel Ofosu-Apea commander of the Second Infantry Battalion, based in Takoradi, about 125 miles from Accra, arrested nineteen men from the two military bases in the city, causing the coup makers to postpone their attempt. He would later be one of the few officers to oppose Rawlings's coup.[78]

---

[77]Interview with Colonel (retired) Seth Kwahu. September 4, 2000. Accra, Ghana.

[78]Interview with Colonel (retired) S.K. Ofosu-Apea. August 15, 2001. Accra, Ghana.

After this incident, the government decided to arrest Rawlings after the holiday season was over. Rawlings, however, pre-empted the government's action by striking during the official armed forces holiday party.[79]

Attack

The conspirators struck around midnight on the night of December 30. The core group directly involved in the attack included roughly ten men, although it may have fluctuated between six and twelve over the course of the event.[80] With the exception of Rawlings, all were enlisted men or enlisted men who had been recently discharged.[81] Most belonged to ethnic groups from the north of Ghana, like the president.

With the help of an ally inside, the conspirators sneaked into the armored regiment and overpowered the guards, taking over the three armored cars that were on standby.[82] They then took control over the entire unit simply by firing a few warning shots in the air. The only opposition came from the commanding officer, Major Pat Collison, who was shot and killed when he refused to stop advancing on the coup makers.[83]

Having taken control, the coup makers broke into the unit's armory to arm themselves. They were unable to increase the number of armored cars under their control, however, because the national security adviser had previously ordered most of the armored cars immobilized.[84] Lastly, the rebels repaired the armored cars they had captured, since the firing pins on at least one of the vehicles had been damaged or removed as a coup-proofing measure. The challengers were extremely vulnerable in this early phase, given that they had lost the advantage of surprise but were still poorly equipped.[85]

---

[79] Interview with KSP Jantuah, former minister of the interior under Limann. December 3, 1999. Accra, Ghana.

[80] One report states that this number swelled to a total of 33 men at maximum. See Kent Mensah. May 23, 2003. *Former Rawlings coup mate says the Ex-Flt. Lt. should acknowledge his "crimes" and "guilt" and apologise to the people of Ghana* <http://allafrica.com/stories/printable /200305240120.html>. Accra: Accra Mail. Accessed May 26, 2005.

[81] Rawlings's role in the coup attempt has been challenged by other members of the group, who claim that he went into hiding and had to be coerced into joining the attack. Alfred Ogbamey. June 16, 2003. *Adabuga Vrs Cudjoe: Who Is Committing Perjury ?* <http://www.ghana web.com/GhanaHomePage/NewsArchive/printnews.php?ID=37827>. Accra: Gye Nyame Concord. Accessed June 16, 2003.

[82] There is some disagreement about whether they captured two or three armored cars. My informant inside the unit claims that three armored cars were captured but one remained inside the unit to guard against possible opposition (Interview with Corporal (retired) Stanley Okyere. August 15, 2001. Accra, Ghana).

[83] Interview with Corporal (retired) Stanley Okyere. August 15, 2001. Accra, Ghana.

[84] Alfred Ogbamey. June 16, 2003. *Adabuga Vrs Cudjoe: Who Is Committing Perjury ?* http:// www.ghanaweb.com/GhanaHomePage/NewsArchive/printnews.php?ID=37827. Accra: Gye Nyame Concord. Accessed June 16, 2003.

[85] Interview with Kweku Baaku. August 9, 2000. Accra, Ghana.

Response

Opposition to the coup attempt was amazingly feeble on the night of the attack. The government, which did not expect a coup attempt during the holidays, was caught unawares. The president, vice president, cabinet, and top brass were all at the armed forces holiday party, and there was no state of alert for the military, even though a plot had been foiled less than a week earlier. However, because the armored regiment was in the middle of the main military base, shots were overheard, and the government learned that Rawlings was mounting a coup sometime shortly after 1 a.m.[86] At this point, the coup makers were fairly weak and could easily have been stopped by an organized, coherent, and coordinated governmental resistance.[87] This did not happen.

The main reason for the distinct lack of vigor in the government's response was that many officers (possibly most) decided not to fight back this time. Instead of resisting the coup attempt, they simply walked away from their posts.[88] They were afraid that enlisted men would flock to Rawlings and that those resisting the coup would be punished even more gravely than before. One officer explained that he had been beaten badly after June 4 even though he had done his best for his soldiers and had tried to better their conditions, so this time he collected his family and left, returning four months afterward.[89]

On the first night of the coup, most of the attempts to oppose Rawlings were uncoordinated and limited in scale. The unit best suited to challenge the armored regiment would have been the main infantry unit in the capital. Infantry had prevailed against armor in the previous coup, and the rebels had only two armored cars in the field, so defeating the rebels was well within their capacity. Nonetheless, the unit put up only minor resistance and folded after a few gunshots.[90]

To the extent that President Limann had a contingency plan, it revolved around a group of northern enlisted soldiers whom he had organized into a counter-coup unit. The head of this group was Sergeant Alolga Akata-Pore, a prominent figure among radical soldiers because of his role as a grassroots leader in the previous mutiny. The president, trusting that these men were loyal to him out of ethnic and regional solidarity, assigned them to spy on Rawlings and to block the attack if one came.[91] It is a sign of Ghana's tangled politics that this group was also working

---

[86]A variety of sources concur on when the government found out about the coup attempt and who they believed to be responsible. Interview with Kweku Baaku. August 9, 2000. Accra, Ghana. Interview with Air Vice Marshall (retired) Odaate-Barnor. July 21, 2000. Accra, Ghana. Interview with KSP Jantuah, former minister of the interior under Limann. December 3, 1999. Accra, Ghana.

[87]Alfred Ogbamey. June 16, 2003. *Adabuga Vrs Cudjoe: Who Is Committing Perjury ?* http://www.ghanaweb.com/GhanaHomePage/NewsArchive/printnews.php?ID=37827. Accra: Gye Nyame Concord. Accessed June 16, 2003.

[88]Interview with anonymous (retired) army sergeant. August 14, 2001. Accra, Ghana.

[89]Interview with Colonel (retired) Seth Kwahu. September 4, 2000. Accra, Ghana.

[90]Interview with Lance Corporal (retired) Rexford Ohemeng. August 13, 2001. Accra, Ghana.

[91]There are strong claims that Akata-Pore had been working with Rawlings all along and that he relayed everything he heard from Limann to Rawlings. Interview with KSP Jantuah, former minister of the interior under limann. December 3, 1999. Accra, Ghana

with a radical group that opposed Rawlings and wanted to stop future military coups.[92] When Rawlings struck, however, Akata-Pore switched sides and actively supported the coup because he was convinced it would succeed.[93]

Although military intelligence had long anticipated a coup attempt and had contingency plans in place, these appear to have failed. One account claims that they had troops in the hills about twenty miles outside of the capital, ready to counter-attack but that they disbanded when they were misled into believing that the Libyan government had interceded on Rawlings's behalf.[94] There may also have been a small group of men from military intelligence who, riding in a white Peugot passenger car, clashed with the rebels and were either defeated or backed down.[95]

The most serious resistance faced by the coup makers in the first few hours came from the engineering regiment, which was not even a combat unit. Forty soldiers armed with light arms and shoulder-mounted recoilless rifles were sent in a truck to engage the challengers at the air force base, to which they had moved. But the truck was spotted and pinned between two armored cars, and the soldiers surrendered after warning shots were fired. A second group of soldiers from engineering was sent after the first, but these were also spotted from a distance; they retreated after shots were fired. According to one of the captured soldiers, the engineers had been scared into surrendering by just six coup makers riding in two armored cars. Of the forty soldiers who were sent, roughly ten escaped and thirty were conscripted into the mutiny, although Rawlings did not trust them enough to arm them, so they played little or no role in the events that followed.[96]

The Fifth Infantry Battalion, the main infantry unit in the capital, put up only minor resistance and folded after a few gunshots. The best explanation for this is that officers in the unit chose to flee and enlisted men had no incentive to organize and mount resistance to Rawlings on their own.

Another sign that the military command structure had entirely fallen apart comes from the actions of the head of the armed forces, Air Vice Marshall Odaate-Barnor, who personally drove an armored car into the conflict. Militaries operate on a strict hierarchical principle, so for the head of the armed forces to leave his office and drive into the fray demonstrates that either he could not communicate with his subordinates or he did not trust them. Given that he, an air force general, had taken the time to be trained in how to use an armored car and kept one at his residence suggests that a lack of trust is the more likely explanation. As he did not try to rally loyalist troops in the field or suppress the mutiny by personally appearing

---

[92] Akata-Pore was a member of the Movement on National Affairs (MONAS), a left-wing group allied with the retired major Boakye-Djan. Boakye-Djan had been one of the key figures in the June 4th coup attempt and the government that followed. While he had once been one of Rawlings's closest friends, they were now implacable opponents, and Rawlings was later to execute Boakye-Djan's younger brother for plotting to overthrow the government. MONAS argued that there should be no further coup attempts in Ghana, and they strongly backed civilian rule.

[93] Interview with Kweku Baaku. August 9, 2000. Accra, Ghana.

[94] Interview with Major (retired) Courage Quashigah. August 1, 1980. Accra, Ghana.

[95] Interview with Corporal (retired) Adam Al-Hassan. August 17, 2001. Accra, Ghana.

[96] Interview with Corporal (retired) Adam Al-Hassan. August 1,7 2001. Accra, Ghana.

and exercising authority, it is not clear exactly what Odaate-Barnor's intentions were. He claims that he had been working with another officer to coordinate a counter-attack, but there is no evidence of this and it was strongly denied by the officer in question.[97] According to Odaate-Barnor, he almost engaged rebel forces himself, personally turning the turret and aiming the gun, before deciding that the conditions were not advantageous. He claimed that operating the hand-cranked turret had caused him injury so he could no longer drive the vehicle and he did not trust the soldiers in the vehicle to follow his orders, so he simply abandoned the armored car at 2 a.m., after which he was no longer involved in the events of the coup.[98]

At 10 a.m., the rebels sent an armored car and a large truck to the broadcasting facilities, where they engaged in a minor skirmish with defending troops. After some sporadic firing, government troops surrendered control of the radio station (Ziorklui 1988, 314).[99] Rawlings made his broadcast at 1 p.m., announcing that the incumbent had been replaced by a new revolutionary order. He explained that he was not playing the national anthem, as was typical during coup announcements, because this was not a coup but a revolution, a "holy war" to transform Ghanaian society (Ziorklui 1988, 312). The country would not be ruled by the military, he claimed, but by the people (Yeebo 1991, 48). Despite this claim, a new junta was announced, comprising many of the same men who had been in charge after the June 4 mutiny (Shillington 1992, 80). As to the old government, listeners were told that President Limann was on the run, but that nobody should harm him and that ministers from his government should turn themselves in.

The coup makers were surprised to find their coup attempt greeted largely with indifference by many enlisted men. They had expected soldiers to rise up en masse, much as they had toward the end of the last mutiny. The radio broadcast had instructed enlisted men to assemble and arm themselves as part of the revolution (Ziorklui 1988, 312), but when the coup makers went into the barracks, they did not pick up enthusiastic volunteers (Yeebo 1991, 47). The soldiers appeared more interested in celebrating New Year than joining the coup, and the number of new recruits to the mutiny was low, probably in the tens rather than hundreds (Government of Ghana 2004, 54).[100]

Because the coup makers were so weak, pockets of resistance continued through the late afternoon of December 31. The army operations room remained functioning until it was shelled around 3 or 4 p.m., causing the death of one major there. The headquarters building for the First Infantry Brigade was able to hold out until

---

[97]Odaate-Barnor claims to have been working with Colonel Samuel Ofosu-Apea, the officer who foiled Rawlings's earlier plot on Christmas Eve and who would later intervene against the mutiny. Colonel Ofosu-Apea rejects this claim, saying that not only were they not coordinating but that Marshall Barnor had been entirely unsympathetic to his efforts earlier.

[98]Interview with Air Vice Marshall (retired) Odaate-Barnor. September 14, 2000. Accra, Ghana.

[99]An alternate source claims that the radio station was guarded by three police armored cars whose occupants ran away rather than fight back. Interview with Corporal (retired) Adam Al-Hassan. August 17, 2001. Accra, Ghana

[100]Interview with anonymous (retired) army sergeant. August 14, 2001. Accra, Ghana.

6 p.m. by firing their recoilless rifles at any armored car that came near, thus blocking four separate attempts by the mutineers to take over. Much to the infantrymen's frustration, however, they had only anti-personnel shells for their recoilless rifles, not anti-tank munitions. This was apparently another coup prevention effort, but one that backfired. Loyalists were able to keep the mutineers at bay but could not knock out any of the rebel armored vehicles with the munitions they had.[101]

In the end, the officers at the First Infantry Brigade also gave up. By this point the central locations for coordinating resistance, army headquarters and the Ministry of Defense operations room, had already surrendered. The brigade commander was unable to contact either the head of the military or the army commander and had become panicked. The number of men remaining at the First Infantry Brigade headquarters had dwindled from roughly 150 in the morning to only 8 by 6 p.m. No longer able to get any information about what was happening, the defenders thought that further resistance was futile if all the other officers had already given up and simply left.[102]

Although the coup makers now dominated the capital, they had yet to face their strongest resistance. Colonel Ofosu-Apea, the same officer who had scuttled the plot scheduled for December 24, brought troops 150 miles from the city of Takoradi to try to block Rawlings.[103] Colonel Ofosu-Apea had first heard about the coup attempt at 6 a.m. on December 31, when the brigade commander, Brigadier Michael Abanah, called to let him know that there was some unspecified trouble in the capital. When the brigade commander called a second time to request that Ofosu-Apea send an anti-tank team (four men, working in two pairs, using Carl Gustav shoulder-mounted recoilless rifles) to Accra, he decided that there must be something seriously wrong. If the brigade commander could not find two recoilless rifles and the men to work them among all the soldiers stationed at the capital, he needed to mobilize his entire battalion for action. Sounding the alarm, he had all his men ready to move by 10 a.m., fabricating a cover story as a pretext for the activity and omitting any mention of Rawlings.

This counter-coup effort faced significant logistical difficulties. A decade of sustained military neglect had left the Second Infantry Battalion with little functioning transport.[104] In the end, Colonel Ofosu-Apea was able to cobble together a force consisting of one three-ton truck, one Pinzgauer transport vehicle, and two Land Rovers to move sixty-seven enlisted men and four officers. Because the truck broke down repeatedly, the 150-mile journey to the capital took all day and the troops arrived after dark on December 31. They engaged in some skirmishes along the way, arresting two groups of rebels who were manning roadblocks on the outskirts of town.

---

[101] Interview with Brigadier (retired) Joseph Odei. August 7, 2000. Accra, Ghana.

[102] Interview with Brigadier (retired) Joseph Odei. August 7, 2000. Accra, Ghana.

[103] This section is based entirely on Ofosu-Apea's account of events. The broad strokes of his story—the size of his force, the time of their arrival, the conditions of their defeat—have been confirmed elsewhere.

[104] Military rule had been bad for operational readiness within the armed forces.

If Ofosu-Apea's battalion had been able to arrive within a reasonable amount of time, there is no doubt that it would have had a significant impact. Unlike other units, this group had anti-tank munitions that would have given them the edge if they had not been ambushed. While the colonel had been able to move only a small number of men, they would have been sufficient for the task, and he was unlikely to have backed down easily. Unfortunately for them, however, the delays gave the coup makers enough prior warning that the battalion was on their way to plan accordingly.

Colonel Ofosu-Apea divided his forces into two groups. The first and smaller group recaptured the radio station, but they were unable to hold it for long. After thirty minutes, they were challenged by a rebel armored car and were defeated after twenty or thirty minutes of heavy firing. The larger group went in the three-ton truck to attack the headquarters of the armored unit, but they were ambushed by an armored car in the vicinity of the military hospital, their truck destroyed, and a small number of the soldiers in it killed. At this point, the last holdouts decided to retreat rather than fight until the bitter end, and Ofosu-Apea went into exile. This was the end of the last military resistance to the coup attempt.[105]

For the first time in Ghana, coup makers also faced civilian opposition. In the past, successful coup attempts (with the exception of the palace coups that went unmarked by the public) had been welcomed by enthusiastic civilian demonstrations. This time, anti-coup demonstrations took place for two days in the north of Ghana, including calls for the population to engage in resistance to the new government. In the capital, a member of the displaced ruling party attempted to organize similar protests, but his efforts were quickly crushed (Yeebo 1991, 48-49). These protests seemed to have no impact on the viability of the new regime.

Analysis

From both a tactical and popular perspective, Rawlings's victory was extremely unlikely. A successful coup by ten largely unarmed men without any command authority cannot be accommodated within the paradigm that coups are like battles. And while the incumbent was extremely unpopular, Rawlings was anathema among the officer corps, and officers far outnumbered the challengers and their allies. Enlisted men also were largely unenthusiastic about the coup attempt at first, responding to Rawlings's broadcast mostly by continuing with their holiday festivities.

Rawlings's real strength was that the officers believed that the enlisted men would support him and therefore decided not to oppose the coup and risk the penalties attached. This expectation was based on the successful June 4 coup attempt and the repeated public warnings about Rawlings made by the incumbent government. The challengers started with a strong edge in expectations, which were further reinforced when they made the only radio broadcasts during the course of

---

[105]Interview with Colonel (retired) Samuel K. Ofosu-Apea. August 20, 2001. Accra, Ghana.

the attempt, giving them clear dominance over the airwaves. Rawlings succeeded because the officer corps believed he would win, a belief which became self-fulfilling.

Coups as Battles

That roughly ten original conspirators managed to take control of a military that was roughly 9,000 men strong is entirely inconsistent with the idea that coups are like battles. As one conspirator admitted, there is no way "to explain militarily why that operation was successful."[106]

The theory does better at predicting the targets of the coup attempt, almost all of which (except the radio station) were on a military base and could have had some tactical importance. It does less well at predicting the nature and intensity of the clashes. Although the confrontation between coup makers and the late-arriving loyalists from the Second Infantry Battalion was intense and resulted in a truck riddled with bullets, the death toll was only a handful of the forty or soldiers in the truck, and the remaining soldiers were allowed to disperse. Contrary to this theory's predictions, coup makers did not try to hunt them down and kill them to prevent them from regrouping and attacking again. Furthermore, most encounters between the two sides were not bloody. For example, the loyalist engineers surrendered after the challengers fired a single warning shot, rather than digging in and fighting hard, the way they would have done if the country was being invaded.

In general, the intensity of the conflict and the resulting death toll were limited by the fact that many officers ran away. Casualties occurred when direct confrontations did take place, but these were rare. While tactical factors were important, Rawlings's tactical weakness did not prevent him from taking over, nor did it mean that most clashes were bloody and fought like military battles.

Coups as Elections

The theory that coups are like elections also does not fit the events of the 1981 coup attempt. It is true that there was little love for President Limann, but enlisted men also had little enthusiasm for Rawlings and officers were strongly opposed to another mutiny. If an election had been held within the military, enlisted men would likely have stayed home, while officers (admittedly less numerous) would have turned out at high rates to vote against the challenger. There was a similarly low demand for Rawlings's return in the population at large. Rawlings had expected his broadcast to set off a "spontaneous uprising from the workers and oppressed groups," but instead there were several days of protests against him (Yeebo 1991, 47).

The challengers' success also contradicts another claim of the theory, namely that preferences correspond to actions. Although officers were strongly opposed to the coup, most gave up rather than fight back. Lastly, Rawlings's broadcast was not intended to convince listeners to support him and would have worked poorly as a campaign speech during an election. He did not appeal to the undecided, and

---

[106]Interview with anonymous (retired) air force officer. June 26, 2000. Accra, Ghana.

while he did instruct his supporters to arm themselves and join the revolution, he did not tell them that the success of the uprising required their active participation, nor did they heed his call.

Coups as Coordination Games

Rawlings's victory can best be understood in terms of the way expectations of his success became self-fulfilling. At the start of the coup, it was widely believed within the military that enlisted men would support a coup by Rawlings. In part this was based on history, since the previous mutiny had succeeded and Rawlings had left office even more popular than when he had taken power. These expectations were further reinforced repeatedly and publicly by the actions of the incumbent government. The administration repeatedly accused Rawlings of plotting coups and being behind various security incidents without doing anything to stop him, making him seem both powerful and elusive and making themselves seem weak. These broadcasts, which went so far as to publicly beg enlisted men to remain loyal to the administration, helped create expectations and meta-expectations that the coup was bound to succeed and that opposition would be futile.

Once the coup started, therefore, it is unsurprising that even the president's own counter-coup force bandwagoned behind Rawlings, convinced that they had no other feasible option. The head of the group told his radical allies that the coup was going to succeed and advised them that it would be most prudent for them to support it and try to seize power from within at a later date.[107]

As the coup attempt got under way, the challengers were adept at further building expectations in their favor via broadcasts. They controlled the radio station from 10 a.m. on, with the exception of half an hour when it was wrested from them by late-arriving loyalist troops from the Second Infantry Battalion. The only broadcast that was actually made was by Rawlings, and it was consistent with the aim of making a fact: Rawlings announced that the Limann government had been overthrown, announced the members of the new government, and even extended his protection to the person of the president, who, Rawlings claimed, was on the run. This claim of victory was premature, as Rawlings had only tens of soldiers on his side and controlled little territory, but it was a plausible statement because it was consistent with prior expectations. As time went on and no counter-broadcast was made, both the officers and the soldiers in loyalist units just stopped fighting. As one of the enlisted men in the capital infantry said to me while explaining the lack of resistance, "Unless he [a soldier] sees his brother take the lead ... he is not prepared to take the lead."[108]

Also consistent with coordination, most of the skirmishes during the coup were low in intensity. When loyalist troops from the engineering regiment attacked, they

---

[107]Interview with Kweku Baaku. August 9, 2000. Accra, Ghana.

[108]The source was a member of the Fifth Infantry Battalion who was not present at the time, so his information is second-hand. Interview with Lance Corporal (retired) Rexford Ohemeng. August 13, 2001. Accra, Ghana.

surrendered after the first warning shot. The most intense clash of the coup attempt was when troops from the Second Infantry were ambushed by coup makers, but even then bloodshed was limited, because rebels did not press their advantage and slaughter the remaining loyalist troops. For their part, the loyalists chose to retreat and abandon the fight after they lost the initial confrontation, rather than fight to the last man. Although there are no definitive sources of casualty figures from this coup attempt, one somewhat unreliable source estimates the total death toll at fifteen: eleven enlisted men and four officers (Awoonor 1984). If that total is true, this was one of Ghana's bloodier coup attempts, consistent with the claim that coups from the bottom tend to have more casualties than other types of coups.

As in all the other coups we have looked at, the constraints associated with rank influenced the dynamics of the coup in that the challengers faced logistical obstacles of the sort not faced by coup makers from the middle or top. For example, coup makers were concerned that they would not be able to access the armory of the armored regiment once they captured the base.[109] In addition, their tactical weakness meant that there were several points during the coup when the coup makers were extremely vulnerable. Had the small group of conspirators been detected as they came into the armored unit, for instance, they could easily have been stopped. Had the loyalist forces from the engineering unit not been detected or the forces from Takoradi arrived sooner, or had the First Brigade possessed a few armor-piercing shells, it would have been much harder for the mutiny to succeed. In an attempt with so few conspirators and such ad hoc organization, chance can play a larger role and "for want of a nail" stories more likely. This is part of what makes a coup from the bottom so risky.

The one area where the coordination game explanation falls short is that the coup makers did not attack any symbolic targets besides the radio station, even though a civilian government was in power and symbols of state authority existed outside the military base. In this case, it is possible that expectations so favored Rawlings already that this was not necessary or perhaps that he lacked the manpower necessary to capture symbolic targets.

Conclusion

Coups from the bottom are the least likely to succeed, because mutineers have the fewest organizational resources with which to make a fact and they face the greatest number of obstacles. Coups from the bottom are more chaotic and relatively bloodier, despite efforts made by both sides to reduce bloodshed.

On a tactical level, a mutiny resembles a coup from the middle more than a coup from the top because mutineers have some hard power but almost no soft power. Mutineers cannot lay the groundwork effectively for the mutiny beforehand the

---

[109] Alfred Ogbamey. June 16, 2003. *Adabuga Vrs Cudjoe: Who Is Committing Perjury?* http://www.ghanaweb.com/GhanaHomePage/NewsArchive/printnews.php?ID=37827. Accra: Gye Nyame Concord. Accessed June 16, 2003.

way a general could, nor can they call a meeting. In fact, they can barely conspire without attracting attention. While they can capture and hold targets by force the way a colonel can, they have to work against a system that is designed to prevent the bottom of the hierarchy from operating autonomously. As a result, mutineers will always be more disorganized and tactically weaker than challengers from the middle would be.

Because of the tactical weakness of mutineers, the success of coups from the bottom is usually explained by the elections model, in terms of the breadth and intensity of grievance held by junior officers, non-commissioned officers, and enlisted men. But, as demonstrated by the three cases in this chapter, widespread support for the coup attempt is neither necessary nor sufficient for it to succeed. That grievance is not a sufficient explanation for coup outcomes is particularly clear from the two mutinies in 1979, which had different outcomes even though they took place under roughly the same conditions. Even the successful coup attempt in the second of those attempts had difficulty attracting support at first, despite support for the grievances articulated by the mutineers. Conversely the coup attempt in December 1981 succeeded without much support.

Instead of grievances or guns, the critical factor in these three coups was beliefs. In May 1979, nobody believed that other enlisted men would join in a mutiny, and so even members of other conspiracies failed to join the aborted rebellion. Because Rawlings did not capture the radio station, he also was unable to use public information to try to make a fact. By June, however, the informational context was entirely different, thanks to the trial of the May conspirators, which had made common knowledge of the willingness among enlisted men to support a mutiny. Then, two years later, in 1981, Rawlings succeeded because the precedent of June 1979 helped create expectations favorable to his coup attempt, as did the government's misguided campaign to portray him as public enemy number one and Rawlings's own broadcast during the coup. In 1981, Rawlings won, not because he was strong or popular, but because everybody expected him to and acted accordingly.

Chapter 7

USSR, 1991: Three Days That Changed the World

The 1991 Soviet coup attempt was arguably the most important coup attempt of the twentieth century. The Union of Soviet Socialist Republics was one of the world's two superpowers, geographically larger by far than any other country, and in possession of the biggest nuclear arsenal in the world. At stake in this coup attempt was not just control over one of the most powerful political entities in the world but the very survival of the Soviet Union. Yet the outcome of this coup is puzzling. That this coup attempt, undertaken by a coalition that included every major senior military and political figure in the country short of its target, Soviet Union president Mikhail Gorbachev, did not succeed is hard to understand. Indeed, even opponents of the coup believed that it would succeed, and at least one went so far as to call the failure of the coup a miracle.[1]

In the context of this book, this coup attempt is also of interest because it is very different from the Ghanaian cases presented earlier. The Soviet state was twice as old as any in post-colonial Africa and extremely well institutionalized. Despite its economic decline, the Soviet Union was still one of the wealthiest countries ever to experience a coup attempt, and the Soviet military was one of the largest, strongest, and most professional in the world. This attempt was also different in that it was a failed coup from the top and involved high levels of civilian mobilization and multiple mass media outlets. Given these differences, the Soviet coup attempt of 1991 would appear to provide a challenging test for the argument that coups are like coordination games. That the theory provides useful insights even in this seemingly least likely case suggests that it truly captures something universal about coups.

The novel reading of the Soviet coup of 1991 in this chapter argues that the attempt failed because the junta behind it was less adept at manipulating expectations than its adversaries. As we shall see, because the conspirators represented virtually the entire state apparatus, they were overconfident and failed to use the resources at their disposal to make a fact as effectively as possible. This left room

---

[1]Frontline. 2000. *Yevgenia Albats.* <http://www.pbs.org/wgbh/pages/frontline/shows/yeltsin/interviews/albats.html>. Boston: WGBH. Accessed: December 16, 2002.

for the Russian president, Boris Yeltsin, and his allies in the media to hijack the content of public broadcasts and create self-fulfilling expectations that the junta was not in control. Yeltsin's faction understood what the junta did not: that during a coup attempt nominal control over the armed forces is not sufficient by itself to take over a country.

The conventional wisdom about why the Soviet coup attempt failed is that the coup makers lacked popular legitimacy and lacked support beyond a handful of old generals and bureaucrats. According to this account, Gorbachev's liberalizing reforms had so dramatically transformed Soviet society that it was impossible to return to the old system, as the old guard figures behind the attempt hoped to do. As a result, the coup attempt was rejected by virtually everybody: common citizens, the middle class, even most of those in the military. The coup was doomed when the people rallied to Yeltsin, surrounding the Russian parliament building with large crowds and defending it with impregnable barriers. Supposedly, this led military officers and their men to defect to the democratic movement, openly switching sides and vowing to protect the people against any attack from those who had illegitimately usurped power. The coup attempt, in this telling, revealed how hollow the Soviet system had become. Once the coup attempt was rejected by the people, it collapsed.

However, the truth of what happened is far more interesting than this myth. This chapter demonstrates that the conventional account does not accurately depict what happened but is a story that was strategically deployed by anti-coup forces to try to block the takeover. An examination of the facts makes clear that the coup did not fail simply because of Yeltsin's ability to rally civilians to his side. While Yeltsin did gather some crowds around him, they were smaller than was claimed, and they and the barricades they set up could have been moved by a determined military. (Indeed, Yeltsin crushed another challenge at the same location two years later.) Nor did it fail because the military switched its allegiance and deserted the junta, since only a handful of officers and men actually defected to Yeltsin. Even at the very end of the coup attempt, when it appeared that military action would be used to crush the opposition, most military officers offered no more support than engaging in some shirking and foot-dragging as they paused to find out what other military actors were doing.

Instead, the coup failed because those who opposed it proved far better at manipulating information and expectations than the junta did. Pro-democracy forces, most significantly those in the Soviet media (even the state-run media) kept up a steady drum beat of stories designed to make the junta seem far weaker than it was and Yeltsin far stronger than he was. They flooded the airwaves with false claims that particular military leaders did not support the coup or had even gone over to Yeltsin's side. These repeated assertions that the junta was not in control of the military became widely believed and they shaped expectations.

As we shall see, the junta proved completely incapable of countering this propaganda campaign and showed little understanding of how important it was. Without adequate refutation, these stories picked up steam until they were believed inside the junta itself. Fearing that an attack on Yeltsin might trigger a civil war, the junta ultimately canceled their scheduled assault at the last minute, and the coup attempt collapsed. Repeated public assertions that the junta was not in control had become a self-fulfilling reality.

In short, although there are many differences between the USSR and Ghana and this coup attempt was quite unusual in a number of ways, viewing the 1991 Soviet coup as a coordination game provides considerable insights into the dynamics and outcome of this attempt. Against all odds, the side that was best able to manipulate information and expectations prevailed against the might of the Soviet state. Soviet officers engaged in fence-sitting and bandwagoning (i.e., coordination) just as officers in Ghana had. Despite the enormously high stakes in this coup attempt, the whole affair was resolved with only a handful of accidental civilian casualties and no military deaths. In the end, the junta backed down rather than risk a civil war, and they surrendered without making a last stand. Although important aspects of the coup attempt are idiosyncratic, much of the behavior that has puzzled other scholars is coherent and consistent with this theory. In both Ghana and the Soviet Union, the theory that coups are coordination games is more effective in explaining observed behavior than the competing explanations.

Background

The 1991 coup attempt emerged from a surfeit of grievances against Mikhail Gorbachev held by members of the Soviet national security organizations. In the two decades before Gorbachev came into power and began enacting his liberalizing policies, the institutional interests of the military had prospered. The armed forces had been provided with ample resources, granted a great deal of control over their own affairs, and enjoyed a good deal of prestige because of their victory in World War II and important role in Cold War politics (Taylor 2003b, 22-23). However, Gorbachev had had to transfer significant resources from military to civilian use to implement his economic reforms. To accomplish this, he asserted control over defense policy, a policy arena traditionally left to the military, to diminish Soviet military commitments. Gorbachev's government reduced the army by 500,000 soldiers, cut arms spending by almost a third, and began to convert the defense industry into civilian production (Taylor 2003b, 23).

The political changes that accompanied Gorbachev's policy of *glasnost* posed a further challenge to the military. *Glasnost*, or openness, led to public scrutiny of the military for the first time. The press was intensely critical, blaming the military for the USSR's ignominious failure in Afghanistan and for the bloated military-industrial complex. The result was a decline both in morale within the military and in respect for the military within society (Taylor 2003b, 24).

Another source of grievance was the collapse of the Warsaw Pact, which followed glasnost, and the abrupt way in which it was handled. Not only did the withdrawal of troops from the countries of Eastern Europe weaken the USSR's strategic position, but it also meant that twenty entire divisions had to be repatriated in a short time span, which was very disruptive (Taylor 2003b, 25).

The country's chief intelligence arm, the KGB, shared the military's sense of disquiet over the end of the Warsaw Pact. In addition to believing it a bad policy decision, they also were upset that the collapse had exposed some members of the intelligence services in former member nations of the pact, some of whom were arrested and tried. Continued domestic changes, they feared, might lead to a similar fate for them in the Soviet Union (Knight 2003, 74-75).

Lastly, one of the strongest causes of grievance for members of the state security organs was the increase in ethno-nationalism that had arisen within the Soviet Union. Regional movements directly challenged the authority of the military; many of them opposed the draft and even constituted their own regional armed bodies (Taylor 2003*b*, 25). The armed forces were used repeatedly to intervene within the republics, notably in Tbilisi in 1989, Baku in 1990, and Vilnius in 1991. In each of these cases, the resulting bloodshed had been blamed on the military rather than the government, further harming the military's reputation while Gorbachev managed to keep his hands clean. Each of these actions had been joint operations between the regular armed forces and the MVD, the separate forces of the interior ministry. The regular military, however, felt that internal policing was the MVD's role alone and that the use of military troops for what one general called "gendarme" functions was "humiliating."[2]

What most worried those within the security organizations, however, was what they saw as the impending dissolution of the Soviet Union as a political entity, and of the Soviet military with it. Gorbachev had negotiated a new Union Treaty with a number of the republics, giving them sovereign status. Under this agreement, power would devolve to the republics themselves and Soviet institutions such as the KGB would cease to have any authority within them. Those at the top of the security apparatus saw this as an obvious threat to the territorial integrity of the union. Although they had tolerated domestic reform and the end of Soviet hegemony in Eastern Europe, dissolution of the union, according to those who hatched the coup, was the final straw. It was their job to protect the Soviet Union, and they would not sit back and watch it being dismantled (Knight 2003, 85).

According to some observers, Gorbachev was also unhappy with the Union Treaty and thus manipulated conservatives within the Soviet power structure into taking action to save the Soviet Union, thereby giving Gorbachev his desired outcome without involving him in the process. By that reading, although Gorbachev found himself under intense pressure from members of his government to prevent this erosion of their (and his) powers, he also recognized that any effort on his part to put the independence genie back in the bottle would be political suicide. According to Amy Knight, Gorbachev therefore decided on a third option, manipulating hard-liners into invoking a state of emergency that "might create the kind of crisis that would lead the West to reconsider bailing the Soviet Union out of

---

[2]The quoted words are those of General Lebed discussing the military action in Baku (Taylor 2003*b*, 30).

its economic crisis for the sake of political stability" (Knight 2003, 82). When the Soviet conservatives did take action, however, Gorbachev failed to back them up. Some conspirators and analysts have come to view Gorbachev's refusal to endorse the junta as strategic—that, once again, he wanted somebody else to do the dirty work while he kept his own hands clean. What is significant for the sake of this analysis, however, is that the conspirators believed that Gorbachev would give his blessing to their actions and were surprised when he refused to cooperate.

Conspiracy

The conspiracy to stage a coup began in the spring of 1991. The original conspirators included key members of the Soviet state, including the head of the KGB, the defense minister, the prime minister, the secretary of the Central Committee, and the chief of the president's staff. When conservative attempts to block the Union Treaty at the Central Committee plenum and the Supreme Soviet failed, those in power became more alarmed, and the plot expanded to include the chairman of the Supreme Soviet, the minister of the interior, two deputy ministers of defense, and six others (Odom 1998, 310).

On August 5, the day after Gorbachev left for his annual vacation in the Crimea, the conspiracy went into full swing. That day, the plotters met at a KGB safe house in Moscow. They had approximately two weeks in which to plan and execute their takeover before Gorbachev was due to return on August 20. The plan of action the conspirators decided upon was to confront Gorbachev and ask him to either declare martial law or resign. If Gorbachev did neither, the vice president would declare that Gorbachev was sick and take over in Gorbachev's place. The plotters also agreed on the need to implement martial law nationwide as soon as they took over and to arrest important pro-democracy and nationalist figures. They continued to work on the coup, convening for a final time on August 17 (Odom 1998, 310-311).

The conspirators' plans were far from airtight. By the time of their last meeting, one day before the coup was due to begin, they still had not finalized the list of targets to be occupied or the units that would be responsible for doing so. One reason for this degree of organizational slackness is that they assumed that the coup would generally go as planned—that Gorbachev would cooperate and popular opposition would be muted. This was not an unreasonable assumption; the Soviet Union had a history of extra-constitutional leadership changes that had gone smoothly. Because the conspirators included almost all of the members of the current government *except* Gorbachev, making the coup almost an *autogolpe*, they expected to prevail without any trouble. A second reason for disorganization is that the coup attempt involved three different military forces—the KGB, the interior ministry, and the regular armed forces—which added an extra level of complexity to the planning (Odom 1998, 311-312).

Attempt

The coup began on Sunday, August 18, 1991.[3] That afternoon, five of the conspirators flew to Gorbachev's dacha in the Crimea and demanded that Gorbachev either declare a state of emergency or resign. When he did neither, they took away his nuclear briefcase and put him under house arrest. As noted earlier, Gorbachev's refusal to cooperate came as a surprise to many of the junta members, which led to bickering among them, as some became suspicious that the others might try to back out and avoid responsibility for what they had done (Odom 1998, 312).[4]

At 4:00 a.m. the next morning, Monday, August 19, the junta declared martial law. At 6:30 a.m., the junta issued a press release stating that Gorbachev had been relieved of his duties "due to the condition of his health" and that Vice President Gennadi Yanayev was now in charge. The junta called itself the State Committee on the State of Emergency, or GKChP, its Russian acronym.

The same morning, KGB commandos also surrounded Yeltsin's vacation home near Moscow, but Yeltsin was not immediately arrested as planned.[5] After consulting with his advisors, Yeltsin took advantage of this opportunity and made a dash to the "White House"—the Russian parliament building—where he issued a public statement declaring the junta illegal and asking for popular support. Around noon, Yeltsin climbed atop a tank to make his famous speech denouncing the junta. This image, which became one of the defining images of the coup, was captured by a CNN cameraman and beamed around the world, including within the Soviet Union, thus bypassing domestic censorship. Several thousand people rallied to the White House in response to Yeltsin's plea, including 250 deputies of the Russian parliament. The White House became a center of opposition to the junta and was fortified with barricades and a defensive perimeter. Yeltsin and other coup opponents took up residence in the building.

A number of sectors of civil society opposed the coup attempt, most notably the local media. Afraid that the coup would mean the end of the media freedom that had come with *glasnost*, journalists were openly hostile in their questioning

---

[3]The information presented in this section represents a largely conventional summary of events and is drawn from Odom (1998, 306-310). Additional details are presented in the analysis section as they are germane to the assessment of each theory.

[4]Dunlop (2003, 101-107) points to a number of odd aspects of Gorbachev's "captivity" in Foros. According to Dunlop, both Gorbachev and his wife have stated that the presidential bodyguards could easily have arrested the would-be junta when they came to Gorbachev's dacha. Dunlop also argues that Gorbachev was not cut off from the world but was in fact communicating with his advisors and the some of the presidents of the various Soviet republics for at least part of the coup attempt. Dunlop says, "My tentative conclusion with regard to Gorbachev's isolation at Foros is to agree with the Military Collegium of the Russian Supreme Court, which concluded in August 1994 that Gorbachev had not in fact been under 'house arrest' at Foros, because he had not attempted to break the blockade of the dacha complex" (102).

[5]Why Yeltsin was not arrested remains a mystery. Odom claims that the KGB chief believed that he could come to an agreement with Yeltsin, and so did not issue final orders to arrest him in a timely fashion (Odom 1998, 314). Yeltsin himself claims that the order to arrest him had been canceled, while another source claims that soldiers balked at carrying out their orders (Dunlop 2003, 107).

of the junta during its first press conference on Monday night. Even journalists at the major state-run television station took a stand, deliberately presenting their live coverage of the junta's first press conference in such a way that made the junta leader look weak, drunk, or scared. Their coverage also dwelled on the defiant stance toward the junta taken by reporters at the press conference. During the 9 p.m. news, journalists at the main state-run television station showed images of the crowds that were gathering around the White House, read negative reactions of foreign leaders to the coup attempt, and even went so far as to air footage of Yeltsin calling the junta illegal (Korchagina 2001*b*). This resistance by the media was to prove critical to the junta's downfall, as it showed the junta had lost control over the content of public broadcasts and was having its claims to power undermined.

The soldiers who had been stationed around the White House acted neutrally. They had no orders to suppress the protestors and took pains to let the civilians around them know that they were not about to open fire. Soldiers and protesters mingled, with protestors climbing on tanks and trying to convince soldiers that the junta was in the wrong. Six tank crews even defected, stationing their tanks with the turrets pointing out, away from the White House. These tanks served mainly a propaganda purpose, however, since their guns were not loaded and the soldiers in the tanks did not even have ammunition in their side arms (Felgenhauer 2001).

Later that night, a battalion of airborne troops arrived at the White House, seemingly in support of Yeltsin and his supporters, and was let inside the barricades. These troops did not defect, however, and chose to withdraw the next morning. The troops were there because Boris Yeltsin was on friendly terms with General Grachev, commander of the Soviet Army's airborne infantry forces, and had asked him for assistance. In turn, General Grachev had asked his deputy, General Lebed, to send a battalion of airborne forces to the White House. The forces were not told to support Yeltsin but were given only the ambiguous mission of guarding and defending the White House. Although the troops did spend the night near the White House, they were not transferred to Yeltsin's control, were not told against whom they were defending the White House (in fact, no attack was planned for that night), did not take sides, and were withdrawn by General Grachev the next morning (Odom 1998, 330-332). Grachev, who would later admit to straddling the fence in the coup, was unwilling to openly back Yeltsin at the time and blamed his subordinate General Lebed for the mysterious troop movements.

The junta members were surprised by the extent and speed of Yeltsin's opposition. Miscalculating his resolve, they tried to negotiate with him. By Monday evening, having wasted a day and the opportunity to dislodge him when he was weakest, they finally understood that Yeltsin was not going to budge easily. Even with the presence of the airborne troops and the crowds, the coup opponents inside the White House spent the first night of the three-day coup uneasily, waiting for an attack, and being relieved when morning came without one.

On Tuesday, the anti-coup forces increased their activity level. The atmosphere outside the White House was tense but festive as crowds continued to gather. Prominent speakers addressed the crowd, including the famous exiled cellist Mstislav

Rostropovich, who was coincidentally in Moscow for a conference (Korchagina 2001*a*). To show their pro-Western leanings, all day long people brought take-out food from Pizza Hut and McDonald's to feed the defenders holed up in the White House.[6] Inside the White House, Yeltsin and others were on the phone constantly, speaking with the media, foreign leaders, and contacts within the Soviet state, trying both to get across their argument against the junta and to find out what was going on elsewhere.[7]

For their part, military officers who had joined the anti-coup forces were similarly calling every officer they knew, trying to get intelligence on what was happening, trying to convince them that the coup was a bad idea, and telling them that many units were joining the resistance (Felgenhauer 2001). They waged a campaign of psychological warfare against the coup makers, planting false stories in the media about the defection of key junta members and top generals in the armed forces. Efforts to strengthen the defense of the White House continued, including placement of armed groups on the roof to foil helicopter landings. Yeltsin also reached out to the military in his speeches, warning that the junta was leading the armed forces into bloodshed and civil war (Yeltsin 1992, 106).

Meanwhile, instead of waging an information or propaganda battle of their own, the junta spent the day finally planning an attack on the White House. The planning was laborious; the attack would employ forces from the regular military, the KGB, and the MVD.[8] An attack was set for 3 a.m. that night, and troops were ordered into position.

By this point, some opposition to the proposed attack had developed within the military. General Grachev and General Shaposhnikov, the head of the Soviet Air Force, had privately voiced disagreement with the plan, and now General Grachev leaked news of the planned assault to Yeltsin and General Shaposhnikov obstructed logistical support to cause delays in the arrival of troops for the assault. As a result of these delays and of additional shirking by mid-level commanders, not all of the units designated for the attack had arrived at the prescribed location at the 1 a.m. appointed time.

For reasons that are still a matter of debate, the junta never gave the final order for the assault. According to the procurator general, the defense minister, Marshall Yazov, suspended the attack at 2 a.m. (Odom 1998, 320).[9] Afterward, a number of

---

[6]BBC News Online. 2001. *Three days that shook the world.* <http://news.bbc.co.uk/1/hi/world /europe/1478422.stm> London: British Broadcasting Corporation. Accessed January 13, 2005.

[7]Another mystery about the coup concerns why communications to the White House were not cut off, at least when it was clear that Yeltsin was not going to cooperate, if not before. Oddly, I have not encountered any significant commentary on this issue, despite how thoroughly every aspect of this coup attempt has been debated. The only reference to Yeltsin's communications capacity that I have found is Seymour Hersh's claim that the Americans enabled Yeltsin to make secure phone calls, but this does not explain why he had the ability to make regular calls all over the world (Dunlop 2003, 111).

[8]The use of all three forces together was tactically awkward and was likely done to make sure that the blame would be shared in the event something went wrong.

[9]Elsewhere, Odom claims that Yazov sent the order to suspend the attack at 1 a.m. (Odom 1998, 335).

officers would step forward to claim credit for having stopped the attack, but there are good reasons to be skeptical of such claims, especially as their intentions were never put to the test (Hough 1997, 444).

By Wednesday morning, it was clear to all that the coup attempt had collapsed. Troops had begun to leave the city at dawn, following Defense Minister Yazov's orders. The USSR vice president and several junta members surprised Yeltsin by flying to meet with Gorbachev. Yeltsin responded by sending Aleksandr Rutskoi, the Russian Republic's vice president, and a supporting delegation after them. Once there, Rutskoi arranged for the arrest of the junta members and then returned to Moscow with the captives and a liberated Gorbachev. The coup attempt that had once seemed guaranteed of success had collapsed in disarray.

Analysis

Neither of the competing theories about coups adequately explains the events of the 1991 coup attempt. The failure of the coups as battles approach to predict the conduct and outcome of the coup is clear: the junta had overwhelming force on its side and yet lost without firing a shot. Although the coups as elections explanation seems more applicable in this case, a closer look at each period of the coup demonstrates that the model does not fit actual events. Contrary to popular opinion, the military largely followed the junta's orders during the coup attempt and never defected en masse in support of Yeltsin, not even at the very end. Instead, I argue, the failure of the coup can best be understood in terms of expectations. While the coup makers had overwhelming military superiority, they did not use this to make a fact, and therefore the opposition was able to use the media to create the mistaken but widespread impression that the junta was weak, military units were defecting to Yeltsin, and an attack on the White House might lead to a split within the armed forces and maybe even to fratricide.

Coups as Battles

From a tactical perspective, there was no reason for this coup attempt to have failed. The junta included the minister of defense, the interior minister, and the chairman of the KGB, giving them the institutional support of all the major military organizations in the country. One of the key conspirators, Deputy Defense Minister General Valentin Varennikov, was commander of all the military ground forces in the Soviet Union. During the coup, the junta called upon a crack commando unit of the KGB, troops from the MVD, armored forces, airborne troops, and *spetnaz* (special operations forces from army intelligence). The amount of force represented by the coup makers was overwhelming. As Defense Minister Dmitry Yavoz said, "You understand ... KGB troops, the KGB itself, the Army—all together. Who could resist them?" (Odom 1998, 313).

By contrast, at no point did Yeltsin have the forces necessary to mount a competent military defense of his position. According to William Odom, "the forces ...

described should have been able to storm the building successfully if they were willing to spill blood" (Odom 1998, 319). Indeed, Yeltsin himself later agreed that the White House would not have held against an assault (Taylor 2003*b*, 52, n 79). Any of the three units tasked with removing Yeltsin—MVD, KGB, or Airborne—had the capacity to take over the White House had they been resolved to do so.

Further proof of the junta's capacity to easily overwhelm the defenders was provided by an incident two years later, in October 1993, when positions were reversed and Yeltsin, using an attack plan very similar to the one drawn up by the junta to dislodge him in 1991, ordered an assault on parliamentarians who had blockaded themselves in the White House. On that occasion, according to Odom, "two or three tanks firing at the [White House] broke the defense of the barricaded parliament very quickly" (Odom 1998, 338). Although Yeltsin had more civilians supporting him in 1991 than the rebellious parliamentarians had in 1993, these additional civilians would hardly have made a difference to the tactical bottom line as long as the military was willing to use force against them.[10]

This analysis of the 1991 coup attempt is at variance with the widespread myth of Yeltsin's courageous stand. Some accounts made it appear that Yeltsin had been protected by impenetrable barriers, supported by an unassailable body of Russian civilians organized into an impromptu armed militia and backed by a sizable contingent of Russian troops. Radio Liberty correspondent Andrei Babitsky reported, "The entrance to the building is already blocked with layers of material and all the nearest points are firmly secured. Granite blocks are surrounding the building, cars have been turned on their side . . . The defenders have at their disposal automatic weapons and bottles of homemade incendiary liquid" (Bransten 2001). A similar view was echoed by one of Yeltsin's military advisors, Colonel Burkov, who "described the crowds around the White House as growing, spirited, and able to stand off an assault" (Odom 1998, 327).

Although Yeltsin encouraged the David and Goliath narrative, both during and after the coup attempt, the barricade around the White House would have done little more than momentarily slow down an attack. That the defense of the White House was organized by veterans of the Afghan campaign did more to encourage morale among the protestors than to actually provide Yeltsin substantial military strength (Odom 1998, 338). And, while a handful of troops did cross over to Yeltsin's side, they were small in both number and strength compared to the forces commanded by the junta. Yeltsin's tanks, for instance, were only for show (Felgenhauer 2001). The junta's decision to withdraw and concede defeat cannot be explained by military factors alone.

In terms of the other predictions of the theory that coups are like battles, every major military target in the country was under the control of the junta, but this

---

[10]Not all militaries are willing to use force against civilians, but the Soviet military had fired on civilians in Tbilisi in 1989, Baku in 1990, and Vilnius in 1991. Later on, the Russian military opened fire on civilians in 1993. It is possible that they would have balked in 1991, given the number of Yeltsin supporters—between 50,000 and 70,000 Russians—but they certainly had the tactical ability to easily capture the White House (Taylor 2003*b*, footnote 67).

did not help them succeed. Rather, the site that proved most important during the coup was the White House, whose importance was purely symbolic.

Lastly, the opposition to the coup was not quickly and ruthlessly suppressed. Instead, the coup makers hesitated and then backed down, declining to issue the final orders for an assault on the White House. By the end of the coup, there had been only three casualties, all them of civilians (Odom 1998, 315). A greater degree of ruthlessness would undoubtedly have helped the junta succeed, but this observation only prompts the question of why they chose to capitulate rather than attack, especially given the very high stakes involved.

Coups as Elections

The dominant explanation given for the failure of the 1991 coup attempt is that the reforms of the previous six years had so changed Soviet society, including the military, that the junta had no support beyond the most senior members of the military. Gorbachev himself subscribed to this view, saying, "If the coup d'etat had happened a year and a half or two years earlier it might, presumably, have succeeded. But now society was completely changed ... including the Army that was part of it. Officers and privates refused to go against their own people despite the threat of court martial." According to this common view, most members of the military had abandoned communism, much like society at large. Having once tasted the fruits of freedom, officers and their men were not willing to support an effort to go back.

Although this interpretation of the 1991 Soviet coup attempt possesses a fair amount of intuitive appeal, it does not correspond well with what actually occurred. There is little evidence that members of the military were opposed to the coup attempt. In fact, we see quite the opposite, that military corporate interests were threatened by *perestroika* and that members of the military had been grumbling for quite some time about the impact of its various reforms. There is little evidence that, even after popular protests began, a majority of soldiers rejected the junta or embraced Yeltsin. Furthermore, even if we posit that a massive preference shift took place within the military, it is not matched by corresponding actions. During the coup, most members of the military were compliant, neither verbally disagreeing with their orders nor refusing to carry them out, until the very end of the coup attempt. Even then, opposition to the junta was limited to fence sitting and shirking by military units rather than outright opposition and defiance.

Because of the popularity and the persistence of the coups as elections explanation of why the coup failed, it is worth examining five different phases of the coup attempt, looking for evidence that actors were against the coup and that they acted upon those preferences.

Stage 1: Before the Coup Attempt

There is little evidence that the military had rejected the old system and embraced Gorbachev before the coup attempt. To the contrary, as previously discussed, a number of significant developments had taken place under Gorbachev that could reasonably be presumed to have made members of the military unhappy. Military spending was being slashed, and military prestige and morale had declined substantially. Changes in the military were being made at great speed, with little apparent consideration for their impact on soldiers' lives. For example, no facilities had been made ready for the hundreds of thousands of soldiers who were demobilized from Eastern Europe (Zolotov 2001). Finally, the growing nationalist movements within the Soviet Union were intensely problematic for the military. To the extent that soldiers were governed by notions of duty, their obligation was to preserve the Soviet Union, and yet the new Union Treaty threatened to virtually dismantle it. Young men in the republics were refusing to comply with the draft, which had always been a grave offense. Some republics even went so far as to try to create their own military bodies and to declare that the national security agencies no longer had any authority in that republic. Members of the military were also concerned that nationalism would lead to more violence, which they were not eager to have to suppress (Taylor 2003b, 23-25).

Admittedly, there were constituencies within the military that supported these changes, but they were small and had little leverage. Some younger officers were supporters of Gorbachev, and others were affiliated with anti-Soviet nationalist groups and became involved with politics in various republics (Taylor 2003b, 23-25). None of these pro-reform movements within the military, however, was very large or powerful. They did little to generate clear support for Gorbachev (or the reform process) within the military, even though the possibility of a coup attempt loomed so clearly that the Bush administration warned Gorbachev of such a possibility three times over the summer of 1991 (Dunlop 1993, 194). Nor was there a huge wellspring of support for Yeltsin among the armed forces. Although Yeltsin was popular among civilians (he had mobilized more than a hundred thousand demonstrators during a confrontation with Gorbachev in March [Dunlop 2003, 98]), only General Kobets had openly sided with Yeltsin before the coup (Odom 1998, 340). Since Kobets was deputy chief of communications for the Soviet armed forces, no forces were actually under his command and his alliance with Yeltsin had little impact on the rest of the military. Contrary to Gorbachev's assertion, there is little evidence that the deep-seated social changes in society had transformed the military into a pro-reform constituency.

Stage 2: Early in the Coup Attempt

If there had been widespread opposition to the coup attempt within the military, and if soldiers had been willing to act upon it, then one might expect to have seen opposition to the coup attempt just as it began. Given that this coup attempt had been strongly foreshadowed, members of the security forces would have had plenty of time to decide where their loyalties lay. Any opponents of the coup would have wanted to challenge the junta early on, before it became entrenched. Also, the revelation came early that Gorbachev was being held hostage by the junta members, news that would surely have outraged loyalists, yet there was neither overt nor covert opposition to the coup attempt at this point. Virtually all military and security personnel followed their orders as directed.[11] For example, when General Yazov called a meeting to inform the military high command of their missions in the coup, nobody objected, nor did they refuse orders when troops were brought in from outside Moscow (Brusstar & Jones 1995, 14).

Stage 3: The Beginning of Mass Protests

The next likely point at which the elections theory might lead us to expect opposition was when civilians began to protest the coup in large numbers. The most common variant of the elections story argues that soldiers were strongly affected by their encounters with large crowds of civilians opposed to the coup. If this were true, by Monday night there should have been a sharp shift in military preferences and behavior.

Monday presented a number of opportunities for soldiers to be exposed to and persuaded by dissenting civilians. Yeltsin stood on a tank and called for mass resistance to the coup around noon on Monday. Throughout the afternoon and evening, civilians responded by assembling around the White House and building barricades. Later that afternoon, Yeltsin issued a decree declaring authority over all Soviet government organizations based on Russian soil. On Monday evening, Leningrad Mayor Anatoly Sobchak came out in opposition to the coup attempt and called for a general strike in Leningrad the next day. That evening, Russian vice president and decorated war hero Aleksandr Rutskoi gave a fiery speech calling specifically upon soldiers to oppose the coup, the sort of broadcast that the coups as elections theory would predict should change preferences:

> Comrades, I am an officer of the Soviet army, a colonel, a Hero of the Soviet Union, vice president of the Russian Federation. I have walked through the fiery path of Afghanistan and seen the horrors of war. I call on you, my comrade-officers, soldiers, and sailors, do not take action against the people — against your fathers, mothers, brothers, and sisters. I appeal to your honor, your reason, and your heart. Today the fate of the country, the fate of its free and democratic development, is in your hands. I call on you to cross over to the side legally elected by the people, the organs of power, the president of the Russian Federation and the Council of Ministers of the Russian Federation of Soviet Socialist Republics. (Bransten 2001)

Some opposition to the coup within the military had surfaced by Monday night, but it was either minor or ambivalent, hardly what one would expect if the coups as elections theory is correct. Some of the soldiers outside the White House, for instance, promised that they would not fire upon the Russian people after having

---

[11]General Karpukhin of the KG later claimed that he had stopped Yeltsin from being arrested at his dacha, however, there are ample reasons to be skeptical of this claim (Dunlop 1993, 212).

been browbeaten repeatedly by *babushkas* in the crowd.[12] As noted earlier, six tanks defected to Yeltsin's side and took up defensive positions around the White House (Korchagina 2001*a*). Higher up the chain of command, the head of the air force, General Shaposhnikov, delayed the arrival of some of the transport planes carrying forces to Moscow.

The most significant development on Monday was the arrival of the airborne troops sent by General Grachev in response to a request by Yeltsin. Nonetheless, the airborne forces did not side with the opposition, insisting that their mission was simply to guard and defend the White House. When pressed by members of the opposition as to what that entailed, General Lebed gave a very vague and non-committal answer.[13] These troops were never fully trusted by Yeltsin's supporters, who suspected they might be a Trojan horse, and they were withdrawn by Grachev the next day.

Significantly, there was no widespread movement by troops to back Yeltsin, despite his belief that an attack on the White House was imminent. Nor did Generals Shaposhnikov and Grachev take any public or irreversible actions to support Yeltsin. Although they assured him of their support in private, they continued largely to cooperate with the junta. The only officer to switch sides and make a serious commitment to the anti-coup forces was Major Yevdokimov, who commanded an armored company within the elite Tamanskaya division and was responsible for the tanks stationed in front of the White House. Even in this most overt case of support, however, Major Yevdokimov was able to bring over only six tanks, even though he commanded ten tanks and an armored vehicle (Korchagina 2001*a*).

Stage 4: Planning of the Assault on the White House

There was no opposition among military players to the coup during the planning of the White House attack, either. According to one commentator, at a meeting of military commanders and KGB officials to put together an attack plan, no one openly dissented: "Grachev himself later testified that he thought the operation a 'dubious idea' but said 'I kept my opinion to myself.'" This account is confirmed by an eyewitness: "Not one of [the meeting] participants refused to perform the task assigned to him" (Brusstar & Jones 1995, 14).

The closest thing to disagreement during the planning process was General Lebed's remark that an attack "would lead to a grandiose bloodletting" (Taylor 2003*b*, 47). In response, General Varennikov criticized Lebed's attitude, saying that Lebed was "obligated to be an optimist, and you [Lebed] have introduced pessimism and lack of confidence here" (Taylor 2003*b*, 48). Yet Lebed's objection to storming the White House could not have been very strong, as he was later assigned

---

[12]O'Connor, Eileen. 2001. *Never argue with a babushka.* <http://www.cnn.com/SPECIALS/ 2001/russia/stories/babushka/> Atlanta: Cable News Network, Inc. Accessed November 19, 2004.

[13]Lebed said, "Against whom does a guard post defend? Against any person or group of persons who encroach on the post or the sentry" (Odom 1998, 331). This could have applied equally to the junta and the defenders.

to draft the final assault plan and did so without any further objection. There may also have been some foot dragging by officers during the planning process, when they complained that they did not have the right number or type of resources for an attack, but none of these objections bottlenecked the planning process (Taylor 2003b, 48).

Stage 5: Assault on the White House

The final opportunity for those in the military to oppose the coup attempt was the planned assault on the White House Tuesday night. If a majority of the military had been opposed to the coup and had been prepared to act on that opposition, then we would expect to have seen widespread and overt opposition to the coup on Tuesday night. Given that the attack did not go ahead as planned and that the coup did fail, this is also the juncture within the coup attempt where we might most expect to find evidence in support of the coups as elections theory. Nonetheless, even this final period of the coup attempt provides at best weak support for the coups as elections theory.

The conventional wisdom is that the coup attempt failed when the military refused to execute the attack on the White House. In fact, of the three generals in charge of the forces scheduled to be used in the attack—General Grachev of the airborne forces, General Gromov of the MVD paramilitary forces, and General Karpukhin of the KGB—not one openly refused their orders or defected to the opposition. Although they were unwilling to take bold action to protect the White House, the generals were also not strong supporters of the assault. General Grachev had promised Yeltsin that he would not attack, and he even had General Lebed leak news of the attack to the opposition (Taylor 2003b, 48). Grachev also dragged his feet and encouraged General Gromov not to attack, claiming that neither the airborne forces nor the KGB forces were going to participate (Odom 1998, 334). General Gromov seems to have agreed with Grachev and may also have obstructed the assembly of some MVD troops (Taylor 2003a, 238). General Karpukhin's position is more ambiguous; although Karpukhin later claimed that he blocked the assault (Bonnell, Cooper & Freidin 1994, 18), other reports say he was enthusiastic (Dunlop 2003, 110).

In the end, the generals were never given the final order to attack the White House, so their private opposition to the coup attempt was never put to the test and we cannot say how they would have acted in that eventuality. What we can say is that their actions did not foreclose any possibilities even though the attack appeared to be imminent. Nor can we say that their delays were instrumental in bringing about an end to the coup attempt. At best, they would have bought Yeltsin a few hours' breathing room, but the fact remains that Yeltsin had few military resources at his disposal with which to defend himself and his supporters. The only thing that saved the White House was the lack of a final order to attack, according to Yevgeny Lisov, chief investigator in the inquiry by the Russian government into the failed coup (Dunlop 1993, 244). Although others disagree with this assessment, it is difficult to see how mere fence sitting by officers would have protected the White House given that the junta could simply have brought in a different set of military forces the next day to mount the attack. As long as officers were unwilling to openly back Yeltsin, the most the opposition could have done was delay an assault on the White House, so the key element in its survival must have been the decision by the junta not to give the final order to attack.

In short, the examination of these five stages demonstrates that the notion that the military turned against the junta en masse is a myth. Rather, it was promulgated for strategic reasons by Yeltsin's side both during and after the coup and was taken up by the military in the aftermath so as to distance themselves from the junta and disclaim institutional responsibility for the coup attempt. This argument is confirmed even by those who opposed the coup, one of whom said afterwards that "commanders and servicemen carried out all orders of the Minister of Defense to the letter" when he was asked if officers or soldiers had defected to Yeltsin's side during the coup attempt.[14]

At best, the 1991 coup attempt provides only weak support for the theory that coups operate like elections. While the presence of large numbers of civilians around the White House undoubtedly raised the costs of military action and played an important role in the resolution of the coup, there is little evidence at any stage during the coup that a majority of soldiers rejected the junta and switched allegiances to those fighting the coup. Even those generals who were opposed to the attack on the White House did nothing to stop it, demonstrating a disconnect between their preferences and their actions that is inconsistent with the basic assumptions of the theory. Lastly, while Yeltsin, Rutskoi, and others did in fact use broadcasts to try to assert a moral claim over the military and get them to switch sides (as the theory predicts), these broadcasts were apparently ineffective in getting them to do so.

Coups as Coordination Games

In this case, as in those in Ghana discussed in the previous chapters, both the dynamics and the outcome of this coup attempt are best understood as a coordination game. Because of the complexity of this case, this section examines each of the six major predictions that this theory makes about how the junta failed to make its victory appear a fait accompli and how the opposition used the media to make the military leaders appear weak and without the support of the armed forces. As these discussions demonstrate, with the outcome of the coup in doubt, members of the security forces began to sit on the fence, unwilling to fully support either side. Afraid that an attack on the White House would provoke an open split within the military and a possible fratricidal conflict, the junta then pulled back, leading to the collapse of the coup attempt.

---

[14]The quote is from Moscow Military District Chief of Staff Zolotov (Brusstar & Jones 1995, 51-52).

Control over Public Information

Despite the junta's formal control of the state apparatus, "no aspect of their plans failed more dismally" than their efforts to control the news media (Dunlop 1993, 228). Yeltsin, on the other hand, was able to dominate the airwaves, because members of the fourth estate were implacable opponents of the junta (Dunlop 1993, 219). As we will see, the coup opponents' message permeated not only the foreign and independent media but also the state media as well. It is worth reviewing each of these types of media in turn.

Although the junta promulgated a strict media policy, they made the mistake of allowing foreign journalists to remain in the country (Tolz 1991). As a result, CNN, the BBC, and the VOA/Radio Free Europe/Radio Liberty (among others) were all able to broadcast from within the White House for the duration of the entire coup attempt. Two Russian journalists working for Radio Liberty arrived in Moscow early on the morning of August 19 and began broadcasting from Munich using a telephone connection via Prague (Dunlop 1993, 220). The BBC managed something quite similar, with their reporter broadcasting continuously for fear that his international telephone connection would go dead if he stopped talking.[15] By noon on August 20, four different radio stations were broadcasting live from within the White House (Bonnell, Cooper & Freidin 1994, 348).

Foreign journalists broadcast more than just the voices of the opposition to the coup; they transmitted iconic images as well. CNN carried Yeltsin's famous speech from atop a tank and also received and aired footage from Russian television journalists that the local journalists were not allowed to air themselves.[16]

The junta took greater measures to restrict domestic independent media. In their second official declaration, they banned all but the nine official newspapers from publishing.[17] The junta also sent soldiers to surround several Moscow- and Leningrad-based independent radio stations and interrupt their broadcasts (Tolz 1991). The radio station Moscow Echo was shut down several times but kept coming back on, broadcasting declarations from Yeltsin and exhortations to the people (Varney & Martin 2000). Yeltsin even had his own ham radio station, dubbed "Radio White House," which was manned by two respected and high-profile Russian

---

[15]BBC News Online. 2001. *Eyewitness: Inside Yeltsin's bunker.* <http://news.bbc.co.uk/1/hi/world/europe/1477729.stm> London: British Broadcasting Corporation. Accessed January 13, 2005.

[16]O'Connor, Eileen. 2001. *Three days that shook the world.* <http://www.cnn.com/SPECIALS/2001/russia/stories/flashback.coup> Atlanta: Cable News Network, Inc. Accessed November 19, 2004.

[17]Because the coup attempt spanned three days, even the print media were able to come out with issues during this period. The eleven banned newspapers pooled their resources to create the *Common Newspaper* which appeared for free. One of the most outspoken newspapers came out in leaflet form, photocopied at the Library of Foreign Literature (photocopying machines were still tightly controlled by the government at that time). The Moscow City Soviet also put out a photocopied issue, headlined "The Plot of the Doomed," which they handed out to soldiers on the street (Munro 2001). To get around the censors, the city council later disguised one of their issues as an apolitical rural newspaper (Varney & Martin 2000).

journalists (Dunlop 1993, 220). This station could not generate common knowledge because of its limited range, but it helped to propagate the resistance's point of view, and its claims were picked up and repeated by other media outlets.

Most importantly, and surprisingly, the state-owned media also challenged the junta. The main Soviet television station, Channel One, took a line against the coup from the beginning. Even though the morning news was designed to be light and entertaining, newscasters wore black and spoke with solemn expressions while reporting the official announcement of the coup. When the junta held a press conference to explain what had occurred, it was shot in such a way as to expose the junta leaders to ridicule, as discussed previously and revisited in greater detail in the next section. In the main nightly news program, the newscaster read the official announcements by the junta but punctuated them with statements by various world leaders condemning the coup. Channel One showed footage of the civilians who had assembled around the White House to resist the coup, describing them as "human waves that kept rolling in, one after another." They even aired footage of Yeltsin condemning the change of government as an illegal coup. Amazingly, this program passed the KGB censor who had arrived at the station in the morning. Since Channel One was the main state-run television station and was being repeated on other channels whose programming had been canceled, anything broadcast on Channel One could be seen by almost any Soviet citizen (Korchagina 2001b).[18]

Content of Broadcasts

Not only did the junta lose effective control over most of the mediasphere, but it proved fairly inept at using the broadcasts it did make to favorably shape expectations within the military. Again, this was a reflection of how poorly they understood the task in front of them. They thought they were involved in a largely civilian policy dispute, one in which they would have Gorbachev's support, and they had no idea what would actually be involved in taking effective power.[19] Having come up through the Soviet system, the conspirators confused nominal command with actual authority, not understanding that obedience during a coup attempt is contingent and that they had to convince military actors that the coup had widespread military support.

As a result, the junta missed successive opportunities to make a fact in their broadcasts. For example, senior military commanders found out about the coup only half an hour before the rest of the nation did, when Defense Minister Yazov addressed the Military Collegium (Odom 1998, 322). Yazov told them little at this time, mainly that martial law had been declared, that the Union Treaty was creating problems and would not be signed, and that the Soviet constitution justified the junta's actions.

---

[18]The junta also faced disobedience at *Izvestia*, which was one of the nine authorized papers. The newspaper came out with the text of the junta's official declarations on the first page but with Yeltsin's appeal to the people on the second page (Munro 2001).

[19]They never publicly admitted to seizing control from Gorbachev, stating repeatedly instead that Gorbachev was ill. Thus, even their claim to be in charge was weak and half-heartedly made.

In treating the defense minister's remarks to the Military Collegium as perfunctory, the junta squandered an opportunity to convince senior military commanders that there was widespread military support for the coup attempt. As a result, only a few hours later the head of the air force made a not-for-attribution remark to a journalist that he was unenthusiastic about the junta. It is unlikely that Shaposhnikov would have spoken this way if he believed that the junta was popular and its victory a fait accompli.

The junta compounded its poor management of military expectations during its first press conference, which did not include KGB chief Vladimir Kryuchkov, Defense Minister Dmitry Yazov, or Soviet Prime Minister Valentin Pavlov, leading to rumors that they had resigned and that the junta no longer had the support of the KGB or the military.[20]

The opposition exploited the conspirators' poor management of expectations. Repeatedly, they broadcast claims that the junta was weak and not in control, that the military was steadily defecting to Yeltsin's camp, that the White House was strong and well defended, and that quashing the resistance would lead the country into a bloody civil war. As the coup attempt continued and Yeltsin's stand at the White House continued, these claims gained enough currency that people acted as if they were true, thus changing the course of events.

This process started with the subversion of the junta's first press conference to the nation. Employees at the state-run television station used their coverage of this event to make the GKChP look feeble and incompetent. According to the *Moscow Times*:

> While experienced in covering up leaders' failures in the past, the Ostankino television crew chose not to apply this skill that day. Instead, an observant lens went after Yanayev's weakness—his constantly trembling hands.
>
> There must have been a way to send a different message—perhaps by showing the stern face of Gorbachev's replacement. But what viewers saw was a group of agitated elderly men who did not look at all sure of what they were doing. The most exciting point of the news conference came when young Nezavisimaya Gazeta reporter Tatyana Malkina, just out of journalism school, bluntly asked Yanayev, "Could you please say whether or not you understand that last night you carried out a coup d'etat?"
>
> Not only did this particular question get aired, but as Yanayev mumbled something incoherent, the camera kept showing Malkina's face bearing an expression of disdain. (Korchagina 2001b)

The mere fact that Yanayev's hands were shaky no more prevented him from acting vigorously and decisively than did Franklin Roosevelt's polio. Still, those who

---

[20]PBS NewsHour. 1991. *The coup: the US perspective.* <http://www.pbs.org/newshour/bb/europe/russia/1991/americans_8-20.html>. Washington: MacNeil/Lehrer Productions. Accessed October 31, 2004.

saw the broadcast remembered Yanayev's hands and interpreted this as a sign that he was either drunk or terrified. The broadcast undermined the junta's credibility, convincing people that the junta was not fully in charge. Meanwhile, Yeltsin— who *was* drunk for most of the coup attempt—was portrayed as strong and in charge (Interview with Yevgenia Albats. 2000).

From the start, the opposition's top objective was to deliberately create fractures within the Soviet military (Dunlop 1993, 246). Yeltsin's top military advisor, General Kobets, and his aides successfully employed "'psychological warfare' by spreading rumors among the military officers around the country about various units changing sides" (Zolotov 2001). For three days, the news reported a steady drumbeat of alleged defections at all levels of the military and security services. At various times, claims were made that the defense minister, the head of the KGB, the head of the air force, the entire air force, the airborne forces commander General Grachev, and Grachev's deputy commander general, Aleksandr Lebed, had joined Yeltsin's forces. Broadcasts also said that units from the Tula Quick Reaction Division and the Taman Motorized Rifle Division—two of the major units stationed around Moscow—had openly sided with Yeltsin (RFE/RL Daily Report No. 158, August 21, 1991). Similarly, it was claimed that the White House was "guarded by some thirty tanks and armored personnel carriers" (Foye 1991).

These broadcasts were persuasive enough that even Defense Minister Yazov believed some of the claims, and, while announcements of high-level defections were usually followed by retractions, they still succeeded in creating a good deal of uncertainty about the extent of military support for the coup (Odom 1998, 325, 333).[21]

There were, of course, limits to what the opposition to the coup attempt could claim. They could not credibly say that they were actually in charge or that they had defeated the junta. They were already stretching the truth far enough. However, what they could do was to make statements that the junta was not in control, that it did not have the support of the armed forces, that resistance was far from futile, and that in fact efforts to quash resistance would lead to civil war.

Targets

The junta also proved poor at maintaining control over symbolic targets, which made them appear weak publicly. As with their underestimating of the importance of the media, the junta did not understand why symbolic targets were important; and in any case, they did not expect any opposition to their efforts, from within the state or without. Although they did position tanks at all bridges in Moscow early on, they imposed a curfew too late without much thought as to how they would

---

[21]Not all of the opposition broadcasts were effective in making a fact. Aleksandr Rutskoi, the vice president of Russia and a war hero, openly appealed to the men of the armed forces to switch sides without making any claims that the coup was doomed to fail (Yeltsin 1992, 56). However, these appeals also did not seem to be very persuasive, since there was no widespread defection, even by soldiers who might have sympathized with the content of the appeal.

implement it, and then they failed to keep people off the streets. As a result of this lack of control over the public, according to one description, "demonstrators clambered onto the tanks to speak more intimately with their occupants and, towards the end of the coup, when the tanks had already become a strange component of the social pastiche of resistance, flowers adorned them and children played on them" (Varney & Martin 2000).

The most important symbolic target, of course, was the Russian parliament building. Given that it lacked tactical importance, the junta did not think to capture it at the start of the coup, and it quickly became a center of opposition to the coup attempt. They compounded this mistake by not isolating and cutting off the building, which would have decreased its symbolic importance and arrested the flow of civilians. By the time they planned to attack the White House, it had become a test of the capacity of the junta, a symbol that they did not control the country and that opposition was not futile.

For their part, Yeltsin and his allies did everything they could to increase the salience of the White House as a symbol of government impotence. They claimed that the White House was defended by 100,000 civilians as well as veterans of the Afghan wars and private security. They played up the number of military defectors who were protecting the building, going so far as to call upon the horse regiment of the Mosfilms studio, using actors to make it seem as if the military Cossack regiment had switched sides. To make the building appear impregnable, they built sixteen barricades out of trolleys, cars, scrap metal, cobblestones, bricks, concrete blocks, tree trunks, and branches. They said the only way the White House could be assaulted would be if the junta used enough force to cause massive bloodshed, and that would never happen, because it would split the military and bring matters to civil war. In Yeltsin's appeal to the military to join the opposition to the coup, he argued:

> There is a choice before you: either you give support to the group of conspirators, usurpers of power and carry their criminal order and thus go against the will of the people, or you defend democracy and power legally elected by the people. The first path will lead the country into a **fratricidal civil war and severe bloodshed**. The second path guarantees civil peace and constitutional order and security ... I give you the order: quickly and without hesitation come over to the side of legal power, observing with this order and discipline. (Yeltsin 1992, 106, emphasis mine)

Casualties

As this theory predicts, very few casualties occurred during this coup attempt. There were no military deaths, and while three civilians were killed, their deaths were most likely accidental (Odom 1998, 315). This is consistent with Defense Minister Yazov's instructions to the Military Collegium that "he did not want to see any blood spilled and that confrontations should be avoided" (322).

For most of the coup attempt, the lack of military injuries can be ascribed to the one-sided nature of the coup. The junta simply had few adversaries to clash with, and they did not attack any targets that were defended.[22] However, the absence of casualties at the end of the coup attempt was clearly due to a deliberate effort by members of the military to avoid actions that might lead to open fighting, such as attacking the White House. Even hard-liners who were willing to spill civilian blood were unwilling to give the final order to attack Yeltsin (Odom 1998, 320). In addition, the junta members accepted defeat gracefully rather than staging a last-ditch effort to salvage the coup attempt. Interior Minister Boris Pugo killed himself (and his wife) rather than face trial, but he did not try to use MVD forces to protect himself.

Similarly, the anti-coup forces also went far out of their way to avoid causing harm. The head of the air force, Air Marshall Shaposhnikov, is credited by some with stopping the final attack on the White House by threatening to bomb the Kremlin if the attack went forward (Dunlop 1993, 248). Yet the orders that Shaposhnikov actually issued were different: he authorized two *unarmed* aircraft to take off and fly low over the Kremlin as a bluff. Even with the fate of the anti-coup forces hanging in the balance, Shaposhnikov was unwilling to use the force at his disposal to try to defeat the coup. And in fact, Shaposhnikov never issued the final orders for these planes to take off (Odom 1998, 327-328).

This explanation for the low bloodshed during the coup attempt has several advantages. To most commentators, Yazov's unwillingness to spill blood was a sign of personal weakness, an indication of the amateurish nature of the coup. But understanding the low casualty count in the context of coordination can account for the unwillingness of actors on both sides—including those clearly not squeamish about civilian deaths—to use force. In addition, it emphasizes the continuity between this coup attempt and others around the world, rather than seeing the lack of casualties here as a sign of the pathological irresoluteness of the conspirators.

History

The hypothesis least relevant to this coup attempt concerns the impact of precedent. Expectations during this coup attempt were not shaped by the experience of prior coup attempts, because it had been almost forty years since the military had been involved in a forcible change of leadership in the Soviet Union, during the 1953 removal of Lavrentiy Beria from the government.

This lack of experience with coup attempts was also reflected in the challengers' ineptness at mounting a coup. After Gorbachev's unexpected refusal to cooperate

---

[22]Dunlop claims that there was one confrontation, right at the end of the coup attempt. At 3 a.m., three companies of *spetnaz* wearing plain clothes tried to infiltrate the White House posing as volunteers. They were detected and confronted by Russian special-ops troops loyal to Yeltsin and other armed volunteers and withdrew without firing a shot (Dunlop 1993, 246). While this incident is not included in other accounts of the coup, if it is true, it is consistent with what we would expect to observe during a coordination game.

in an *autogolpe*, they foundered quickly, repeatedly making errors that demonstrated that the junta had neither experience with nor an understanding of the central dynamics of military coups. Not only did they largely ignore the security services, but they wrongly assumed that civilians would support them, believing that almost 80% of Russian civilians were against the transition to a market economy (Dunlop 1993, 198). As a result, they were poorly prepared for any sort of opposition.

Rank

The Soviet coup attempt of 1991 showcases nicely both the advantages and disadvantages of launching a coup from the top of the military. This is true even though this coup failed while the theory predicts that most coups from the top will succeed, because the failure was due to the challengers' inability to adequately use the prerogatives of their position to make a fact.

Since this coup originated at the very apex of the military hierarchy, military actors were generally cooperative with the junta, especially at the beginning, when they had a strong presumption of success. The junta was able to convene the Military Collegium and issue orders without having to fight for access or worry about getting locked up, something that wouldn't have been true for conspirators from the middle or bottom of the hierarchy. The junta's orders were accepted and largely followed; even commanders who opposed the coup did not openly disagree. These strengths shaped the initial successes of the junta, their ability to assume control over the state apparatus and to cover the streets of Moscow with tanks and soldiers.

The conspirators' main weakness was also intrinsic to their position: they lacked direct command over any troops, and so they were unable to enforce their will at critical junctures when officers began to drag their feet or refuse to carry out orders. This was compounded by the fact that the junta included relatively few members of the military hierarchy below its apex, and so they did not even have the allegiance of some of the service commanders.

In other areas, Gorbachev's challengers were less typical. Because they ignored the military aspects of the coup, they failed to take advantage of the privileges associated with their rank. Because they assumed unconditional obedience to commands, they did not bother to find out in advance how much support they would have or to try to convince key actors that a coup would be well supported. After the coup started, they did a very poor job of controlling public information. Steeped in the old Soviet mindset, they had no idea how different the post-*glasnost* media were and could not imagine that they would be betrayed even by the state-owned media outlets. This failure to control public information was central to the failure of the coup attempt, because it robbed the junta of its most important asset. Once the opposition made the junta look as if it did not have the support of the military, key actors began to sit on the fence and delay. In the end, even the junta leaders were convinced that to move ahead would risk a civil war, and they backed down.

Understanding the Overall Trajectory of the Coup Attempt

Together, these insights provide a coherent explanation for both the outcome and the dynamics of the coup attempt. Despite appearances, the coup leaders started out with a weak hand, because they did not lay the groundwork for the coup within the military, trusting instead that obedience would be automatic. They compounded this error at several points early on by missing opportunities to make a fact within the military: neither the address to the Military Collegium nor the junta's first press conference was designed to create public belief in unanimous support for the coup within the various security agencies. In fact, they created an impression of military disunity, which freed the head of the air force to speak disapprovingly about the coup, albeit anonymously.

The coup leaders then lost further ground as the coup attempt dragged on without resolution, each day undermining further their claim to being in control. The White House became the hub of anti-junta activity, increasingly fortified with tanks, barricades, armed supporters, and unarmed civilian volunteers. That this added little to defense of the White House from a tactical standpoint was irrelevant; what mattered was the appearance of impregnability and the coup opposition's visibility in a key symbolic location. Most important, the challengers lost the battle for the airwaves; the message that the junta was weak was broadcast by state-owned, independent, and foreign media.

Without clear expectations to provide a focal point for coordination, many members of the military began to sit on the fence, unwilling to commit themselves to either side.[23] As Odom says of the officer corps, "Rather than act to save the system, they waited and watched, seeking to join the winning side" (Odom 1998, 345). Perhaps the most overt example of this behavior is that of General Grachev, who afterwards admitted having "tried to tack between the army leadership and the Russian government" (Taylor 2003*a*, 237).

This fence sitting continued right up to the scheduled time for the attack on the occupied parliament building. While the victory of the junta was in question among the military, so too was Yeltsin's political, and actual, survival. As a result, even officers who had privately given assurances that there would be no attack on the White House did not take any irreversible steps that would publicly commit them to opposing the coup. They may have dragged their feet and delayed, but they neither openly sided with Yeltsin, told the junta they were unwilling to attack, nor ordered their forces out of Moscow.

Even General Shaposhnikov, Yeltsin's strongest supporter, held back (Hough 1997, 444). He assured both sides that he was loyal to their cause and took no action more direct than delaying the scheduled arrival of troops to attack the White House. While he threatened that he would bomb the Kremlin if the junta insisted

---

[23]While there is a good deal of disagreement about what happened during the coup attempt and why, multiple scholars have remarked on the prevalence of fence sitting within the officer corps by the second day of the coup (Odom 1998, Taylor 2003*a*, Hough 1997). It is difficult to assess how widespread such behavior was, but one commentator says a majority of officers were engaged in fence-sitting (Taylor 2003*a*, 241).

on going ahead with the assault on the White House, he took no action to do so before the attack was finally canceled (Odom 1998, 327).

The generals who were assigned to carry out the attack had an additional concern, namely, that none of them wanted to attack the White House alone for fear of being blamed afterward for the civilian bloodshed. The military had been scapegoated for their actions in the Baltics, and such concerns were especially salient in the face of an illegal junta that might not survive. This desire to spread possible blame was undoubtedly at the root of the unnecessarily complicated force structure planned for the attack. Grachev seems to have used this coordination dynamic to further slow things down. He told Gromov that neither airborne forces nor the KGB would actually join the attack, though they were both expected to report to the scene. Gromov was reportedly unwilling to participate under those conditions (Odom 1998, 334). According to one account, Grachev played a similar game with Karpukhin, who refused to attack without Grachev's and Gromov's forces. Afterward, Grachev took credit for this tactic, explaining, "If I had gone, then everyone would have followed after me" (Dunlop 2003, 110). It is likely that Grachev was inflating both his importance and his resolve to oppose the coup attempt, but there is circumstantial evidence that all three generals were concerned about the costs involved in acting alone, even though each of them commanded sufficient force to take the White House on their own.

In the end, the critical decision to stop the attack came from the junta, which backed down rather than give the final order to proceed. Several different explanations have been given for this last minute about-face. Some observers argue that Yazov was stopped by the refusal of his subordinates to execute the assault, but none of officers involved had told Yazov that they would disobey and the command was never given, let alone refused (Odom 1998, 320). Others claim that it was Yazov who lacked the stomach for civilian casualties, yet Odom, looking at Yazov's behavior over the entire course of the conspiracy and coup attempt, claims that "Yazov showed more determination to use force than did most of the . . . [junta], even if that meant spilling blood" (337). And even if Yazov suffered a change of heart, this still does not explain why the other hard-line members of the junta also backed down when they could have proceeded using just MVD and KGB troops.

Rather, the most convincing explanation for the junta's decision not to attack the White House is that they were afraid it might cause a fight among different security forces, possibly leading even to a civil war (Brusstar & Jones 1995, 36). Although we lack any direct account of the junta's deliberative process that would establish this explanation conclusively, we do know that the conspirators had been hearing claims of defections (albeit false ones) and were in at least partial knowledge of shirking within the military. Yazov knew that he no longer had total obedience within the organization and was displeased about it (Odom 1998, 320). Contemporaneous accounts about the fear of a civil war include Yeltsin's warning about the possibility of a civil war, General Lebed's statement that he did not want to get dragged into a civil war (333), and remarks from commentators like Henry Kissinger and McGeorge Bundy who openly said that they were worried about a civil war breaking out.[24] This is the only rationale that can account for why even the most hard-line junta members, those willing to sacrifice civilian lives for their cause, were unwilling to order the assault.

Conclusion

This analysis of the 1991 Soviet coup attempt highlights many of the similarities between what happened in the Moscow coup attempt and in coup attempts elsewhere in the world. As in the Ghana cases, the coup could succeed only if the coup makers were able to make a fact and would fail if they did not. Soviet officers coordinated among themselves and went out of their way to ensure low casualties. As we have seen, information and expectations were central to the dynamics of the coup attempt, and the rank of the coup makers shaped their ability to make a fact. This last point is worth emphasizing. Even within the Soviet military, one of the most professional in the world, the top level could not assume that their orders would be unquestioningly carried out by their subordinates. This argues that contingency of command is a structural obstacle for all coups from the top, not just those in poor, young countries.

Also worth explicating are the differences between this case and some of those discussed earlier. The first and major one of these is that this coup from the top failed, unlike Ghana's coup attempts of 1975 and 1978. In contrast to coup makers in Ghana, who successfully used their institutional position to make a fact, the Soviet junta assumed that things would be accomplished simply by removing Gorbachev and taking his position. As a result, they made no effort to mold expectations, or even to correct them once people started to think that the junta was losing control. This lack of consideration for the power of information and beliefs is in some ways similar to Rawlings's failure to seize the broadcasting station during the failed May 1979 coup attempt.

Another difference has to do with the number of broadcast media outlets in the country. The Soviet Union had multiple television and radio stations in operation, both domestic and foreign. In Ghana, there was only one media corporation during the period of the coup attempts, and that was state-owned. While it broadcast on multiple channels, they were all controlled from a single facility. The multiple radio and television organizations in the Soviet Union made it harder for the junta to dominate public information and allowed Yeltsin's counterargument to be heard. Once Yeltsin was on the air, he was able to contest the junta's claims to be in control, thus increasing the duration of the coup attempt to the very long period of three days. This variety of media outlets and the difficulty in controlling them appears to have reduced the advantage usually held by coup makers at the top. Also worth noting is that, instead of producing a cacophony of opinion, this multitude

---

[24]PBS NewsHour. 1991. *The coup: the US perspective* <http://www.pbs.org/newshour/bb /europe/russia/1991/americans_8-20.html>. Washington: MacNeil/Lehrer Productions. Accessed October 31, 2004.

of media outlets were all telling the same story and supporting Yeltsin's claims, demonstrating that the existence of multiple mass media broadcasters is not an insurmountable obstacle to making a fact.

A third area of difference between the Soviet and Ghanaian coups is the prominent involvement of civilians on both sides of the Soviet coup. The coup makers included both civilians and military men, and they worked together from the beginning to plan the coup attempt; in fact, civilians were even more prominent than military men within the junta if not within the coup attempt. Similarly, the mainly civilian opposition to the coup attempt was led by a civilian politician, used civilian media rather than soldiers to manipulate public information, and featured large crowds of civilians demonstrating against the coup.

Nonetheless, the presence of civilians in the junta and in the opposition did not change the essential dynamics of the coup nor shift its locus from the military. While Yeltsin was a prominent civilian, he executed the same strategy as a coup maker from the top of the military. Like a general, he had no troops of his own, but he could use information and expectations to manipulate key unit commanders within the military. To actually execute this propaganda strategy, however, Yeltsin relied on the small number of military men working with him. They were the ones who made the claims that the White House was well defended or that various units had defected. Although most of these claims were false, they were more credible for being made by military personnel.

It is true that the presence of large numbers of civilians surrounding Yeltsin had an effect and that the junta was not eager to kill large numbers of civilians if it could be avoided, but the presence of civilians did not stop the junta from planning an attack on the White House, nor did it bring about the end of the coup. Instead, the masses were important only in conjunction with the public claim that military units were unwilling to attack them. Although this was actually not true, it strengthened expectations within the military that the country was on the verge of civil war.

A fourth way in which this coup was unusual is that it took place in one of the world's largest countries. The coup was contested not just in Moscow but in Leningrad and the republics as well. This was different from events in Ghana, where there was little action outside of the capital during the coup attempts. Yet, even in the Soviet Union, it was events in Moscow that proved pivotal in the end. Even the large Soviet military ended up coordinating fairly well around a small set of signals.

A fifth and final way in which the Soviet coup attempt was different from any of the Ghanaian coups was its duration. Consistent with the argument made earlier about the impact of time, however, the longer the coup went on, the greater doubt there was about the junta's claim to be in control and the more plausible it seemed that the coup would fail.

In short, despite all these differences and the unprecedented nature of the Soviet coup attempt more generally, the theory that coups are coordination games does a better job of explaining its dynamics and outcome than does either of the competing hypotheses.

Chapter 8

Conclusion

In this book I have argued that coup attempts are best understood as resembling coordination games rather than battles or elections. During a coup attempt, each actor wants to be on the same side as everybody else, both to prevent a deep split from developing within the military and to avoid the punishment associated with supporting the loser. This imperative to coordinate creates a point of leverage for both the challengers and the incumbent. The side that prevails does so by "making a fact," that is, by publicly creating the impression that the victory of their side is inevitable and that resistance is futile. If actors believe that everybody will support one side, and that everybody else believes that everybody will support that side, this will create self-fulfilling expectations in favor of that side, making it the side that wins.

As the previous chapters have demonstrated, this theory is the only theory that adequately explains the likely dynamics and outcomes of military coups. This explanation allows us to understand why some coups fail despite the coup makers' having a preponderance of tactical might and why others fail despite the unpopularity of the incumbent government. It also goes beyond observing that rank matters in coup making to explain why coups launched by military actors nearer the top of the military hierarchy have a better, though never guaranteed, chance of success. It also provides both a theoretical and an empirical argument for why factors extraneous to the military do not determine the trajectory and outcomes of coup attempts.

In this final chapter, I discuss some of the broader implications of this theory for the study of civil-military relations more generally, for how the proliferation of electronic and social media might affect future coups, and for social and political policy making.

Implications for the Study of Civil-Military Relations

Having extensively discussed the reasons why some coups fail and others succeed, I next want to venture some conclusions about the theoretical implications of this work for the study of civil-military relations more generally. The first of these is that there are important theoretical reasons why coup failure, not merely coup success, should be central to our understanding of civil-military relations, not peripheral to it. Although failed coups may not leave their mark on history by changing governments, the fact that coups sometimes fail is what creates the necessity for coup attempts and successful coups at all. It is only because coups can fail—and in fact fail quite often—that civil-military relations is an arena of negotiation rather than one in which military actors can dictate outcomes by fiat.

To understand this point, imagine a hypothetical world where coup failure was absent and all coup attempts succeeded. Such a vision is implicitly the basis for much of the existing work on civil-military relations. Gaetano Mosca, for example, said, "The class that bears the lance or holds the musket regularly forces its rule upon the class that handles the spade or pushes the shuttle" (Mosca 1939, 228). If the military is the six-hundred-pound gorilla of domestic politics, then it must either be socialized into voluntary compliance or appeased. Scholars have spent considerable energy discussing strategies for the former; Samuel Huntington's analysis of objective and subjective control of the military occupies center stage in both academic and policy debates on the subject (Huntington 1957). What is missing from these debates, however, is an understanding that if all coup attempts succeeded, then, in equilibrium, there would never be any coup attempts. Some militaries would be recruited and trained in such a way that they accepted the norm of civilian supremacy and they would not mount any coup attempts. Those that did not, however, would always be appeased by the government, since they could never be denied. In neither situation would there rationally be any coup attempts at all.

Of course, this is not how the world actually looks. In the real world, coup attempts do occur, and half of them fail. It is precisely because coups can and frequently do fail that members of militaries can neither automatically dictate policies they want nor veto policy they dislike.[1] With half of all coup attempts failing, and many more conspiracies being nipped in the bud, there are clear limits to the coercive powers of a threatened coup attempt (Acemoglu & Robinson 2006, 248). Peter Feaver argues that it is the ability to mount a successful coup that makes the challenges of controlling the armed forces unique among the various tasks of governance (Feaver 1999). If he is right, then failed coups should also be central to our understanding of civil-military relations, since it is the possibility of coup failure that allows civilian governments to govern unruly militaries.

Secondly, the frequency of coup failure also demonstrates that intra-military dynamics must be an important level of analysis within civil-military relations. This is not a novel suggestion, as a considerable corpus of scholarship already pays close attention to the interactions between military factions. Yet the suggestion does bear repeating, especially in light of how difficult it is for researchers to penetrate military organizations and get actors to discuss matters that bear on national security. Unfortunately, such a perspective has been absent in recent influential scholarship, in which scholars appear to assume either that the entire military has

---

[1] The existence of coup attempts also reveals the clear limitations of socialization to tame the military.

been captured by class interests (Acemoglu & Robinson 2006) or that the most important threats to an incumbent come from civilian elites with large civilian constituencies (Magaloni & Kricheli 2010). While it is always necessary to simplify the world in order to analyze it, we need always to remember that such simplifications have their dangers. Treating the military as a unitary actor, or worse yet, ignoring it, creates models divorced from the reality of regime stability and change in the world.

Implications for Future Coups

As the previous chapters have discussed at length, coordination is most fundamentally a matter of information and expectations. The critical role played by mass media in many coup attempts naturally raises the question of whether changes in the media landscape will make the process of coup making different in the future. In particular, we may wonder how coups may be changed by various forms of social media, like Facebook and Twitter, that have been credited with playing important roles in recent political upheavals, such as the Arab Spring.[2] A careful examination of the available evidence suggests, however, that even though new information technologies, the Internet, and social media have proven to be important resources for civilian political dissidents, they will not fundamentally transform the way coups are conducted. While the manipulation of information and expectations is central to coup making, we are unlikely to see the place of mass media broadcasts replaced by tweets any time soon.

In a coup attempt, the goal of the challengers is to entirely dominate public information. That means gaining control over the major broadcast channel and shutting down all others or forcing them to repeat the same message. The broadcast becomes common knowledge when it gains such widespread distribution that everybody not only has heard or seen it but can assume that everybody else has, and that everybody knows that everybody else has, etc. This is best done when the announcement of the coup displaces the morning news, since this is the broadcast that virtually everybody watches or listens to.

Social media are very different from radio and television. They do not create common knowledge in a short time frame and therefore cannot alone make a fact. Imagine a coup that used social media exclusively to disseminate information, one in which challengers announced their coup attempt by sending a tweet from the official government Twitter handle and posting the news on the official national Facebook page. Obviously, such a media strategy could not help make a fact, and therefore would not help the coup succeed. Unlike the morning news, it is unlikely that large

---

[2]As an example of how important this technology has been, the U.S. State Department convinced Twitter to postpone scheduled maintenance that would have disrupted service to Iran in the midst of anti-government protests in 2009 (Grossman 2009). For its service during this uprising, when traditional journalism was suppressed, former U.S. national security advisor Mark Pfeifle suggested that Twitter receive the Nobel Peace Prize (Pfeifle 2009).

numbers of people would at the same time see the Twitter and Facebook announcement that the incumbent had been overthrown, and such messages definitely would not reach the level of ubiquity necessary to generate common knowledge and therefore would not engender coordination. In many ways, social media are best understood as variants of small-scale traditional print media, much like a small newspaper printed out of a basement. They can inform the people who receive the messages, but the shared information does not quickly change their expectations about the likely behavior of large numbers of other people.

Another problem with using social media to shape expectations in a coup attempt is that even those members of the military who did receive news of the attempt would be disinclined to take it seriously. A radio or television broadcast is credible in part because it is costly; it requires having or seizing control over a broadcasting facility and usually involves a broadcast by an identifiable individual who could be thrown into jail if the coup attempt failed. An announcement on a government webpage or government Twitter handle could easily be the work of hackers, and therefore is too cheap a gesture to have much effect. The voice and face of an identifiable important person carries immediate credibility.

In addition, given that social media are designed to increase the number of voices speaking at once, the only way to attain dominance over social media would be to shut them down, so that the coup announcement was the only message appearing on social media in the country. Even then, the government could use traditional broadcast media to broadcast a counterclaim, one that would become common knowledge and therefore could push military actors to coordinate around the government.

Furthermore, if we look more specifically at how social media have facilitated protest movements, we see that they are unlikely to have a similar impact on coup making, because most of the things that social media have done for protests are related to the fact that protests are open and public. One of the key contributions of social media during the Arab Spring was to build public awareness and therefore attract recruits to the movement in ways that bypassed government restrictions. Wael Ghonim, one of the key architects of the overthrow of Egypt's President Mubarak, claimed that the "revolution started on Facebook" (Gustin 2011), as Facebook pages and YouTube videos allowed dissidents in Egypt to circumvent the censored national media and put their message directly in front of a wider audience. For example, a Facebook page called "We Are All Khaled Said" (named for a martyr of the movement) gained 350,000 followers.[3] Members of this Facebook group were then organized into smaller units of 100 and educated about techniques of non-violent resistance (Giglio 2011). All of this would have been very difficult for the opposition in Egypt to do in the physical world without attracting the attention of the police. Instead, the nascent movement was able to grow unmolested until it survived even the shutting down of the Internet in Egypt.

---

[3]Khaled Said was a young Alexandrian businessman who was murdered by the police after posting a video on the Internet showing them stealing from a drug dealer. Since Said was killed for his use of the Internet to expose wrongdoing, he became a symbol of the cause for other netizens.

However, this use of social media does not lend itself well to coup making. Membership in a coup conspiracy is not just an act of dissent, it is an act of treason. These conspiracies are not public, and membership is by invitation only. A coup attempt cannot be organized over Facebook, using the real names or even traceable pseudonyms of those involved, because it is a secret and dangerous affair. Not even mutinous conspiracies would fare well on social media, even though a mutiny is the closest type of coup to a revolution. Soldiers are already forbidden from discussing politics in the mess hall, so soldiers who joined a Facebook page devoted to airing grievances over pay would find themselves facing disciplinary proceedings very quickly.

The other major use of social media by protest movements has been to publicize dissident activity, bringing it to the attention of the world press in the hope that this would offer a modicum of protection for the protesters. This is the primary way that Twitter has been used during protests; it informs the world media of events rather than being a mobilization tool within the country.[4] But a successful coup does not require the sympathy of the international public. This is fortunate for coup makers, since they are unlikely to become international causes célèbres. In addition, coups are over quickly, and there is a substantial lag between when tweets on protests begin to appear and when the international media notices the story. It took weeks before the U.S. media paid any attention to tweets about protests in Tunisia (Zuckerman 2011). In short, coups and revolutions differ enough in their key tactical elements that the aspects of social media that have been quite helpful to dissidents are unlikely to be of much help to coup makers.

This does not mean that coup makers and incumbents should entirely ignore the advent of social media once the coup attempt is under way. One interesting recent development is the advent of what is called "citizen journalism," in which members of the public report on current events they observe. For example, both the Mumbai terrorist attacks of 2008 and the capture of Osama bin Laden in Abbotabad in 2011 were covered live by eyewitnesses who narrated events on Twitter as they occurred. If this information reaches an international media outlet that is still broadcasting into the country, facts recorded by bystanders can become public.

It certainly is possible that citizen journalism could limit the ability of challengers to use exaggeration to appear bigger and more powerful than they are. On the other hand, countering such claims would require the amateur reporter to both observe and understand salient facts about the size and identity of the challengers. Even if citizen journalists had been present for the 1967 coup attempt in Ghana, it is unlikely that they would have understood enough of what was happening to realize that the challengers were weaker than they appeared to be.

---

[4]There is considerable misunderstanding on this point. The 2009 protests in Moldova were called a "Twitter Revolution," even though there were only 100-200 Twitter users in the entire country of Moldova, and none of the demonstrators were able to tweet from the protest venue because of limited cell phone coverage there (Zuckerman 2009). Journalists were reading tweets coming from Moldovans overseas, not in country. Similarly, in Iran the primary language of the tweets was English (instead of Farsi) and they were sent primarily by Iranians abroad (Esfandiari 2010).

And in fact, it is possible that citizen journalism might even decrease the veracity of news broadcasts during a coup, since it would provide a channel for misinformation to be distributed, much like what happened during the 1991 Soviet coup attempt. Because of the anonymity of the Internet, one person could send out multiple tweets and even faked photos from a variety of different Potemkin identities purporting to show that the challengers are strong and in control of a variety of different symbolic targets. Such dissimulation could be persuasive for a few days, long enough to have an impact on the coup attempt. The net effect of citizen journalism on the veracity of international news broadcasts is therefore also unclear.

Lastly, any discussion of the effect of new communication technologies during a coup attempt assumes that domestic phone networks and the Internet remain functional during a coup attempt. In many coup attempts, the challengers disable domestic and international phone service. In the future, this could include domestic mobile networks and Internet service, especially with an increasing number of countries creating "kill switches" that allow the government to disable these networks during a time of national emergency.[5] For all these reasons, then, coup makers are unable to replace mass media with social media in the conduct of a coup. Until social media attains the penetration and ubiquity of the traditional broadcast media, it cannot create common knowledge, and therefore cannot be used to make a fact during a coup attempt.

Implications for Policy

The analysis of past coups contained in this book offers few suggestions for outsiders, governmental and non-governmental, attempting to sway the outcome of future military coup attempts. Generally speaking, coups are over quickly and all the critical actors are internal to the military, offering outsiders little opportunity to try, for example, to protect an allied incumbent, short of direct military intervention. As a result, it is probably more fruitful for countries and multinational organizations wishing to protect democracy to focus on heavily penalizing military governments and offering incentives for a rapid transition back to representative civilian rule.

The one exception is that outsiders may have some leverage if a coup attempt is not resolved quickly and factions within the military appear to be deadlocked. If an incumbent leader is still at liberty, his or her allies can try to provide additional international media coverage and room to make a fact. In addition, outside governments that are allied with the incumbent may try to shape expectations themselves,

---

[5]Domestic cellular communications are fairly easy to turn off. Because the architecture of the Internet is decentralized, it was earlier believed that it would be difficult, if not impossible to disable easily. This has been proven false recently, as governments in Iran, Libya, Egypt, and Syria have all turned off the Internet during periods of national emergency (Hunt 2011). The capacity to disable access to the Internet is likely to spread, even to democratic countries, in the future. In the United States, legislation has been proposed in the past that would give the president the ability to shut off communications from a foreign country, and it was rumored to contain an undisclosed capacity to turn off the entire Internet, as well (Lawson 2011).

saying, for instance, that they believe the military does not support the coup and that forces are steadily switching sides to the incumbent. However, all of this is a long shot; even in the USSR in 1991, outside governments and media played a smaller role than did domestic actors and media. Outside attempts to shape expectations must be credible, and they run the risk that their messages will be tagged by the news media as transparent propaganda, in which case they may hurt more than they help their cause. In the end, however, because the dynamics of coups are intra-military, there are few points of leverage that can be used by outside actors. Such actors are best advised to wait until the coup is over and then use traditional modes of diplomacy to try to influence the new government that emerges.

That said, the central argument in this book, that the manipulation of expectations can be used to create or prevent change, does provide some valuable advice for how outside actors can fruitfully engage with other scenarios that can be understood as coordination games. The examples discussed below demonstrate the applicability of this insight in widely different fields and how making a fact can be used in efforts to create new social norms and in developing effective counter-insurgency strategy.

Changing Deep-Seated Social Practices

As discussed at the start of this book, social norms can best be understood as coordination games. Traditionally, most efforts to change social practices deemed as harmful have focused on public education, following in essence what is an elections approach, with limited results. In situations in which social or political actors have attempted to change not only individuals' preferences but also their expectations about the behavior of others, their efforts to produce social change have proven more successful.

One arena where these basic insights are being employed is the campaign to end female genital cutting (FGC), a practice sometimes also called female circumcision or female genital mutilation. The traditional approach of educating families about the health dangers involved in FGC has proven largely ineffective, because the practice is a societal one and therefore cannot easily be addressed at the level of the individual household. Even if the adults in a family are convinced by the outreach efforts, they will still not change their behavior, out of fear that it will leave their daughters unmarriageable if they are the only ones violating the norm. Similarly, in places where FGC has been banned by law, adults have had to weigh the slim chance that they will be caught and punished against the far larger chance that obeying the law will exclude their daughters from most possible marriages. There is evidence, however, that if the norm is changed in a public fashion within an intra-marrying group, the practice will end quickly (Mackie 2000).[6]

---

[6]I refer to families and adults as the decision making actors because, while the girl herself usually has little say in the matter, various adults in the family do. In particular, it is a mistake to act as if the father is solely responsible for the decision. Stopping the practice involves reaching out to parents, aunts and uncles, grandparents, etc.

A group of activists in West Africa have developed a successful approach to eliminating FGC by coupling education with a public pledge made by a large number of families. This pledge makes common knowledge of these families' decision not only to end FGC in their own homes but also not to require it from girls from other families. A similar discovery about the effectiveness of public pledging in changing norms was made by anti-footbinding reformers in China over a century ago. In both cases of using this strategy to eradicate a socially promoted practice, it was found that the reforms were durable over time; groups persisted with the new practice rather than backsliding (Mackie 2000).[7]

Fighting Insurgencies

Another policy area in which insights into coordination could fruitfully be applied is counter-insurgency strategy. During a civil conflict, the side that can gather more popular support is more likely to win, even if civilian support is neither necessary or sufficient.[8] Mao referred to guerrillas as fish swimming in a sea of civilians, implying that the insurgency was sustained by its relationship with the overall population. When civilians support a rebellion, they can provide its members with food, shelter, recruits, money, and information. When deprived of this support, the rebellion is weakened, especially if the citizenry actively support the government by providing tactical intelligence and joining local self-defense militias. To win over civilian support, however, requires more than information campaigns designed to win hearts and minds; it must also engage with civilian expectations. For their part, civilians have a strong interest both in backing the winner and in avoiding the punishment associated with being on the losing side, and therefore are more likely to support the government attempting to put down the rebellion when they think others will do so as well.

Given that civilians in such situations will engage in coordination, government efforts to win "hearts and minds" should be coupled with efforts to shape their expectations. As with the campaign against FGC, governments might do well to attempt to bring entire communities to their side by using public pledges. In addition, their mass media propaganda strategies should go beyond touting the virtues of the government (and the evils of the rebels) to making claims that the government has widespread support and extensive strength. This has to be done carefully

---

[7] In the West, efforts to change norms have generally involved the mass media, rather than public pledges. For example, the widespread adoption of mouthwash in America followed a massive advertising campaign in 1920 that was designed to "make a fact" around the new norm (Chwe 2001, 39).

[8] In a civil war, coordination by civilians is an important but not decisive factor. Civilians often provide financial support and recruits, but their support is not necessary for rebel survival. Insurgents with external patrons or control over lootable resources can purchase food, shelter, information, and mercenaries. They can also use coercion to obtain a certain amount of support, however unwilling. Some civilians also support one side out of pure ideological conviction; the fact that they are in a civil war means that the fear of civil war no longer serves to override their principles, as it would during a coup. Since civilian support is not the only factor determining rebel survival, the outcome of a civil war cannot be reduced solely to civilian coordination. This is an important difference between civil wars and military coups.

to remain credible and not be dismissed outright, but such claims can work even if individuals are skeptical about government claims that they have civilian support.

When expectations are ignored, however, even a powerful army with some reason to expect civilian support may find that such support is not forthcoming. The architects of the U.S. invasion of Iraq paid little attention to the management of expectations, as became abundantly clear by their response to the looting of Baghdad in the wake of the April 2003 invasion. Theft was extensive, leaving "virtually no industrial plant, government ministry or cultural institution" untouched (Hendrickson & Tucker 2005, 10). To Secretary of Defense Donald Rumsfeld, this looting was a minor matter, to which he famously responded, "stuff happens" (Dyson 2009). He did not view looting, and the expectations it created, as relevant to the successful occupation of Iraq.

What Rumsfeld and U.S. military leaders failed to understand was that, while the United States had overthrown a hated dictator and attained clear military dominance, the looting sent a public signal that the United States was either unwilling to protect Iraqi civilians or uninterested in doing so because it would soon leave. Not only did this discourage Iraqis from supporting U.S. efforts in their country, but, because the response to the looting was common knowledge, it also decreased each citizen's expectation that others would give such support. The United States had made public its lack of connection to the Iraqi people. Especially as the disorder spread and persisted, a rational civilian would have formed the belief that few others would support the occupying forces, weakening the possibility of an equilibrium in which civilians would work with the United States to stamp out the insurgency at an early stage. Thus, as other commentators have noted, "a critical window of opportunity was lost" (Hoffman 2006, 104) and "the US ... never recovered from ... [its failure] to prevent the looting of Baghdad in the early days of the occupation" (Galbraith 2004, 42). It was a clear mistake for the government of the United States to regard the occupation solely in terms of battles and elections rather than in terms of coordination.

In short, then, this analysis of coup attempts through the lens of coordination game theory offers new and potentially powerful insights, not only into the major cause of irregular regime and leadership change in the second half of the twentieth century, but into other significant issues of interest to political scientists, other scholars, and policy makers.

Appendix

Description of Variables Used in Analyses

Economic Variables

Per capita national income. The primary indicator for log(GDP/capita) was taken from Gleditsch (2002), because of its coverage and thorough data checking. Additional measures of the same concept were taken from the Penn World Table (PWT), Maddison and Fearon, all as provided by the Quality of Government (QoG) dataset (Teorell, Holmberg & Rothstein 2008).

Percentage urban. Percentage of population living in cities with population greater than 100,000. Derived from Correlates of War data on National Material Capabilities (v3.02).

Trade openness. Calculated from Gleditsch (2002) which had the most thorough approach and the best coverage. The Penn World Table's measure of trade openness (provided by QoG) was also used as a cross check.

Economic growth. Calculated from Gleditsch's (2002) data, checked against the PWT measure of the same.

Resource dependence. The primary measure was oil production per capita, taken from Wimmer (Wimmer, Cederman & Min 2009). A secondary measure was Fearon & Laitin's (2003) measure of oil dependence as measured by country years in which oil exports were greater than one-third of total exports.

Regime/Election Variables

Democracy. The primary measure of the level of democracy was the mean democracy score from the Unified Democracy Scores project (Pemstein, Meserve & Melton 2008). This was cross-checked with Polity and to a lesser extent with Coppedge's measures of democracy, both taken from the QoG dataset. The Democracy^2 variables are generated from the respective democracy level variables.

Regime subtype. Dummies for parliamentary democracy, presidential democracy, mixed democracy, civilian dictatorship, military dictatorship, and monarchy were taken from Cheibub and Gandhi's classification of regime institutions, via the QoG dataset.

Election. Golder's presidential elections variable indicates the number of direct presidential elections held in that year, via QoG.

Ethnicity Variables

Ethnic heterogeneity. Fearon and Laitin's (2003) and Alesina et al.'s (1996) measures of ethnic heterogeneity, taken from QoG. Ethnicity squared was generated from the two ethnic heterogeneity terms and cross checked using Fearon's measures of the size of the largest and second largest ethnic groups.

Strategic Variables

Cold War. Dichotomous variable. Coded 1 if the year is before 1990 and after 1949.

Closeness to superpower. This measure is derived Gartzke's United Nations voting affinity S-scores. Alignment is taken to be the absolute value of the difference between affinity with the United States and with the USSR. Countries who vote strongly with one superpower and against the other would have a high affinity score; countries that vote with both or neither would have a low score.

Former French colony. Based on Hadenius and Teorell's measure of colonial origin, taken from QoG.

International war. Generated from the interstate armed conflict variable in the PRIO Armed Conflict Dataset (Version 3-2005), taken from QoG.

Civil war. The main measure was generated from the maximum of the internal armed conflict and the internationalized internal armed conflict variables from the the PRIO Armed Conflict Dataset (Version 3-2005). This variable has four levels, indicating no conflict, minor conflict, intermediate conflict, and severe conflict. Other proxies were Sambanis's and Fearon's measures of civil wars. All of these were taken from the QoG dataset.

Military Variables

Relative military size. log(military personnel / population). The military personnel variable is taken from the Correlates of War data on National Material Capabilities (v3.02).

Relative military budget. log(military expenditure / total GDP). The military expenditure variable is taken from the Correlates of War data on National Material Capabilities (v3.02).

Recent successful coups. Count of the number of successful coups in the previous five years. Other proxies to measure the same concept included a count over a ten year window, and moving average rather than count versions of the same concept to pro-rate the number of incidents for younger countries.

Recent failed coups. Same as above but for past failures.

References

Aboagye, Festus. 1999. *The Ghana Army: A Concise Contemporary Guide to Its Centennial Regimental History, 1897–1999*. Accra, Ghana: Sedco Publishing.

Acemoglu, Daron & James A. Robinson. 2006. *Economic Origins of Dictatorship and Democracy*. New York: Cambridge University Press.

Afrifa, Akwasi. 1966. *The Ghana Coup*. London: Frank Cass.

Aguero, Filipe. 1995. *Solders, Civilians and Democracy: Post-Franco Spain in Comparative Perspective*. Baltimore, MD: Johns Hopkins University Press.

Alesina, Alberto, Sule Ozler, Nouriel Roubini & Phillip Swagel. 1996. "Political Instability and Economic Growth." *Journal of Economic Growth* 1(2):189–211.

Anderson, Benedict. 1983. *Imagined Communities: Reflections on the Origin and Spread of Nationalism*. New York: Verso.

Angeletos, George-Marios & Alessandro Pavan. 2007. "Efficient Use of Information and Social Value of Information." *Econometrica* 75(4): 1103–1142.

Angeletos, George-Marios, Christian Hellwig & Alessandro Pavan. 2006. "Signaling in a Global Game: Coordination and Policy Traps." *The Journal of Political Economy* 114(3):452–484.

Angeletos, George-Marios, Christian Hellwig & Alessandro Pavan. 2007. "Dynamic Global Games of Regime Change: Learning, Multiplicity, and the Timing of Attacks." *Econometrica* 75(3):711–756.

Associated Press. 1970. "Argentine Chief Is Forced To Quit In Military Coup." *The New York Times*, June 9, p. A1.

Aumann, Robert. 1976. "Agreeing to Disagree." *Annals of Statistics* 4(6):1236–1239.

Awoonor, Kofi. 1984. *The Ghana Revolution: A Background Account from a Personal Perspective*. Bronx, NY: Oases.

Bates, Robert H. 2001. "Annual War and Political Instability Survey." Computer file, available from http://africa.gov.harvard.edu/.

Bates, Robert H. 2005. *Markets and States in Tropical Africa: The Political Basis of Agricultural Policies*. Berkeley: University of California Press.

Baynham, Simon. 1988. *The Military and Politics in Nkrumah's Ghana*. Boulder, CO: Westview Press.

BBC News. 2009a. "Masses Mourn Protesters in Iran." http://news.bbc.co.uk/2/hi/middle_east/8108115.stm.

BBC News. 2009*b*. "Timeline: The Tiananmen Protests." http://news.bbc.co.uk/2/hi/asia-pacific/8057148.stm.

Belkin, Aaron & Evan Schofer. 2003. "Toward a Structural Understanding of Coup Risk." *Journal of Conflict Resolution* 47(5):594–620.

Belkin, Aaron & Evan Schofer. 2004. "Coup Risk, Counterbalancing, and International Conflict." *Security Studies* 14:140–177.

Bennett, Valerie Plave. 1975. "Epilogue: Malcontents in Uniform." In *Politicians and Soldiers in Ghana, 1966–1972*, ed. Dennis Austin & Robin Luckham. London: Frank Cass, pp. 300–313.

Biddle, Stephen D. 2004. *Military Power: Explaining Victory and Defeat in Modern Battle*. Princeton, NJ: Princeton University Press.

Bikhchandani, Sushil, David Hirshleifer & Ivo Welch. 1998. "Learning from the Behavior of Others: Conformity, Fads, and Informational Cascades." *The Journal of Economic Perspectives* 12(3): 151–170.

Bonnell, Victoria E., Ann Cooper & Gregory Freidin. 1994. *Russia at the Barricades: Eyewitness Accounts of the August 1991 Coup*. Armonk, NY: M.E. Sharpe.

Bransten, Jeremy. 2001. "Russia: A Chronology of 1991 Failed Soviet Coup (Part 1)." http://www.rferl.org/features/2001/08/1508200 1123554.asp.

Brownlee, Jason. 2007. *Authoritarianism in an Age of Democratization*. Cambridge, UK: Cambridge University Press.

Brusstar, James H. & Ellen Jones. 1995. *The Russian Military's Role In Politics*. Washington, DC: Institute for National Strategic Studies.

Cabrales, Antonio, Walter Garca-Fontes & Massimo Motta. 2000. "Risk Dominance Selects the Leader: An Experimental Analysis." *International Journal of Industrial Organization* 18(1):137–162.

Cabrales, Antonio, Rosemarie Nagel & Roc Armenter. 2007. "Equilibrium Selection through Incomplete Information in Coordination Games: An Experimental Study." *Experimental Economics* 10:221–234.

Calvo, Guillermo A. 1988. "Servicing the Public Debt: The Role of Expectations." *The American Economic Review* 78(4):647–661.

Carlsson, Hans & Eric VanDamme. 1993. "Global Games and Equilibrium Selection." *Econometrica* 61(5):989–1018.

Cass, David & Karl Shell. 1983. "Do Sunspots Matter?" *The Journal of Political Economy* 91(2):193–227.

Central Intelligence Agency. 2000. "CIA Activities in Chile (General Report)." http://bit.ly/cia-chile-shortlink.

Chamley, Christophe. 1999. "Coordinating Regime Switches." *Quarterly Journal of Economics* 114(3):869–905.

Chazan, Naomi. 1983. *An Anatomy of Ghanaian Politics: Managing Political Recession, 1969–1982*. Boulder, CO: Westview Press.

Cheibub, Jose Antonio. 2007. *Presidentialism, Parliamentarism, and Democracy*. Cambridge Studies in Comparative Politics. New York: Cambridge University Press.

Chwe, Michael. 2001. *Rational Rituals*. Princeton, NJ: Princeton University Press.

Clark, John. 2007. "The Decline of the African Military Coup." *Journal of Democracy* 18(3):141–155.

Cole, Harold L. & Timothy Kehoe. 2000. "Self-Fulfilling Debt Crises." *Review of Economic Studies* 67(1):91–116.

Collier, Paul. 2009. *Wars, Guns, and Votes: Democracy in Dangerous Places*. New York: Harper Collins.

Collier, Paul & Anke Hoeffler. 1998. "On Economic Causes of Civil War." *Oxford Economic Papers* 50(4):563–573.

Cooper, Russell. 1999. *Coordination Games*. Cambridge: Cambridge University Press.

Cooper, Russell & Andrew John. 1988. "Coordinating Coordination Failures in Keynesian Models." *The Quarterly Journal of Economics* 103(3):441–463.

Cooper, Russell, Douglas V. DeJong, Robert Forsythe & Thomas W. Ross. 1990. "Selection Criteria in Coordination Games: Some Experimental Results." *The American Economic Review* 80(1):218–233.

Cooper, Russell, Douglas V. DeJong, Robert Forsythe & Thomas W. Ross. 1992. "Communication in Coordination Games." *The Quarterly Journal of Economics* 107(2):739–771.

Crano, William D. & Radmila Prislin. 2006. "Attitudes and Persuasion." *Annual Review of Psychology* 57(1):345–374.

Dale, Stacy Berg & Alan B. Krueger. 2011. "Estimating the Return to College Selectivity Over the Career Using Administrative Earnings Data." *SSRN eLibrary*.

David, Steven R. 1987. *Third World Coups d'Etat and International Security*. Baltimore: Johns Hopkins University Press.

Decalo, Samuel. 1975. "Praetorianism, Corporate Grievances and Idiosyncratic Factors in African Military Hierarchies." *Journal of African Studies* 2(2):247–273.

de Meza, David & Clive Southey. 1996. "The Borrower's Curse: Optimism, Finance and Entrepreneurship." *The Economic Journal* 106(435):375–386.

DeNardo, James. 1985. *Power in Numbers: The Political Strategy of Protest and Rebellion*. Princeton, NJ: Princeton University Press.

Desch, Michael C. 1999. *Civilian Control of the Military: The Changing Security Environment*. Baltimore, MD: Johns Hopkins University Press.

Devetag, Giovanna & Andreas Ortmann. 2007. "When and Why? A Critical Survey on Coordination Failure in the Laboratory." *Experimental Economics* 10:331–344.

Diamond, Douglas W. & Philip H. Dybvig. 1983. "Bank Runs, Deposit Insurance, and Liquidity." *The Journal of Political Economy* 91(3):401–419.

Dickson, Eric S. Forthcoming. "Leadership, Followership, and Beliefs About the World: An Experiment." *British Journal of Political Science*

Duffy, John & Eric O'N. Fisher. 2005. "Sunspots in the Laboratory." *The American Economic Review* 95(3):510–529.

Dunlop, John B. 1993. *The Rise of Russia and the Fall of the Soviet Empire*. Princeton, NJ: Princeton University Press.

Dunlop, John B. 2003. "The August 1991 Coup and Its Impact on Soviet Politics." *Journal of Cold War Studies* 5(1):94–127.

Dunning, Thad. 2008. *Crude democracy: Natural Resource Wealth and Political Regimes*. New York: Cambridge University Press.

Dyson, Stephen Benedict. 2009. "'Stuff Happens': Donald Rumsfeld and the Iraq War." *Foreign Policy Analysis* 5(4):327–347.

Edmond, Chris. 2007. Information Revolutions and the Overthrow of Autocratic Regimes. Working Papers 07-26. New York: New York University.

Edmond, Chris. 2008. Information Manipulation, Coordination and Regime Change. Working Papers 07-25. New York: New York University.

Esfandiari, Golnaz. 2010. "The Twitter Devolution." http://www.foreignpolicy.com /articles/2010/06/07/the_twitter_revolution_that_wasnt.

Esseks, John. 1975. "Economic Policies." In *Politicians and Soldiers in Ghana, 1966–1972*, ed. Dennis Austin & Robin Luckham. London: Frank Cass, 37–62.

Farcau, Bruce W. 1994. *The Coup: Tactics in the Seizure of Power*. Westport, CT: Praeger.

Fearon, James D. & David D. Laitin. 2003. "Ethnicity, Insurgency, and Civil War." *American Political Science Review* 97(01):75–90.

Feaver, Peter D. 1999. "Civil-Military Relations." *Annual Review of Political Science* 2(1):211–241.

Felgenhauer, Pavel. 2001. "Moscow in 1991, Grozny in 1995." *The Moscow Times*, August 16, 2263:8.

Ferguson, Gregor. 1987. *Coup d'Etat: A Practical Manual*. Poole, UK: Arms & Armour.

Finer, Samuel. 1962. *The Man on Horseback: The Role of the Military in Politics*. London: Pall Mall Press.

First, Ruth. 1970. *The Barrel of a Gun*. London: Allen Lane.

Fitch, John Samuel. 1977. *The Military Coup d'Etat as a Political Process: Ecuador, 1948–1966*. Baltimore: Johns Hopkins University Press.

Fitch, John Samuel. 1986. "The Military Coup d'Etat as a Political Process: A General Framework and the Ecuadorian Case." In *Armies and Politics in Latin America*, ed. Abraham F. Lowenthal & John Samuel Fitch. New York: Holmes, & Meier, 151–164.

Fossum, E. 1967. "Factors Influencing the Occurrence of Military Coups d'Etat in Latin America." *Journal of Peace Research* 4(3):228–251.

Foye, Stephen. 1991. "A Lesson in Ineptitude: Military-Backed Coup Crumbles." http://www.funet.fi/pub/culture/russian/politics/ coup/rlr/91-0824A.RLR.

Frimpong-Ansah, Jonathan. 1991. *The Vampire State in Africa*. London: James Curry.

Galbraith, P. W. 2004. "How to Get Out of Iraq." *New York Review of Books* 51(8): 42–45.

Galetovic, A. & R. Sanhueza. 2000. "Citizens, Autocrats, and Plotters: A Model and New Evidence on Coups d'Etat." *Economics and Politics* 12(2):183–204.

Gandhi, Jennifer. 2008. *Political Institutions under Dictatorship*. Cambridge: Cambridge University Press.

Geddes, Barbara. 1999. "What Do We Know About Democratization After Twenty Years?" *Annual Review of Political Science* 2:115–144.

Geddes, Barbara. 2003. *Paradigms and Sand Castles: Theory Building and Research Design in Comparative Politics*. Analytical Perspectives on Politics. Ann Arbor: University of Michigan Press.

Geddes, Barbara. 2009. "How Autocrats Defend Themselves Against Armed Rivals." *SSRN eLibrary*.

Giglio, Mike. 2011. "The Facebook Freedom Fighter." *Newsweek* 157(8):14.

Gleditsch, Kristian Skrede. 2002. "Expanded Trade and GDP Data." *Journal of Conflict Resolution* 46(5):712–724.

Gleditsch, K. S. & M. D. Ward. 1999. "Interstate System Membership: A Revised List of the Independent States since 1816." *International Interactions* 25(4):393–413.

Goemans, H. E. 2008. "Which Way Out?: The Manner and Consequences of Losing Office." *Journal of Conflict Resolution* 52(6):771–794.

Goemans, H. & R. Marinov. 2008. "Putsch for Democracy: The International Community and Elections After the Coup." Working paper, Yale University.

Goemans, Hein, Kristian Gleditsch & Giacomo Chiozza. 2009. "Introducing Archigos: A Data Set of Political Leaders." *Journal of Peace Research* 46(2): 269–283.

Goldstein, Itay & Ady Pauzner. 2005. "Demand Deposit Contracts and the Probability of Bank Runs." *The Journal of Finance* 60(3):1293–1327.

Gott, Richard. 2005. *Hugo Chavez and the Bolivarian Revolution*. London: Verso.

Government of Ghana. 2004. *Report of the National Reconciliation Commission*. Accra, Ghana.

Granovetter, Mark. 1978. "Threshold Models of Collective Behavior." *The American Journal of Sociology* 83(6):1420–1443.

Grossman, Lev. 2009. "Iran Protests: Twitter, the Medium of the Movement." *Time Magazine*, June 17, p. 17.

Guimaraes, Bernardo & Stephen Morris. 2007. "Risk and Wealth in a Model of Self-fulfilling Currency Attacks." *Journal of Monetary Economics* 54(8):2205–2230.

Gustin, Sam. 2011. "Social Media Sparked, Accelerated Egypt's Revolutionary Fire." http://www.wired.com/epicenter/2011/02/ egypts-revolutionary-fire/.

Hansen, Andrew. 2008. "The French Military in Africa." http://www.cfr.org /publication/12578.

Hebditch, David Leroy & Ken Connor. 2008. *How to Stage a Military Coup: From Planning to Execution*. London: Frontline Books.

Hegre, Havard & Nicholas Sambanis. 2006. "Sensitivity Analysis of Empirical Results on Civil War Onset." *Journal of Conflict Resolution* 50(4):508–535.

Hendrickson, David C. & Robert W. Tucker. 2005. "Revisions in Need of Revising: What Went Wrong in the Iraq War." *Survival: Global Politics and Strategy* 47(2):7.

Herbst, Jeffrey. 1993. *The Politics of Reform in Ghana: 1982–1991*. Berkeley: University of California Press.

Hoffman, Bruce. 2006. "Insurgency and Counterinsurgency in Iraq." *Studies in Conflict and Terrorism* 29(2):103.

Horowitz, Donald. 1980. *Coup Theories and Officers' Motives*. Princeton, NJ: Princeton University Press.

Hough, Jerry F. 1997. *Democratization and Revolution in the USSR, 1985–1991*. Washington, DC: Brookings Institution.

Hunt, Naomi. 2011. "IPI on World Press Freedom Day: Naomi Hunt Speaks at Oviedo Press Association on 3 May." http://www.freemedia.at/singleview /5505/.

Huntington, Samuel P. 1957. *The Soldier and the State: The Theory and Politics of Civil-Military Relations*. Cambridge, MA: Harvard University Press.

Huntington, Samuel P. 1968. *Political Order in Changing Societies*. New Haven, CT: Yale University Press.

Huntington, Samuel P. 1991. *The Third Wave: Democratization in the Late Twentieth Century*. Norman: University of Oklahoma Press.

Hutchful, Eboe. 1973. "Military Rule and the Politics of Demilitarization in Ghana, 1966–1969." PhD thesis. University of Toronto.

Hutchful, Eboe. 1997. "Reconstructing Civil-Military Relations and the Collapse of Democracy in Ghana, 1979-81." *African Affairs* 96(385):535–560.

Hutchful, Eboe. 1998. "Institutional Decomposition and Junior Ranks' Political Action in Ghana." In *The Military and Militarism in Africa*, ed. Eboe Hutchful & Abdoulaye Bathily. Dakar, Senegal: CODESRIA.

Interview with Yevgenia Albats. 2000. http://www.pbs.org/wgbh/pages/frontline /shows/yeltsin/interviews/albats.html.

Jackman, Robert W. 1978. "The Predictability of Coups d'Etat: A Model with African Data." *The American Political Science Review* 72(4):1262–1275.

Jackson, Kofi A. 1999. *When Gun Rules: A Soldier's Testimony*. Accra, Ghana: Woeli Publishing Services.

Janowitz, Morris. 1964. *The Military in the Political Development of New Nations: An Essay in Comparative Analysis*. Chicago: University of Chicago Press.

Jenkins, J. Craig & Augustine J. Kposowa. 1990. "Explaining Military Coups d'Etat: Black Africa, 1957-1984." *American Sociological Review* 55(6):861–875.

Jenkins, J. Craig & Augustine J. Kposowa. 1992. "The Political Origins of African Military Coups: Ethnic Competition, Military Centrality, and the Struggle over the Postcolonial State." *International Studies Quarterly* 36(3):271–291.

Johnson, Dominic D. P. 2004. *Overconfidence and War: The Havoc and Glory of Positive Illusions*. Cambridge, MA: Harvard University Press.

Johnson, Thomas H., Robert O. Slater & Pat McGowan. 1984. "Explaining African Military Coups d'Etat, 1960-1982." *The American Political Science Review* 78(3):622–640.

Kandori, Michihiro, George J. Mailath & Rafael Rob. 1993. "Learning, Mutation, and Long-Run Equilibria in Games." *Econometrica* 61(1):29–56.

Karl, Terry Lynn. 1997. *The Paradox of Plenty: Oil Booms and Petro-States.* Berkeley: University of California Press.

Katz, Michael L. & Carl Shapiro. 1986. "Technology Adoption in the Presence of Network Externalities." *The Journal of Political Economy* 94(4):822–841.

Kebschull, Harvey G. 1994. "Operation 'Just Missed': Lessons from Failed Coup Attempts." *Armed Forces and Society* 20(4):565–579.

Kennedy, Gavin. 1974. *The Military in the Third World.* London: Duckworth.

Kimenyi, M. S. & J. M. Mbaku. 1993. "Rent-seeking and Institutional Stability in Developing Countries." *Public Choice* 77(2):385–405.

King, Gary, Robert Keohane & Sidney Verba. 1994. *Designing Social Inquiry: Scientific Inference in Qualitative Research.* Princeton, NJ: Princeton University Press.

Kirk-Greene, A. H. M. 1981. *Stay by Your Radios: Documentation for a Study of Military Government in Tropical Africa.* Cambridge, UK: African Studies Centre.

Knight, Amy. 2003. "The KGB, Perestroika, and the Collapse of the Soviet Union." *Journal of Cold War Studies* 5(1):67–93.

Kojima, Fuhito. 2006. "Risk-Dominance and Perfect Foresight Dynamics in N-Player Games." *Journal of Economic Theory* 128(1):255–273.

Korchagina, Valeria. 2001*a*. "The Coup That Changed Our World." *The Moscow Times* August 14, 2261:1.

Korchagina, Valeria. 2001*b*. "State TV Stages a Revolt of Its Own." *The Moscow Times* August 14, 2261:1.

Kristof, Nicholas. 1989. "A Reassessment of How Many Died In the Military Crackdown in Beijing." *The New York Times*, June 21, p. A8.

Kuran, Timur. 1989. "Sparks and Prairie Fires: A Theory of Unanticipated Political Revolution." *Public Choice* 61(1):41–74.

Kuran, Timur. 1997. *Private Truths, Public Lies: The Social Consequences of Preference Falsification.* Cambridge, MA: Harvard University Press.

Lawson, Sean. 2011. "Is America Really Building An Internet Kill Switch?" http://blogs.forbes.com/firewall/2011/02/11/is-america-really-building-an-internet-kill-switch/.

Lefever, Ernest. 1970. *Spear and Scepter.* Washington, DC: The Brookings Institution.

Lehoucq, Fabrice & Anbal Prez Lin. 2009. "Regimes, Competition, and Military Coups in Latin America." *SSRN eLibrary.*

Levine, John M., Lauren B. Resnick & E. Tory Higgins. 1993. "Social Foundations of Cognition." *Annual Review of Psychology* 44(1):585–612.

Li, Quan & Rafael Reuveny. 2003. "Economic Globalization and Democracy: An Empirical Analysis." *British Journal of Political Science* 33(01):29–54.

Lichbach, Mark. 1998. *The Rebel's Dilemma.* Ann Arbor: University of Michigan Press.

Linz, Juan J. 1978. *The Breakdown of Democratic Regimes: Crisis, Breakdown, and Reequilibration.* Baltimore: Johns Hopkins University Press.

Linz, J. J. 1990. "The Perils of Presidentialism." *Journal of Democracy* 1(1):51–69.

Londregan, John & Keith Poole. 1990. "Poverty, the Coup Trap, and the Seizure of Executive Power." *World Politics* 42(2):151–183.

Lunde, Tormod K. 1991. "Modernization and Political Instability: Coups d'Etat in Africa, 1955-85." *Acta Sociologica* 34(1):13–32.

Luong, Pauline Jones & Erika Weinthal. 2006. "Rethinking the Resource Curse: Ownership Structure, Institutional Capacity, and Domestic Constraints." *Annual Review of Political Science* 9(1): 241–263.

Luttwak, Edward N. 1979. *Coup d'Etat: A Practical Handbook.* London: Wildwood House.

Mackie, Gerry. 1996. "Ending Footbinding and Infibulation: A Convention Account." *American Sociological Review* 61(6):999–1017.

Mackie, G. 2000. "Female Genital Cutting: The Beginning of the End." In *Female "Circumcision" in Africa: Culture, Controversy and Change,* ed. B. Shell-Duncan and Y. Hernlund, pp. 253–281. Boulder: Lynne Rienner.

Magaloni, Beatriz. 2008. "Credible Power-Sharing and the Longevity of Authoritarian Rule." *Comparative Political Studies* 41(4-5):715–741.

Magaloni, Beatriz & Ruth Kricheli. 2010. "Political Order and One-Party Rule." *Annual Review of Political Science* 13(1):123–143.

Mainwaring, Scott & Matthew Shugart. 1997. *Presidentialism and Democracy in Latin America.* Cambridge Studies in Comparative Politics Cambridge: Cambridge University Press.

Marshall, Monty G. & Donna Ramsey Marshall. 2010. "Coup d'Etat Events, 1946-2009: Codebook." http://www.systemicpeace.org/inscr/CSPCoupsCodebook 2009.pdf.

McGough, Laura. 2001. "Ananse's Web: The Interplay of Civil Society and State in Post-Colonial Ghana." Working paper, University of Ghana; revision of Engineer's Society paper.

McGowan, Patrick J. 2003. "African Military Coups d'Etat, 1956–2001: Frequency, Trends and Distribution." *The Journal of Modern African Studies* 41(3):339–370.

Meredith, Martin. 2005. *The Fate of Africa: From the Hopes of Freedom to the Heart of Despair: A History of Fifty Years of Independence.* 1st ed. New York: Public Affairs.

Moreno, Erika, Michael Lewis-Beck & Jacque Amoureux. 2004. "Latin Rhythms: Coup Cycles in the Americas." Presented at the Midwest Political Science Association Conference in Chicago, IL.

Morris, Stephen & Hyun Song Shin. 1998. "Unique Equilibrium in a Model of Self-Fulfilling Currency Attacks." *The American Economic Review* 88(3):587–597.

Morris, Stephen & Hyun Song Shin. 2004. "Liquidity Black Holes." *Review of Finance* 8(1):1–18.

Mosca, Gaetano. 1939. *The Ruling Class.* New York: McGraw-Hill.

Munro, Robin. 2001. "The Press Also Was Beyond Control." *The Moscow Times*, August 17, 2264:1.

Nagel, Rosemarie. 1995. "Unraveling in Guessing Games: An Experimental Study." *The American Economic Review* 85(5):1313–1326.

Needler, Martin C. 1966. "Political Development and Military Intervention in Latin America." *The American Political Science Review* 60(3):616–626.

Nkrumah, Kwame. 1990. *Kwame Nkrumah: The Conakry Years, His Life and Letters*. London: Zed Press.

Nordlinger, Eric A. 1977. *Soldiers in Politics: Military Coups and Governments*. Prentice-Hall Contemporary Comparative Politics Series. Englewood Cliffs, NJ: Prentice-Hall.

Nugent, Paul. 1996. *Big Men, Small Boys and Politics in Ghana*. Accra, Ghana: Asempa Publishers.

Nun, Jose. 1986. "The Middle-Class Military Coup Revisited." In *Armies and Politics in Latin America*, ed. Abraham F. Lowenthal & John Samuel Fitch. New York: Holmes & Meier, pp. 59–95.

Obstfeld, Maurice. 1996. "Models of Currency Crises with Self-fulfilling Features." *European Economic Review* 40(3-5):1037–1047.

Ocran, Albert. 1977. *Politics of the Sword*. London: Rex Collings.

Odom, William E. 1998. *The Collapse of the Soviet Military*. New Haven, CT: Yale University Press.

O'Kane, Rosemary H. T. 1987. *The Likelihood of Coups*. Aldershot, UK: Avebury.

O'Kane, Rosemary H. T. 1993. "Coups d'Etat in Africa: A Political Economy Approach." *Journal of Peace Research* 30:251–270.

Okeke, Barbara. 1982. *4 June: A Revolution Betrayed*. Enugu, Nigeria: Ikenga Publishers.

Oquaye, Mike. 1980. *Politics in Ghana: 1972–1979*. Accra: Tornado Publications.

Pemstein, Daniel, Stephen Meserve & James Melton. 2008. "Democratic Compromise: A Latent Variable Analysis of Ten Measures of Regime Type." http://www.clinecenter.uiuc.edu/research/affiliatedresearch/UDS/uds.pdf.

Peski, Marcin. 2010. "Generalized Risk-dominance and Asymmetric Dynamics." *Journal of Economic Theory* 145(1):216–248.

Petchenkine, Youry. 1993. *Ghana In Search of Stability, 1957–1992*. Westport, CT: Praeger.

Pfeifle, Mark. 2009. "A Nobel Peace Prize for Twitter." *The Christan Science Monitor*, July 6, p. 9.

Potash, Robert A. 1980. *The Army and Politics in Argentina, 1945–1962: Peron to Frondizi*. Stanford, CA: Stanford University Press.

Quantson, Kofi. B. 2000. *Ghana: Peace and Stability*. Accra: Napascom.

Quinlivan, James T. 1999. "Coup-Proofing: Its Practice and Consequences in the Middle East." *International Security* 24(2):131–165.

Ray, Donald. 1986. *Ghana: Politics, Economics, and Society*. Boulder, CO: Lynne Rienner.

Reed, Thomas C. & Danny B. Stillman. 2009. *The Nuclear Express: A Political History of the Bomb and Its Proliferation*. Minneapolis: Zenith Press.

Rimmer, Douglas. 1992. *Staying Poor: Ghana's Political Economy, 1950–1990*. Oxford: Pergamon Press.

Risen, James. 2000. "New York Times Special Report: The C.I.A. in Iran." http://www.nytimes.com/library/world/mideast/ 041600iran-cia-index.html.

Ross, Michael Lewin. 1999. "The Political Economy of the Resource Curse." *World Politics* 51(2):297–322.

Scheina, Robert L. 2003. *Latin America's Wars*. Vol. 2: *The Age of the Professional Soldier, 1900–2001*. 1st ed. Washington, DC: Brassey's.

Schelling, Thomas. 1960. *The Strategy of Conflict*. Cambridge, MA: Harvard University Press.

Schirmer, Jennifer G. 1998. *The Guatemalan Military Project: A Violence Called Democracy*. Pennsylvania Studies in Human Rights. Philadelphia: University of Pennsylvania Press.

Schmidt, David, Robert Shupp, James M. Walker & Elinor Ostrom. 2003. "Playing Safe in Coordination Games: The Roles of Risk Dominance, Payoff Dominance, and History of Play." *Games and Economic Behavior* 42(2):281–299.

Shillington, Kevin. 1992. *Ghana and the Rawlings Factor*. London: Macmillan.

Simons, G. L. 1996. *Libya: The Struggle for Survival*. 2nd ed. Houndmills, Basingstoke, Hampshire: Macmillan.

Sondrol, Paul C. 1992. "The Paraguayan Military in Transition and the Evolution of Civil-Military Relations." *Armed Forces and Society* 19(1):105–122.

Stepan, Alfred C. 1974. *The Military in Politics: Changing Patterns in Brazil*. 1st Princeton pbk. ed. Princeton, NJ: Princeton University Press.

Stepan, Alfred & Cindy Skach. 1993. "Constitutional Frameworks and Democratic Consolidation: Parliamentarianism versus Presidentialism." *World Politics* 46(1):1–22.

Straub, Paul G. 1995. "Risk Dominance and Coordination Failures in Static Games." *The Quarterly Review of Economics and Finance* 35(4):339–363.

Svolik, Milan. 2008. "Power-Sharing and Leadership Dynamics in Authoritarian Regimes." *SSRN eLibrary*.

Svolik, Milan. 2010. "Contracting on Violence: Authoritarian Repression and Military Intervention in Politics." *SSRN eLibrary*.

Taylor, Brian D. 2003*a*. *Politics and the Russian Army Civil-Military Relations, 1689-2000*. Cambridge: Cambridge University Press.

Taylor, Brian D. 2003*b*. "The Soviet Military and the Disintegration of the USSR." *Journal of Cold War Studies* 5(1):17–66.

Teorell, Jan, Soren Holmberg & Bo Rothstein. 2008. "The Quality of Government Dataset, version 15May08." http://www.qog. pol.gu.se.

Thyne, Clayton L. 2009. "Supporter of Stability or Agent of Agitation? The Effect of US Foreign Policy on Coups in Latin America, 1960–1999."

Tolz, Vera. 1991. "The Soviet Media Under Emergency Rule." http://www.funet.fi /pub/culture/russian/politics/coup/rlr/91-0820A.RLR.

Transparency International. 2004. *Global Corruption Report 2004*. London: Pluto Press.

Valentino, Benjamin A. 2004. *Final Solutions: Mass Killing and Genocide in the Twentieth Century*. Ithaca, NY: Cornell University Press.

Varney, Wendy & Brian Martin. 2000. "Lessons from the 1991 Soviet Coup." *Peace Research* 32(1):52–68.

Wick, Katharina & Erwin Bulte. 2009. "The Curse of Natural Resources." *Annual Review of Resource Economics* 1(1):139–156.

Wimmer, Andreas, Lars-Erik Cederman & Brian Min. 2009. "Ethnic Politics and Armed Conflict: A Configurational Analysis of a New Global Data Set." *American Sociological Review* 74:316–337.

World Bank. 2004. "World Development Indicators 2004."

Yankah, Kojo. 1986. *The Trial of JJ Rawlings: Echoes of the 31st December Revolution*. Tema, Ghana: Ghana Publishing Corporation.

Yeebo, Zaya. 1991. *Ghana: The Struggle for Popular Power*. London: New Beacon Books.

Yeltsin, Boris. 1992. *Putsch: The Diary: Three Days That Collapsed the Empire, Aug. 19–21, 1991*. Mosaic Press.

Zimmerman, Ekkart. 1983. *Political Violence, Crises, and Revolutions: Theories and research*. Cambridge, MA; Schenkman; Boston: GK Hall.

Ziorklui, Emmanuel Doe, ed. 1988. *Ghana: Nkrumah to Rawlings*. Accra, Ghana: Em-Zed Books Centre.

Zolotov, Andrei. 2001. "GKChP Couldn't Finish What It Started." *The Moscow Times*, August 17, 2264:1.

Zuckerman, Ethan. 2009. "Unpacking "The Twitter Revolution" in Moldova." http://www.ethanzuckerman.com/blog/2009/04/09/unpacking-the-twitter-revolution-in-moldova/.

Zuckerman, Ethan. 2011. "The First Twitter Revolution?" *Foreign Policy*, January 14.

Index